Using Technology in the Classroom

Sixth Edition

Gary G. Bitter

Arizona State University

Melissa E. Pierson

University of Houston

PEARSON
A and B

Boston   New York   San Francisco
Mexico City   Montreal   Toronto   London   Madrid   Munich   Paris
Hong Kong   Singapore   Tokyo   Cape Town   Sydney

Series Editor: *Arnie Burvikovs*

Series Editorial Assistant: *Megan Smallidge*

Marketing Manager: *Tara Whorf*

Production Administrator: *Mary Beth Finch*

Editorial-Production Service: *Omegatype Typography, Inc.*

Composition and Prepress Buyer: *Linda Cox*

Manufacturing Buyer: *Andrew Turso*

Cover Administrator: *Linda Knowles*

Electronic Composition: *Omegatype Typography, Inc.*

For related titles and support materials, visit our online catalog at www.ablongman.com.

Between the time Website information is gathered and then published, it is not unusual for some sites to have closed. Also, the transcription of URLs can result in typographical errors. The publisher would appreciate notification where these errors occur so that they may be corrected in subsequent editions.

Library of Congress Cataloging-in-Publication Data

Bitter, Gary G.
    Using technology in the classroom / Gary G. Bitter, Melissa E. Pierson.—6th ed.
      p. cm.
    Includes bibliographical references and index.
    ISBN 0-205-41915-1
    1. Computer-assisted instruction. 2. Microcomputers. 3. Educational technology. I. Pierson, Melissa. II. Title.

LB1028.5.B47   2005
371.33'4—dc22

                      2004043664

Photo and text credits are found on page 345, which should be considered an extension of the copyright page.

Printed in the United States of America

10 9 8 7 6 5 4 3 2 1   09 08 07 06 05 04

CONTENTS

CHAPTER 2
Basic Productivity Operations 35

CHAPTER 3
Internet Basics and Electronic Messaging 47

CHAPTER 7
Selecting and Using Educational Software 127

SECTION 3 Teaching, Learning, and the Curriculum 191

PREFACE

Using Technology in the Classroom was written to help prospective and practicing classroom teachers, school personnel, and parents understand the role of technology in PreK–12 education. Based on the authors' experiences with teaching children and adults in schools at all levels, an attempt is made to explain clearly the most important information about technology and its application in the educational environment, with technical jargon avoided as much as possible. The book may be read from cover to cover for a comprehensive perspective, or topics may be selected and returned to as needed.

This sixth edition is organized to reflect the new International Society for Technology in Education (ISTE) National Educational Technology Standards for Teachers (NETS-T). It is especially designed for the introductory undergraduate or graduate education student who needs an overview of the role and use of technology in education. Specific education examples and applications at all levels are provided throughout the book. New to this edition is a DVD, included at the back of the book, filled with video case examples of real teachers and students using technology. The video excerpts, noted throughout the book with the designation DVD/Video Vignette, are aligned with the ISTE's NETS for Students. Readers are encouraged to view the video lessons again and again as their understanding level grows. Learner activities have been designed for students to further explore specific educational understanding and applications.

Section 1, Technology Operations and Concepts, introduces readers to educational technology issues. The first chapter gives an overview of technological literacy and its effect on education. A discussion of computer applications in society as a whole is included, as is a discussion of the computer's potential contributions to the school and home. Chapter 1 concludes with a brief historical discussion of early computing devices and an overview of hardware components. Chapter 2 serves as an introduction and resource for basic operations of the most common productivity software: word processors, spreadsheets, and databases. Educational uses are discussed, and a table of terms is presented for each application. Electronic communication already plays a significant role in all levels of education. Chapter 3 introduces the basic concepts of electronic mail, focusing on email procedures, etiquette, and educational applications. Listservs are introduced and their relevance for education is detailed. The chapter defines the structure of the Internet, introduces search strategies for locating specific information, and discusses security issues with regard to students' exploring the online world. Chapter 4 rounds out Section 1 by tipping educators off to emerging trends, with a look at new technologies and what these advancements might mean for students of the future.

Section 2, Planning and Designing Learning Environments, deals with the planning and designing processes of using technology in the classroom. At the outset of the planning process, it is vital that new teachers understand what research has shown regarding the use of technology in education. Chapter 5 summarizes recent findings. Chapter 6, new to this edition, addresses planning for technology-rich instruction, a vital component to the teaching sequence. Educational software is one of the first technologies that teachers new to technology attempt to use, and Chapter 7 advises the reader about the unique features of each educational software type with descriptions of each category, tips for practical classroom integration, and illustrative classroom vignettes. Criteria and a detailed evaluation instrument are presented so educators can make well-informed buying decisions. The resources available on the World Wide Web hold much promise for educators at all levels; Chapter 8 highlights a selection of exemplary web resources, presented according to a helpful organizing framework, and instructs on evaluating the quality of online sources. Following the discussion of using web resources, Chapter 9 focuses on creating original web-based instruction. Helpful considerations are suggested for planning an effective website, and specific instructions are given for creating a web page using a variety of web editing software solutions.

Section 3, Teaching, Learning, and the Curriculum, discusses the various uses of technology. Chapter 10 explores strategies for technology integration in the content areas and across disciplines in multidisciplinary units. The lesson plans given as examples should be used as a springboard to develop your own lessons that meet the unique needs of your students. Chapter 11 takes a closer look at using technology to support data analysis and simulations, and Chapter 12 extends the discussion to the use of computers for mathematical modeling. Chapter 13 aims to supply very practical procedures for keeping the technologically enhanced class organized. Specific emphasis is on using computers both in computer labs and classroom settings. Finally, Chapter 14 highlights multimedia projects and computer-based presentation techniques. Its aim is both teachers and learners, reflecting the blurring of the leadership roles in new educational philosophy.

Section 4, Assessment and Evaluation, demonstrates how technology can make the assessment process more efficient, either as the focus of assessment or as an instructional tool. In Chapter 15 ways that technology can impact alternative assessment methods as well as more traditional test-taking uses are given, as are practical tips on using productivity tools to record both quantitative and qualitative assessment, including portfolios.

The teacher's roles beyond teaching form the basis for Section 5, Productivity and Professional Practice. Chapter 16 suggests ways to use basic productivity software, as well as newer specific-purpose software, to perform a myriad of daily administrative tasks, such as keeping records and producing materials.

The online world brings teachers increased opportunities for communication, collaboration, and professional growth that they have not traditionally had in previously isolated classrooms; Chapter 17 focuses on the professional educator.

Section 6, Social, Ethical, Legal, and Human Issues, discusses the role of technology in these important contextual issues facing the educational field in Chapter 18. Along with all of the ways that technology makes certain tasks easier and brings people closer, come new questions of the ways its presence impacts people both in classrooms and in society at large. Teachers need to be aware of the challenges and mixed messages that students in today's classrooms will face in their information-saturated lives.

Acknowledgments

We would like to express our appreciation to the persons and organizations that have contributed in some way to this publication. Specifically, we thank the preservice teachers of the University of Houston and Arizona State University for challenging us to constantly examine the ways in which technology can be included in their education. Marcie Bump contributed to the piece on assistive technologies, and we are grateful for her thoughts. We are appreciative to Alysa McLachlan at the University of Houston for reviewing and selecting the video case studies, to Soo Kim for checking website links and indexing, and to Deborah Stirling for overall contributions to the book.

For reviewing the sixth edition of *Using Technology in the Classroom,* we would like to thank Devon C. Dunhaney, State University of New York at New Paltz, and Kai Sai Un, Texas A&M University.

We hope you will find ways to make technology a meaningful and authentic part of your teaching and your students' learning. The possibilities technology presents for bringing the world into the classroom are endless.

CHAPTER 1

Getting Started with Technology

FOCUS QUESTIONS

1. How have societal trends during the Information Age been influenced by technological advances?

2. In what ways can basic technology standards and profiles be used to plan for technology integration at all levels of education?

3. What terminology is necessary for successful operation of current computer hardware components?

Technology is an agent of change, spurring our redefinition of time and space. In 1998, for the first time in 50 years, young people's television viewing time declined. Television viewing gave way to the Internet, video games, palm pilots, pagers, cell phones, wireless technologies, and personal digital assistants (PDAs). As emerging technologies rapidly become commonplace, how do we keep pace? One method of forecasting the future is by predicting computing power advances.

In 1965, Gordon Moore, one of the founders of Intel, observed a striking trend. Each new chip contained roughly twice as much computing power and twice the number of transistors on a chip as its predecessor, and each chip was released within 18 to 24 months of the previous chip. If this trend continued, he reasoned, computing power would rise exponentially over relatively brief periods of time. Moore's observation, now known as Moore's Law, predicted a trend that has continued and is still remarkably accurate. It is the basis for many planners' performance forecasts. In 29 years, as Moore's Law predicted, the number of transistors on a chip has increased from 2,250 on the 4004 in 1971 to 42 million on the Pentium 4 processor. Today's chips have over 100 million transistors. Intel's cofounder predicted transistor density on microprocessors would double every 2 years. This prediction, so far, has proven amazingly accurate. The website at **www.intel.com/research/silicon/mooreslaw. htm?iid=sr+moore&** has a graph of Moore's Law and related information.

Trends of the Information Age

The formative years of the Information Age, 1956 and 1957, were marked by the launching of *Sputnik* and the increased numbers of white-collar workers in relationship to blue-collar workers. The *Sputnik* launch marked the beginnings of satellite communications applications, other opportunities to develop global perspectives, and the space industry. The number and capability of workers are indicative of a change in the nature of the kind of commodity being produced. As we moved from the Industrial Age into the Information Age, more workers became involved in the creation, management, and transfer of information than in the manufacturing of products. An economy built on information rather than goods and services began to emerge. Knowledge (cognition) and knowing how to learn and think (metacognition) increased in global importance, significance, and value.

Three significant trends with implications for education mark the Information Age: (1) a shift in demographics; (2) an acceleration of technology; (3) and an ever-expanding base of available data through which to search, sift, sort, and select. It is estimated that the amount of information in the world doubles every 900 days. Therefore, by the time a first-grader progresses through the traditional public educational system and is preparing for high school graduation, the information base will have quadrupled.

Most of today's children have never lived in a noncomputerized society. Great portions of their leisure time are spent viewing television and playing electronic interactive adventure games within imagined, virtual environments. Sophisticated, modern computers and other technological peripherals and devices are the norm, and schools are as responsible for providing access to and the opportunity to learn and use technology as are families.

The acceleration of technology increases the pace of change. Within the Agrarian Society, the pace of change was established by the seasons; each season had specific activities, events, and purposes. The yearly calendar and the almanac were used to mark time. Time orientation moved to the present within the Industrial Age. The 40-hour workweek and time clocks were used to measure productivity and profit. In the Information Age, the orientation has become the future. Satellite communications now allow information to travel across time, space, and distance as the information float collapses.

Racing toward the Biotechnology Age: The Third Millennium

The third millennium is being viewed as a time to close the door on the past and begin anew. The acceleration of technology has allowed the communication and application of information, especially within the fields of science and mathematics, to be rapidly disseminated. Scientists are able to share knowledge and to build cooperative projects wherein information explodes as problems are addressed, breakthroughs are made, and problems are solved.

Within the Biotechnology Age, the valued resources will be mind and life. The mind as a resource of value demands that people be not only literate but also competent, critical, and creative thinkers. People must become independent, lifelong learners, constantly updating their skills, knowledge, and experiences. The ability to participate fully in a technologically rich society will require people to scan entire landscapes of information; to select that which is pertinent, meaningful, and applicable to the tasks and their thinking; to construct problems and simulations that test hypotheses; to analyze and integrate information; to evaluate results; and to compose and communicate their thoughts to form new knowledge.

What Is of Such Intrinsic Value?

Knowing that information will quadruple within a student's traditional school experience has teachers asking what skills, concepts, and information students will need as participants within such a society. What knowledge is of such intrinsic value that each child from every culture must have and share it within the "global village"? What skills will teachers need? What responsibility must teachers share? What will be the role of the teacher? How will educators effect responsiveness in such an expansive, ever-changing environment? Many educators believe the traditional, basic three R's will no longer be the end products students possess but will become means to create the qualities of independence, integrity, image, and invention within each student. The development of students as thinkers, problem solvers, and creators requires teachers to create projects in which students work with ideas, symbols, and abstractions. Students' work will require them to do something with the information they access and acquire.

How Is This Affecting Education and Educators?

The educational system is regarded as the force that, when functioning properly, promotes literacy or, when failing, allows illiteracy. Many U.S. corporations have undergone a transformation to respond to the changes in the world marketplace and have installed state-of-the-art technology to make the workplace more efficient, economical, and safe. They have retooled the workplace and are presently retraining their workers. With the installation of new technology, the training of employees needs to be at a compatible level. There are very few places within the workplace now for the unskilled and the high school dropout. Many of those jobs are now exported to Third World nations in which the labor laws are few and the costs are minimal. Business has accepted the double financial burden of both retooling and retraining. However, the enormous retraining costs cannot be incurred indefinitely solely by industry. Education must share the responsibility of developing technologically literate people, not only to help people maintain a standard of living but also to help people create a balanced lifestyle.

Since the inception of the personal computer in 1977, two "generations" (two 12-year cycles) of students have completely progressed through the school system. Their experiences with computers depended on the visions and financial priorities of their teachers, administrators, and state and community leadership. In many cases, they left high school less prepared than their parents for the demands of the workplace and the decisions of the lifestyle they dreamed of enjoying.

Business and government interests are forming new coalitions for the purposes of raising the educational standards for determining proficiency. Professional organizations for educators have issued position statements regarding the desired availability and use of computers in the classroom. One of the most prominent groups that has developed standards for teachers and students is the International Society for Technology in Education (ISTE) (Roblyer, 2003).

 ## ISTE National Educational Technology Standards for Teachers (NETS–T)

The ISTE National Educational Technology Standards for Teachers (NETS–T) (**http://cnets.iste.org/teachers/pdf/Sec_1-1_Establishing_NETST.pdf**) provide guidelines for applying information technology in educational settings. All candidates seeking initial certification or endorsements in teacher preparation programs should have opportunities to meet these standards. NETS for Teachers are organized into six broad categories with twenty-three performance tasks.*

Technology Operations and Concepts.   Teachers demonstrate a sound understanding of technology operations and concepts. Teachers:

1. Demonstrate introductory knowledge, skills, and understanding of concepts related to technology (as described in the ISTE National Educational Technology Standards for Students).
2. Demonstrate continual growth in technology knowledge and skills to stay abreast of current and emerging technologies.

Planning and Designing Learning Environments and Experiences.   Teachers plan and design effective learning environments and experiences supported by technology. Teachers:

1. Design developmentally appropriate learning opportunities that apply technology-enhanced instructional strategies to support the diverse needs of learners.
2. Apply current research on teaching and learning with technology when planning learning environments and experiences.
3. Identify and locate technology resources and evaluate them for accuracy and suitability.

*Reprinted with permission from *National Educational Technology Standards for Teachers,* copyright © 2000, ISTE (the International Society for Technology in Education), 800.336.5191 (U.S. & Canada) or 541.302.3777 (Int'l), iste@iste.org, www.iste.org. All rights reserved. Permission does not constitute an endorsement by ISTE. For more information about the NETS Project, contact Lajeane Thomas, Director, NETS Project, 318.257.3923, lthomas@latech.edu.

4. Plan for the management of technology resources within the context of learning activities.
5. Plan strategies to manage student learning in a technology-enhanced environment.

Teaching, Learning, and the Curriculum.   Teachers implement curriculum plans that include methods and strategies for applying technology to maximize student learning. Teachers:

1. Facilitate technology-enhanced experiences that address content standards and student technology standards.
2. Use technology to support learner-centered strategies that address the diverse needs of students.
3. Apply technology to develop students' higher-order skills and creativity.
4. Manage student learning activities in a technology-enhanced environment.

Assessment and Evaluation.   Teachers apply technology to facilitate a variety of effective assessment and evaluation strategies. Teachers:

1. Apply technology in assessing student learning of subject matter using a variety of assessment techniques.
2. Use technology resources to collect and analyze data, interpret results, and communicate findings to improve instructional practice and maximize student learning.
3. Apply multiple methods of evaluation to determine students' appropriate use of technology resources for learning, communication, and productivity.

Productivity and Professional Practice.   Teachers use technology to enhance their productivity and professional practice. Teachers:

1. Use technology resources to engage in ongoing professional development and lifelong learning.
2. Continually evaluate and reflect on professional practice to make informed decisions regarding the use of technology in support of student learning.
3. Apply technology to increase productivity.
4. Use technology to communicate and collaborate with peers, parents, and the larger community in order to nurture student learning.

Social, Ethical, Legal, and Human Issues.   Teachers understand the social, ethical, legal, and human issues surrounding the use of technology in PreK–12 schools and apply that understanding in practice. Teachers:

1. Model and teach legal and ethical practice related to technology use.
2. Apply technology resources to enable and empower learners with diverse backgrounds, characteristics, and abilities.

3. Identify and use technology resources that affirm diversity.
4. Promote safe and healthy use of technology resources.
5. Facilitate equitable access to technology resources for all students.

Teacher education should emphasize these standards in technology courses, integrated technology-content methods courses, and classroom experiences. To facilitate this emphasis, the chapters in this book are organized by the ISTE categories just presented. Teachers must be prepared to use technology in their teaching (**http:// cnets.iste.org/intro.html**).

Tom Carroll, past director of the U.S. Department of Education's Preparing Tomorrow's Teachers to Use Technology (PT3), said, "The power of technology for student learning doesn't come from the presence of classroom computers or the Internet. The real power of technology in education will come when teachers have been trained well and have captured the potential of technology themselves" (**www.pt3. org/stories/lessonslearned.html**).

NETS Profiles of Technology-Literate Teachers

A major component of the ISTE NETS–T project is the creation of performance profiles at key developmental points in teacher preparation programs to determine whether candidates are meeting the standards.

Technology Performance Profiles for Teacher Preparation

Note: Numbers in parentheses listed after each performance task in the following profiles refer to the standards categories to which the performance is linked. The categories are:

1. Technology operations and concepts
2. Planning and designing learning environments and experiences
3. Teaching, learning, and the curriculum
4. Assessment and evaluation
5. Productivity and professional practice
6. Social, ethical, legal, and human issues

General Preparation Performance Profile

Performance Tasks.   Upon completion of the general preparation component of their program, prospective teachers:

1. Demonstrate a sound understanding of the nature and operation of technology systems. (1)*
2. Demonstrate proficiency in the use of common input and output devices; solve routine hardware and software problems; and make informed choices about technology systems, resources, and services. (1)*

3. Use technology tools and information resources to increase productivity, promote creativity, and facilitate academic learning. (1, 3, 4, 5)
4. Use content-specific tools (e.g., software, simulation, environmental probes, graphing calculators, exploratory environments, web tools) to support learning and research. (1, 3, 5)*
5. Use technology resources to facilitate higher-order and complex thinking skills, including problem solving, critical thinking, informed decision making, knowledge construction, and creativity. (1, 3, 5)*
6. Collaborate in constructing technology-enhanced models, preparing publications, and producing other creative works using productivity tools. (1, 5)*
7. Use technology to locate, evaluate, and collect information from a variety of sources. (1, 4, 5)*
8. Use technology tools to process data and report results. (1, 3, 4, 5)*
9. Use technology in the development of strategies for solving problems in the real world. (1, 3, 5)*
10. Observe and experience the use of technology in their major field of study. (3, 5)
11. Use technology tools and resources for managing and communicating information (e.g., finances, schedules, addresses, purchases, correspondence). (1, 5)
12. Evaluate and select new information resources and technological innovations based on their appropriateness to specific tasks. (1, 3, 4, 5)*
13. Use a variety of media and formats, including telecommunications, to collaborate, publish, and interact with peers, experts, and other audiences. (1, 5)*
14. Demonstrate an understanding of the legal, ethical, cultural, and societal issues related to technology. (6)*
15. Exhibit positive attitudes toward technology uses that support lifelong learning, collaboration, personal pursuits, and productivity. (5, 6)*
16. Discuss diversity issues related to electronic media. (1, 6)
17. Discuss the health and safety issues related to technology use. (6)

Professional Preparation Performance Profile

Performance Tasks.   Prior to the culminating student teaching or internship experience, prospective teachers:

1. Identify the benefits of technology to maximize student learning and facilitate higher-order thinking skills. (1, 3)
2. Differentiate between appropriate and inappropriate uses of technology for teaching and learning while using electronic resources to design and implement learning activities. (2, 3, 5, 6)
3. Identify technology resources available in schools and analyze how accessibility to those resources affects planning for instruction. (1, 2)
4. Identify, select, and use hardware and software technology resources specially designed for use by PreK–12 students to meet specific teaching and learning objectives. (1, 2)
5. Plan for the management of electronic instructional resources within a lesson design by identifying potential problems and planning for solutions. (2)

6. Identify specific technology applications and resources that maximize student learning, address learner needs, and affirm diversity. (3, 6)
7. Design and teach technology-enriched learning activities that connect content standards with student technology standards and meet the diverse needs of students. (2, 3, 4, 6)
8. Design and peer teach a lesson that meets content area standards and reflects the current best practices in teaching and learning with technology. (2, 3)
9. Plan and teach student-centered learning activities and lessons in which students apply technology tools and resources. (2, 3)
10. Research and evaluate the accuracy, relevance, appropriateness, comprehensiveness, and bias of electronic information resources to be used by students. (2, 4, 5, 6)
11. Discuss technology-based assessment and evaluation strategies. (4)
12. Examine multiple strategies for evaluating technology-based student products and the processes used to create those products. (4)
13. Examine technology tools used to collect, analyze, interpret, represent, and communicate student performance data. (1, 4)
14. Integrate technology-based assessment strategies and tools into plans for evaluating specific learning activities. (4)
15. Develop a portfolio of technology-based products from coursework, including the related assessment tools. (4, 5)
16. Identify and engage in technology-based opportunities for professional education and lifelong learning, including the use of distance education. (5)
17. Apply online and other technology resources to support problem solving and related decision making for maximizing student learning. (3, 5)
18. Participate in online professional collaborations with peers and experts. (3, 5)
19. Use technology productivity tools to complete required professional tasks. (5)
20. Identify technology-related legal and ethical issues, including copyright, privacy, and security of technology systems, data, and information. (6)
21. Examine acceptable use policies for the use of technology in schools, including strategies for addressing threats to security of technology systems, data, and information. (6)
22. Identify issues related to equitable access to technology in school, community, and home environments. (6)
23. Identify safety and health issues related to technology use in schools. (6)
24. Identify and use assistive technologies to meet the special physical needs of students. (6)

Student Teaching/Internship Performance Profile

Performance Tasks.   Upon completion of the culminating student teaching or internship experience, and at the point of initial licensure, teachers:

1. Apply troubleshooting strategies for solving routine hardware and software problems that occur in the classroom. (1)

2. Identify, evaluate, and select specific technology resources available at the school site and district level to support a coherent lesson sequence. (2, 3)

3. Design, manage, and facilitate learning experiences using technology that affirm diversity and provide equitable access to resources. (2, 6)

4. Create and implement a well-organized plan to manage available technology resources, provide equitable access for all students, and enhance learning outcomes. (2, 3)

5. Design and facilitate learning experiences that use assistive technologies to meet the special physical needs of students. (2, 3)

6. Design and teach a coherent sequence of learning activities that integrates appropriate use of technology resources to enhance student academic achievement and technology proficiency by connecting district, state, and national curriculum standards with student technology standards (as defined in the ISTE National Educational Technology Standards for Students). (2, 3)

7. Design, implement, and assess learner-centered lessons that are based on the current best practices on teaching and learning with technology and that engage, motivate, and encourage self-directed student learning. (2, 3, 4, 5)

8. Guide collaborative learning activities in which students use technology resources to solve authentic problems in the subject area(s). (3)

9. Develop and use criteria for ongoing assessment of technology-based student products and the processes used to create those products. (4)

10. Design an evaluation plan that applies multiple measures and flexible assessment strategies to determine students' technology proficiency and content area learning. (4)

11. Use multiple measures to analyze instructional practices that employ technology to improve planning, instruction, and management. (2, 3, 4)

12. Apply technology productivity tools and resources to collect, analyze, and interpret data and to report results to parents and students. (3, 4)

13. Select and apply suitable productivity tools to complete educational and professional tasks. (2, 3, 5)

14. Model safe and responsible use of technology and develop classroom procedures to implement school and district technology acceptable use policies and data security plans. (5, 6)

15. Participate in online professional collaboration with peers and experts as part of a personally designed plan, based on self-assessment, for professional growth in technology. (5)

First-Year Teaching Performance Profile

Performance Tasks. Upon completion of the first year of teaching, teachers:

1. Assess the availability of technology resources at the school site, plan activities that integrate available resources, and develop a method for obtaining the additional necessary software and hardware to support the specific learning needs of students in the classroom. (1, 2, 4)

2. Make appropriate choices about technology systems, resources, and services that are aligned with district and state standards. (1, 2)
3. Arrange equitable access to appropriate technology resources that enable students to engage successfully in learning activities across subject/content areas and grade levels. (2, 3, 6)
4. Engage in ongoing planning of lesson sequences that effectively integrate technology resources and are consistent with current best practices for integrating the learning of subject matter and student technology standards (as defined in the ISTE National Educational Technology Standards for Students). (2, 3)
5. Plan and implement technology-based learning activities that promote student engagement in analysis, synthesis, interpretation, and creation of original products. (2, 3)
6. Plan for, implement, and evaluate the management of student use of technology resources as part of classroom operations and in specialized instructional situations. (1, 2, 3, 4)
7. Implement a variety of instructional technology strategies and grouping strategies (e.g., whole group, collaborative, individualized, and learner centered) that include appropriate embedded assessment for meeting the diverse needs of learners. (3, 4)
8. Facilitate student access to school and community resources that provide technological and discipline-specific expertise. (3)
9. Teach students methods and strategies to assess the validity and reliability of information gathered through technological means. (2, 4)
10. Recognize students' talents in the use of technology and provide them with opportunities to share their expertise with their teachers, peers, and others. (2, 3, 5)
11. Guide students in applying self- and peer-assessment tools to critique student-created technology products and the process used to create those products. (4)
12. Facilitate students' use of technology that addresses their social needs and cultural identity and promotes their interaction with the global community. (3, 6)
13. Use results from assessment measures (e.g., learner profiles, computer-based testing, electronic portfolios) to improve instructional planning, management, and implementation of learning strategies. (2, 4)
14. Use technology tools to collect, analyze, interpret, represent, and communicate data (student performance and other information) for the purposes of instructional planning and school improvement. (4)
15. Use technology resources to facilitate communications with parents or guardians of students. (5)
16. Identify capabilities and limitations of current and emerging technology resources and assess the potential of these systems and services to address personal, lifelong learning, and workplace needs. (1, 4, 5)
17. Participate in technology-based collaboration as part of continual and comprehensive professional growth to stay abreast of new and emerging technology resources that support enhanced learning for PreK–12 students. (5)
18. Demonstrate and advocate for legal and ethical behaviors among students, colleagues, and community members regarding the use of technology and information. (5, 6)

19. Enforce classroom procedures that guide students' safe and healthy use of technology and that comply with legal and professional responsibilities for students needing assistive technologies. (6)
20. Advocate for equal access to technology for all students in their schools, communities, and homes. (6)
21. Implement procedures consistent with district and school policies that protect the privacy and security of student data and information. (6)

In addition to these standards, the International Society for Technology in Education (ISTE) has developed performance assessment standards for initial and advanced educational computing and technology programs including (1) the technology facilitation initial endorsement; (2) the technology leadership advanced program; and (3) the secondary computer science education preparation programs. Institutions offering one or more of these programs should respond to the corresponding set of program standards (**http://cnets.iste.org/ncate/**).

The National Educational Technology Standards (NETS) Project also has been developing technology performance standards for PreK–12 students, establishing specific applications of technology through the curriculum, providing standards for support of technology in schools, and addressing student assessment and evaluation of technology used to improve learning (Bitter et al., 1997; Thomas & Bitter, 2000). The following are recommended standards and profiles for students in grades PreK–12.*

 ## ISTE National Educational Technology Standards for Students (NETS–S)

The technology standards for students are divided into six broad categories. Standards within each category are to be introduced, reinforced, and mastered by students. These categories provide a framework for linking performance tasks found within the Profiles for Technology-Literate Students to the standards. Teachers can use these standards and profiles as guidelines for planning technology-based activities in which students achieve success in learning, communication, and life skills.*

Technology Standards for Students

1. Basic operations and concepts
   - Students demonstrate a sound understanding of the nature and operation of technology systems.
   - Students are proficient in the use of technology.

2. Social, ethical, and human issues
   - Students understand the ethical, cultural, and societal issues related to technology.
   - Students practice responsible use of technology systems, information, and software.
   - Students develop positive attitudes toward technology uses that support life-long learning, collaboration, personal pursuits, and productivity.
3. Technology productivity tools
   - Students use technology tools to enhance learning, increase productivity, and promote creativity.
   - Students use productivity tools to collaborate in constructing technology-enhanced models, preparing publications, and producing other creative works.
4. Technology communications tools
   - Students use telecommunications to collaborate, publish, and interact with peers, experts, and other audiences.
   - Students use a variety of media and formats to communicate information and ideas effectively to multiple audiences.
5. Technology research tools
   - Students use technology to locate, evaluate, and collect information from a variety of sources.
   - Students use technology tools to process data and report results.
   - Students evaluate and select new information resources and technological innovations based on the appropriateness to specific tasks.
6. Technology problem-solving and decision-making tools
   - Students use technology resources for solving problems and making informed decisions.
   - Students employ technology in the development of strategies for solving problems in the real world.

NETS Profiles of Technology-Literate PreK–12 Students

A major component of the NETS project for students grades PreK–12 is the creation of general profiles of technology-literate students at key developmental points in their precollege education. These profiles provide rather broad descriptions of technology competencies that students should have developed by the time that they exit the target grades.

These profiles reflect the underlying assumption that all students should have the opportunity to develop technology skills that support learning, personal productivity, ethical behaviors, decision making, and daily life. They prepare students to be lifelong learners and make informed decisions about the role of technology in their lives.

These profiles are indicators of achievement at certain points in PreK–12 education. Technology skills are to be developed by coordinated activities that support learning throughout a child's education. They must be introduced, reinforced, and finally mastered and integrated into an individual's personal learning and social framework. The profiles reflect the following basic principles and assumptions:

1. Students acquire steadily increasing skills and knowledge related to the use of technology for enhancing personal and collaborative abilities.
2. Students acquire steadily increasing ability to make quality decisions related to managing their own learning.
3. Students acquire steadily increasing skills to work in collaboration with others, with hardware and software and information resources, and to solve problems with the support technology tools.
4. Students become responsible citizens and users of technology and information.
5. Students have access to current technology resources, including telecommunications and multimedia enhancements.
6. Students acquire skills that prepare them to learn new software and hardware technology to adapt to the complex technology environments that emerge in their lifetime.

 ## Profiles for Technology-Literate Students

Note: Numbers in parentheses listed after each performance task in the following profiles refer to the standards categories to which the performance is linked. The categories are:

1. Basic operations and concepts
2. Social, ethical, and human issues
3. Technology productivity tools
4. Technology communication tools
5. Technology research tools
6. Technology problem-solving and decision-making tools

Grades PreK–2

Performance Indicators. All students should have opportunities to demonstrate the following performances. Prior to completion of Grade 2, students will:

1. Use input devices (e.g., mouse, keyboard, remote control) and output devices (e.g., monitor, printer) to successfully operate computers, VCRs, audiotapes, and other technologies. (1)
2. Use a variety of media and technology resources for directed and independent learning activities. (1, 3)
3. Communicate about technology using developmentally appropriate and accurate terminology. (1)

4. Use developmentally appropriate multimedia resources (e.g., interactive books, educational software, elementary multimedia encyclopedias) to support learning. (1)
5. Work cooperatively and collaboratively with peers, family members, and others when using technology in the classroom. (2)
6. Demonstrate positive social and ethical behaviors when using technology. (2)
7. Practice responsible use of technology systems and software. (2)
8. Create developmentally appropriate multimedia products with support from teachers, family members, or student partners. (3)
9. Use technology resources (e.g., puzzles, logical thinking programs, writing tools, digital cameras, drawing tools) for problem solving, communication, and illustration of thoughts, ideas, and stories. (3, 4, 5, 6)
10. Gather information and communicate with others using telecommunications, with support from teachers, family members, or student partners. (4)

Grades 3–5

Performance Indicators.   All students should have opportunities to demonstrate the following performances. Prior to completion of Grade 5, students will:

1. Use keyboards and other common input and output devices (including adaptive devices when necessary) efficiently and effectively. (1)
2. Discuss common uses of technology in daily life and the advantages and disadvantages those uses provide. (1, 2)
3. Discuss basic issues related to responsible use of technology and information and describe personal consequences of inappropriate use. (2)
4. Use general-purpose productivity tools and peripherals to support personal productivity, remediate skill deficits, and facilitate learning throughout the curriculum. (3)
5. Use technology tools (e.g., multimedia authoring, presentation, web tools, digital cameras, scanners) for individual and collaborative writing, communication, and publishing activities to create knowledge products for audiences inside and outside the classroom. (3, 4)
6. Use telecommunications efficiently and effectively to access remote information, communicate with others in support of direct and independent learning, and pursue personal interests. (4)
7. Use telecommunications and online resources (e.g., email, online discussions, web environments) to participate in collaborative problem-solving activities for the purpose of developing solutions or products for audiences inside and outside the classroom. (4, 5)
8. Use technology resources (e.g., calculators, data collection probes, videos, educational software) for problem-solving, self-directed learning, and extended learning activities. (5, 6)
9. Determine when technology is useful and select the appropriate tool(s) and technology resources to address a variety of tasks and problems. (5, 6)
10. Evaluate the accuracy, relevance, appropriateness, comprehensiveness, and bias of electronic information sources. (6)

Grades 6–8

Performance Indicators. All students should have opportunities to demonstrate the following performances. Prior to completion of Grade 8, students will:

1. Apply strategies for identifying and solving routine hardware and software problems that occur during everyday use. (1)
2. Demonstrate knowledge of current changes in information technologies and the effect those changes have on the workplace and society. (2)
3. Exhibit legal and ethical behaviors when using information and technology, and discuss consequences of misuse. (2)
4. Use content-specific tools, software, and simulations (e.g., environmental probes, graphing calculators, exploratory environments, web tools) to support learning and research. (3, 5)
5. Apply productivity/multimedia tools and peripherals to support personal productivity, group collaboration, and learning throughout the curriculum. (3, 6)
6. Design, develop, publish, and present products (e.g., web pages, videotapes) using technology resources that demonstrate and communicate curriculum concepts to audiences inside and outside the classroom. (4, 5, 6)
7. Collaborate with peers, experts, and others using telecommunications and collaborative tools to investigate curriculum-related problems, issues, and information, and to develop solutions or products for audiences inside and outside the classroom. (4, 5)
8. Select and use appropriate tools and technology resources to accomplish a variety of tasks and solve problems. (5, 6)
9. Demonstrate an understanding of concepts underlying hardware, software, and connectivity, and of practical applications to learning and problem solving. (1, 6)
10. Research and evaluate the accuracy, relevance, appropriateness, comprehensiveness, and bias of electronic information sources concerning real-world problems. (2, 5, 6)

Grades 9–12

Performance Indicators. All students should have opportunities to demonstrate the following performances. Prior to completion of Grade 12, students will:

1. Identify capabilities and limitations of contemporary and emerging technology resources and assess the potential of these systems and services to address personal, lifelong learning, and workplace needs. (2)
2. Make informed choices among technology systems, resources, and services. (1, 2)
3. Analyze advantages and disadvantages of widespread use and reliance on technology in the workplace and in society as a whole. (2)
4. Demonstrate and advocate for legal and ethical behaviors among peers, family, and community regarding the use of technology and information. (2)
5. Use technology tools and resources for managing and communicating personal/ professional information (e.g., finances, schedules, addresses, purchases, correspondence). (3, 4)

6. Evaluate technology-based options, including distance and distributed education, for lifelong learning. (5)
7. Routinely and efficiently use online information resources to meet needs for collaboration, research, publications, communications, and productivity. (4, 5, 6)
8. Select and apply technology tools for research, information analysis, problem solving, and decision making in content learning. (4, 5)
9. Investigate and apply expert systems, intelligent agents, and simulations in real-world situations. (3, 5, 6)
10. Collaborate with peers, experts, and others to contribute to a content-related knowledge base by using technology to compile, synthesize, produce, and disseminate information, models, and other creative works. (4, 5, 6)

This NETS project is ongoing and will continue to be updated as technology continues to change, which causes basic skills to change. The ISTE NETS project represents this movement as well as an articulated clear vision through its development of the following standards:

- NETS for Students (ISTE, 1998) describes what students should know about technology and be able to do with technology.
- NETS for Students: Connecting Curriculum and Technology (Thomas & Bitter, 2000) describes how technology can be used throughout the curriculum for teaching, learning, and instruction management using the student standards with subject matter standards.
- NETS for Teachers (ISTE, 2000) describes what teacher candidates should know about technology and be able to do with technology.
- NETS for Teachers: Preparing Teachers to Use Technology (Thomas, 2002) describes how technology can be used throughout teacher education programs.
- Educational Technology Support Standards (2004) describes systems, access, staff development, and support services essential to support the effective use of technology.
- Standards for Student Assessment and Evaluation of Technology (2004) describes various means of assessing student progress and evaluating the use of technology in learning and teaching (**http://cnets.iste.org/state/st_overview.html**).

Most states have developed their own student technology standards or use some form of the International Society for Technology in Education (ISTE) student standards. You can access your state's standards by visiting your state's education website. States using the NETS standards can be found at **http://cnets.iste.org/docs/States_using_NETS.pdf**. For example, the Texas state standards can be found at **www.tea.state.tx.us/teks/index.html.**

Technology Standards for School Administrators (TSSA)

The Technology Standards for School Administrators (TSSA) collaborative followed the student and teacher standards with the development of administrator professional standards. These standards provide specific leadership guidelines for school administrators including principals, district program directors, and superintendents. The standards, performance indicators, and role-specific tasks can be found at **http://cnets.iste.org/administrators.**

 ## Technology Standards for Administrators*

I. Leadership and Vision:

Educational leaders inspire a shared vision for comprehensive integration of technology and foster an environment and culture conducive to the realization of that vision.

Educational leaders:
A. facilitate the shared development by all stakeholders of a vision for technology use and widely communicate that vision.
B. maintain an inclusive and cohesive process to develop, implement, and monitor a dynamic, long-range, and systemic technology plan to achieve the vision.
C. foster and nurture a culture of responsible risk-taking and advocate policies promoting continuous innovation with technology.
D. use data in making leadership decisions.
E. advocate for research-based effective practices in use of technology.
F. advocate, on the state and national levels, for policies, programs, and funding opportunities that support implementation of the district technology plan.

II. Learning and Teaching:

Educational leaders ensure that curricular design, instructional strategies, and learning environments integrate appropriate technologies to maximize learning and teaching.

Educational leaders:
A. identify, use, evaluate, and promote appropriate technologies to enhance and support instruction and standards-based curriculum leading to high levels of student achievement.
B. facilitate and support collaborative technology-enriched learning environments conducive to innovation for improved learning.
C. provide for learner-centered environments that use technology to meet the individual and diverse needs of learners.
D. facilitate the use of technologies to support and enhance instructional methods that develop higher-level thinking, decision-making, and problem-solving skills.
E. provide for and ensure that faculty and staff take advantage of quality professional learning opportunities for improved learning and teaching with technology.

*This material was originally produced as a project of the Technology Standards for School Administrators Collaborative.

III. Productivity and Professional Practice:

Educational leaders apply technology to enhance their professional practice and to increase their own productivity and that of others.

Educational leaders:
A. model the routine, intentional, and effective use of technology.
B. employ technology for communication and collaboration among colleagues, staff, parents, students, and the larger community.
C. create and participate in learning communities that stimulate, nurture, and support faculty and staff in using technology for improved productivity.
D. engage in sustained, job-related professional learning using technology resources.
E. maintain awareness of emerging technologies and their potential uses in education.
F. use technology to advance organizational improvement.

IV. Support, Management, and Operations:

Educational leaders ensure the integration of technology to support productive systems for learning and administration.

Educational leaders:
A. develop, implement, and monitor policies and guidelines to ensure compatibility of technologies.
B. implement and use integrated technology-based management and operations systems.
C. allocate financial and human resources to ensure complete and sustained implementation of the technology plan.
D. integrate strategic plans, technology plans, and other improvement plans and policies to align efforts and leverage resources.
E. implement procedures to drive continuous improvements of technology systems and to support technology replacement cycles.

V. Assessment and Evaluation:

Educational leaders use technology to plan and implement comprehensive systems of effective assessment and evaluation.

Educational leaders:
A. use multiple methods to assess and evaluate appropriate uses of technology resources for learning, communication, and productivity.
B. use technology to collect and analyze data, interpret results, and communicate findings to improve instructional practice and student learning.
C. assess staff knowledge, skills, and performance in using technology and use results to facilitate quality professional development and to inform personnel decisions.
D. use technology to assess, evaluate, and manage administrative and operational systems.

VI. Social, Legal, and Ethical Issues:

Educational leaders understand the social, legal, and ethical issues related to technology and model responsible decision making related to these issues.

Educational leaders:

A. ensure equity of access to technology resources that enable and empower all learners and educators.

B. identify, communicate, model, and enforce social, legal, and ethical practices to promote responsible use of technology.

C. promote and enforce privacy, security, and online safety related to the use of technology.

D. promote and enforce environmentally safe and healthy practices in the use of technology.

E. participate in the development of policies that clearly enforce copyright law and assign ownership of intellectual property developed with district resources.

No Child Left Behind (NCLB)

No Child Left Behind (NCLB) **(www.ed.gov/nclb/landing.jhtml?src=fb)** is education legislation enacted in 2002 which established technology literacy as fundamental to learning. This legislation called for academic excellence in the context of today's technologies. Lemke (2003) outlined four skill clusters for surviving in the twenty-first century: Digital-Age Literacy, Inventive Thinking, Effective Communication, and High Productivity. These skills are emphasized as a critical pathway to success in a highly technological age. NCLB has a strong accountability component for which technology will play a significant role (Education Week, 2003). (See **www.edweek. org/sreports/TC03/article.cfm?slug=35exec.h22.**)

In 2003, a Learning for the 21st Century report (**www.21stcenturyskills.org**) outlined six key elements of twenty-first-century learning:

1. Emphasize core subjects.
2. Emphasize learning skills.
3. Use twenty-first-century tools to develop learning skills.
4. Teach and learn in a twenty-first-century context.
5. Teach and learn twenty-first-century content.
6. Use twenty-first-century assessments that measure twenty-first-century skills.

All of these reports emphasize the role that technology is expected to play in education. Now is the time for schools to be retooled and educators retrained. For some time, education may face the same double financial burden that business has been shouldering: tools and training. Financial constraints have spurred educational systems to set priorities and develop strategies that encourage the acquisition of new technological skills and information. Some school systems are finding that some of the ideas of the 1960s and 1970s, such as open-space classrooms, peer tutoring, modular scheduling, and individualized instruction, are now more likely to succeed because instructional strategies such as cooperative learning and state-of-the-art technology can meet the logistical, managerial, and instructional needs of large numbers of students, sources, and faculty. Outside funding, business partnerships, and foundation grants are being promoted as sound investments in the development of a cooperative, interdependent system of human enterprise based on Francis Bacon's premise: Knowledge is power.

Computer Generations

The First Generation of Computers

Developed in 1944, the Mark I, made up of mechanical switches that opened and closed by electrical current, was 51 feet long, 8 feet high, and contained 1 million components and over 500 miles of electric wire. At approximately the same time, Grace Hopper and others were beginning to develop the computer languages that were necessary to program these new electronic computers. The next major development in computer technology culminated in the Electronic Numerical Integrator and Computer (ENIAC). Designed by John W. Mauchly and J. Prespert Eckert, Jr., ENIAC was intended to be used by the military. It was programmed by means of switches and connections. ENIAC was more than 1,000 times faster than the Mark I, performing 5,000 calculations per second. Weighing 60,000 pounds and containing nearly 2,000 vacuum tubes, ENIAC required tremendous amounts of electricity and gave off large amounts of heat (see Figure 1.1). The most significant feature of ENIAC was that it introduced vacuum-tube technology, and no longer were calculations and operations performed by moving mechanical parts. This gesture allowed for greatly increased speed of performance.

The first generation of computers, which thrived from 1951 until 1959, was characterized by vacuum-tube technology. Although they were amazing devices in their

FIGURE 1.1 (a) The Electronic Numerical Integrator and Computer (ENIAC), designed by John W. Mauchly and J. Prespert Eckert, Jr. (b) The ENIAC contained nearly 2,000 vacuum tubes.

(b)

(a)

time, they were large, were expensive to operate, and required almost constant maintenance to function properly. The next generation of computers attempted to resolve some of these problems.

The Second Generation of Computers

The second generation of computers extended from 1959 until 1964 and was characterized by transistor technology. The transistor was developed in 1947 by John Bardeen, Walter H. Brattain, and William B. Shockley at Bell Laboratories in New Jersey. Bardeen, Brattain, and Shockley studied substances that permitted a limited flow of electricity through semiconductors. Transistors that used semiconductor material could perform the work of vacuum tubes and took up much less space.

Because transistors were smaller, the distance between operating parts was reduced, and speed of performance was increased significantly. Transistors were also much cooler than vacuum tubes, reducing the need for expensive air conditioning in areas where computers were housed (see Figure 1.2).

Transistors did present several problems, though. They were relatively expensive because each transistor and its related parts had to be inserted individually into holes in a plastic board. Also, wires had to be fastened by floating boards in a pool of molten solder. The number of parts required for even the simplest transistors was staggering. The next generation of computers helped to alleviate some of these problems.

The Third Generation of Computers

The development of integrated circuits in 1963 spawned the third generation of computers, lasting from 1964 until 1975. The production process begins when tubes of silicon are sliced into wafer-thin disks that are chemically pure and cannot hold electrical charge. A preconceived design is etched onto the surface of the wafer with the use of light rays and the wafer is placed in an acid bath to eliminate all unexposed areas. To enable the wafer to carry an electrical impulse, slight traces of impurities must be added in a specified pattern. Finally, a fine diamond saw slices through the wafer and divides it into dozens of blocks, like postage stamps in a large sheet. Each tiny piece is now a chip, which is encased and connected to the outside of the case with gold wires (see Figure 1.3).

FIGURE 1.2 Electronic panel containing transistors. Invention of the transistor made possible a decrease in the size and an increase in the power of computers.

FIGURE 1.3 (a) One step in the manufacture of integrated circuits. (b) The integrated circuit led to smaller computers. (c) Magnified view of an integrated circuit.

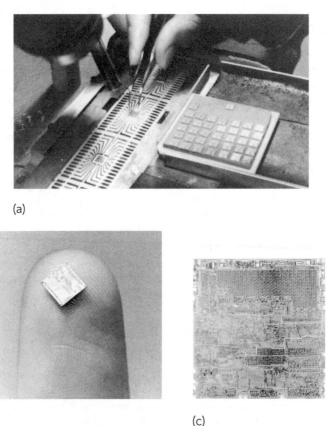

(a)

(b)　　　　　　　　　　　　　(c)

Third-generation computers were designed as general-purpose computers, representing a giant leap forward in the data-processing field. Not only were speed and reliability enhanced, but power consumption was decreased markedly. Computers became smaller and less expensive, putting computer power into the hands of a greater number of users than ever before.

The Fourth Generation of Computers

As engineers learned how to manufacture chips more easily, they conceived the idea of grouping an assortment of functions on a single chip, creating a microelectronic "system" capable of performing various tasks required for a single job. This technology became known as large-scale integration (LSI). Thus, the fourth generation of computers was born in the mid-1970s.

LSI has many applications other than large-scale computers, such as the pocket calculator and the digital watch. Still another innovation of LSI technology was the computer-on-a-chip. Its manufacturers compress nearly all the subsystems of a computer into 1/20 square inch. This led to Intel developing in 1971 the world's first microprocessor. The 4004 was made up of 2,250 transistors while today the Pentium 4 processor has over 42 million transistors (see Figures 1.4, 1.5, and 1.6). LSI technology is responsible for the popularity of the computer as prices have continued to decline and computers are easier to maintain. (See Table 1.1 for a summary of this decline in computer costs.)

Future Generations of Computers

A hint of tomorrow's computer capability can be found in very large-scale integrated (VLSI) circuitry, which further increased the speed at which computers were able to function.

Multiprocessing, the simultaneous running of several programs by one computer, is being developed further in fifth-generation computers. Today, the personal computer has become an important interactive tool for teaching and learning. Multimedia

FIGURE 1.4 Original Apple I.

FIGURE 1.5 Apple I board.

FIGURE 1.6 Steve Jobs's garage, where the original Apple computer was produced.

TABLE 1.1	Decreasing Cost of Computer Operations	
Generations	**Technology**	**Cost per 100,000 Computations**
First	Vacuum tubes	$1.25
Second	Transistors	0.25
Third	Integrated circuits	0.10
Fourth	LSI	Less than 0.01

peripherals, CD-ROM (compact disc read-only memory), CD-RW (compact disc rewritable), and DVD (digital versatile disc) can be interfaced with the personal computer and the World Wide Web, which greatly expanded its utilization. Personal computers with their multimedia capabilities are continually being integrated into the classroom curriculum. Using personal computers and the World Wide Web, educators are creating new learning environments. Within these environments, teachers become facilitators and students become constructors of knowledge. Together, teachers and students become knowledge navigators, a term coined by John Sculley, past CEO of Apple Computers.

Certainly, the trend of miniaturization witnessed throughout the past several generations of computers will also continue in the next generations, concentrating greater amounts of computer capacity in ever smaller spaces (Moore's Law).

Finding Your Way around a Computer

There are a number of terms that are basic to an understanding of computer operations.

Software

Software, also called computer programs, refers to the commands that instruct the computer to perform tasks in a specific logical sequence. People who write these instructions are called computer programmers.

Hardware

In contrast to software, computer hardware is the physical machinery that makes up the computer system. Hardware is the equipment that you see when you visit a computer room or computer retail store. Computer hardware is sophisticated electronic equipment that must be handled and used appropriately and safely, and maintained properly in order for the computer system to operate with optimal efficiency.

CPU

The heart of the computer system is the central processing unit (CPU). The CPU controls all the computer's functions because it is made up of circuitry that interprets and

FIGURE 1.7 The central processing unit (CPU).

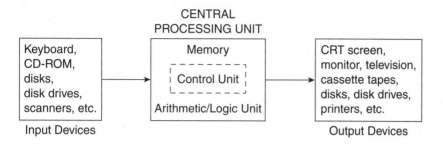

carries out instructions written into software. The CPU also retrieves software instructions before decoding and executing them. The components of the CPU are the arithmetic/logic unit (ALU), the memory, and the control unit (see Figure 1.7).

The ALU is that part of the CPU capable of performing mathematical calculations required for many data-processing applications. The memory of the CPU is made up of integrated circuitry in which information can be stored. The control unit of the CPU controls the flow of the computer's operations, including data transfer, acceptance of input, functioning of the ALU, and other related functions (see Figure 1.8).

FIGURE 1.8 Primary components of a computer system.

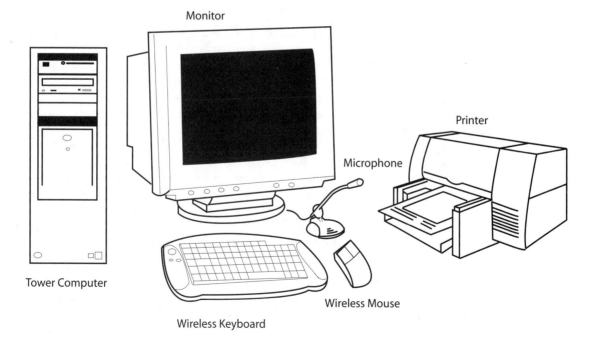

The Microphone and Keyboard

Through microphones and keyboards, instructions and data are entered into the computer system. Advances in speech technology have made hands-free control of systems, applications software, and web searching possible. The personal computer keyboard is made up of keys that represent letters of the alphabet and numbers, as well as special symbols such as @, $, %, and *, and special-function keys that instruct the computer to perform specific tasks. Wireless technologies now provide untethered keyboard communication with other computers, printers, notebooks, and peripherals.

Computer Memory

A greater amount of memory capacity can be included in the CPU than was previously possible. Adding memory to a personal computer is a simple and affordable process that most users can perform themselves. To determine the memory size of a personal computer system, it is necessary to understand several quantitative terms that apply to computer capability. A digital computer operates using a binary system of 0's and 1's. A binary digit is called a bit and is the smallest unit of digital information. A byte is the number of bits necessary to store one character of text.

- one byte = 8 or 16 bits
- one kilobyte (KB) = 1,024 bytes
- one megabyte (MB) = 1 million bytes
- one gigabyte (GB) = 1,024 MB

A major advantage of personal computer systems is that extra memory space can be added simply and quickly as the needs of the user expand. Extra memory space allows the system to operate with greater speed and efficiency. More complex programs with lengthier instructions can be stored and run on a system to which extra memory space has been added.

There are two major types of semiconductor memory: random-access memory (RAM) and read-only memory (ROM). RAM is designed to store new data and programs. Data and program instructions are entered into the memory of the central processing unit and then accessed, or retrieved from memory, in random fashion. RAM is not permanent memory. For example, if the computer system loses power during operation, the information stored in RAM is lost forever. To maintain program instructions and data in the assigned RAM locations, the system must "refresh" its memory. The system does this by supplying small amounts of electricity to memory locations at the rapid speed of several hundreds or even thousands of times per second. In contrast to RAM, ROM (read-only memory) is comprised of computer chips that have had program instructions manufactured into them permanently. Information stored on ROM chips cannot be lost in the event of a power failure.

Memory Storage Devices

Another essential part of computer hardware is the memory storage device. Storage devices retain data and instructions outside of the computer's central processing unit so that information is not lost when the computer is turned off. The most popular storage device in use for computers in general is the magnetic disk drive. Each disk has two recording surfaces: top and bottom. On the recording surfaces are concentric circles moving outward from the center of the disk to its edge. Inside the disk drive are mounted several read/write heads that record and retrieve information on magnetic disks.

Information stored on magnetic disks is relatively safe from loss. Loss of stored material may result from writing too much information onto a disk. Disks may also be erased by a computer-controlled device called a bulk eraser. Accidental loss of information stored on magnetic disks is unusual, though, and this factor adds to the popularity of magnetic disk storage.

The floppy disk functions similarly to the hard disk. Floppy disks today (or diskettes) have a diameter of 3.5 inches and are enclosed within a hard plastic container. Floppy disks can now hold over one hundred times the information once stored on a 5.25-inch disk. Many other types of memory devices exist with even greater storage capacities. They include CD-ROMs with rewrite capabilities, DVD-ROMs, various types of data cards, and the use of network capabilities. Pocket and mobile drives can be used to externally store data (see Figures 1.9 and 1.10).

Scanners are another method of entering information into the computer. Text scanners can "read" textual information printed on a page from any source. Image scanners "read" black-and-white and color images. These scanners convert the analog information to digital information. Some scanners also convert text to speech.

FIGURE 1.9 (left) 100-disk CD changer. (right) 50-disk CD changer.

FIGURE 1.10 CD-rewritable recorder.

Still other methods of inputting information are optical character readers (OCRs), optical mark readers (OMRs), and bar-code readers. For example, OCRs "read" the characters on the bottom of personal checks as well as all mail sent to a post office. Some uses of OMRs are to score objective tests for which the answers have been blacked in, to control the inventory of library books, and to monitor classroom attendance.

Display Devices

Display devices enable humans to see what instructions are being given to the computer; to respond to erroneous information; to enter data and verify data for correctness; and to see the output, or final product, of the computer's operation. Personal computer systems rely on a variety of video screens for display purposes. Many computers can be adapted for use with ordinary television screens, the most common video screen in our society. Video games that plug into the family television set are popular examples (see Figure 1.11).

With improvements in flat panel technology and lower-cost versions, liquid-crystal displays (LCDs) will continue to replace cathode-ray tube screens (CRTs). LCDs are often used to project for presentations and classroom lessons (see Figure 1.12). The next generation of displays for television and computers is HDTV (high-definition television). This display provides much clearer images and displays. The advent of HDTV will mean the demise of one of the last vacuum tubes—the television picture tube.

FIGURE 1.11 Flat panel multimedia monitor.

Printing Devices

Once the computer has completed its data-processing function, it is necessary to generate some human-readable, permanent copy of the resulting output. A record of computer transactions printed onto paper is referred to as hard copy, often necessary for filing purposes or for reporting the results of data processing to others.

Reliance on dot-matrix printers, which printed text by actually impacting the paper with a printing element, has shifted now to two common printer types, the inkjet and laser. Inkjet printers electrostatically spray small ink droplets from a nozzle onto the paper. Laser printing employs some design concepts that have been used in photocopying machines. Laser printing is much quieter than impact printing and is capable of printing copy of nearly typeset quality. The initial purchase of a laser printer is more expensive than the matrix and inkjet printers. However, the dura-

FIGURE 1.12 (a) LCD projector. (b) LCD panel.

(a) ⠀⠀(b)

bility of the laser copy and the avoidance of smudging and fading problems give laser printers the advantage over inkjet printers.

An emerging color printing technology is High Fidelity or Hi-Fi. Although still expensive, Hi-Fi color technology provides an alternative to traditional four-color offset printing methods. By increasing the number of standard colors from four (cyan, magenta, yellow, and black) to six, seven, or even eight colors, the accuracy of reproducing screen images increases.

Conclusion

Now that you have a moderate vocabulary of computer terminology and can recognize the function of various kinds of computer hardware, you are ready to explore the uses of computers for teaching and learning. Modern computers are user friendly with help options and automatic features, along with sophisticated software that allows the average user to bypass complicated programming of the past. Later chapters will cover uses of emerging hardware, interactive software, and the quickly growing online environment, advances those early pioneers in the computer area would have been amazed to witness.

Summary

Because computers are pervasive in our society, there is a great need for people, young and old, to become computer literate. Computer awareness refers to the ability to recognize computers and work comfortably with them. Computer literacy, often referred to as technology literacy, refers to a fundamental understanding of computer operations and terms, applications of computers in society, and uses and limitations of technology. Educational technology standards and profiles are essential for all students. Technology literacy is a given in our society.

One reasonable place to begin with computer and technology literacy is to gain an understanding of the history of the machines themselves. Although many primitive mathematical devices contributed to the development of computer technology, the first generation of computers was considered to have begun with the introduction of vacuum-tube technology. The second generation of computers incorporated transistor technology in an attempt to resolve some of the problems presented by vacuum tubes. The third generation of computers was based on integrated-circuit technology, which was enhanced in the large-scale integrated (LSI) circuits of the fourth generation of computers.

We can speculate about the future generations of computers based on the trends that are currently emerging. Very large-scale integration (VLSI) technology has continued the trend toward miniaturization, making computer systems smaller, more powerful, and more affordable. As this occurs, computers will gain even more popularity. The logical consequence of this trend will be an increased need for computer literacy for people of all ages and occupations.

Computers are a vital part of our society today. The personal computer industry with the advent of electronic mail and the World Wide Web is booming, indicating that a great number of people are discovering the benefits of computing and technology. This will require that technology users acquire a greater degree of technological literacy.

Software refers to the written instructions that tell a computer how to operate. Hardware refers to the electronic equipment that carries out the software instructions. The central processing unit, the brains of the computer system, is made up of the arithmetic/logic unit, the control unit, and memory. Other hardware devices include storage devices such as magnetic disk drives and display devices such as the video screen, input devices such as keyboards, and output devices such as thermal printers, inkjet printers, and laser printers.

DVD/VIDEO VIGNETTE

Commutative Properties of Multiplication Using Graphing Calculators

In this lesson, students use graphing calculators to enhance their understanding of the commutative property of multiplication.

Challenge Yourself!

1. Interview a local businessperson and write a report about how his or her company uses personal computers.
2. Write a report comparing the national, your state, and a local District Technology Plan.
3. Determine the technology teacher standards required in your state. How do they compare to the ISTE requirements?

4. Research the contributions of women (other than those discussed in this chapter) to the development of computers.

5. Design a sequence of lessons for one ISTE Technology Foundation standard for students.

6. Spend some time in reflective analysis of the DVD/Video Vignette. When you first view the video segment, stop the DVD player at various stages and write down what your next step would be in this lesson if you were the teacher. After viewing the DVD Video Vignette, list the changes you would make in teaching this lesson.

7. Review the DVD Video Vignette for this chapter. Identify and list the NETS Student Standards that are covered in the lesson. List the strengths and weaknesses of the lesson. Compare your results with those of your classmates.

8. Develop a portfolio assessment plan for one of the technology-literate student profiles.

9. Select one of the performance tasks and provide student activities to determine a student's understanding of the content listed.

10. Outline the need for computer literacy education in the public schools. At what age should students be introduced to computers?

11. Design a lesson plan that introduces one major application of computers in our society.

12. Research and prepare a report on how extensively computers are used in your local school district for administrative functions and curriculum enhancement.

13. Research and prepare a report on the extent to which the International Society for Technology in Education (ISTE) National Educational Technology Standards for Teachers have been implemented in college and university teacher preparation programs.

14. Research and prepare a report on how computers are used in the musical and/or visual arts. In what ways are computers being used in the composition of music? How are computers used in teaching piano keyboarding skills? How are textile artists and weavers using computers to design their hand-woven pieces?

15. Visit a retail store that sells primarily electronic equipment. Observe and prepare a report on how the use of the computer-on-a-chip has influenced the size and capability of electronic "gadgets."

16. Outline a plan for implementing the NETS PreK–12 student profiles into education in the United States. Include factors of cost, availability, and education implications.

17. Review the No Child Left Behind (NCLB) legislation and prepare a list of programs in which technology plays a role.

18. Compare the student, teacher, and administrator standards. Prepare a PowerPoint presentation showing the similarity and differences of the standards for each group.

19. Research current developments in computer memory technology. Identify major trends.

20. Prepare a report including a time line of the evolution of the computer.

References

Association for Supervision and Curriculum. (1997, November). Integrating technology into teaching. *Educational Leadership, 55*(3).

Bitter, G. G. (1991). Vision: Technologically enriched school of tomorrow (TEST) communicator. *Journal of the California Association for the Gifted, 21*(1), 20–21.

Bitter, G. G. (1992). *Macmillan encyclopedia of computers.* New York: Macmillan.

Bitter, G. G., Thomas, L., Knezek, D. G., Friske, J., Taylor, H., Wiebe, J., & Kelly, M. G. (1997). National educational technology standards: Developing new learning environments for today's 1998 classrooms. *Bulletin of the National Association of Secondary Principals, 81*(592), 52–58.

Brady, M. L. (1991). Keeping current with technology. *Mathematics Teacher, 84,* 92–96.

Brush, T., & Bitter, G. G. (2000). An innovative approach to high-tech learning. *Learning and Leading with Technology, 28*(1), 22–30.

Bush, G. (1991). *America 2000—Source book.* Washington, DC: U.S. Department of Education.

CEO Forum on Education and Technology. (2000, June). *The power of digital learning: Integrating digital content.* Washington, DC: Author.

Chung, J. (1991). Collaborative learning systems: The design of instructional environments for the emerging new school. *Educational Technology, 31*(12), 15–22.

Clements, D. H. (1991). Enhancement of creativity in computer environments. *American Educational Research Journal, 28,* 173–187.

Collins, A. (1991). The role of technology in restructuring schools. *Phi Delta Kappan, 73,* 28–36.

Collins, A., Hawkins, J., & Frederickson, J. R. (1991). *Three different views of students: The role of technology in assessing student performance.* New York: Center for Children and Technology, Bank Street College of Education.

Cradler, J., et al. (2002). Research implications for preparing teachers to use technology. *Learning and Leading with Technology, 30*(1), 50–53.

David, J. L. (1991). Restructuring and technology: Partners in change. *Phi Delta Kappan, 73,* 37–40.

Dichard, N. (2003). *The sustainability challenge: Taking ed tech to the next level.* Boston, MA: Education Development Center/Benton Foundation.

Flagg, B. N. (1990). *Formative evaluation for educational technologies.* Hillsdale, NJ: Lawrence Erlbaum.

Frand, J. L. (2000). The information age mindset: Changes in students and implications for higher education. *Educause Review, 35*(5), 15–24.

Friesen, J. (2003). Giving students 21st century skills: A practical guide to contemporary literacy. *Multimedia Schools, 10*(3), 22–26.

Fuller, H. L. (2000). First teach their teachers: Technology support and computer use in academic subjects. *Journal of Research on Computing in Education, 32*(4), 511–537.

Education Week. (2003). (Eds.). Pencils down: Technology's answer to testing. *Education Week, 22*(35).

Fulton, K. (1997). *Learning in a digital age: Insights into the issues.* Santa Monica, CA: Milken Exchange on Educational Technology.

Griffin, H., et al. (2002). Using technology to enhance cues for children with low vision. *Teaching Exceptional Children, 35*(2), 36–42.

International Society for Technology in Education. (1998, June). *National Educational Technology Standards for Students.* Eugene, OR: Author.

International Society for Technology in Education. (2000, June). *National Educational Technology Standards for Teachers.* Eugene, OR: Author.

Johnson, D. L., & Maddux, C. D. (Eds.). (1997). *Using technology in the classroom.* New York: Haworth Press.

Johnson, D. L., & Maddux, C. D. (Eds.). (2003). Technology in education: A twenty year retrospective. *Computers in the Schools, 20*(1/2), 1–186.

Kinnaman, D. E. (1990). What's the research telling us? *Classroom Computer Learning, 10*(6), 31–39.

Lee, L., et al. (2002). Taking the leap into meeting state standards. *Multimedia Schools, 9*(4), 12–16.

Lemke, C. (2003). Standards for a modern world: Preparing students for the future. *Learning and Leading with Technology, 31*(1), 6–9, 21.

McCarthy, R. (1990). The hardware dilemma. *Electronic Learning, 9*(5), 20–24.

The National Commission on Excellence in Education. (1983, April). A *nation at risk: The imperative for educational reform.* Washington, DC: U.S. Department of Education.

Papert, S. (1980). *Mindstorms: Children, computers, and powerful ideas.* New York: Basic Books.

Quality Counts 2003. (2003). *Education Week 22*(17).

Roblyer, M. D. (2003). Getting our netsworth: The role of ISTE's National Educational Technology Standards. *Learning and Leading with Technology, 30*(8), 6–13.

Serim, F. (2002). No child left behind—the implications for educators. *Multimedia Schools, 9*(4), 26–29.

Sheekey, A. (2003) (Ed.). *How to ensure ed/tech is not oversold and underused.* Lanham, MD: Scarecrow Press.

Software and Information Industry Association. (2000). *2000 report on the effectiveness of technology in schools: Executive summary.* Washington, DC: Author.

Solomon, C. (1986). *Computer environments for children.* Cambridge, MA: MIT Press.

Sutton, R. E. (1991). Equity and computers in the schools: A decade of research. *Review of Educational Research, 61*(4), 475–503.

Taylor, R. (1980). *The computer in the school: Tutor, tool, tutee.* New York: Teachers College Press.

Thomas, L. (2002). (Ed.). *National Educational Technology Standards for Teachers: Preparing teachers to use technology.* Eugene, OR: International Society for Technology in Education.

Thomas, L., & Bitter, G. G. (2000). (Eds.). *National Educational Technology Standards for Students: Connecting curriculum and technology.* Eugene, OR: International Society for Technology in Education.

Technology Counts 2002. (2002). (Eds.). *Education Week, 21*(35).

Vockell, E. L. (1990). Instruction principles behind computer use. *The Computing Teacher, 18*(1), 10–15.

Webb, B. (2000). Planning-and-organizing-assistive technology resources in your school. *Teaching Exceptional Children, 32*(4), 50–55.

Wissock, C., & Gardner, J. E. (2000). Multimedia or not multimedia: That is the question for students with learning disabilities. *Teaching Exceptional Children, 32*(4), 34–43.

Websites

Intel Corporation   **www.intel.com**

International Society for Technology in Education   **www.iste.org**

National Educational Technology Standards for Teachers and Students   **http://cnets.iste.org**

NCATE Technology Report   **www.ncate.org**

Technology Based Learning and Research   **http://tblr.ed.asu.edu**

Basic Productivity Operations

CHAPTER 2

FOCUS QUESTIONS

1. How can productivity software be used for teaching and learning?

2. How can spreadsheets and databases be used to address different learning goals?

Productivity software is readily available on new computers and relatively easy to learn for new computer users. Fortunately, these tools are also some of the most versatile ways to put computers to work making your personal and professional life more efficient. The authors believe that learning disconnected software procedures out of context is not the most effective way to become a technologically proficient teacher. Students will remember what they learn longer if they learn it for a real purpose. This chapter, therefore, is not intended as a step-by-step tutorial. For such detailed direction, students are encouraged to consult the Help features of the specific software they are using or other software procedure manuals. Instead, this chapter serves as an overview of the educational possibilities of the most common productivity applications: word processing, spreadsheet, and database applications.

Most productivity software is now available as an integrated suite of software from one publisher, designed to function together to provide the user the most effective options and compatibility. All of the tools in the suite share some features in common so that the user can move easily among the suite components. The following terms describe functions common to most productivity software tools. These commands are generally available from pulldown menus, buttons on a toolbar, and keyboard shortcuts. (See Table 2.1.)

Word Processing

Word processing is the writing, manipulating, and storing of textual material in a computerized medium, and it is a tool that has become a vital everyday function in classrooms, offices, and homes. Advanced software features now allow users to move beyond these simple operations to interact with other software, to embed multimedia elements into documents, and to easily save files in web-ready format. (See Table 2.2.)

TABLE 2.1	Common Productivity Features
Bold	An individual character, a word, or a block of text may be printed in bold type for emphasis.
Center	Centering means automatically placing titles and other text evenly between the left and right margins.
Copy	The user can highlight and copy text already entered in one part of a document to be pasted into another part of the document automatically without having to retype it.
Find	Given the Find command, the software will locate and pause at every occurrence of a particular character, word, phrase, or number in a text.
Footer	The footer is the text at the bottom of a page, such as a page number or section title. Footers may be programmed to appear on all or any number of specified pages.
Header	The header is the text at the top of a page; this space can consist of a heading, image, page numbers, or any other text that the user wishes to have appear on every page or specified pages of a document.
Macro	A macro is a shortcut for entering frequently used commands by recording and saving a sequence of keystrokes in a file that can be recalled for future use. Each macro is assigned a name that the user types to implement the series of keystrokes or data that it represents.
Margins	The space around the text at the edge of the paper may be specified, left and right, as well as top and bottom.
Paste	The user can insert text that has been copied or cut from another part of a document without having to retype it.
Print	The Print command directs the computer to print an entire document, or a portion of it, in multiple copies and various formats.
Replace	This command will find every occurrence of a particular character, word, phrase, or number in a document and replace it with another character, word, phrase, or number.
Save	The Save command copies the document to a disk for storage. Documents can generally be saved in a variety of formats to be accessible in other software programs or to be displayed on the World Wide Web.
Scroll	Scrolling is moving quickly through a document vertically or horizontally.
Type Style	Type style refers to the font, the design of the characters, and the size of the text.
Underline	Characters, words, or blocks of text may be underlined, either continuously (words and spaces) or separately (words only).

TABLE 2.2   Word Processing Fundamentals

Many characteristics are common to most word processing software, so that once learned, users can typically transfer similar skills among different programs.

Break	A break is a mark inserted to manually separate pages, columns, or sections so that text can be segmented or formatting can be customized.
Bullet	An individual character that marks the items in a list is a bullet.
Columns	It is often desirable to present text in multiple vertical sections on one page, similar to newspaper text. Text in columns can continue from one column to another on the same page and onto subsequent pages, with the word wrap function keeping the text within the defined column width.
Grammar Check	The Grammar Check command identifies grammatical mistakes in the document and suggests alternate wording.
Insert	The insert feature allows the user to add items to the text of a document, such as pictures, other files, objects, comments, and symbols.
Justify	The word processor can easily produce text with even, or justified, right and left margins.
Merge	The merge function allows information from two or more documents to be combined. The classroom teacher can use the merge function to combine a form letter with a document containing student and parent names and addresses so that the letters appear to be individualized for each family.
Spacing	Spacing refers to how many blank line spaces there are between lines of text. The usual defaults are single spacing and double spacing, although there are capabilities for half-line spacing options as well.
Spell Check	Spell checking features use a preloaded dictionary of common words. The spell checker will highlight words that are spelled incorrectly or that are not recognized, either when manually activated or automatically as words are typed. The user may then select the correct word from a list of choices or type the correct spelling. Some common words can be automatically corrected as they are typed.
Tab	Similar to a typewriter tab, the cursor moves a predetermined number of spaces to the right each time the tab key is pressed.
Tables	Tables consist of individual cells arranged in any configuration of rows and columns, limited only by the width of the document itself. Table columns and rows can be manipulated in much the same way as other text, such as inserted, deleted, moved, and copied. When revising a document, each column is treated as a separate block of text or media elements and can be changed without affecting other columns.
Thesaurus	The thesaurus will, on command, produce a list of words of similar meaning that may be substituted for a given word. If the list contains a more appropriate word, the user may then instruct the computer to exchange a word for the given word.
Track Changes	This feature allows multiple writers to edit a single document, marking insertions and deletions in different colors for each user.

Word Processing in Education

Word processing is often the first use of computers in classrooms because its capabilities can quickly improve efficiency of PreK–12 students and teachers alike. Word processors in the classroom can expand the horizons of learning in ways not possible before this technology was available. Users can produce professional-quality documents with the limitless ability to edit, change layouts, and reformat. As students and teachers create documents, the word processor prompts them to consider how the material will appear on the printed page, including choices about margins, spacing, and font.

Spelling and vocabulary are other areas in which students are provided with instant feedback. By using the *spell check* feature, students can tell whether a word is spelled incorrectly and often can select the correct spelling. The *thesaurus* feature provides a list of words with similar meanings, allowing students to vary word choice and to augment their written vocabulary. *Grammar check* features highlight any problematic sentence structure, encouraging students to consider options for rewording. The immediacy of these individualized help options promotes continuous learning, prevents students from repeating errors, and extends the teacher's capabilities by offering another dimension of assistance to students.

By using a word processor's many functions, students can produce better first drafts that are eye-pleasing and easy for the teacher to read and grade. Students are able to see their work as valued and are more able and likely to make revisions, retrieving the original and making the necessary changes, without having to reproduce the whole text.

FIGURE 2.1 A student composes a story using a word processor.

Composing text on the screen is a new skill made possible by word processors (see Figure 2.1). Depending on the age and abilities of students and the type of work being done, the steps of handwriting a rough draft and then typing a final version can be bypassed. On-screen composition requires different organizational and mental skills, which likely will be necessary for future employment. Teachers also might prefer to evaluate text on screen rather than from a printed copy. The editing feature enables collaborative writing processes between teachers and students as well as among peer teams. One piece of writing can be edited by multiple people, thereby encompassing a variety of expertise and viewpoints. The time saved for both student and teacher is one of the positive aspects of word processing.

Content areas such as history, social studies, English, foreign languages, science, and the arts also benefit from the use of word processing. On any level, teachers can prepare lesson

How Does This Look in the Classroom?

1. Teach students peer editing by using the editing features in word processing software. Have one student electronically distribute a piece of writing to a series of partners. The Track Changes feature automatically saves each editor's contributions in a different color. If students have the ability to change their User Information, each student's comments will additionally appear with the author's initials.
2. Experiment with different fonts and text formatting as a design study. Have students discuss how the perception of a piece of text changes when formatted in various ways.
3. Tables are simple ways to format student work pages, from fill-in-the-blanks to lab reports to flash cards. Either print for students to work with on paper, or protect the document as a Form so students can fill in on screen.
4. Design templates for reuse in a range of assignments, such as a template for a picture story book or report in which students can enter their text and insert clip art or photos. Teach students to open templates from an easy-to-find folder and Save As to their own directory or disk.
5. Use the Auto Style formatting to demonstrate the organization of a paper with multiple heading levels. Students can quickly see whether their headings are organized by viewing the paper in Outline view.

plans, examinations, and other classroom materials using a word processor (see Chapters 10–12). The material can be updated from year to year as necessary without having to re-create the whole body of information. In addition, teachers can administer and grade exams and quizzes using a word processor (see Chapter 15). Word processing can assist educators to meet professional and administrative needs, including writing manuscripts, research reports, grant proposals, and public relations materials (see Chapter 17).

Spreadsheets

Perhaps the best way to describe an electronic *spreadsheet* is to visualize on the computer screen an accountant's ledger sheet with its array of horizontal rows and vertical columns. Each row and column contains information, either letters or numbers, which may be organized in such a way as to be meaningful to the user. Although the electronic spreadsheet performs exactly such a function, that is only the beginning of its capabilities. Each piece of data entered into the spreadsheet is considered as it relates to all the other data contained therein. In this way, any change made in one cell can affect the whole spreadsheet, with the spreadsheet automatically able to re-compute and update any data affected by an entry. It takes little imagination to recognize the time saved and errors avoided over doing the same task on a ledger sheet, with an eraser and calculator at hand. (See Table 2.3.)

TABLE 2.3 Spreadsheet Fundamentals

The spreadsheet has three modes of operation: *ready, entry,* and *command.* The user always begins in the ready mode, in which the directional, or arrow, keys can be used to move around within the spreadsheet. When the user begins to enter data into the spreadsheet, the entry mode is activated automatically. The command mode is used to manipulate or perform calculations on data for various purposes.

Analysis	Analysis is the examination and evaluation of data.
Cell	A cell is the point on the spreadsheet at which a row and column intersect. Most programs provide letter designations for columns and number designations for rows. Thus, the cell location D3 can be found at the intersection of column D and row 3.
Chart	A graphics option allows the user to create visual aids, such as pie charts, based on the figures represented in the spreadsheet so that the data can be compared and evaluated at a glance.
Copy	Copying in spreadsheets is done in two ways: *duplicating* (or exact copying of data) and *replicating* (sometimes called relative copying). Duplicating is the copying of a block of data—defined by a cell, row, column, or a range of these—exactly as it appears. Replicating is the copying of formulas and functions, so that once pasted, the calculation will be performed on the data contained in a new column or row.
Cursor Movement	The directional arrows move the cursor to the left or right and up or down. Some programs allow the cursor to move more rapidly when the Home, End, Page Up, or Page Down keys are pressed. In addition, most programs allow the user to move directly to any specific cell location with a Go To command.
Fill	Clicking a *fill handle* on the corner of a cell and dragging to adjacent cells allows formulas to be copied and series of predictable information, such as a number, date, or time series, to be extended automatically.
Format	The Format command is used to define the arrangement and placement of a selection of data. The user can also format the way data is interpreted, such as numerical or dates.
Formulas	Formulas used in spreadsheets are much like the mathematical formulas used elsewhere. Formulas are entered into the cell where the result is to be displayed. Although the cell actually contains the formula, the user does not see it but rather sees its numeric result on the screen. Whenever a value is changed in any of the cells that the formula uses, the resulting numerical value changes automatically.
Functions	Functions are preprogrammed formulas that are most commonly used in spreadsheets (e.g., the function *SUM* adds numbers in a designated group of cells).
Graph	A graphics option allows the user to create visual aids, such as line graphs and vertical and horizontal bar graphs, based on the figures represented in the spreadsheet so that the data can be compared at a glance.
Insert	The insert feature allows the user to insert an entire row or column without disturbing data that have already been entered.
Labels	Labels are titles, names, or other identifying information that describe the contents of rows or columns.
Modeling	Users can employ what-if statements to create a model of what might occur if certain conditions existed. The value can be a change in actual numbers or an increase or decrease by a specified percentage rate.

TABLE 2.3	Continued
Projection	Projection is the use of spreadsheet calculations to predict what may be logically expected to occur in the future based on data that have been collected.
Status Line	An aid for entering data correctly is the status line, telling the user where the cursor is located and what that cell contains.
Values	Values are numbers entered into any cell. The computer always interprets numeric entries as values, unless indicated otherwise.
Worksheet	Spreadsheets allow one open file to contain a number of different worksheets, or the documents used to store and manipulate data. Calculations can be performed on multiple worksheets simultaneously.

Spreadsheets in Education

One of the most obvious uses for spreadsheets in education is for numerical applications, such as for manipulating math and science information and understanding mathematical formulas. By entering instructions in the form of formulas, students reinforce the learning of mathematical symbols and the standard order of precedence. Decimals, percentages, and the computation of simple and compound interest are other mathematical areas expedited and explained more fully when displayed in spreadsheet format.

In addition to math, other subjects may also be better explained, as well as made more interesting, with the use of spreadsheets. The analysis of social studies data (such as population growth, income distribution, census information) and the results of scientific studies are only a few of the potential uses for spreadsheets in classroom teaching. Another educational function for spreadsheets is the management of research data. Large amounts of demographic and statistical information can be gathered through survey questionnaires and entered into a computer's database. The spreadsheet can be used to compile and analyze the data in whatever way fits the purpose of the research project (see Figure 2.2).

Students will be working in the real world—in business and industry, in education, or in government or nonprofit agencies. Because spreadsheets will inevitably be a part of their world, students will benefit from hands-on classroom experience with spreadsheet software.

Teachers can use spreadsheets to maintain student records and grade reports. To use the computer's power to manipulate data most effectively, grades can be combined to compute average, mean, median, and various ranges in a class or group of classes. Specific data can also be isolated from the rest, for example, to view an individual student's records. Virtually any piece of information desired is at the user's fingertips.

Databases

Before the advent of computers, information files had to be maintained manually, with paper-based files kept on index cards stored alphabetically in boxes or drawers or file

How Does This Look in the Classroom?

1. Locate and download raw data online (try the Raw Data link on the Landmarks for Schools site at **www.landmark-project.com/index.php**). Have students pose questions and then manipulate data to find answers.
2. Students can compose a survey based on a topic they are studying. Survey data can be entered into a spreadsheet and then graphed to assist analysis of what the data mean.
3. Design a multisheet workbook in which student grades from a main grade book feed into individual student grade sheets to protect the confidentiality of other students. Using their own grade tracking templates, students can monitor their progress and experiment with what-if scenarios for necessary grades on future assignments.
4. Have students experiment with the functions to design a mathematical calculator template. Student teams can compete to design the most useful computational tool.
5. Create an interactive map with pop-up data, such as city names and population data (see **www.infotday.com/MMSchools/jan02/lehmann.htm** for more details).

FIGURE 2.2 Spreadsheets can be used to compile and analyze research data.

cabinets. With the creation of *database* software, files can now be manipulated by the computer, thus saving hours of physical labor in handling, updating, and moving information when changes are made. (See Table 2.4.)

Databases in Education

The educational community has been a beneficiary of the database's ability to compile, store, and manipulate huge amounts of demographic and statistical information. For example, once student records are entered into a database, they can be accessed by any criteria the user wishes and compiled to generate specific and individually designed reports. School districts and universities have built databases to handle student files, which can include currently enrolled students, classes, financial accounts, grades, and schedules.

Databases are also an invaluable new tool for the classroom teacher. A database can be created for members of an individual class and used to arrange information, as the teacher requires. Curriculum enhancements are available through library databases and other sources of reference

TABLE 2.4   Database Fundamentals

Database software enables users to create new files; add, delete, or change entries in files; perform limited calculations using data; sort records according to varying criteria; and merge two or more files into one.

To create, test, and manage a successful database, it is necessary to have a thorough understanding of the data to be stored, the reason for their existence, and how they can be managed to provide the desired end product. Based on the type of information to be stored, three types of database structures are available: *hierarchical*, *network*, and *relational*.

Hierarchical Databases.   The simplest database is the hierarchical, or tree-structured, model in which information is accessed from the top down. For example, a social security number may be used to identify a record followed by a student's name and address. If the user wants to search the records and knows only a student's name, the system must follow the hierarchical path. This method is said to be a parent—child relationship; that is, each item relates only to the one above and below it in the hierarchy.

Network Databases.   Network databases allow multiple, explicit relationships to exist, rather than only top-to-bottom relationships. The network model also uses a less rigid search structure. The shortest distance to the required information is followed, rather than a top-to-bottom route. The complexity of this system makes modification a more involved procedure.

This model works well for standardized operations wherein transactions predictably follow a preconceived path for each occurrence, such as banking transactions, airline reservations systems, and inventory control.

Relational Databases.   A relational model allows multiple associations among common fields in more than one database. Relational databases are arranged in table format, two-dimensionally, with rows and columns. What was referred to in the previous two models as a file is now a *relation*. A record is now termed a *row*; a field is now a *column*. In order to avoid confusion, we will continue to refer to files, records, and fields throughout this description. The relational database performs three basic functions:

>   **Joining.**   Two files are merged into one.
>
>   **Projection.**   Fields are extracted from various files to form a new file.
>
>   **Selection.**   Various records may be chosen according to the user's own criteria; this is called selection.

A relational database is useful for data such as school records. Student information, course information, class information, and instructor information can all be stored in a database, and grades can be maintained, averaged, compared, printed, and mailed to students. Libraries are another area in which relational databases are used so that resources can be accessed according to the interest of the user.

Common commands and operations associated with most database programs:

>   **Edit.**   The Edit command is used to change or modify data that are already part of a file. The system displays the entire record and fields can be altered as necessary. Entered changes replace the earlier entries.
>
>   **Enter.**   When the user chooses the Enter command, a new record is created and stored in the file.
>
>   **Field.**   A field is a category of information. Multiple fields make up a single record.
>
>   **File.**   A group of related records is called a file.
>
>   **Form.**   Forms can be created to assist entry and viewing of data. Forms contain input areas based on the database fields.

(continued)

TABLE 2.4 Continued

Query. Running a query allows the user to select only certain records within a file based on a set of criteria. For example, a principal may want to generate a mailing list of parents of a specified segment of the student population; however, the database files contain addresses of parents of all the students. A query can be used to search for only the specified parents.

Record. A record is the basic unit of database organization. The information for each person in a contact database, for example, would be a separate record.

Report. Once a query has been run, the selected data can be displayed and printed in a formatted report.

Sort. The user can reorder records by performing a sort based on any one field of a record. For example, student records might be arranged alphabetically according to students' names or numerically according to zip codes for mailing purposes. Sorting can be done in ascending or descending order according to the chosen field.

materials. By implementing a database search for content-relevant information, a teacher can locate multiple sources of material in much less time than that required for a physical library search. Educators and students should be aware of the use of databases in other sectors of society; information from online databases frequently can be accessed for educational purposes. Government agencies, nonprofit organizations, businesses, and private individuals all store information in databases.

How Does This Look in the Classroom?

1. Have students collect information from other students in the school about their physical characteristics (e.g., eye color, height). Design a database in which each type of characteristic is a field. Students can manipulate the data to draw some conclusions about the makeup of the school.
2. Students can conduct a neighborhood study and record information about the types of businesses and other attractions around the school.
3. Catalog all of the classroom books on a Classroom Library Database. Work with students to devise an appropriate checkout system that they think will work.
4. Keep track of facts learned about a topic studied. Have all students contribute to the fact bank, and generate reports to answer questions about the data.
5. Compare student experiences with search engines. Challenge students to think through what database operations happen when they search for information on an Internet search engine.

Online Databases

Most people who use the Internet are quite proficient at using online databases without even realizing it. Have you ever used a search engine? Ordered a book online? Booked airline reservations? If you answered yes to any of these questions, you have used an online database. Any time you use a search button or box to enter search terms, you are interacting with a database. Your requested terms are compared with those in the database, and any similarities are displayed to you as "hits." Whenever you enter personal information, such as setting up an account or entering your credit card information, you are inputting data into another database. Companies compile customers' information in databases for their use and for your use. They can keep track of customer profiles, and you can save your preferences so that the site will "remember" you the next time you visit. For example, if you want to enter your mailing address only once, you can ask the database to automatically display the mailing address when you log in to purchase an item.

More complex websites are even built on a database structure, although they appear as though they are simple web pages to the lay user. These websites use template pages with database fields tagged into the page. When the page is accessed, those field tags automatically query the database for information saved in that field.

Databases are a key to organizing and making sense of the vast amount of information available online. Although the lay user does not need to understand the intricate workings of the database itself, he or she should be aware that once information is entered online, it is saved and can be potentially used in a whole variety of ways. Users may want to consult a website's information use policies to be sure they are comfortable with how their personal information will be shared with other entities.

Summary

This chapter provides an overview of possibilities of the most common productivity applications: word processing, spreadsheet, and database applications. Productivity software is readily available and easy-to-use for new computers users. It is also a versatile way to use computers for personal and professional effectiveness. Most productivity software is available as an integrated suite designed to function together, with all of the tools in the suite sharing common features so the user can move easily among the suite components. Writing, editing, storing, and copying text can all be done efficiently by computer. Advanced software features move users beyond these simple operations to interacting with other software, embedding multimedia elements, and saving as web-ready documents.

Word processing is often the first use of computers in classrooms because its capabilities can so quickly improve work for students and teachers. Word processing features can give students instant feedback on spelling and vocabulary, and other functions allow students to produce eye-pleasing and easy-to-read drafts. Depending on student age and ability, as well as the type of work being done, the steps of handwriting a rough draft and then typing a final version might be bypassed in favor of on-screen composition.

Electronic spreadsheets are electronic versions of an accountant's ledger sheet. One of the most obvious education uses for spreadsheets is for numerical applications, such as for manipulating math and science information.

Database files can be manipulated electronically, thus saving time in handling, updating, and moving files. The educational community has been one of the primary beneficiaries of the database's ability to compile, store, and manipulate huge amounts of demographic and statistical information. Educators should also be aware of the use of databases in other sectors of society, as information from online databases frequently can be accessed for educational purposes. Databases are a key to organizing and locating the vast amount of information online.

Challenge Yourself!

1. Open a word processing program and type some sample text. Practice formatting the text with the Bold, Italic, and Underline commands. Use the pulldown menu commands, the toolbar icons, and the keyboard shortcuts for these formatting features.
2. Type a block of text. Try formatting the text as aligned left, centered, aligned right, and justified. In what situations would each style be appropriate?
3. Using a long document, use the Replace feature to substitute another word for a word you suspect you use too frequently. How many instances of that word were replaced?
4. Run a Spell and Grammar Check on a document you have completed. How many incorrect items were identified?
5. Open a new database document to practice. Insert at least five fields to hold information about yourself or your students. Now, enter this information for at least five individual records. Once entered, attempt to sort the information according to at least two different fields.
6. Enter student grade information into the cells of a spreadsheet. Use column headings to organize the data. Now, insert simple sum and average formulas. Try to copy exact numerical and relative formula information.
7. Insert a chart to illustrate the relationships among data in a spreadsheet document. Format the chart, and insert it into a word processing document.
8. To represent related lists of information, such as days and times of classes, insert a table into a word-processed document. Adjust the column widths, and format the column and row headings for readability.
9. After you have created a database of student contact information, type a form letter in the word processing program. Insert the merge fields for the fields of information you would like, and run the merge. Did the merge successfully create unique letters for each contact in your database?
10. How many online databases do you use regularly? What database fields can you identify among the search fields?

CHAPTER 3

Internet Basics and Electronic Messaging

FOCUS QUESTIONS

1. How does the hypertext structure of the World Wide Web facilitate nonlinear, dynamic access to information?

2. How can email be used to enhance communication in educational communities?

3. What privacy issues must be considered when communicating electronically?

From its humble beginnings as a government experiment to provide strong, transparent connections among military and research institutions, yet impenetrable enough to withstand a nuclear attack, the Internet has grown to be an incomprehensibly strong and far-reaching information network that bonds computers virtually everywhere. Someone sitting at one computer screen can travel to any computer that is connected to the Internet in mere seconds. The dynamic nature of the Internet, however, implies a future of continual growth beyond even what can be imagined today. Even with the understanding that the Internet may yet be in its developmental infancy, educators cannot ignore the limitless resources available from the worldwide community. This section gives an introduction to what the Internet is and how it is structured, and later chapters in this book invite educators to explore resources available online and to participate in designing their own web-based instruction.

In its most simplistic form, the Internet can be seen as a network of networks. Most offices and many schools have found that by linking all of their computers together to form a local area network (LAN), they can increase communication and thus increase efficiency. These LANs connected to other LANs connected to yet other LANs make up the basic structure of the Internet. But the Internet is more than just the physical wires and machines. It is also composed of the resources available through these connections. Information on any topic, no matter how specialized or obscure, can be found somewhere on some computer connected to the Internet, and clearly these pieces of information are made possible by the people who create them. It is people who choose to make connections to others. It is people who place information online for others to access. Finally, it is people who make decisions on how to use the resources available to them. The Internet, then, can be really seen as a partnership among physical, informational, and human elements.

In the true spirit of this partnership, and as a key feature of the original military design, there exists no central Internet entity. There is no "home" computer at which all of the wires ultimately converge; instead, each host computer shares equally the authority and the responsibility for successful connections. Because of this, the network is perpetually strong, able to bypass any wires or machines that are not functioning by routing information in other directions. The Internet also lacks a main receptacle of knowledge and information. Its users both provide and draw from the vast selection of resources that make the Internet dynamic and rich with substance. Finally, there is no presiding human authority in charge of maintaining the Internet. It is a cooperative environment, with its participants governing themselves for the most part. The Internet Society (ISOC) is a nonprofit organization of volunteers that assumes responsibility for guiding the technical and practical growth of the Internet. Members of the ISOC make recommendations regarding what protocols will be necessary to support communication with new technology and also organize and assign unique addresses to Internet host computers. Other than these "housekeeping" functions, the ISOC does nothing to regulate, rate, or otherwise rule on the kinds of information that bounce throughout the world connections. The absence of a central overseer leads to quite an excess of duplicated, poor-quality, and even objectionable material that can be accessed online, but it also has created a democratic environment, for the people and by the people, the likes of which the world has never seen.

Unfortunately, for simplicity's sake, computers around the world are not all manufactured by the same company or with the same speed and capabilities, so there exists a need for a consistent way that they all can communicate. The Internet allows for standard communication by operating according to standard rules, or protocols. Every bit of information that is sent through the Internet must be broken down into manageable pieces, or packets, that can fit through the communication lines that are used to connect. These packets must conform to the Transmission Control Protocol/Internet Protocol, or TCP/IP. By formatting messages according to this protocol, any computer with the ability to connect to the Internet will have the ability to receive and reassemble the packets, resulting in a complete message. It is in this way that the Internet is able to be platform-independent.

The World Wide Web

There are a number of "entrances" onto the mighty network of networks known as the Internet. One is through email, as was discussed earlier. Another, which is quickly becoming the most popular way to locate many types of information, is through the World Wide Web (WWW) or also referred to as the web.

Hypertext

The web is an attractive, graphically arranged, nonlinear way to access information available on the Internet. The key to navigating through the web is *hypertext*. The prefix *hyper* means "above" or "beyond" and *text* refers to words on a web page, which is the basic unit of the web structure. Hypertext, then, is the word or words that when clicked on, present some information beyond the word itself. In today's increasingly multimedia-enhanced web environment, that information might be audio or video, but the most frequent use of hypertext is to link one web page with another. By clicking on a word identified as hypertext, usually underlined and of a different color than other text, you can jump to another page of information. You might even be taken to a completely different website. A website is a collection of a number of web pages at one address location introduced or organized by a homepage. In many cases, an image or icon provides the hyperlink between web pages. The hyperlinks, or hypertext that links to other pages, allow you to immediately see additional information on just exactly what you choose, rather than having to page through irrelevant information as you might need to in a reference book. It is exactly this freedom to explore documents in a three-dimensional way that gives the web its appeal.

The Purpose of Web Browsers

In keeping with the goal of consistent accessibility of the Internet, documents on the web are accessible to any computer that has browser software. Browsers do two things that allow you to see web documents. First, the software seeks out and retrieves a document requested by clicking on a hyperlink or by entering a web address, called a *Uniform Resource Locator (URL)*. A URL is similar to an email address in that it identifies the specific location of the requested document by computer-domain designations separated by periods. The address does not include a person's log-on name followed by the @ sign, as in an email address, but instead may identify a particular document name at the end of the address (see Figure 3.1). Additionally,

FIGURE 3.1 The hypertext transfer protocol prefix and URL displayed in Netscape.

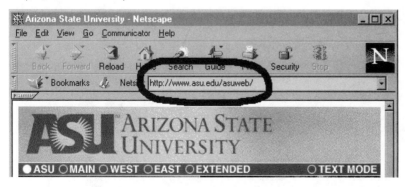

a URL must begin with *http://*, which shows that this document follows the *hypertext transfer protocol*, or the specific rules that are set up for transferring documents in the WWW environment.

The second thing a browser does is allow you to see the document you have requested. Documents on the web must be written in *hypertext markup language (HTML)*, which is a coded language that gives the directions necessary for documents to have specific layouts, including graphics and formatted text (see Chapter 9 for more information on creating HTML documents). HTML allows any document on the web to be viewed by any computer that has a browser. The browser interprets the HTML code in which the page has been tagged and displays the page on your computer screen as the person who wrote the page intended (see Figures 3.2 and 3.3).

How to Use a Web Browser

When the browser software is launched, it first shows the website that has been identified as its homepage, or starting point. This starting page can be changed to be any website, but often is the homepage of the school where the computer is located or can even be someone's personal homepage. From here, there are two main ways a browser helps you to see web documents: simple browsing, or "surfing," and going directly to a website.

If you have the URL for the site you wish to visit, type it directly into the Location text box and then press Enter. If the address is correct and the site is still current, you will be taken directly to it. If you have mistyped the URL, or if the site is no longer being maintained by its operator, you will be taken to a page that says that you have requested an invalid address. If this happens, check the address you typed to see if you made a mistake.

To avoid having to continually input the long address to a favorite site you visit frequently, you can click on Bookmarks or Favorites then Add a bookmark at that site, thus saving the URL. The next time you want to go to that site, click on Book-

FIGURE 3.2 A portion of the source document for a web page.

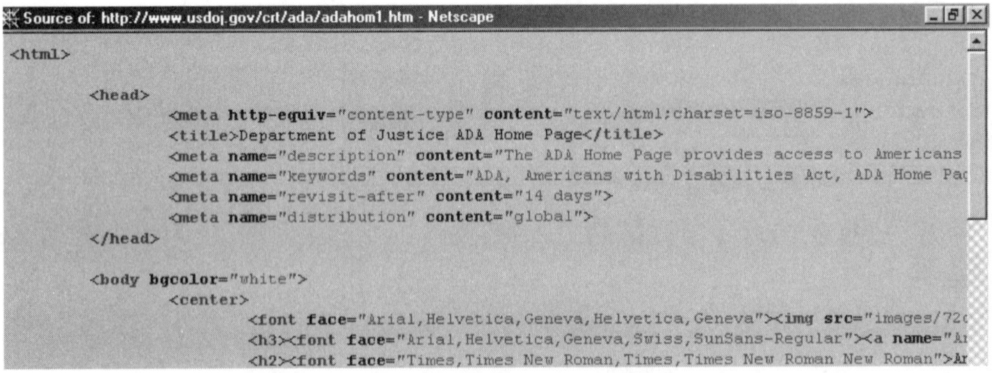


```
<html>

        <head>
                <meta http-equiv="content-type" content="text/html;charset=iso-8859-1">
                <title>Department of Justice ADA Home Page</title>
                <meta name="description" content="The ADA Home Page provides access to Americans
                <meta name="keywords" content="ADA, Americans with Disabilities Act, ADA Home Pa
                <meta name="revisit-after" content="14 days">
                <meta name="distribution" content="global">
        </head>

        <body bgcolor="white">
                <center>
                        <font face="Arial,Helvetica,Geneva,Helvetica,Geneva"><img src="images/72
                        <h3><font face="Arial,Helvetica,Geneva,Swiss,SunSans-Regular"><a name="A
                        <h2><font face="Times,Times New Roman,Times,Times New Roman New Roman">A
```

FIGURE 3.3 The same document as rendered in a browser.

marks or Favorites again, and just choose the name of the desired site to go there automatically.

Searching the World Wide Web

If you do not have the URL for the website you need, you will want to perform a web search. In addition to searching for textual information, you can also search for graphics, sounds, and other kinds of files. There are essentially two approaches to searching for information on the Internet (Pierson, 1997). The first is to use a hierarchical subject directory, such as Yahoo! or LookSmart, which first shows a list of very general subjects. Choosing from these subjects will narrow the search until actual web-page links are given. Be prepared to spend some time looking through the threads of topics to find what you want because the directory designers may have a different idea of the organization of information than you do. A subject directory is handy if you want quick, general information.

The other, more directed, approach to finding information on the Internet is to use a search engine or a meta-search engine, such as the currently popular Google, Excite, Lycos, AltaVista, or Dogpile. In a meta-search engine such as Dogpile, you submit keywords and the search spiders send your search simultaneously to several individual search engines such as Google and AltaVista. Almost instantaneously, you view the results from all the search engines. Clicking on the Search button in your web browser should take you to a site with links to all of the largest engines, or look at Table 3.1 for the URLs to take you directly to the engine websites.

Search engines and meta-search engines are actually enormous indices of information locations that have been amassed by computer programs designed to go out and find these sources automatically. Lawrence and Giles (1999) estimated the size of indexed information at 800 million pages in 1999. Search engine sites allow you to input keywords, or *search strings,* to guide the search of the indexes. All of the available search engines vary according to size, speed, options, and how documents are actually indexed. Some engines, for example, search for terms only on the headers or page titles, whereas others thoroughly inspect the entire page text for the requested keywords. Many of the major search engines are also becoming known as "Internet Portals" because they provide a number of popular services on a centralized website.

Searching Strategies

Once you have located a search engine site, the best thing to do is to check the help section available on all sites for search tips specific to that engine. Being aware of an engine's features will help you to perform searches that are more efficient. With the constant updates and improvements being made to each engine, however, it is nearly impossible to be an expert on every feature of every engine. It makes good sense, then, to become familiar with general properties and basic search strategies common to most search engines. Table 3.2 describes some helpful search tips and gives examples of the search strings you would enter into the search engine. Figure 3.4 shows the results of a simple query using one popular search engine. There is no one best search engine that will serve your needs every time. For the best results, enter the term you want into several different search engines to ensure a complete and well-rounded search.

TABLE 3.1	World Wide Web Search Engines		
Search Engines			
AltaVista	www.altavista.com	Lycos	www.lycos.com
Excite	www.excite.com	Netscape Search	search.netscape.com
Google	www.google.com	Northern Light	www.northernlight.com
GoTo	www.goto.com	Yahoo!	www.yahoo.com
Hotbot	www.hotbot.com		
Meta-Search Engines			
Metacrawler	www.metacrawler.com	Dogpile	www.dogpile.com
Subject Directories			
LookSmart	www.looksmart.com	Yahoo!	www.yahoo.com

TABLE 3.2 World Wide Web Search Strategies	
Search for the singular form of a term. This search will give you both *convertible* and *convertibles*.	**convertible**
Enter all of the spellings you think might apply for a given term, separating each by a space.	**Hanukkah Hanukah Chanukah**
Enclose a phrase in double quotes; otherwise the engine will find every occurrence of each individual word.	**"Grand Canyon"**
Be as precise as possible. Entering a common word, such as *book*, would give you far too many useless sites. Include the word in a specific phrase to help narrow the search.	**"antique book dealer"**
Require that a term must be contained in every document by preceding it directly with a + sign.	**+ mineral**
Prohibit a term, meaning that no documents found will contain it, by preceding it with a – sign.	**– music**
Require some terms and prohibit others within one search string. This example will give you documents about rocks that are minerals, but will not include anything about rock music or rock bands.	**"rock" +mineral –music –band**
Use wildcard characters at the end of a phrase to substitute for several missing letters. AltaVista, for example, uses the asterisk (*) as a wildcard character. This search will give you *vegetable*, *vegetarian*, *vegetation*, etc.	**vege***
Use Boolean operators AND, OR, AND NOT, and NEAR to narrow searches. • Use AND to find documents containing more than one term occurring together. • Use OR to specify one term or the other found separately. • Use AND NOT to exclude a term from the search. • Use NEAR to find documents that contain two terms in close proximity to each other, usually within ten words.	 **scholarship AND loan** **Kansas OR Illinois** **farming AND NOT wheat** **"United Nations" NEAR Bosnia**
Combine Boolean operators and phrases into logical groupings with parentheses.	**(African OR Asian) AND elephant**

In the ever-evolving search engine market, there are now available specialized search engines that allow you to focus your search on documents related to very specific topics (Vaughan-Nichols, 1997). A list of the most current specialized engines, such as ones that locate health-related sites or information on computer-related searching, to name a couple, can be found by clicking on the search button on your browser or the website at **www.searchenginewatch.com/webmasters/index.php.** In addition, searchable databases such as Ask Jeeves provide answers to natural language questions. For

FIGURE 3.4 Results from using the AltaVista search engine to search for the string "Grand Canyon."

instance, if you wanted to know about portals, you would enter the question "What is a portal?" Your inquiry will result in a listing of related links.

Electronic Messaging

Professional isolation is an unfortunate hallmark of teaching. Traditional school practices require teachers to work alone with their own students, inside the four walls of their classrooms, with little contact among colleagues on any given day. The technology that has the most potential to bridge physical distances between teachers and learners and to provide a method for collegial collaboration is electronic messaging. As easy as it is to learn to use, email can quickly be mastered even by novice computer users. With a little awareness of the privacy issues that could affect its use, email can successfully be used for planning and instruction among teachers, students, and experts worldwide.

Electronic mail, commonly known as *email*, is a way of sending paperless "letters" from one computer user to another. The concept of email is often compared to the familiar traditional mail to better understand its similarities and differences. For instance, an email message must be sent to a unique address, and the recipient "opens" his or her mail once it has arrived in a "mailbox." However, the speed and ease with which messages can be sent and organized using email software truly separate this communication medium from anything seen previously. A number of email software packages are currently available, but once the basic procedures of sending, replying, forwarding, and organizing messages are mastered, they can be easily transferred for use in any email program.

Sending a Message

Everyone who has an email account has a unique email address that allows mail to be sent directly to that address, either to a desktop computer or to a server account that the recipient may access remotely. An email address has two parts that are separated by the @ sign and essentially represents a particular person at a particular location. An address begins with a person's name or user ID, often a shortened version of a name, such as the first initial and the last name (see Figure 3.5). Following the @ sign is the domain name, which identifies the server (a computer connected to a network) that houses the person's email account and may consist of a number of subdomain, or third-level domain, names.

Finally, the address ends with an extension identifying the domain type. Domain types within the United States are identified by the nature of their business: .com for commercial companies, .edu for educational and research institutions, .gov for government facilities, .int for international or intergovernmental, .mil for military agencies, .net for gateway or host, and .org for other miscellaneous and nonprofit organizations. Outside the United States, domain type names are identified by two-letter codes: .ca for Canada, .es for Spain, .tw for Taiwan, .uk for the United Kingdom,

FIGURE 3.5 Components of an email address.

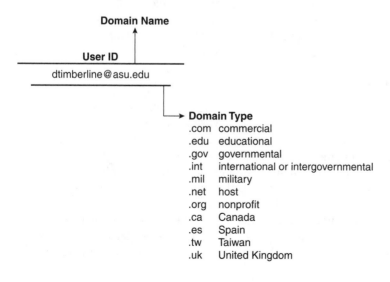

and so forth. However, the use of .k-12.__.us for the United States where the state code goes in the middle is becoming more common especially for educational email addresses. All components of the domain name of an email address are separated by periods, and there are no spaces in the entire address.

Electronic messages require all of the components of an address to be present. A message sent to an incorrect or incomplete address almost surely will not reach the person for whom it was intended, but instead will be returned to the sender as "undeliverable mail" or lost forever in cyberspace.

Because accuracy is so critical, it is helpful to use an email program's capability of saving addresses to an address book. Generally, you can save the email address of a person to whom you frequently write under a simpler nickname, so that instead of remembering a long, multidomained address, you can type a nickname, and the address of the person will automatically be inserted.

Completing the header information, the sender can list other addresses of people to whom copies of the message should be sent, usually marked Cc for "carbon copy" or Bcc for "blind carbon copy." Use the Bcc option when you want a recipient not to be identified to the other recipients, including those in the Cc list. Other files, such as word processing documents or spreadsheet worksheets, can be attached to the message. Finally, a brief subject is listed, giving the recipient some idea of what the message contains. The subject is not required to be completed in order for the message to be sent, but it is a courtesy to the person reading the message not to have to guess at a message's content.

Composing is essentially the same as using a word processor, as errors can be easily corrected, text manipulated to some degree, and text formatted, such as boldfaced or put in a different font. Email conventions do not demand strict adherence to formal letter writing rules.

One distinct advantage that email holds over traditional mail is the ability to easily send identical messages to more than one person. If you find that you frequently send messages to the same group of people, you can make a distribution list of the addressees so they will not need to be input each time. The distribution list can be given a name, and from then on, only the name has to be entered into the address line in the header to send the message to the entire list.

Responding to a Message

When you access your email account, the first thing you will want to do is check your inbox to see whether you have any messages. Messages can generally be viewed in a list with the date the message was sent, the name or email address of the sender, and the subject line. New messages that have not yet been "opened" are marked as such so they can be easily distinguished from messages that have already been read. Clicking on the message line will bring up the complete text of the message. After reading the message, a decision can be made as to what to do next.

If you choose to reply, you can usually choose whether to include a copy of the original message along with your response, to remind the sender what was said, or you can simply send the answer by itself. The header is supplied automatically with the recipient's return address already listed, and the subject line usually includes a prefix of RE: indicating to the recipient that this message is a reply to the earlier message. Sometimes a message you receive might be of interest to another party. In this case, you can forward an exact copy of the message to that other person.

If the message is important, it can be saved. Saved messages can be organized into folders, like other computer files, so that they will be easy to retrieve at a later date. A message can also be saved by just leaving it where it is in the inbox, where it can stay until it is removed. If a message is no longer needed, the inbox can be cleaned out by deleting the message.

Advanced Features of Email Software Applications

Email software available today ranges from the very basic to that with the "bells and whistles" found in high-end software tools, although the end product, an electronic message, is virtually the same. New programs rapidly appear on the market, each bringing new and improved features to email users. Streaming technologies make it possible to send audio and video email messages just as easily as text email. The best advice is to investigate the program to which you will have access to make yourself familiar with the options available to you.

Most Internet browser programs, which began evolving in the early 1990s, offer an email component to give their users a more complete communications package. Icons, or pictures, show whether messages are new or have already been read and give navigational clues to perform standard email functions. High-priority messages can be marked with a flag as they are sent, so that the recipient is aware of messages that should be answered right away. The text of a message is easier to manipulate in the graphical programs such as Netscape, because you can highlight and drag text just like in a word processor. URLs (Uniform Resource Locators), or Internet addresses, sent within an email message are hotlinked to take the user directly to that website with just a click. Netscape's AOL Instant Messenger feature (also available with other email programs) lets you chat with people. Chat is synchronous, meaning that the messages are answered the moment they are received.

Microsoft Outlook (see Figure 3.6) allows the user to customize the interface, or what the user sees on the screen, to fit the individual's purposes. An "inbox assistant" lets you organize your messages even before you receive them. For instance, if you get quite a few messages from a listserv to which you subscribe, you may want to have those messages automatically sorted into a separate folder so you can go through them at your leisure without having them get in the way of your other messages. Outlook has a diary/scheduling system, which is extremely helpful when trying to arrange a meeting with colleagues. Other programs, such as Lotus Notes, allow the sender to easily attach files, such as spreadsheets or graphic files. You can find numerous free email programs on the Internet, such as Eudora Light, Pegasus Mail, and Phoenix Mail. As programs continue to evolve, new models for the navigation and organization of mail will appear, as well as multimedia capabilities including audio and video email options. Fancy features aside, though, whichever email program you have access to will always be able to perform the basic functions of sending, replying, forwarding, and saving.

FIGURE 3.6 Composing a message in Microsoft's Outlook Mailbox.

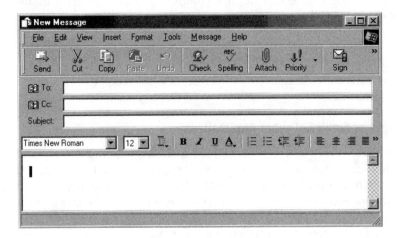

As you become more familiar with email programs, you will start to pick up on some of the standard practices and conventions of email discourse. Table 3.3 offers a number of good tips to get you started.

Listservs

Once you have an email account and are comfortable with the basic email procedures, you might want to try participating in a listserv. A *listserv* is like a giant conversation among many people with a common interest. The ongoing dialogue that listservs facilitate keeps teachers in touch with the most current educational issues. When you subscribe to a listserv, your email address is added to the list of members. Any time a message is sent to the list address, a copy of the message is sent to every email address on the list.

Joining a Listserv

Subscribing procedures vary slightly with each list, but generally you send a regular email message to the address of the list manager, who may be a person who moderates the list screening messages to see whether they are relevant to the list topic, or may be a computer that automatically distributes an identical copy of every sent message to every member. In your request, leave the subject line blank and in the body of the message, type:

subscribe listname firstname lastname

Because you are most likely "talking" to a computer, your instructions must be exact or they might not be interpreted correctly, and you will not be subscribed. Most

TABLE 3.3	Good Email Habits

- Check your email regularly. Once people know you have email, they will start using it and expect you to do the same.
- Include a subject line so the person who is receiving your message can quickly prioritize the messages in his or her inbox.
- Use all capital letters sparingly, only when what you are saying is extremely important. When an email message written in all capital letters is read, it appears as though the sender is "SHOUTING!"
- Read your messages before you send them. Spelling and grammatical errors make a message seem poorly written and can reflect on your intelligence.
- Give yourself time to calm down before responding to a controversial or inflammatory message. Sometimes the written message does not appear on-screen the way it sounded in your head. Virginia Shea, author of *Netiquette* (1994), suggests asking yourself whether you would say to the person's face what you have written in the message. If not, you should rewrite it until you are sure it is acceptable. Once you send a message, it cannot be retrieved, and once it arrives at another person's inbox, it is out of your control and can be easily forwarded on to others you may not have intended to see it.
- Use sarcasm with caution and preferably with people who have personally met you or are familiar with your sense of humor. Facial gestures that help give meaning to a sarcastic remark made in person do not transmit through email, and sarcastic words alone could easily be misinterpreted.
- Remove the previous headings from messages that have been forwarded several times so your recipient does not have to scroll through a lot of useless text trying to find the message.
- If you are replying to just the sender of a message from a listserv or distribution list, be sure to choose the option to reply to the sender only. Others on the list will appreciate the courtesy of not cluttering their inboxes with personal messages intended for other people.

listservs will send you a confirmation message asking you to reply within a certain time frame confirming that you do want to be a member of that list. Once you have subscribed, expect to start receiving messages, sometimes quite a few messages, every day. The level of participation in the discussions will vary depending on the topic of the list and the individuals involved. Listserv members have the option to be active participants, contributing opinions and advice to the list regularly, or to remain passive observers, or "lurkers," who read all messages without actually sending a message. Any level of participation with which a person is comfortable is acceptable on a listserv. Keep in mind, however, that the information and viewpoints presented on the listserv come from other members of the list. These people are not necessarily experts in the field and may or may not be relaying accurate information.

Many lists have rules, both formal and informal, for participating. As a courtesy to those who have already subscribed, participate in the list at first in a silent mode. Watch for the "code of conduct" that is accepted and for the type of information and comments that are typical. Pay attention to the tone of the messages. Regular listserv members are often intolerant of newcomers who do not play by the rules, and they may flame you, or send you a message that in no uncertain terms lets you know what part of your message was not welcome.

When you are ready to participate in the list, just send a message to the list address. This address should have been given to you in the information sent when you subscribed. Note that it is not the same address as the list manager's address to which you subscribed. Try subscribing to a listserv for a while. If you find the topic or tone of the discussion is not quite what you had expected, you can take yourself off the list at any time by following the unsubscribing instructions sent to you when you subscribed. You should also note that most listserv users are encouraged not to unsubscribe or to respond to spam email messages. Responding to spam encourages the sender to continue sending messages to your email address because you have verified that it is a valid address.

Conversations for Everyone

Lists are available for every conceivable interest area, from professional to personal. Public lists cover topics from medicine and politics to religion and recreation and allow anyone with an email address to subscribe. Private lists restrict membership to just certain groups, such as particular college graduating classes or groups that use the list to stay in touch between annual meetings. Performing an Internet search on "listservs" will yield a staggering array of lists that might be of interest. A more defined search can be done at library-sponsored websites such as the Arizona State University Library homepage at **www.asu.edu/lib** or at a directory of listservs such as the tile.net website at **http://tile.net/lists.** Table 3.4 provides a selection of general education and subject-specific listservs that might be of professional interest to educators.

Implications for Education

With access to email in their classrooms, teachers have the opportunity to communicate with colleagues at their school, educators at other schools, parents, administrators, and educational contacts worldwide. The ease and immediacy of email can have an enormous impact on the sharing of ideas, the making of requests, and the completion of other daily communication, both educational and managerial. Email allows teachers to be more productive and time-efficient, leaving more time that can be spent working for and with students. Meetings can now be organized through email, mailing out the plans to several people at once. Consensus on decisions between groups of teachers can be made without even dragging the plastic school chairs together to sit down. The opinions and contributions of even shy participants can be given equal weight in the final decision. Some schools are now sending attendance in via email, making it possible to very quickly identify students who are absent. Parents with email access can contact a teacher with a question without having to wait until after school to call. Because email is asynchronous, meaning that the messages do not have to be answered the moment they are received, teachers can respond at their convenience.

TABLE 3.4 General Education and Subject-Specific Listservs

Under each list description is the listname in capital letters followed by the email address of the list manager.

General Education	Subject Specific
Educational Administration Discussion ADMIN listproc@bgu.edu	**Discussion of Middle School-Aged Children** MIDDLE-L listserv@postoffice.cso.uiuc.edu
Early Childhood Education (8–9 years) ECENET-L listserv@postoffice.cso.uiuc.edu	**Multicultural Education Discussion** MULTC-ED listserv@umdd.umd.edu
Updates from the U.S. Department of Education EDINFO listproc@inet.ed.gov	**Teaching Whole Language Discussion** TAWL listserv@listserv.arizona.edu
Legal Issues in Education EDLAW listserv@ukcc.uky.edu	**Ideas, Research, and Questions about Teaching** TEACHNET listserv@byu.edu
Integrating Technology in the Schools ITS listserv@unm.edu	**Talented and Gifted Education Discussion** TAG-L listserv@vm1.nodak.edu
NETFUTURE: Technology and Human Responsibility NETFUTURE listserv@maelstrom.stjohns.edu	**Geography Education List** GEOGED listserv@lsv.uky.edu
Biology and Education Discussion BIOPI-L listserv@ksuvm.ksu.edu	**National Forum on Information Literacy** INFOLIT listproc@ala1.ala.org
Foreign Language Teaching Forum FLTEACH listserv@ubvm.cc.buffalo.edu	**The Reading Teacher** RTEACHER listserv@bookmark.reading.org
Teaching Social Studies in Secondary Schools H-HIGH-S listserv@h-net.msu.edu	**Using the Internet for Teaching Mathematics** UIME listproc2@ecnet.net
The World Wide Web and Education WWWEDU listserv@lists.lightspan.com	**Special Education Discussion List** SPECED-L listserv@listserv.uga.edu
Music Education Discussion MUSIC-ED listserv@artsedge.kennedy-center.org	**Educational Technology** EDTECH listserv@h-net.msu.edu
Language Learning and Technology International LLTI listserv@listserv.dartmouth.edu	**History of Science, Medicine & Tech** H-SCI-MED-TECH listserv@h-net.msu.edu
Teachers of ESL to Children TESLK-12 listserv@cunyvm.cuny.edu	**Math and Science Education Alerts** MATH-SCI-ALERTS listserv@lists.rbs.org

Students, too, can make use of email. Before giving out email accounts, schools require students to sign an Acceptable Use Policy (AUP). The school- or district-developed AUP defines acceptable behaviors by students and states the rules for email and Internet use. Parents are also required to sign the AUP granting permission for their sons or daughters to access their email accounts and use the Internet. (See Chapter 18 for details.) The possibilities for email to support and inspire educational inquiry are virtually endless. Activities such as the following demonstrate the authentic uses of technology in the classroom.

Classes can participate in telementoring projects that connect experts in every conceivable field of knowledge to students in classrooms everywhere, all through email. The International Telementor Program (**www.telementor.org**) has been facilitating electronic mentorships between professionals and students since 1995. The teachers, students, and experts work as a team to design projects that are goal-oriented and curriculum-based, with the teachers and students sharing their work with and looking for guidance from the experts. This program utilizes online facilitators who serve as liaisons between the classes and the experts, bridging the gaps between the ages of participants and the different environments. Students in such relationships with real-life mentors gain not only content-oriented knowledge but also authentic communication skills, career encouragement, and motivation to learn.

Much of the collaboration needed for projects with students in other classes can be accomplished via email messages. Students can interact with other students from other grades without having to leave their classrooms and walk around campus by themselves. Writing can be sent through email by one student, modified by a student at the other end, and sent back for a continuous cooperative effort. Older students might even submit complete assignments and receive teacher feedback entirely electronically, all without using a single sheet of paper (Dowden & Humphries, 1997). Teachers having assignments submitted in this way have less paperwork and an accurate documentation of when assignments were received.

Videoconferencing and Internet Relay Chat are alternative collaboration tools. *Videoconferencing* is a live, two-way, interactive electronic means of message exchange. Global and national videoconferencing exchanges can be set up through lists available at the Global Schoolhouse Lightspan website located at **http://gsh.lightspan.com/cu/index.html.**

Internet Relay Chat (IRC) is a synchronous or real-time conferencing conversation tool that lets multiple discussions go on at the same time. The Kidlink IRC located at **www.kidlink.org/IRC** encourages students to participate in a global network of friends using IRC.

Students in classes across the country and around the world can be "key pals," the electronic version of pen pals. Even young students are able to work on writing skills in a fun, meaningful activity, without the problems of deciphering developing handwriting or even paying for postage. Students learn that they have to use conventional spelling in order for their key pals to be able to understand their messages. Key pals can serve as cultural guides to their part of the state or country or world, exchanging pictures and brochures, and making faceless parts on the globe come alive. Because electronic messages are communicated through text, students with different racial, ethnic, or religious backgrounds can learn to meet the person inside rather than perpetuating any stereotypes about outside appearances. Thinking critically about the circumstances of lives in other places or cultures helps students to identify and better understand what they believe to be important in their own lives (Rice, 1996). Keypal programs can be set up privately between two teachers, or teachers can apply for key pals for their students through teaching magazines, the ePALS website at **www.epals.com,** listservs such as KIDINTRO (subscribe to **listserv@sjuvm.stjohns. edu**), or the Intercultural E-Mail Classroom Connections website located at **www. teaching.com/iecc.**

Other Internet Services

In addition to presenting hypertext web documents, browsers also offer easy access to resources available through the older, text-based services. Access to services such as transferring files, logging on to systems remotely, and reading news are so seamless that you might not even realize you have left the web.

File Transfer Protocol (FTP)

If you want to send or receive an entire file, such as a database or graphics file, you will want to use *file transfer protocol (FTP)*. FTP is the set of Internet rules governing the sending of files from one computer to another. You can use FTP through the World Wide Web to download files, or copy them to your system from another remote system. You can also use an FTP program, such as WS-FTP for Windows and Fetch for Macintosh. FTP programs are available for download from the Tucows website at **www.tucows.com.** The software window on either program prompts you to log in and give your password to gain access to files on the remote system. Some systems allow you to use FTP anonymously by giving the word *anonymous* for your login name and your email address as your password, if you do not have an account on that system. This will give you access to the archives of files that the institution has made available to the public. FTP also lets you upload files from your computer to a computer on another system.

Telnet

Another way of accessing remote systems is through *Telnet,* which is yet another Internet protocol. Rather than just letting you download files as with FTP, Telnet actually lets you log in to other systems, using programs they have, searching databases, such as library holdings, or even checking email from remote locations. Some versions of Telnet come preloaded as part of Windows or Macintosh operating systems, and others are available for free download at numerous websites. As with other communication applications, an online connection must already be established in order to use Telnet to connect to remote locations. In addition to Telnet, a *virtual private network (VPN)* is yet another way of accessing remote systems using your Internet provider. A VPN provides a secure connection and allows connectivity behind a gateway or firewall.

Newsgroups

Newsgroups, like listservs, are a way to discuss timely issues related to a topic of your choice with other people who share similar interests. The difference with newsgroups is that the messages are not automatically distributed to each member's email account, but rather "posted" on something like an electronic bulletin board for others to see at their leisure. You can look at messages only or choose to post a reply for all to see. Most browser software also includes a newsreader component that allows you to choose which newsgroups you wish to peruse on a regular basis. When you enter a newsgroup, you will see the messages listed by subject, the name of the author, and the length of the message in lines. These messages are arranged in threads, with replies to particular messages listed underneath the originals so you can follow the line of dialogue. You can click through the messages, reading only the ones that interest you and skipping the others.

Web Logs or Blogs

Web logs (also *weblogs* or, more commonly, *blogs*) (Holzberg 2003) offer a personal way to express opinions, communicate ideas, and share interesting links. Free web log publishing software at **www.noahgrey.com/greysoft** makes it possible for anyone to create a web log and continually update the blog with relevant information or web links.

The site Using Web Logs in Education, at **www.weblogg-ed.com,** provided the following responses to frequently asked questions.

What is a web log? Web logs are easily created, easily updated web pages or websites that can be accessed and edited from the web browser of any Internet-connected computer. Think of them as digital paper.

Who uses web logs? Almost anyone can create and maintain a web log with minimal technical experience. For that reason, in an educational setting, web logs are used by students and teachers of all ages, K–16.

How have web logs been used in the classroom? Classroom uses of web logs are varied. They can be used as online student portfolios or filing cabinets where assignments and projects are stored. They can be class portals where teachers keep homework assignments, links, handouts, syllabi, and so on. Teachers have also used web logs as collaborative writing spaces where students read and give feedback to one another. Web logs have served as reader's guides for literature study, as newspapers, and as project sites where students create and contribute all content.

Privacy and Security

Because the Internet has become a true community of people, it faces some of the same serious issues that plague real communities. Just as people put up fences around their yards and alarm their cars to protect their families from outside harm, so will they also need to take care to protect themselves from potential privacy invasions and other dangers lurking within the Internet society.

Web Privacy

Even though you may be sitting by yourself at your home computer, if you are exploring the Internet, many people may know exactly who you are and what you are doing. Some of the information they find out about you is given by you voluntarily, when you fill out an online registration form, such as to receive complimentary software. This personal information is often sold to marketing companies, who will probably begin sending you piles of junk email. To keep your information from being sold, inspect online registration forms carefully to see whether they have a policy of not selling the information that they receive. If you do not see any type of disclaimer, you might want to resist divulging your personal data.

Other information can be collected from you without your even knowing about it. Websites are able to detect what type of computer you are using, what browser software you have, and what other sites you have recently visited, all from your browser (Mann, 1997). After some sites get this information, they are happy to leave your computer with a little treat, called a cookie. Cookies are pieces of text that a website you visit actually stores on your computer. The next time you visit that location, the site requests the cookie from your hard drive, getting the information on who you are and the specifics on the business you might have done with it in the past. In certain instances it is helpful to have particular sites know who you are, such as when a frequently visited site can customize the path it presents to you to fit your particular interests. It may be a little unsettling, however, that this information exchange is being done right under your nose without your even knowing it. All of these privacy issues can be dealt with by using a variety of software tools, available online or commercially. The first step to understanding the potential privacy invasions is being aware that you are not alone out there.

In 1997, over 4 million children accessed the Internet from school and 5.7 million from home (FTC, 1998). Between 1997 and 1999 the availability of classroom computers and connectivity had increased more than 12 percent and will continue to increase (Williams, 2000). With growing numbers of children online, safety and privacy issues become serious concerns for educators and parents. The Federal Trade Commission voiced its concern in its historic 1998 report to Congress. Congress responded by passing the Children's Online Privacy Protection Act (COPPA). This act of legislation, effective April 2000, established rules to safeguard children's privacy online. Websites catering to children 12 and under must get "verifiable parental consent" before obtaining any personal information from a child. To help educators and parents better understand privacy issues, Classroom Connect and TRUSTe published the

Parents' and Teachers' Guide to Online Privacy (**www.truste.org/education/users_ parents_teacher_guide.html**).

Email Privacy

Mail tampering is a federal offense. Barring any unforeseen natural disasters or lawbreakers, we feel safe that our mail will reach its intended receiver unmolested. Once that letter is in the hands of that person, he or she owns it and can throw it away or save it, thus ending the story of the letter. Not so with an electronic message. An email message is not the sole property of the person who sent it or the person who received it. In fact, if it is sent from a school, which is a public institution, it may even be considered to be public information (Descy, 1997). Just because you send your message to one person's email address, it is possible for any of a number of people to read your supposedly confidential message. Building administrators, district network supervisors, even people operating computers through which your message passes on its way to its final destination, all may have access to your message. Unlike the laws that govern tampering with traditional mail, it is perfectly legal to monitor the content of your email messages. Even messages that have been deleted from the receiver's account can be recovered if necessary because the files on server computers are regularly saved on backup files. The advice email users should heed is to be very cautious about writing anything in an email message that they would not want other people to see. If you hear a rumor that your principal is peeking into people's messages, believe that it is indeed possible! When instructing even young students how to use email, the issue of privacy must be discussed.

Security

Because the Internet operates in an essentially unregulated arena, material that is objectionable to or inappropriate for students can be stumbled upon. Parents and educators alike will need to make proactive choices to ensure that the computer world is a protected place to explore. Although supervision is unquestionably the best way to know what students are coming across on the Internet, an *Acceptable Use Policy (AUP)* clearly defines appropriate and inappropriate use of classroom computers. Additionally, Internet "filtering" software gives varying amounts of control over the sites students can access. The software can be programmed to keep students from venturing to sites with certain objectionable words in their titles, and some can keep track of what sites have been visited. Even as these programs progress in their sophistication, none of them is designed to be a substitute for watchful, responsible adult supervision while children are using the computer. The frequency with which new and potentially dangerous sites are added to the Internet makes that goal a practical impossibility. Instead, this software is meant to provide some convenient safeguards to keep students safe in their pursuit of information on the Internet.

Summary

The Internet is essentially a large network linking together all of the smaller networks that connect computers around the world. The physical wires that form the Internet carry information composed by and for people. There is no central authority that governs Internet activity or operation, nor is there a central information repository. The spirit of the Internet requires its users to monitor the quality of their own contributions to the collective information available through the Internet. The World Wide Web offers nonlinear access to information through hypertext links. Web browsers allow you to travel to other sites either by clicking on a hyperlink or by inputting a URL. The browser then displays the requested document as the page designer intended it to look.

You can search for sites on specific information by using a search engine, a web application that indexes websites and allows you to search for information by inputting keywords. A number of strategies lets you narrow your search to more efficiently find what you are looking for. Other Internet applications let you transfer files (FTP), access other computers remotely (Telnet), discuss topical issues with others (newsgroups), and communicate through the use of web logs. All online activity should be undertaken with the understanding that it is not entirely secure or private. With the open community inspired by the Internet, some available material may be inappropriate for some audiences. Being aware of such issues will help educators constantly seek ways in which to allow students to safely explore the Internet.

Email has the potential to provide for regular and quick communication among all members of the educational community. All email programs allow for the basic operations necessary to compose, open, respond to, and save electronic messages. Higher-end software allows for more control over a user's mail management, such as graphical icons, direct links to the World Wide Web for URLs included as part of a message, and automatic mail sorting according to categories. By joining a listserv, you can use email to participate in ongoing conversations with people on an unlimited array of topics. Once you have subscribed by sending an appropriate message to the list manager, you will begin receiving copies of all messages sent to the list. You can either sit back and read passively or actively participate by sending your own contributions. Attention to the implicit and explicit rules of the list community will make the experience productive and pleasant for you and for other list members. Educators should remain aware of and make sure their students are aware of the privacy issues related to the use of electronic messages. With thoughtful use, email can provide a forum for quality collaborative work among students, teachers, colleagues, and the resource-rich community outside the walls of the school.

Postcards from the Net

In this video, students email an attached postcard to other students to share familiar landmarks of their community. How does technology allow students to broaden their learning in this lesson?

DVD/VIDEO VIGNETTE

School Stories

The classroom door is pushed open, and the hot, sweaty fifth-graders pile inside after lunch recess. Ms. Gomez calls out to the class as she stands at the door talking to a student, "Let's continue where we left off before lunch. If you need to check your email, you may wait at the computers." One or two still-chattering students have already plopped down at each of the four computers in the room.

"I probably won't have an answer yet from Mr. Carter because I just sent my message this morning," Ming says to Lindsay as she confidently clicks her way into the email program and her own inbox. "Sometimes he doesn't check his mail until the afternoons because he has so many meetings."

As she says this, she sees the lone message sitting in her mailbox, the envelope icon still unopened. "He did write!" she exclaims and quickly opens the message from Mr. Carter, their class Emissary match. Mr. Carter is a state senator and he is working with students in Ms. Gomez's class to help them to understand the election process and to plan their own mock campaigns. Ming had asked him just that morning whether he got nervous during speeches, because she has one scheduled in front of another class for the next day, and she is starting to get butterflies in her stomach.

In his brief email reply, Mr. Carter says that he does, in fact, still feel nervous right before he has to speak in public, but that it usually goes away after he sees the audience become interested in what he has to say. He gives her a couple of ideas that always work for him so she can rehearse that night. Ming immediately clicks on the reply button and thanks him for the advice, promising to let him know how it goes after the speech the next day.

On the next computer, Antonio and Blake have just read the latest installment of their cooperative email story and are discussing what twist the plot should take next. The two take turns with students in four other classes, two of which are not even at their school, adding a paragraph or two each time to a continuing story. When they are finished with each installment, they forward the updated story on to the next group. So far, the two fictional boys in the story entitled "Escape from the Jungle" have made their way down a mountain, dodging gold smugglers and enemy aircraft in the process, only to find out that they forgot their walkie-talkies back by the bridge.

Antonio's eyes light up. "I know! They could hike back up the mountain, but come up to the bridge by a different trail, just in time to see some gorillas trying to eat their walkie-talkies!"

"Yeah!" agrees Blake. "But maybe the gorillas are really spies undercover!" The boys type in what they have come up with, make a few minor modifications, and send the story on its way to the next authors.

As they finish, Ms. Gomez looks up from the groups of students she is working with. "Boys, could you send an email to Mrs. Dillon to ask whether we can schedule a time to use the art room to paint our campaign signs? I didn't see her at lunch today."

Challenge Yourself!

1. Experiment with two different email packages. Compare features and evaluate the effectiveness of each.
2. Find a listserv of either a professional or personal interest. Join and watch the messages passively for several weeks, or until you feel comfortable to contribute a message of your own.
3. Spend some time in reflective analysis of the DVD Video Vignette. When you first view the video segment, stop the DVD player at various stages and write down what your next step would be in this lesson if you were the teacher. After viewing the DVD Video Vignette, list the changes you would make in teaching this lesson.
4. Research contacts for student key pals. Are there many organizations or individuals that exist to set up such relationships? Are there key pals available for all ages of students?
5. Research current privacy laws governing electronic communications. How often does your school or university back up email files?
6. Develop a learning activity that incorporates the use of email for the level student you plan to teach. What special help might they need to be successful? To what extent will email be a part of your comprehensive educational plan?
7. Organize a virtual meeting between professional colleagues entirely through email. Include sending out an agenda, encouraging discussion on the topics, summarizing key points, and providing a summary of conclusions reached. Then solicit reaction from those involved as to how email might contribute to or detract from decision-making processes.
8. Refer to the URLs for the popular search engines given in this chapter. Enter a very general keyword in a search engine of your choice. Using the strategies described in this chapter, along with any noted in the search engine's help section, continue to narrow your search. How many modifications to your search string did it take until you were satisfied with your search results?
9. Choose one keyword string that interests you and enter it into at least three different search engines. How do the search results compare? What types of information would you have missed by using only one engine? What opinions are you forming about the features that define a good engine?
10. Review an Internet filtering application. Test it thoroughly to see what types of objectionable material it intercepts and what is allowed to pass through its screens. Does the software live up to its claims of safety?

References

Abilock, D. (1996). Integrating email into the curriculum. *Technology Connection, 3*(5), 23–25.

Anderson, B. (1996). The Internet: Trends and directions. *Behavioral and Social Sciences Librarian, 15,* 59–64.

Barbeite, F. G., & Weiss, E. M. (2004). Computer self-efficacy and anxiety scales for an internet sample: Testing measurement equivalence of existing measures and development of new scales. *Computers in Human Behavior, 20*(1), 1–15.

Besnard, C. (1996). Students' empowerment: Email exchange and the development of writing skills. *Mosaic, 3*(2), 8–12.

Bjorner, S. (1997). Day tripping to Internet world. *Searcher, 5*(2), 50–61.

Bogyo, J. (1997). So you want to use the Internet in the elementary school. *Technology Connection, 4*(2), 10–12.

Brandt, D. S. (1997). What flavor is your Internet search engine? *Computers in Libraries, 17*(1), 47–50.

Carroll, R. (1997). Documentation of electronic sources. *Business Education Forum, 5*(4), 7–10.

Collis, B. (1996). The Internet as an educational innovation: Lessons from experience with computer implementation. *Educational Technology, 36*(6), 21–30.

Coulter, B., Konold, C., & Feldman, A. (2000). Promoting reflective discussions. *Learning and Leading with Technology, 28*(2), 44–49, 61.

Cowan, G. (1996). How the web works. *Social Education, 60,* 113.

Descy, D. E. (1997). The Internet and education: Some lessons on privacy and pitfalls. *Educational Technology, 37*(3), 48–52.

DeZelar-Tiedman, C. (1997). Known-item searching on the World Wide Web. *Internet Reference Services Quarterly, 2,* 5–14.

Dowden, R., & Humphries, S. (1997). Using email in computer assisted freshman composition and rhetoric. *T.H.E. Journal, 24,* 74–75.

Ekhaml, L. (1996). Making the most of email: How to be concise, courteous, and correct online. *Technology Connection, 2*(10), 18–19.

Falcone, M. (2003). The role of the delete key in blog. *New York Times, 153*(52,621), 39.

Falk, H. (1997). World Wide Web search and retrieval. *Electronic Library, 15*(1), 49–55.

Fargen, T. (1996). Surfing the Internet in gym class: Physical education email keypals. *Teaching and Change, 3,* 272–280.

Gillmor, D. (2003). Weblogs, RSS and the rise of the active web. *Release 1.0, 21*(7), 2–29.

Glenn, D. (2003). Scholars who blog. *Chronicle of Higher Education, 49*(39), A14.

Federal Trade Commission. (1998). Privacy online: A report to Congress June 1998. Chapter II.C.1.

Hackett, L. (1996). The Internet and email: Useful tools for foreign language teaching and learning. *On-Call, 10*(1), 15–20.

Hamilton, M. C. (1996). The trouble with email. *CUPA Journal, 47*(2), 1–5.

Harris, J., O'Bryan, E., & Rotenberg, L. (1996). It's a simple idea, but it's not easy to do! Practical lessons in telementoring. *Learning and Leading with Technology, 24*(2), 53–57.

Hill, J. A., & Misic, M. M. (1996). Why you should establish a connection to the Internet. *TechTrends, 41*(2), 10–16.

Holzberg, C. (2003). Education web logs. *Tech Learning Forum.* Retrieved August 1, 2003, from www.techlearning.com/story/showArticle.jhtml?articleID=12803462.

Kafai, Y., & Bates, M. J. (1997). Internet web-searching instruction in the elementary classroom: Building a foundation for information literacy. *School Library Media Quarterly, 25,* 103–111.

Kuntz, K. (2003). Pathfinders helping students find paths to information. *Multimedia Schools, 10*(3), 12–15.

Laverty, C. Y. C. (1996). Internet primer: Workshop design and objectives. *Internet Reference Services Quarterly, 1*(3), 35–53.

Lavooy, M., & Newlin, M. (2003). Computer mediated communication: Online instruction and interactivity. *Journal of Interactive Learning Research, 14*(2), 157–165.

Lawrence, S., & Giles, C. E. (1999). Accessibility of information on the web. *Nature, 400,* 107–109.

Lindroth, L. (1997). Internet connections. *Teaching PreK–8, 27*(5), 68–69.

Mann, B. (1997, April). Stopping you watching me. *Internet World, 6,* 42–44.

Miller, S. (2003). *Web searching strategies—An introductory curriculum for students and teachers.* Eugene, OR: International Society for Technology in Education.

Mondowney, J. G. (1996). Licensed to learn: Drivers' training for the Internet. *School Library Journal, 42,* 32–34.

Pierson, M. E. (1997). The honeymoon is over: Leading the way to lasting search habits. *Technology Connection, 4*(4), 10–12, 25.

Reed, J. (1995). Learning and the Internet: A gentle introduction for K–12 educators. *Distance Educator, 1, 2,* 8–11.

Rice, C. D. (1996). Bring intercultural encounters into classrooms: IECC electronic mailing lists. *T.H.E. Journal, 23*(6), 60–63.

Rogers, F. (1996). Email to the neighborhood. *TECHNOS, 5*(4), 33–36.

Sanchez, R. (1996). Students on the Internet: Can you ensure appropriate access? *School Administrator, 53*(4), 18–22.

Scott, J. (1996). Creating your own Internet projects with email. *School Library Media Activities Monthly, 12*(9), 43–48.

Shea, V. (1994). *Netiquette.* San Francisco: Albion.

Simpson, C. (1996). Full speed ahead on the Internet. *Book Report, 15*(2), 3, 5–7, 9–11, 13–14.

The Software and Information Industry Association (SIIA). (2000, August 3). *Building the Net: Trends Report 2000.* Washington, DC: Author. Retrieved September 29, 2000, from www.trendsreport.net.

Tobiason, K. (1997). Tailoring the Internet to primary classrooms. *Technology Connection, 4*(2), 8–9.

Truett, C., Allan, S., Tashner, J., & Lowe, K. (1997). Responsible Internet use. *Learning and Leading with Technology, 24*(6), 52–55.

Van Horn, R. (2003). Gateways, portals, and websites. *Phi Delta Kappan, 84*(10), 727, 792.

Vaughan-Nichols, S. J. (1997, June). Find it faster. *Internet World, 8,* 64–66.

Williams, C. (2000). *Internet access in public schools: 1994–1999* (NCES 2000-086). U.S. Department of Education. Washington, DC: National Center for Education Statistics.

CHAPTER 4

Emerging Technologies

FOCUS QUESTIONS

1. In what ways are emerging technologies helping computers to mimic human capabilities?

2. How might computer innovations impact classrooms of the future?

3. What effects will the increased storage capacities of computers have on the transmission of information in various media?

Technological advancement is constantly offering challenges to teaching and learning. With the advent of computers in science and industry, technological developments occur almost daily. The present and future are sometimes hard to distinguish: What was science fiction 10 years ago is reality today and will be obsolete in 10 years. For example, Kurzweil (2003) prophesies that $1,000 of today's computing power, if measured in brainpower, would be between that of the brain of an insect and that of a mouse. Nanotechnology has been known only since the 1980s. Yet, miniaturizion in technology continues to exceed our imaginations. Engineering and computer science students are often told that their educations will be outdated by the time they graduate and enter their professional fields. The lightning speed of technological advancements in our age makes predictions of the future tentative and difficult. However, some technological trends have emerged over the past several years that permit us to speculate about how technology will revolutionize our society and our daily lives in the future.

One fact is certain: Computers are here to stay! The work of our complex society could not be accomplished without the speed and accuracy that computers allow. In addition, the multifaceted work of computers in research and development, coupled with the research of scientists and engineers, will produce the next generation of computers, more capable than those in use today. Their work is oriented toward several areas: continued miniaturization, greater memory capacity, speech recognition and synthesis, enhanced graphics displays, as well as many emerging technologies.

One of the most noticeable characteristics of computers during the past 20 years has been their decreasing physical size. Many of the powerful computers of the 1960s were room-sized; in the 1980s, a home computer owner could own and operate an equally powerful personal computer that could be set up in the corner of a study or family room! The 1990s saw the introduction of portable computers and notebook-sized computers that fit into a briefcase or backpack. Currently, we are seeing the advancement of ubiquitous computing with palm-sized computers. What has accounted for this decrease in size of computer hardware?

Speech Recognition and Synthesis

Speech recognition refers to the computer's ability to recognize and interpret human speech (see Figures 4.1 and 4.2). Computers that recognize speech circumvent the need for a keyboard. A computer that recognizes speech and does not have a monitor uses the concept of a hologram to project text into space. This has a number of advantages. For example, speech recognition just may make house keys obsolete and, at the same time, cut down on home burglaries. Imagine a computerized "lock" that opens doors only to those people whose voices it recognizes as members or guests of a household.

Speech synthesis, on the other hand, refers to the computer's ability to duplicate sounds similar to the human voice. The speech synthesizers of today are rudimentary and often difficult to understand, but researchers are constantly improving their quality. Computer speech has the potential for great impact on the lives of people who are voice-impaired, and experiments are now being conducted with computers that speak for those who have no voice.

Speech recognition capabilities continue to improve. Early speech recognition worked by the method of discrete speech. The user had to pause between words.

FIGURE 4.1 SpeechMagic—Phillips speech recognition engine.

FIGURE 4.2 SpeechFlow—the PC-LAN–based digital dictation system.

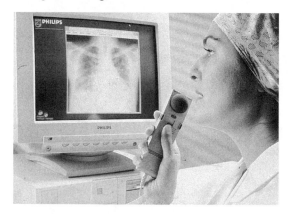

Phone companies utilize this approach. Continuous speech recognition is more sophisticated. A user can speak in a natural rhythm with close to normal speaking pace. Speech and voice recognition software usually allows the computer to be "trained" to recognize your individual voice patterns, rhythm, syntax, and vocabularies. The legal and medical professions actively utilize this software. Legal briefs, letters, patient charts, and data collection are applications in practice. In education, Kurzweil and Microsoft have developed voice recognition products (see the discussion later in this chapter and websites listed after the references at the end of the chapter). The future of this emerging technology is unlimited. We will see this technology applied to cars, appliances, and software; it will especially have an impact on educational software. This software will engage the learner in conversations that provide unlimited educational potential. A newer technology, "digitized" speech, has an improved, humanlike quality.

Graphics

Yet another area of technological advancement is graphics. With the phenomenal popularity of video games, both at home and in game arcades, computer graphics is becoming a popular art form. Researchers are working to make computer graphics more sophisticated (see Figure 4.3). Graphics will display a wider range of colors and effects that are more realistic. This will also have a great impact on classroom computers; spectacular graphics displays attract children to the computer and hold their attention.

The personal computing era is giving way to the ubiquitous computing era, which is the availability of data and information generating, storing, transmitting, or processing anywhere, anytime. In the future, more people will be using a variety of "in-

FIGURE 4.3 (a) Image processing steps of human-interface system. (b) Human-interface system.

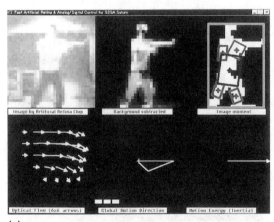

(a)

(b)

formation appliances," such as automobile navigational systems, personal digital assistants (PDAs), digital cameras, and mobile phones. Computers will be physically smaller and less expensive, have greater memory capacity, be able to recognize and produce speech, generate more sophisticated graphics displays, as well as take advantage of other emerging technologies. As the price of computers declines, more and more people will take advantage of the seemingly infinite benefits of computer technology.

Other Emerging Technologies

The network computer, handheld devices such as personal digital assistants and palm-sized personal computers (PCs), flash memory cards, DVD, digital video, Internet 2, and wireless technologies are a few of the emerging technologies that will have an impact on education. The *network computer (NC)* is a fully functional, low-priced multimedia computer that accesses and uses internal and external networks. It works similarly to a television or telephone. Individual students would have their own NCs. Each NC is an intelligent system connected to networks and it gains all its power from the network. The unit cost is minimal and provides a means for web browsing, electronic mail, applications software, and educational software that is on the network. Students could do their assignments offline and download to the school network for teacher or peer review. The NC can potentially have a major impact on education.

FIGURE 4.4
Wireless personal digital assistant (PDA).

Personal digital assistants (PDAs), or knowledge navigators, will become available to everyone. These represent smaller, more compact computers that function as message centers, personal secretaries, and passports to electronic networks to access and share information (see Figure 4.4). Palm-sized PCs equipped with sensing probes will help students gather field data such as water or soil temperature. Flash memory cards are high-capacity diskettes with the ability to transfer data between information appliances as well as PCs. Flash memory devices such as Sony's Memory Stick will enable students to share digital pictures instantly and easily and SmartMedia cards to share CD-quality music. Flash memory devices will help students create and share electronic portfolios and multimedia presentations.

Digital Versatile Disc (DVD) is the next generation of optical media. Its impact is on multimedia, video games, music, consumer electronics, and entertainment. DVD is slowly expected to replace videotape because of its excellent video quality and its interactive potential. In essence, DVD technology's large data storage capacity provides for high-quality playback of video, audio, images, and text. For PCs, DVD allows for high rates of data transfer, paving the way for the convergence of TV and the computer. Education will be able to combine the interactivity with high-quality video and sound into sophisticated interactive learning programs.

Digital video has the capability to provide full motion, full screen, and full color for desktop computers. Quick Time is a common video file

FIGURE 4.5 Virtual reality for the Internet.

format for computers. The emergence of digital video will play an important role in the delivery of video on the Internet. In education, learning technologies and the World Wide Web (WWW) enable the integration, manipulation, and delivery of various media.

Internet 2 is a collaborative effort of the nation's leading universities, the private sector, and the federal government to develop the next generation of Internet technology and applications. This development will enable schools to send and receive high-quality programs that are now limited due to transmission and delivery capabilities. For example, video will be delivered full screen in real time (see Figure 4.5).

Advancements in wireless technologies will impact classroom connectivity. With increasing frequency and ease, classrooms will be connected to a local-area network (LAN) and a wide area network (WAN) like the WWW. Placing network resources in the classroom will significantly impact students' access to real-time data exchanges. Wireless technologies combined with affordable handheld and NC computers will make equipping every student with computing power a reality. *Wireless Fidelity (Wi-Fi)* is the popular term for a high-frequency *wireless local area network (WLAN)* (see **http://searchmobilecomputing.techtarget.com/sDefinition/0,,sid40_gci213380,00. html**). Presently, Wi-Fi is the most popular built-in wireless capability and is found in many of the newer computers. Many locations have Wi-Fi connectivity, which makes anytime, anywhere computing a dream come true. There are many forms of wireless connectivity, and they will get only faster and more convenient! Of course, these are only a few of the emerging technologies that will impact education.

Data Communications

Another area destined for rapid and significant development in the future is data communications, or the transfer and reception of data by electronic means. Many computer users rely on data communications via network systems. This allows large corporate offices to keep in constant communication with branch offices. It allows for centralized record keeping and enables a corporation to coordinate the efforts of all its branches to best meet the needs of its customers. It is an effective means of keeping business healthy. This trend toward communicating over data networks will continue to grow, becoming faster and more reliable than it is today. Government will certainly work toward developing more effective means of data communication. It is important for governmental agencies to keep in contact with each other, for remote military bases to maintain communication, and even for nations to monitor each other's activities. More sophisticated means of data communications, such as fiber optics and microwave, will make communication faster and more effective in the future.

Artificial Intelligence

Along with databases and data communications, the field of *artificial intelligence (AI)* will undergo rapid changes and development. Artificial intelligence refers to devices capable of imitating human cognitive processes: thinking, remembering, learning, inferring, and so forth. For the past 25 years, researchers have been working to develop a "teachable" computer. Although today's computers process numerical data, the AI computers of the future are expected to process nonnumerical data with technology that is being developed all over the world.

In addition, future generations of computers with artificial intelligence are expected to be able to decode instructions given them in ordinary human language. They may be able to compile their own instructions to perform virtually any task they are asked (literally!) to perform. Researchers say that these computers will be available in the near future.

Much work that has been done by humans is now being performed by robots, and this is expected to increase in the future. The term *robot* calls to most minds an image of a metal humanoid similar to the tin man in *The Wizard of Oz* or the two characters in the *Star Wars* series, R2D2 and C3PO. Yet robots are highly sophisticated machines capable of performing many tasks. They are particularly well suited to jobs that are repetitive, dangerous, or difficult for humans to perform. Robots can be exposed to situations that might injure the health of human workers. In addition, they are capable of working 24 hours a day, seven days a week, with little need for work stoppage. Although the initial purchase price of robots is high, robots are extremely cost-effective workers. The advent of computerized robots in manufacturing raises an important issue. Many people fear computers because they believe that these technological wonders will make human workers obsolete. What will happen to the large percent of the labor force whose jobs are eventually automated? Actually, there will be plenty of employment opportunities available in the future, but the nature of those jobs will be different from the jobs today. This is why the retooling and retraining going on in business and industry are such enormous tasks.

According to the U.S. Bureau of Labor Statistics, the need for qualified people to work in computer-related careers will double in the next decade. Many experts say that that estimate is too moderate and predict that the demand for such workers will easily triple during the next three years. It is logical to assume, then, that those workers who find themselves displaced by automation on the job will be retrained to assume computer-related positions. The robots cannot exist, after all, without human workers to design, manufacture, operate, and maintain them.

However, robots in industry are merely one facet of the fascinating field of artificial intelligence. The impact of AI on computers in the schools will be momentous. Very young children will be able to operate computers without the need for typing skills or knowledge of programming languages. They will be able to "teach" the computer to carry out the activities they want done. Because AI computers function as intelligent aids to their users rather than as merely programmable machines, computers will become more effective teachers, listening to the students, responding according to information stored in memory, and then storing information away for later use. They will no longer rely on rigidly defined software.

Computers for People with Disabilities

The widespread use of technology within the last decade has moved to affect the lives of people with disabilities. Assistive and adaptive technology will continue to increase in capability and versatility into the future. Any item, piece of equipment, or product system that is used to increase, maintain, or improve functional capabilities of individuals with disabilities is considered to be an assistive technology device, according to the Individuals with Disabilities Education Act (PL 101-476) (see **www.ed.gov/offices/OSERS/Policy/IDEA/index.html**).

Here are some examples of assistive technologies:

Screen readers
Screen magnifiers
Adaptive keyboards
Voice recognition software

Generally, the disabilities are categorized into four areas of impairment, which are:

Hearing loss and deafness
Speech disorders
Vision impairment
Cognitive delay and learning impairment

Assistive technology in the hearing-impaired community includes those who are "hard of hearing" and those who are "Deaf" (with a capital D). "Hard of Hearing" describes all levels of hearing loss between normal (unimpaired) hearing and severe or profound deafness. Hard of hearing individuals may be able to understand speech by the use of audio-assistive devices amplifying sound and utilizing residual hearing. Hard of hearing persons may be born with hearing impairment of this level or they may acquire it later in life. In both cases, the impairment may become progressively worse. Usually, hard of hearing individuals can become proficient in speech with appropriate hearing aids, supplemented by lip-reading. It is through this that mainstream education is usually acceptable for hard of hearing students, especially if audio-assistive resources are available. Alternately, for those with a severe to profound degree of hearing impairment, audio-assistive devices are not helpful to the individuals to understand speech. This group of people is divided into those who are "Deaf" (regard themselves as part of the Deaf Culture) and those who are "deaf" (do not regard themselves as part of the Deaf Culture). Those who belong to the Deaf Culture consider their primary language to be sign language, while those who are deaf are usually not fluent in sign. Assistive technology for those who are hard of hearing includes:

- *Telecommunications equipment and peripherals.* This group includes such devices as amplified telephones, text-pagers, and TDDs (telecommunication devices for the deaf).
- *Listening devices, which may be used alone or in conjunction with a student's hearing aids.* They include personal FM systems, sound field FM systems, and t-coils (which

drown out background noise and feedback on the telephone, and are used with hearing aids).
- *Alerting devices.* This category includes those devices that provide visual cues such as a flashing light, amplify sound, and vibrate. If an alarm clock is wired to a vibrator and then placed under the bed pillow, the user is literally shaken awake. Auditory signals are sometimes used together with either visual or vibratory cues. Often, a single flashing light signaling system in a deaf or hard of hearing person's home can be wired to alert the person to several different sounds. For example, when the light flashes a simple code helps identify the source of the sound. Three slow flashes may mean the doorbell, three quick flashes may mean the telephone, or regular on–off flashes may signal that the baby is crying.

Speech impairment is an oral motor function that causes problems in communication, usually caused by hearing loss, brain injury, drug abuse, neurological disorders, mental retardation, physical impairments such as cleft lip or palate, and vocal abuse or misuse. The cause is usually unknown. Assistive and adaptive technology for speech impairments usually is served in the form of an *adaptive or augmentative communication device (AAC).* An AAC is any device, system, or method that improves the ability of a child with communication impairment to communicate effectively. Ideally, an AAC system includes more than one mode of communication, with the child using whichever is the most efficient given the persons, setting, and activity at hand. Very often one of the modes of communication in an AAC program is natural speech.

The factors that help to determine which assistive paths to take for effective communication include the age of the individual user, the cause of the disability, the course of the disability, and the user's environmental demands. Augmentative communication can include a communicative technique (e.g., speech, manual signs, physical boards), a symbol set or system (e.g., Mayer-Johnson Symbols, Signs of American Sign Language), or communication/interaction behavior (e.g., demands/requests, conversations).

Communication aids can include speech output devices, which give the user verbal feedback and are more readily understood by the child's peers. Simple electronic aids such as the *BigMack* and the *One Step Communicator,* which hold one message, or the Step by Step, which holds several messages in sequence, are excellent for classroom activities. Messages can quickly be recorded or replaced. These devices are fairly limited in scope, but they can be used to introduce a child to a low-tech electronic aid.

Visually impaired refers to those people who are partially sighted, low vision, legally blind, and totally blind. "Partially sighted" indicates some type of visual problem has resulted in a need for special education. "Low vision" generally refers to a severe visual impairment, not necessarily limited to distance vision. Low vision applies to all individuals with sight who are unable to read the newspaper at a normal viewing distance, even with the aid of eyeglasses or contact lenses. These individuals use a combination of vision and other senses to learn, although they may require adaptations in lighting or the size of print, and sometimes Braille. "Legally blind" indicates that a person has less than 20/200 vision in the better eye or a very limited field of vision (20 degrees at its widest point). "Totally blind" students learn via Braille or other nonvisual media.

Assistive technology for vision impairment includes special devices that assist with independent reading, communication through printed text, and access of computerized information. Assistive technology products include auditory text access (Talking Books, Kurzweil Reader [Kurzweil, 2003]), text enlargement (handheld magnifiers, large-print books, "Closed Circuit Television (CCTV)" system), tactile-text (Braille-to-letters), portable note-taking devices (Braille and speech note-taker), and computer access (screen magnifier, speech-synthesized voice output, refreshable Braille display that produces hard-copy Braille).

Finally, one of the most promising areas of technological advancement in assistive technologies to watch in the future is the research and development of devices to aid the population with disabilities (see Figure 4.6). Many promising devices are under study today and will become more accessible as computer technology develops smaller and less expensive computers. Speech recognition is one of many future technological developments that will have a major impact on aiding the population with disabilities.

Learning technologies have proven extremely effective in special education environments. Slow learners are comfortable using computers to master academic subjects that have proven difficult for them in the past. In addition, students who are paralyzed or suffer muscle impairment that prevents them from holding a pen are capable of writing essays and solving mathematical problems with a computer. Severely handicapped or special needs students can use computers to learn in their homes if they are unable to attend classes (see Figure 4.7). Computers also help people with disabilities in other ways. Voice synthesizers allow the speech impaired to communicate their thoughts, perhaps for the first time. Still other devices help the vision impaired to read and generate written texts. Because artificial intelligence re-

FIGURE 4.6 Bausch and Lomb PC Magni-Viewer magnifies on-screen information 175 percent.

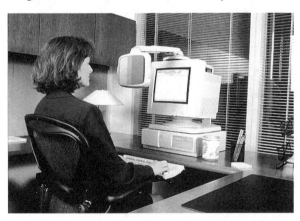

FIGURE 4.7 Voice mail with voice recognition to email software.

search promises to make computers more capable of imitating human activities, more computer aids for those with disabilities are sure to be developed in the future (see Figure 4.8). This gives hope to many today.

The Future Student Personal Computer

The future student personal computer will be a handheld or "tablet" device with wireless Internet access, software programs, input devices, and many mathematical capabilities. The student palmtop will have a calculator, graphing capabilities, productivity tools for word processing and spreadsheets, geometry construction tools, simulations, algebra systems, and intelligent tutor capabilities. The computer will start instantly like a transistor radio (Murray, 2003). It also will be able to adapt to the user's interests and abilities and may even talk to him or her. This wireless device will have a touch screen option like a magic slate, allowing students to input or write without a keyboard. Battery life will be similar to that of pagers—lasting weeks. So merging the organizer, pager, TV, Internet, streaming video, voice recognition, and more advanced handwriting recognition on today's tablet computers (**http://abcnews. go.com/sections/scitech/DailyNews/cybershake021111.html**) will produce a very slim, lightweight student handheld personal computer.

Many of the technologies listed previously will be available on the palmtop or be accessible via this PC and the Internet. Students will have access to resources or digital content required by the school for their academic success. Students will be able to access many of the historical archives as well as download required textbook materials as needed. No more big, heavy backpacks! Students' academic activities and assignments will always be with them and can be sent to the teacher and/or parent

FIGURE 4.8 Foot-controlled mouse.

for evaluation. Special needs functionality will be an integral part of this hand-held PC as well. It is clear that future technologies will become more interactive, promoting exploration, problem solving, communication, and higher-order thinking. By 2006, every student will have his or her own handheld personal computer. This will truly be anytime, anywhere learning.

The current trend to merge the computer lab with the library or media center to create a digital media lab will continue. The media lab exists as both a physical space—a digital media lab—and a virtual space—a collection of web-based resources. The lab will provide access to existing resources and will support the creation of new customized media projects for the faculty, support personnel, and students as well as the community (see Figure 4.9). Tomorrow's media centers will include fewer shelves of books and periodicals and more digital storage and retrieval systems. The process of data storage and retrieval, or databases, will become vital links between information and the people who require that information.

Indeed, every subject that is taught in schools today can be adapted to digital learning. The CEO Forum on Education and Technology (2000) defines digital learning as "the educational approach that integrates technology, connectivity, content

FIGURE 4.9 Emerging technologies support the creation of new customized media projects.

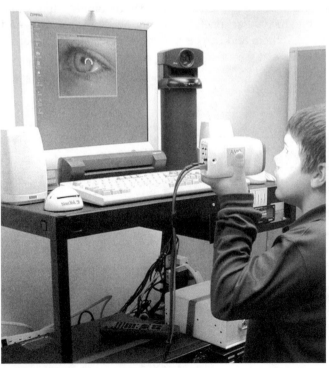

and human resources." Programs such as *math•ed•ology*™ (see **http://tblr.ed.asu.edu/ Projects/MathEdOlogy/?w=1016**) by Technology Based Learning and Research, were designed to provide teachers with anytime, anywhere professional development. Simulations will be designed to give teachers and students opportunities to problem solve and interact with other professionals outside of the school setting. Project-based inquiry, virtual communities-of-practice (Linn, 1997), and other forms of sophisticated pedagogies will support students' development of higher-order cognitive, affective, and social skills necessary for success in a knowledge-based economy.

Clearly, we are in the midst of a technological revolution; the phenomenal advancements in technology that we have witnessed during the past 20 years are only the tip of the iceberg. What technological achievements lie in our future is anyone's guess! Because our technological society will have deep roots in math and science concepts, people of all ages will be expected to become both scientifically and technologically literate.

Summary

In the future, we may expect to see rapid technological advancements in computers. Research and development is geared toward several areas in particular: continued miniaturization, greater memory capacity, speech recognition and synthesis, enhanced graphics displays, and other emerging technologies. Greater amounts of computer power will be built into physically smaller units that will be more affordable and, hence, more accessible to the average person. These smaller computers will be made more powerful by new systems of memory that allow for greater storage. Speech recognition and synthesis will make computers easier to use because they will be able to communicate directly with humans. Finally, improved graphics capabilities will make computers more attractive to those who wish to generate visual displays.

The computers of tomorrow will be used in a great number of applications, both social and personal. Already, computers help regulate traffic flow, control airplane landings and takeoffs, and monitor the vital signs of hospital patients. They serve to diagnose illnesses and prescribe treatment. In addition, they play a more important role in the educational system as a greater number of schools implement curricula that employ emerging information technologies.

We can also expect to see expanded use of databases by the general public. Databases give computer users access to up-to-the-minute information on a wide range of subjects. Not only are databases extremely useful to professionals such as doctors, lawyers, and law enforcement officers but they also provide special-interest information on hobbies, first aid, and current events. Tomorrow's complex society will necessitate fast access to updated information. Data communications, or the transfer and retrieval of data via electronic means, will develop to become an important way for large corporations to keep in constant contact with their branch offices. It will also be used more widely by government agencies and others who must maintain close contact with remote locations.

Yet another promising area of technological advancement is artificial intelligence. Future computers will be capable of imitating human cognitive activities such as thinking, remembering, and inferring. They will be able to compile their own instructions based on commands given them in ordinary human language, allowing more people to "program" computers without extensive knowledge of computer programming languages. In addition, AI robots will continue to be used widely in industry, causing a significant shift of the labor force from industrial work to technically oriented jobs.

Home personal computers will expedite the work of homeowners by keeping records, maintaining budgets, and regulating household inventories. They will also serve as important learning tools either to supplement education received in traditional classrooms or to serve as a medium of taking classes via distance education. This access will be able to provide many forms of entertainment. More people will use their personal computers to work at home without the need for traveling to a work site. DVD will combine the TV and PC into one home entertainment unit, merging excellent video and sound capabilities with interactivity that will revolutionize home entertainment. Education will utilize this technological impact with parent, school, and home communication and interactivity. The classroom of tomorrow will bridge the current learning gap—the difference between available resources and classroom access.

People with disabilities will enjoy numerous new computerized devices that will improve the quality of their lives. Speech synthesizers, for example, will allow the speech impaired to communicate orally. The future holds great promise of technological advancements that will change our lives for the better.

Challenge Yourself!

1. Interview a computer scientist about the future of technology and write a summary of the discussion.
2. Write your own scenario of the technology-based classroom of the future.
3. Research predictions of future technology by several computer experts. Include any research findings on the success or lack of success of emerging technologies. Report on your findings.
4. Consider how the development of artificial intelligence will affect learning technologies.
5. Develop a unit of practice in which students explore the future of technology.
6. Write a report reviewing the literature on the role of learning technologies for special needs students.
7. Write a report on the potential impact of voice recognition on education.
8. Write a report on the impact that the Digital Versatile Disc (DVD) will have on the future of education.
9. Write a report on the implications of web-based instruction via the WWW on business, industry, and education.
10. Design a handheld student computer. Include a drawing, size specifications, and capabilities and applications that this computer will possess.

References

Artificial intelligence goes postal. (1997). *Science, 27,* 1073.

Austin, M. B. (1994). A comparison of three interactive media formats in an RTV/DVI computer-mediated lesson. *Computers and Education, 22,* 319–333.

Benedikt, M. (Ed.). (1991). *Cyberspace: First steps.* Cambridge, MA: MIT Press.

Broadband Editor. (2000). Colorado State University expedites student research with library-wide wireless network. *T.H.E. Journal, 28*(2), 34–37.

CEO Forum on Education and Technology. (2000). *The power of learning: Integrating digital content.* Washington, DC: Author.

Cheng, D., & Yan, H. (1997). Recognition of broken and noisy handwritten characters using statistical methods based on a broken-character-mending algorithm. *Optical Engineering, 36,* 1465–1479.

Collins, H. M. (1990). *Artificial experts—Social knowledge and intelligent machines.* Cambridge, MA: MIT Press.

Decker, R., & Hirschfield, S. (1992). *The analytical engine: An introduction to computer science using toolbook.* Belmont, CA: Wadsworth.

Dede, C. (2000). *Implications of emerging information technologies for states' education policies.* Commissioned paper for the Council of Chief State School Officers' Educational Technology Leadership Conference in January 2000. Retrieved October 17, 2003, from www.ccsso.org/publications/details.cfm?PublicationID=95.

Duchastel, P. (1996). Learning interfaces. In T. Liao (Ed.), *Advanced educational technology: Research issues and future potential.* New York: Springer-Verlag.

East, P. (1990). On the basics of education in the 21st century. *The Computing Teacher, 17*(6), 6–7.

Gader, P. D., Keller, J. M., Krishnapuram, R., Chiang, J.-H., & Mohamed, J. A. (1997). Neural and fuzzy methods in handwriting recognition. *Computer, 30,* 79–86.

Girard, K., & Dillon, N. (1997). Market grows for voice applications. *Computerworld, 31*(32), 55–56.

Haugeland, J. (1986). *Artificial intelligence: The very idea.* Boston: MIT Press.

Hofmeister, A. M. (1991). Expert systems and decision support in special education: Results and promise. *Educational Technology, 31*(10), 23–28.

Hughes, T. (1990). *American genius.* New York: Penguin.

Kim, G., & Govindaraju, V. (1997). A lexicon driven approach to handwritten work recognition for real-time applications. *IEEE Transactions on Pattern Analysis and Machine Intelligence, 19,* 366–379.

Kirkpatrick, S. N., & Biglan, B. (1990). AI in the elementary, middle, and secondary classroom. *The Computing Teacher, 17*(5), 14–19.

Kurzweil, R. (2003). The end of handicaps. *eSchool News, 6*(7), 40–41.

LaBarge, R. S. (1996). *DVD Today,* Vol. 1 [CD-ROM]. Crofton, MD: NB Digital Solutions.

Leedham, D. G., & Qiao, Y. (1992). High speed text input to computer using handwriting. *Instructional Science, 21,* 209–221.

Levert, C., & Pierre, S. (2003). Designing distributed virtual laboratories: Methodological and telecommunications aspects. *International Journal on E-Learning, 2*(3), 18–28.

Levi, K., et al. (2003). Integrating artificial intelligence and intelligent tutoring systems into the air university curriculum. *Journal of Instruction Delivery Systems, 17*(2), 20–29.

Linn, M. C. (1997). Learning and instruction in science education: Taking advantage of technology. In D. Tobin and B. J. Fraser (Eds.), *International handbook of science education.* The Netherlands: Klewer.

Lundsten, A., & Doiel, R. (2000). Digital video and Internet2: Growing up together. *Syllabus, 14*(1), 12–16.

McCullough, M., Mitchell, W. J., & Purcell, R. (Eds.). (1990). *The electronic design studio: Architectural knowledge and media in the computer era.* Cambridge, MA: MIT Press.

Murray, C. (2003). Coming fast: Computers that boot instantly. *eSchool News, 6*(9), 20.

Papert, S. (2003). Learners, laptops and powerful ideas. *Scholastic Administrator, 1*(4), 53–56.

Patterson, J. C. (2000). How digital video is changing education. *Curriculum Administrator, 36*(6), 34–37.

Pearlman, R. (1989). Technology's role in restructuring schools. *Electronic Learning, 8*(8), 9, 12, 14–15, 56

Roberts, G. I., & Samuels, M. T. (1993). Handwriting remediation: A comparison of computer-based and traditional approaches. *Journal of Educational Research, 87,* 118–125.

Schenkel, M. E. (1995). *Handwriting recognition using neural networks and hidden markov models.* Kontanz, Germany: Hartung-Gorre Verlag.

Sheingold, K. (1991). Restructuring for learning with technology: The potential for synergy. *Phi Delta Kappan, 73,* 17–27.

Sin, B.-K., & Kim, J. H. (1997). Ligature modeling for on-line cursive script recognition. *IEEE Transactions on Pattern Analysis and Machine Intelligence, 19,* 623–633.

Solomon, G. (1990). Learning to use the tools of the future. *Electronic Learning, 9*(5), 14–15.

Soloway, E., Grant, W., Tinker, R., Roschelle, J., Mills, M., Resnick, M., Berg, R., & Eisenberg, M. (1999). Science in the palm of their hands. *Communications of the ACM, 42*(8), 21–26.

Szuprowicz, B. O. (1999). *Multimedia networking.* New York: McGraw-Hill.

Tamashiro, R., & Bechtelheimer, L. (1991). Expert systems in the elementary grades: Developing thinking skills and independent learning. *The Computing Teacher, 18*(5), 21–26.

Turkle, Sherry. (2004). How computers change the way we think. *The Chronicle Review Information Technology,* Special Issue, *50*(i21), B26–B28.

Van Horn, R. (2003). A primer on the new television. *Phi Delta Kappan, 85*(1), 7, 89.

VRML industry microcosms in the making. (1998). *New Media, 8*(3), 21–24.

Wildstrom, S. H. (1997, September 22). PC, take a letter to Mr. Jones. *Business Week* (34), 18.

Williams, C. (2000). *Internet access in public schools: 1994–1999* (NCES 2000-086). U.S. Department of Education. Washington, DC: National Center for Education Statistics.

Willis, W. (1998). Speech recognition: Instead of typing and clicking, talk and command. *T.H.E. Journal, 2*(6), 18–22.

Ziegler, Bart. (1998, January 29). New generation of hand-held PCs inches closer to ideal. *Wall Street Journal*, B1.

Websites

About Internet2　**www.internet2.edu/html/about.html**

Canon DV: DV Format　**www.canondv.com/xl1s/f_dv_format.html**

Communication Intelligence Corporation　**www.cic.com**

Handwritten word recognition. Center of Excellence for Document Analysis and Recognition (CEDAR).　**www.cedar.buffalo.edu**

Making Educational Software and Web Sites Accessible: Design Guidelines Including Math and Science Solutions　**http://main.wgbh.org/wgbh/access/access.html**

Memory Stick Information　**www.hightechproductions.com/memorystick.htm**

Panasonic DVD homepage　**www.panasonic.com/consumer_electronics/dvd_players/default.asp**

Rawson, C. E. (1996, July). Breaking down the last document automation barriers! An overview of Natural Handwriting Recognition (NHR).　**www.infotivity.com/hwr.htm**

SmartMedia Technology Primer　**www.pcmcia.org/smartmedia.htm**

Sony DVD　**www2.sony.com/SEL/consumer**

Srihari, S. N., & Kuebert, E. J. (1997, May 31). Integration of hand-written address interpretation technology into the United States Postal Service Remote Computer Reader System. Center of Excellence for Document Analysis and Recognition (CEDAR).　**csdlcomputer.org/proceedings/icdar/7898/78980892abs.htm.**

Ubiquitous Computing　**www.ubiq.com/hypertext/weiser/UbiHome.html**

Zakon, R. H. (2000, July). Hobbes' Internet time line.　**http://www.zakon.org/robert/internet/timeline**

Speech Recognition Sites

Apple Computer Speech Recognition　**www.apple.com/macosx/jaguar/speech.html**

CMU Sphinx　**www.speech.cs.cmu.edu/sphinx**

IBM Voice Systems　**www-306.ibm.com/software/voice/viavoice**

Kurzweil Speech　**www.speech.cs.cmu.edu/comp.speech/Section6/Recognition/kurzweil.html**

Microsoft Speech Technology　**www.research.microsoft.com/research/srg**

Scansoft Speech　**www.scansoft.com**

Wireless Technology Sites

www.intel.com/business/bss/infrastructure/wireless/index.htm
www.zdnet/anchordesk/
www.wired.com/wired/archive/11.05/unwired/wifirevolution.html
www.cio.com/research/communications
www.wi-fiplanet.com
www.internetnews.com/wireless

Handwriting Recognition Sites

www.artcomp.com
http://homepage.mac.com/larryy/larryy/ANHR.html
http://pocket-pc-software.penreader.com/PenReader.html
www.microsoft.com/WindowsXP/expertzone/columns/vanwest/
    03may28hanrec.asp

Research on Technology in Teaching and Learning

CHAPTER 5

FOCUS QUESTIONS

1. How do classroom teaching and learning behaviors alter as a result of incorporating technology-rich curriculum?

2. Does technology use lead to academic gains in all subject areas?

3. What are reasonable effects to expect from integrating technology in typical classrooms?

By the early stages of the twenty-first century, leaders in the field of educational technology have studied the impact of technology on teaching and learning long enough to know that not only is technology not a panacea, but if used as part of an inadequate teaching plan, gains in learning may be jeopardized. These leaders now decry the use of technology for its own sake and espouse instead that educational technology be used with the ultimate goal of improved and enriched student learning.

The CEO Forum on Education and Technology (2001) asserts that when technology is used to support learning objectives, improved student achievement can be anticipated in the form of (1) improved scores on standardized tests; (2) increased application and production of knowledge for the real world; (3) increased ability for students to manage learning; (4) increased ability to promote achievement for special needs students; and (5) improved access to information that increases knowledge, inquiry, and depth of investigation (p. 6). In order for this growth to occur, the CEO Forum suggests attention to the following "building blocks":

- *Alignment.* Ensure that curriculum, technology uses, and assessment work together to support standards and objectives.
- *Assessment.* Involve students in relevant, challenging tasks that measure higher-order thinking skills. Technology should be reflected in assessment as it is in instruction, in a way that provides ongoing feedback.

- *Accountability.* Use technology to monitor progress, collect and analyze performance data, study evidence of what works, and inform continuous school improvement planning.
- *Access.* Equalize opportunity for all students through technology and be conscious of inequity in technology levels that may marginalize certain diverse or special populations.
- *Analysis.* Continue to conduct research on the ways that technology improves student achievement.

The federal education plan *No Child Left Behind (NCLB)*, signed into law on January 8, 2002, addresses technology specifically in the Enhancing Education Through Technology Act of 2001 (*The Facts About 21st-Century Technology,* 2001; *No Child Left Behind,* 2002). The legislation lists as a primary goal, "to improve student academic achievement through the use of technology in elementary schools and secondary schools," and additional goals of having students graduate eighth grade technologically literate and integrating technology effectively into teacher preparation and curriculum development. Technology resources must be aligned to state standards, and the effectiveness of those resources in improving student achievement must be measured with quantitative methods (Cradler, 2003). Unfortunately, large-scale scientific studies of the kind called for in NCLB are expensive, and neither local nor federal funding for this required research is plentiful.

In order to meet these goals, students and teachers must have adequate access to current technology and reliable connectivity. In 2001, 99 percent of U.S. public schools reported that they had access to the Internet, up from 35 percent in 1994 (Kleiner & Farris, 2002). Of those with access somewhere in the building in 2001, 87 percent of schools had Internet access in all instructional rooms. Among those statistics lie some differences in access. Schools with the highest minority enrollment or the highest concentration of poverty had a smaller percentage of instructional rooms connected to the Internet than did schools with lower minority or poverty populations. Approximately 81 percent of classrooms in schools with the highest minority enrollment and 79 percent of classrooms in schools with high poverty concentrations were Internet-connected. Overall, the ratio of students to Internet-ready instructional computers was 5.4 to 1, and three-quarters of public schools posted a website in 2001.

Somewhat surprising is the fact that newer teachers, those with less than 5 years' experience, are no more likely to use technology than are teachers who have been in the classroom over 20 years (Fatemi, 1999). This statistic hints at a more complex challenge than can be met by simply purchasing adequate hardware.

This chapter will first inform educators about characteristics unique to educational technology research so that results can be appropriately interpreted. It will then highlight recent findings on technology's effect on teaching and learning. Any expected change in classrooms as a result of technology hinges on teachers' perceptions and understandings of the potential benefits and barriers. Hence, an awareness of current research findings must be a part of the ongoing dialogue on the benefits of technology in the classroom.

Interpreting the Results of Research on Technology in Education

Unfortunately, as the technology wave crashes into traditional educational practices, teachers are infrequently being made aware of the latest research findings. Dozens of articles are written every year on educational technology–related topics, and although the sheer amount of information can be staggering to new teachers, being aware of the mistakes and successes of others will help to establish sound practices. In order to integrate technology effectively into the lives of students, teachers need to be able to weigh the evidence. Do computers make students smarter? How do actual classroom teaching and learning behaviors alter as a result of introducing technology to the curriculum? Is this technological revolution really good for our children, or is this just education's attempt to stay up with the times? (See Figure 5.1.)

Changing Research Goals

As each new media type has become available to classrooms, educators, along with the general public, have been quick to jump on the bandwagon, hoping that real change in education may be possible this time.

History shows, however, that many educational innovations have come and gone without satisfying the goals for improved student learning. Much of the past research on technology integration has focused on incorporating computers into traditional teaching methods (Berson, 1996) and allowing teachers to do what they normally do, but faster (O'Neil, 1995). Educators are discovering that it is no longer enough merely to place a computer in a classroom and say that students are "using" technology. It is the way computers are used rather than the actual machines themselves that contribute to learning (Proctor & Burnett, 1996; Roblyer, 1997). Researchers are beginning to look more at how technology might change basic teaching and learning processes to better address expectations for what students should learn, moving away from simply investigating whether students have higher test scores with computer-based instruction (Roblyer, 1996).

Rather than asking questions like "Should technology be used in education?" educators now must ask themselves, "How should technology be used to help students achieve higher

FIGURE 5.1 Do computers make students smarter?

levels?" (Fouts, 2000). The discussion of research in educational technology can be expected to continue to be refined as researchers suggest the need for more experimental, quantitative studies on the effects of technology on learning (Waxman, Connell, & Gray, 2002), coming on the heels of the No Child Left Behind legislation that calls for scientifically based evidence of student learning (*No Child Left Behind*, 2002).

New Learning Theory and Practice

Any discussion of the inclusion of technology in classrooms must be informed by an understanding of current learning theories and practices that represent fundamental changes in the ways teachers teach and learners learn. *Constructivism* is a learning theory premised on the understanding that people are participants in their own learning. There is no single true reality that must be imparted to learners, but rather individuals create their own knowledge based on how they relate new information to what they have previously experienced. *Social constructivism* additionally recognizes the value of social interactions in the learning process, meaning that people clarify personal conceptions as they interact with the understandings of others. *Engaged learning* is tied closely to constructivist underpinnings. Students learn best when they are active participants in the learning process, meaning that they make their own decisions, think critically about real learning problems and resources, and operate in contexts that are meaningful to them. Authentic, challenging, and multidisciplinary learning tasks allow students to grasp the subject matter better.

Teachers in constructivist and engaged learning classrooms must build rich learning environments filled with opportunities for authentic, project-based tasks as well as a variety of technology and nontechnology tools. They must then facilitate the management of a range of information by their students, rather than telling students what they need to know. Students need to have a voice in what topics will be explored and ample interaction with peers, adults, experts, and others with whom they can test theories and confirm understanding. Students take ownership of their own learning, with teachers serving a supportive, rather than directive, role.

Clarifying the Research Variables

The changed goals for research on technology use, along with the increasing acceptance of constructivist and engaged learning principles, have implications for interpreting research results on the effectiveness of technology in education. Computers used in traditional classrooms, in which students are expected to converge upon predetermined correct answers, will have a different effect on student learning than computers used in classrooms in which students are expected to participate in their own understandings of various concepts. Technology will be used for different purposes in each situation.

The following three factors must first be accepted in order to interpret research on the effectiveness of technology in student learning (Honey, Culp, & Spielvogel, 1999):

1. *Technology* refers to more than computers, including a range of electronic methods and tools that can be used to support learning (see Figure 5.2).
2. The assessment of how technology impacts student achievement is a complex process that demands alternative methods to standardized assessments of isolated facts.

3. Classroom change correlates with other educational factors, such as teaching and learning roles.

Educators looking to the results of research for the answers about using technology for learning might start by isolating study variables through the following questions:

Who? Who are the leaders in student learning? Do students have ownership and direction in their own learning or are classroom activities primarily teacher-directed?

What? What technology is being used? Are students using productivity software, content-specific software, web-based tools, handheld devices, or scientific probeware?

Where? Where do students have access to technology? Regular, as-needed access to computers in the classroom will impact student learning differently than will limited, weekly visits to the computer lab.

Why? Why is technology being used? Is there a clear learning goal in mind, or is technology being used only for technology's sake?

How? How is technology used by students and teachers? Are electronic information sources used to supplement traditional instruction or as the basis for student-led, meaningful, inquiry-based learning?

Research reports do not always clearly specify the learning conditions in classrooms in which technology use is studied, so as consumers of research, teachers must look carefully for clues. If none exist, the results should not be taken as a complete story but rather as one indication of technology effectiveness.

FIGURE 5.2 Technology refers to more than computers, including a range of electronic methods and tools that can be used to support learning.

Teaching with Technology

Teachers' actions largely influence their students' achievement. Therefore, an understanding of the academic effects of the use of technology for students should begin with an understanding of the impact of technology on the teaching profession. The types of teachers who use technology, how that technology use alters teaching practice, the effects on collegial relationships, and the stages of integration that teachers progress through when adopting technology as a part of their teaching are areas of recent investigation.

Technology-Using Teachers

Becker (1994) looked at how "exemplary computer-using teachers" differ from other teachers in the environment in which they teach, their personal computer experience, and their teaching habits. Using information from surveys of third- through twelfth-grade teachers, this study found four main requirements of a school environment that make it more conducive to exemplary computer-using teachers.

1. Teachers need to be surrounded by other teachers who use computers. Whether expert or novice users, teachers can benefit from the collegial sharing of ideas, resources, and teaching strategies with other computer-using teachers in their building.

2. Teachers benefit by working in a school in which computers are used for authentic, meaningful purposes, such as for writing for a real audience. Exemplary computer-using teachers are more likely to come from a setting like this than from one in which word processing is used only to accomplish predetermined skills or computers are used primarily for games.

3. Financial support for technology at both the school and district levels makes for more proficient computer users. Schools in which exemplary computer users were found frequently had a school or district computer coordinator who assisted teachers in getting started with technology integration. In addition, these teachers had available to them sufficient staff development opportunities, to instruct them in computer applications and to integrate the computer into the content being taught.

4. A "resource-rich" environment supports expert computer users. Teachers often had smaller class sizes and fewer students per computer. It is unclear whether teachers were able to become exemplary computer users because they had smaller classes, or whether they were given smaller classes because they were exemplary computer users.

When surveyed about their personal backgrounds, researchers found that these exemplary computer-using teachers, more than other teachers, spent a great deal of their personal time working on computers, staying after school, or bringing computers home (Becker, 1994). These teachers on the whole also had more training with using computers, higher levels of education, more experience teaching their current subject; and they tended to a large degree to be male. Later studies have supported these characteristics, finding that teachers who were more likely to use computers for teaching had greater personal computer skills, allowed for open-ended learning activities, and saw computers less as an "add-on" and more as an integral component of a learning plan (Higgins, Moseley, & Tse, 2001). In practice, the teachers surveyed who fell into the category of exemplary computer users more often than others made conscious decisions to alter existing curriculum, eliminating less important topics to allow room for more computer-related endeavors (Becker, 1994). They allowed students some choice in their learning and encouraged teams of students to work together on computer assignments. Together, these data imply that both increased personal interest as well as greater amounts of experience, with computers and with general content knowledge, make for a teacher more apt to be successful in technology integration in the classroom. This finding is echoed in other studies that show that the amount of technology used by the teacher positively impacts student achievement in areas such as reading and math (e.g., Middleton & Murray, 1999).

There is a strong need for training to maintain teachers' knowledge of new technology and its use in education, not only for specially designated computer teachers, but extended to all teachers (Yaghi, 1996). Effective integration of technology depends on teachers who have knowledge about how to use technology to meet instructional goals. However, lower socioeconomic schools spend less on teacher development (Anderson & Becker, 2001). Unfortunately, whereas 66 percent of technology expenditures is spent on hardware and 19 percent on software, only 15 percent is allocated to teacher professional development (*Technology in Education 2002*, 2002). Administrators must play a key role in envisioning the effective use of technology and in providing an appropriate environment for technology use (Solomon, 2002; Stolarchuk & Fisher, 2001). Teachers are more successful when they have regular access to technical support (Tiene & Luft, 2001). The leadership role necessary to provide such support, along with extra resources, release time, and encouragement, is vital in teacher success with technology (Higgins et al., 2001).

Changes in Teaching Practice

The Apple Classrooms of Tomorrow (ACOT) project involved giving every teacher and every student from test classrooms across the country two computers each, one to use at school and one to bring home (David, 1995). The intent was to create model, technology-rich learning environments in which teachers and students could use computers on a routine, authentic basis. ACOT researchers found that changes in teaching practices did not take place instantaneously (Ringstaff, Sandholtz, & Dwyer, 1995). New technology was typically slotted into a place determined by old teaching habits. Even teachers who use technology for personal reasons often do not use technology in the classroom, or if they do, they integrate it with traditional teaching methodologies (Pflaum, 2001). Teachers and students initially followed the traditional classroom patterns with which they were familiar (O'Neil, 1995). Gradually, over years of participating in the study, teachers began making noticeable alterations in the dynamics of the learning environments, based on the new thinking the technology sparked. Teachers were finding out that one person, whether it was himself or herself or a student, could not always be the expert on every facet of a new technology medium. Recognizing the potential for student involvement in the teaching of peers was a difficult shift for many teachers who had grown accustomed to the traditional teacher–student relationship structure. When teachers were able to move past that pervasive teacher-centered view of education, students and teachers, as communities of learners, were able to benefit from the range of individual areas of expertise represented by the entire group (see Figure 5.3).

Collegial Relationships

As teachers ventured through this learning process, they discovered new facets of relationships they shared with each other (Ringstaff et al., 1995). In a traditional school, teachers are fairly autonomous; once the classroom doors close, the majority of their time is spent with students. Teachers in the ACOT schools at first communicated

FIGURE 5.3 Students and teachers benefit from the range of individual areas of expertise represented by the entire group.

primarily to commiserate about their unfamiliar experiences and to support each other. As they grew accustomed to having and using the technology, they supported each other using the hardware and software, passed along instructional ideas and strategies, and ultimately collaborated with team members to develop innovative teaching methods and curricula. Technology was the topic of conversation and also the medium through which much of the communication was made possible.

Stages of Integration

Researchers were able to identify five distinct stages through which teachers new to technology developmentally progressed in their pursuit of technology integration (Sandholtz, Ringstaff, & Dwyer, 1997). The *Entry* stage was one of frequently painful growth as experienced teachers ran headlong into the very basic challenges that generally plague rookie teachers. Everyone involved was required to learn to live with very different classrooms than those in which they were used to teaching and learning. Teachers had to contend with students experimenting with new cheating techniques, technical problems, and the annoyances of classroom facilities not built for computers. At this initial stage, teachers found themselves reacting to the small issues and overlooking the larger issues involved with integrating the computers into effective instructional agendas. Teachers transitioned into the *Adoption* stage as they began to take more of a proactive stance toward meeting the challenges presented by the computers. They worked with students to learn to use the hardware and software and began learning from their mistakes to settle into tolerable patterns of classroom life, often accepting a level of movement and activity in the classroom that they might not have found acceptable earlier. Learning to use the technology tends to take precedence over the integration of content, with initial technology projects done with excitement and flash, but meaningful content integration taking perhaps years (Goldman, Cole, & Syer, 1999).

In the *Adaptation* stage, teachers finally began making the technology work for them, instructionally and for administrative duties. The traditional lecture format perpetuated in classes throughout the study, but teachers were able to get past issues of teaching the technology and get back to teaching content. During the *Appropriation* stage, they were able to move beyond simply accommodating computers and squeezing them into the traditional daily routine and began to personally accept the new teaching possibilities technology offers. Ultimately, many teachers arrived at the *Invention* stage, at which they were not only ready but also eager to break out of typical, teacher-controlled classroom routines. At this stage, teachers communicated with each other a great deal, sharing ideas and innovations, and even bringing together groups of students for authentic project-based activities. Working with and learning from other teachers and students characterized this changed philosophy of education whereby technology became the medium for inquiry, collaboration, and constant reflection on what was being accomplished and what was yet attainable. At this final stage, teachers took advantage of new communication capabilities to play the roles of information consultants, team collaborators, facilitators, course developers, and academic advisers (Kook, 1997).

Learning with Technology

Those involved with educational technology policy decisions are frequently concerned with one issue: Do the academic gains brought by the addition of computers into classrooms outweigh the financial expenditures necessary to equip classrooms? Unfortunately, those looking for quick answers will find none. The results from research into the effects of technology on learning are mixed. Whereas a large proportion of researchers are able to demonstrate positive academic results, others have shown no effects or even slightly negative impacts on achievement. The most recent meta-analysis of research on the effects of technology on student outcomes suggests that students who used technology in their learning had modest but positive gains in learning outcomes over students who learned without technology (Waxman et al., 2002).

Overall Academic Effects

Similar to the ACOT study, a study of concentrated computer use took place in Union City, New Jersey, a largely ethnic and impoverished community in the most densely populated city in the United States (Honey, Culp, & Carrigg, 1999). The city embarked on substantive changes in class block length, increased in-service training for teachers, building renovation, and improved class libraries. Union City also began investing in technology resources so that it is now one of the most wired urban school districts in the country. Researchers found that these reforms impacted standardized-test performance, especially for those students with home and school access to technology. Writing was the area in which middle-grade students showed the greatest gains. Increased expectations and teacher preparation combined with other reforms to achieve such improvements. The researchers recommend that technology will have the greatest impact when other reforms happen in concert. Professional development in teaching approaches, not only for technology skills, must be offered to teachers. Students should be assisted in developing learning skills such as creativity through individualized tasks for all ability levels. Information-rich environments including technology and nontechnology tools should be available.

When compared with students in traditional classrooms, students in the technology-rich ACOT classrooms were more apt to work together, which made school more interesting and, consequently, improved students' attitudes about themselves and their learning (Sandholtz, Ringstaff, & Dwyer, 1995b). Rather than merely fulfilling what was asked of them in assignments, these students surpassed original goals, challenging themselves to explore new and creative projects and often choosing to work during their free time. Teachers, in fact, had trouble at times getting students to move on to other projects. Students did not, as was feared at the outset, become solo workers in front of their personal computer screens. Instead, they developed and demonstrated the ability to use social interaction to enhance their learning by sharing knowledge and explaining processes as they were undertaken (see Figure 5.4).

Along with those for whom computers facilitated a richer learning experience, some students became just as bored with technology as they did with traditional teaching. This was the case when the technology was not used as just one of a selection of classroom tools but was focused on in an artificial manner. Students worked best when technology was not the topic itself but was integrated into the entire curriculum.

High school students who had unlimited access to technology during their entire high school careers matured into self-starting problem solvers and self-assured collaborators (Tierney et al., 1995). They were able to verbalize the role computers played in their growth as students, and they saw how the unique abilities they had gained during those four years had empowered them to future success.

A staggering number of studies on educational technology have examined the effects of a whole range of factors on success with technology, from student variables, such as gender and socioeconomic levels, to environmental variables, such as the type of technology being used. Academic and other gains made by various segments

FIGURE 5.4 Students do not become solo workers in front of their computers but use social interaction to enhance their learning.

of students often appear to contradict each other; so, again, the reader is cautioned to interpret such findings as partial indication of effectiveness rather than as absolute truth.

Boys are more likely than girls to see themselves as computer users and to see the world of computer use as male-dominated, although behaviors related to computers do not generally vary according to gender (Whitley, 1997). Boys are more concerned with mastery of computer work and feel more relaxed while working with computers, possibly leading them to feel better about their performance of work on the computer. Girls like to use computers to communicate and to solve real problems (Solomon, 2002). It is believed that differences in how boys and girls perceive their computer competence stem from boys having more opportunities, at home and at school, to use computers (Nelson & Cooper, 1997).

Having a home computer is associated with higher mathematics and reading scores, and in general, children from high- rather than low-socioeconomic-status homes, boys more than girls, and white students more than ethnic minorities, achieve the largest educational gains from home computers (Attewell & Battle, 1999). Families from diverse cultures can use home connectivity to find resources and connect with the school, enhancing language learning for the entire community (Solomon, 2002). Other findings indicate that high school students' skill and experience with computers, parental education, access to computers, and even academic self-concept are all reliable predictors of student use of electronic communication tools (Fishman, 1999). Fifth-graders using an integrated learning system improved test scores, although in this case, lower-achieving students made the greatest gains, and boys and girls achieved equally (Mann, Shakeshaft, Becker, & Kottkamp, 1999).

Both regular and special needs students in technology-rich environments showed positive achievement in all subject areas in preschool through higher education, as well as improved attitudes toward learning and self-concept (Sivin-Kachala, 1998). Students who used educational computer games had more developed comprehension skills and outscored nongame-playing peers in both reading and math, possibly a result of experience with comprehending game instructions and performing game-related tasks (Mayer, Schustack, & Blanton, 1999). Technology has been shown to allow learner control, increase motivation, provide connections to the real world, and lead to increased achievement when tied to content standards and the needs of the learners (Valdez et al., 1999). Students are using computers at home in increasing numbers. Over 17 million teenagers (73 percent) use the Internet (Lenhart, Rainie, & Lewis, 2001), with 94 percent using it for school research (Lenhart, Simon, & Graziano, 2001). The Internet has become the primary research tool for teens.

The Effect of Technology on Language Achievement

Research into the effects of technology on student achievement in language arts has resulted in widely disparate findings. Sixth-grade students who wrote compositions on word processors showed few differences in quality and complexity of compositions, as well as the accuracy of grammar, from students who wrote compositions by hand (Nichols, 1996). Those students using word processors, provided they had ample keyboarding experience, wrote significantly longer compositions than those writing with paper and pencil. Using computers has no conclusive effects on either the quantity or quality of the writing of fifth-graders. This suggests that the difference in students' writing abilities will stem from their teachers' beliefs and dedication toward teaching writing rather than from the decision of whether to use computers (Dybdahl, Shaw, & Blahous, 1997).

A review of research on the effects of word processing programs on students' writing abilities shows that in general, writing using word processing programs improves students' attitudes toward writing, produces longer and more fluent written products, and allows students to revise their writing more easily and quickly than with paper and pencil (Reed, 1996). Despite this success, the potential problem with word processing programs is that they are not completely aligned to writing process theory. The programs offer an open area for drafting compositions, but do not prompt student writers to consider prewriting thoughts or specific revision activities. Teachers should understand the role of this software as a tool in the writing process, not a substitute for the process itself. In fact, first-graders, whose use of computers resulted in longer writing including more words and more sentences, improved in their writing abilities not because they liked using computers, but because specific software features aided the writing process (Barrera, Rule, & Diemart, 2001). When writing on the computer, students reread their writing aloud frequently, which facilitated more writing. Rather than rereading their own writing, students writing by hand spoke to classmates about what they were writing. Handwriters frequently asked their teachers when they could stop writing, whereas their computer-writing counterparts were reluctant to stop. Teachers found that it was more beneficial to sit with students to edit their papers on-screen rather than printing out the writing.

Technology allows students to enhance written words using multiple modalities through which to communicate, such as through video, animation, and sound effects (Baker & Kinzer, 1998). Word processing allows teachers to reevaluate composition methods by viewing the writing process as dynamic and recursive, rather than linear, as it frequently is when students use pencil and paper. Students who word processed rarely considered writing pieces finished, regularly returning to saved files to rework compositions. Peers collaborated more openly, offering feedback to writers as they passed by the computer monitors. These practices signal potentially dramatic changes in assessment, as traditional practices such as grading final papers might not measure student learning sufficiently. A caveat emerging is the tendency for students to put more focus on creating electronic presentations than on attending to the content of the paper.

Researchers have also investigated the effects of technology on reading comprehension. Students had higher comprehension scores after reading the electronic stories versus reading printed texts (Greenlee-Moore & Smith, 1996; Matthew, 1997). The interactive effects of the sound, animation, narration, and additional definitions that make up the electronic texts motivate students to want to read the stories again and again, something researchers found to occur less often with printed books. The educational potential of these stories is jeopardized when insufficient teacher guidance leads to the software being used solely for entertainment.

Ninety percent of kindergarten students using a computer-based reading readiness program achieved grade-level reading ability by first grade (Alfaro, 1999). Third- through sixth-grade students in a low socioeconomic community scored the same reading scores with traditional basal reading preparation and computer-assisted instruction (Hamilton, 1995). Drill-and-practice software was found to be effective with practicing correct spelling (Ediger, 2001). Students using computers in a collaborative context demonstrated superior depth of understanding and reflection, as well as improved reading and language scores (Scardamalia & Bereiter, 1996).

The Effect of Technology on Mathematics Achievement

Research into how computers have affected mathematics learning and teaching examines effects of programming, computer-assisted instruction, and tool software (McCoy, 1996). Students from primary to secondary grades who have programming experience score higher on measures of geometry knowledge and problem solving. A review of research found that experimental groups of students from third grade to high school, using fraction software, problem-solving software, and estimation software, scored significantly higher than did control groups (McCoy, 1996). Simulation programs that allowed students to explore mathematical environments actively were shown to be effective in helping students understand geometric notions and develop intuitive understandings of graphing. Students using mathematical software for algebra, geometry, and calculus were shown to have gained a better understanding of the topic (McCoy, 1996). The tools allowed students to actively participate in mathematical topics that otherwise might be considered stagnant or outdated (Blubaugh, 1995).

Students were more motivated and self-confident about subjects such as calculus, finding them to be more meaningful than they had previously thought (Rochowicz, 1996). Students in math courses in which computers were used were able to tackle more complex problems without spending time on routine exercises. Other studies, however, found no difference between the achievement levels of students using computers in mathematics and those who were not, yet noted improved motivation and participation of the computer users (McCoy, 1996).

The professional development of the teacher and the frequency of home computer use were positively related to academic achievement in mathematics (Education Testing Service, 1998). Fourth-graders achieved better in mathematics when they had experience using math computer games, whereas eighth-graders did better when higher-order thinking skills were stressed. The positive aspects of technology use were more prominent for older students, equivalent to up to 15 weeks above grade level, than younger students.

The Effect of Technology on Science Achievement

Computers have been used in science classrooms in a variety of ways aimed both at helping students learn scientific facts and at giving them experience with the scientific process. Computer-assisted instruction has been shown to have a positive effect for secondary science achievement (Ardac & Sezen, 2002; Bayraktar, 2001–2002; Chang, 2001; Siegle & Foster, 2001). The most effective forms of technology for science achievement are those that engage students in more active learning, such as simulations and tutorials; drill-and-practice software actually had a negative effect on achievement. Simulations lead to learning equivalent to that of hands-on dissection and are more effective when used before other learning experiences (Akpan, 2001). Software developed by teachers themselves was shown to be the most effective because of the awareness of learning objectives. The effects were highest when computers supplemented traditional instruction. Computer-based instruction fostered content knowledge and process skills in secondary science students when accompanied by teacher guidance; students working independently on the computer were less able to gain the content knowledge (Ardac & Sezen, 2002). Problem-based software may encourage students to focus on the central problem and to consider science within a real-world context (Chang, 2001). On the average, students receiving traditional instruction supplemented with computer-assisted instruction attained higher science achievement than did those receiving only traditional instruction (Christmann & Badgett, 1999).

The Effect of Technology on Social Studies Achievement

In a review of recent research involving the effectiveness of computers in social studies (Berson, 1996), drill-and-practice programs were found to be the most prevalent of applications used in social studies education. Use of this type of software was studied largely with secondary students, and results showed modest gains in recall-type skills and motivation. Simulation programs allowed students to go beyond the basic knowledge level to explore environments to which they might not normally be able to go. Although working with these programs also appeared to increase a student's ability to recall facts, students additionally showed improvement in problem solving, curiosity, and personal initiative and control. Computerized simulations resulted in students who could communicate better and at higher levels than those who did not use simulations in social studies (Willis, 1996). Databases were encouraging to the development of students' abilities to search for and analyze the extensive collections of current and historical data (Berson, 1996). Overall, computers allowed students access to information and motivated them to inquire and to learn.

The Effect of Technology for Students with Special Needs

In the areas of composition and reading, the literature has shown positive effects from using technology with students with mild and moderate disabilities (Fitzgerald & Koury, 1996). Improved comprehension, spelling, and collaborative practices were found, along with positive attitudes in students who used multimedia tools to compose. Current advancements in voice transcription technology allow students to compose a piece of writing completely via dictation.

Technology helps students with disabilities participate in collaborative projects and increase independence and communication (Solomon, 2002). Motivation, self-confidence, learning attitudes, and achievement of at-risk students were improved with cooperative-learning computer-search activities (Gan, 1999). Traditionally, schools have had lower expectations for at-risk students and have emphasized the acquisition of basic skills, often in special pullout programs or in lower-level tracks (Means, 1997). Students with special needs may require more coaching in computer-based activities, but they will benefit from the experience of learning with and from other students.

Technology-Enriched Learning Environments

Effective technology-rich educational environments are characterized by: (1) students' active involvement in the learning process through such activities as problem solving and data analysis; (2) collaborative learning activities that tend to increase student motivation, understanding, and self-confidence; (3) immediate and individualized feedback on student performance typically provided by educational software; and (4) material presented in the context of real-world situations or through other authentic sources of information available through the Internet (Roschelle, Pea, Hoadley, Gordin, & Means, 2000). Teachers with access to technology are less likely to present to the whole group and more likely to allow for increased student work time (Tiene & Luft, 2001). They shift into a more facilitative role and feel their teaching is more effective because of the technology. Teachers see their students' learning improve, and some see standardized test performance improve for students with access to technology. Technology facilitates student interactions and task-oriented discussions, and decreases classroom management issues with cooperative groups.

Social context is important when learning with technology (Lou, Abrami, & d'Apollonia, 2001). Students working in small groups had greater cognitive and affective gains than students working individually. Although students working individually accomplished tasks faster, students in small groups found benefits in the social interaction, leading to improved attitudes toward group work and an increase in appropriate learning strategies. Group work was most effective when teachers prepared students with strategies for cooperative learning and when groups were small. Students working in pairs had the greatest learning gains, possibly because groups have to be able to fit around the computer screen to participate equally. The effects on learning in groups were most prominent when students were working with drill-and-practice or tutorial programs. With these characteristics in mind, it is important for teachers to distinguish expected outcomes for the group as opposed to the individual. Students with a 2:1 computer-to-student ratio showed the greatest improvement in writing abilities over time (Owston & Wideman, 2001). Students were willing to assist each other with technical problems and cooperate for learning activities. Higher computer-to-student ratios may have been less effective because of reduced student time on the computer and increased teacher time spent on student management issues.

High amounts of technology do allow teachers to individualize learning opportunities, however, allowing students to work at their own pace and motivating students to focus on work for great periods of time (Tiene & Luft, 2001). Individuals talked less and were more focused on the learning task than were students working in pairs, but took the same amount of time as pairs, apparently taking more time to think while the pairs engaged in off-task discussion (Jackson, Kutnick, & Kington, 2001). Drill-and-practice software was better for individual students. These findings imply that teachers should not require students to work in groups for the sole reason of increasing student time on computers; they should consider instead the student grouping arrangement that makes the most sense for the learning task.

Laptop Computers

There is a growing movement to consider the use of laptop computers in educational settings, citing the appeal of the flexibility and individual access to technology that portable computers provide. A variety of laptop configurations are being tested, including those in which all students and teachers have laptops, only the teachers have laptops, or wireless carts are employed (Rideout, 2002). When teachers are strong leaders, display a willingness to help students using laptops, and are organized and interested in their subject, students were shown to have positive attitudes not only toward the laptops but also toward their content area (Stolarchuk & Fisher, 2001). Teachers with laptop computers increasingly teach with constructivist practices, use discussion rather than lecture, encourage student-led inquiry, and emphasize thinking skills (Walker, Rockman, & Chessler, 2000). They feel they have a greater sense of control over their classroom instruction and use computers more frequently and with greater confidence.

Students with the ubiquitous access to technology that laptop computers provide demonstrated improved writing assessments, increased time doing homework, and increased use of computers and the Internet, at both home and school (Walker, Rockman, & Chessler, 2000). Elementary students with access to laptops from third through fifth grades exhibited an increased writing ability over those with only occasional access (Owston & Wideman, 1997). Secondary students benefited from using laptops to review information, complete assignments, and study for tests (Siegle & Foster, 2001). Access to laptops has been shown to enhance academic gains among sixth-grade students who traditionally have not succeeded in school, with laptop users consistently outperforming nonusers (Stevenson, 1999). Laptops encouraged collaboration among students, working more often in groups and assuming a greater variety of roles teaching their peers and their teachers. Finally, these students were more confident, organized, and motivated. Laptop-using students were more likely to agree with the statement "Computers help me improve the quality of my schoolwork," whereas nonlaptop-using students agreed with the statement "I enjoy playing games on computers" (see Figure 5.5).

Caveats

A growing concern among critics of technology use in education is that the charm of technology might not be so magical after all. Some argue that students become so focused on learning the tricks of a particular software that they are prevented from learning what the software is designed to teach (Oppenheimer, 1997). Another chal-

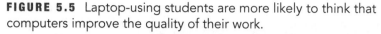

FIGURE 5.5 Laptop-using students are more likely to think that computers improve the quality of their work.

lenge is group computer work, which in reality involves one student centered in front of the computer screen with control of the mouse at any one time. Other students may or may not be attending and participating in the decision-making process and may not get a turn in the "driver's seat" with any regularity. Students may have difficulty paying attention in a classroom filled with the variety of noises, activity, and distractions common to technology-enhanced rooms (Sandholtz, Ringstaff, & Dwyer, 1995b).

The rate of technological advancement is staggering, and in order to provide the best education possible to students, hardware must be maintained, software must be upgraded, and staff must be kept trained in the most current practices. These issues might prove to be too great of a financial burden for the schools and districts to face regularly. There are clearly no easy answers for schools, so it follows that the best advice would be to consider these potential drawbacks as part of a complete and ongoing decision-making process regarding technology integration.

Observations from the ACOT study summarize well the need for caution as we form expectations about computers in the classroom (Sandholtz, Ringstaff, & Dwyer, 1997):

1. Teachers must be ready to make some changes in their teaching beliefs and methodologies in order to give innovations a chance.

2. Technology by itself cannot be expected to revolutionize education, but rather should be seen as one of a collection of tools that might spark and facilitate innovative thinking.
3. An environment of support and sharing will encourage teachers to take risks.
4. Any changes initiated by the introduction of technology to classrooms must be expected to occur over time and with a great deal of dedication and effort.

Teacher as Researcher

The characteristics and trends in educational technology research should certainly be understood by classroom teachers, but more importantly, the growing body of research should signal a call for action. The interaction between the technology and the user is beginning to be seen as a conversation that is different with every user in every situation (Kozma, 1994), which presents difficulties for neat, convenient research. More qualitative, ethnographic-type studies are called for, but the dilemma is encountered that no easy, all-encompassing answer is available to apply to every situation (Roblyer, 1996).

Traditional educational research cannot keep pace with hardware and software development, yet teachers, who generally are on the forefront of innovative methods, often do not write their findings so that others can learn from their insight (Valdez et al., 1999; Willis, 1996). If classroom teachers participate in educational research, that research will be stronger as it reflects their daily lived experiences. Despite the requirements of normal duties, teachers' substantial participation in research is the only way to ensure meaningful and practical research results.

Even more important than enriching the literature base, the process of classroom research serves the vital function of helping teachers learn more about their own teaching by carefully observing their students (Painter, 2000). Teachers who research with colleagues, and even students, can further inform their own understanding, satisfy personal learning goals, and accomplish writing through collaboration.

Summary

This chapter begins with a discussion of characteristics unique to educational technology research so that teachers will be able to interpret the findings. Researchers are beginning to pay closer attention to how technology can change teaching and learning processes to better address expectations for what students should learn, rather than simply investigating whether students have higher test scores with computer-based instruction. Current learning theories and practices, such as *constructivism* and *engaged learning*, represent fundamental changes in the ways we understand teaching and learning. Educators looking to research findings for guidance about using technology for learning should first consider the variables in studies they read about.

Exemplary computer-using teachers have been shown to teach in different environments from other teachers and have greater personal computer experience, greater amounts of personal time working on computers, and unique teaching habits. Teachers in technology-rich classrooms followed the traditional classroom patterns initially, and then gradually began altering classroom practices and forming new collegial relationships. Researchers have identified distinct stages through which teachers new to technology progress in their pursuit of technology integration.

The results from research into the effects of technology on learning are mixed. Whereas a large proportion of researchers are able to demonstrate positive academic results, others have shown no effects or even slightly negative impacts on achievement. A recent meta-analysis demonstrated that students using technology had modest but positive gains in learning outcomes over those students who used no technology. The effects of technology use on language, math, science, and social studies achievement, as well as effects for special needs students, have been recent areas of research.

As teachers learn about the potential of technology, they restructure their physical classroom environments to allow presentation space, group work space, and flexible space for multiple activities. Effective technology-rich environments allow for active student learning, collaborative environments, immediate feedback, and authentic information. Effective environments place value on the social context of learning while still allowing individualized learning opportunities. There is also a growing movement to consider the use of laptop computers in educational settings, due to the appeal of their flexibility and individual technology access.

A growing concern among critics of technology use in education is that the charm of technology might not be so magical after all. Some argue that students focus on the software rather than the content and that students working in groups have unequal access.

Traditional educational research cannot keep pace with hardware and software development. Teachers, who are at the forefront of innovative methods, are urged to write about their experiences so that others can learn from their insights.

Challenge Yourself!

1. Watch both the local and national newspapers and popular news magazines over a month's time for news on educational technology. What are the current issues? How is research on technology's effectiveness being portrayed to the public?
2. Visit a local school and observe the level and amount of technology available. What is the school or district plan for integration? What evidence do you see of its progress?
3. Interview a teacher who has incorporated technology to some extent into his or her teaching. According to the teacher, what challenges have been faced?
4. Research technology's effectiveness in your intended area of specialty.
5. Make a list of how teaching in a high-technology classroom will be different from or similar to the education you had growing up. How will it change daily classroom activities?
6. How might universities and other teacher preparation programs better ready future teachers to take advantage of the technology they will surely have in their classrooms? How are strategies that will be used to introduce technology to students similar to those that can be used to familiarize teachers with it?

7. Write a note to the parents of your future students explaining your philosophy of technology integration.
8. How would you convince a reluctant colleague to utilize computer technology in his or her teaching repertoire?
9. What are your predictions for the future of technology use in education? Will schools always attempt to emulate the degree of technology integration that society achieves?
10. Play the devil's advocate role. Compose a brief argument against the purchase and use of computers in schools.

References

Akpan, J. P. (2001). Issues associated with inserting computer simulations into biology instruction: A review of the literature. *Electronic Journal of Science Education, 5*(3). Retrieved 2/19/03 from unr.edu/homepage/crowther/ejse/ejsev5n3.html.

Alfaro, R. (1999). The technology–reading connection. *Educational Leadership, 56*(6), 48–50.

Anderson, R. E., & Becker, H. J. (2001). *School investments in instructional technology.* Retrieved April 9, 2003, from www.crito.uci.edu/tlc/findings/report_8/startpage.htm.

Ardac, D., & Sezen, A. H. (2002). Effectiveness of computer-based chemistry instruction in enhancing the learning of content and variable control under guided versus unguided conditions. *Journal of Science Education and Technology, 11*(1), 39–48.

Attewell, P., & Battle, J. (1999). Home computers and school performance. *Information Society, 15*(1), 1–10.

Baker, E., & Kinzer, C. K. (1998). Effects of technology on process writing: Are they all good? *National Reading Conference Yearbook, 47,* 428–440.

Barrera, M. T., Rule, A. C., & Diemart, A. (2001). The effect of writing with computers versus handwriting on the writing achievement of first-graders. *Information Technology in Childhood Education Annual,* 215–228.

Bayraktar, S. (2001–2002). A meta-analysis of the effectiveness of computer-assisted instruction in science education. *Journal of Research on Technology in Education, 34*(2), 173–188.

Becker, H. J. (1994). How exemplary computer-using teachers differ from other teachers: Implications for realizing the potential of computers in schools. *Journal of Research on Computing in Education, 26*(3), 291–321.

Berson, M. J. (1996). Effectiveness of computer technology in the social studies: A review of the literature. *Journal of Research on Computing in Education, 28*(4), 486–501.

Blubaugh, W. L. (1995). Use of software to improve the teaching of geometry. *Mathematics and Computer Education, 29*(3), 288–293.

CEO Forum on Education and Technology. (2001). *Key building blocks for student achievement in the 21st century.* Retrieved June 6, 2003, from www.ceoforum.org/downloads/report4.pdf.

Chang, C.-Y. (2001). Comparing the impacts of a problem-based computer-assisted instruction and the direct-interactive teaching method on student science achievement. *Journal of Science Education and Technology, 10*(2), 147–153.

Christmann, E., & Badgett, J. (1999). A comparative analysis of the effects of computer-assisted instruction on student achievement in differing science and demographical areas. *Journal of Computers in Mathematics and Science Teaching, 18*(2), 135–143.

Cradler, J. (2003). Technology's impact on teaching and learning. *Learning and Leading with Technology, 30*(7), 54–57.

David, J. L. (1995). Partnerships for change. In *Apple education research reports* (pp. 45–46). Eugene, OR: International Society for Technology in Education.

Dybdahl, C. S., Shaw, D. G., & Blahous, E. (1997). The impact of the computer on writing: No simple answers. *Computers in the Schools, 13*(3/4), 41–53.

Ediger, M. (2001). Assessing student achievement in spelling. *Reading Improvement, 38*(4), 183–187.

Education Testing Service. (1998). *Does it compute? The relationship between educational technology and student achievement in mathematics.* Wenglinsky, H. (Ed.), Policy Information Center. Princeton, NJ: Author.

The Facts About 21st-Century Technology. (2001). Retrieved June 8, 2003, from www.nclb.gov/start/facts/21centtech.html.

Fatemi, E. (1999). Building the digital curriculum. Technology Counts '99: Building the Digital Curriculum. *Education Week, 19*(4), 5–8.

Fishman, B. J. (1999). Characteristics of students related to computer-mediated communications activity. *Journal of Research on Computing in Education, 32*(1), 73–97.

Fitzgerald, G. E., & Koury, K. A. (1996). Empirical advances in technology: Assisted instruction for students with mild and moderate disabilities. *Journal of Research on Computing in Education, 28*(4), 526–551.

Fouts, J. T. (2000). *Research on computers and education: Past, present and future.* Retrieved June 8, 2003, from www.esd189.org/tlp/images/TotalReport3.pdf.

Gan, S. (1999). Motivating at-risk students through computer-based cooperative learning activities. *Educational Horizons, 77*(3), 151–156.

Goldman, S., Cole, K., & Syer, C. (1999). *The technology/content dilemma.* Retrieved January 27, 2004, from www.ed.gov/Technology/TechConf/1999/whitepapers/paper4.html.

Greenlee-Moore, M. E., & Smith, L. L. (1996). Interactive computer software: The effects on young children's reading achievement. *Reading Psychology, 17*(1), 43–64.

Hamilton, V. (1995). Computers and reading achievement (ERIC Document Reproduction Service No. ED 382 923).

Higgins, S., Moseley, D., & Tse, H. (2001). Computers and effective teaching. *Education Canada, 41*(3), 44–47.

Honey, M., Culp, K. M., & Carrigg, F. (1999). *Perspectives on technology and education research: Lessons from the past and present.* Retrieved January 27, 2004, from www.ed.gov/Technology/TechConf/1999/whitepapers/paper.html.

Honey, M., Culp, K. M., & Spielvogel, R. (1999). Using technology to improve student achievement. *Pathways to School Improvement.* Retrieved January 27, 2004, from www.ncrel.org/sdrs/areas/issues/methods/technology/te800.htm.

Jackson, A., Kutnick, P., & Kington, A. (2001). Principles and practical grouping for the use of drill and practice programs. *Journal of Computer Assisted Learning, 17*(2), 130–141.

Kleiner, A., & Farris, E. (2002). *Internet access in U.S. public schools and classrooms: 1994–2001.* Retrieved February 11, 2003, from http://nces.ed.gov/pubsearch/pubsinfo.asp?pubid=2002018.

Kook, J. (1997). Computers and communication networks in educational settings in the twenty-first century: Preparation for educators' new roles. *Educational Technology, 37*(2), 56–60.

Kozma, R. B. (1994). Will media influence learning? Reframing the debate? *Educational Technology Research and Development, 42*(2), 7–19.

Lenhart, A., Rainie, L., & Lewis, O. (2001). *Teenage life online: The rise of the instant-message generation and the Internet's impact on friendships and family relationships.* Retrieved April 9, 2003, from www.pewinternet.org/reports/toc.asp?Report=36.

Lenhart, A., Simon, M., & Graziano, M. (2001). *The Internet and education: Findings of the Pew Internet & American life project.* Retrieved April 2003, from http://www.pewinternet.org/reports/toc.asp?Report=39.

Lou, Y., Abrami, P. C., & d'Apollonia, S. (2001). Small group and individual learning with technology: A meta-analysis. *Review of Educational Research, 71*(2), 449–521.

Mann, D., Shakeshaft, C., Becker, J., & Kottkamp, R. (1999). *West Virginia's Basic Skills/Computer Education Program: An analysis of student achievement.* Santa Monica, CA: Milken Family Foundation.

Matthew, K. (1997). A comparison of the influence of interactive CD-ROM storybooks and traditional print storybooks on reading comprehension. *Journal of Research on Computing in Education, 29*(3), 263–275.

Mayer, R. E., Schustack, M. W., & Blanton, W. E. (1999). What do children learn from using computers in an informal, collaborative setting? *Educational Technology, 39*(2), 27–31.

McCoy, L. P. (1996). Computer-based mathematics learning. *Journal of Research on Computing in Education, 28*(4), 438–460.

Means, B. (1997). Critical issue: Using technology to enhance engaged learning for at-risk students. *Pathways to School Improvement.* Retrieved January 27, 2004, from www.ncrel.org/sdrs/areas/issues/students/atrisk/at400.htm.

Middleton, B. M., & Murray, R. K. (1999). The impact of instructional technology on student academic achievement in reading and mathematics. *International Journal of Instructional Media, 26*(1), 109–115.

Nelson, L. J., & Cooper, J. (1997). Gender differences in children's reactions to success and failure with computers. *Computers in Human Behavior, 13*(2), 247–267.

Nichols, L. M. (1996). Pencil and paper versus word processing: A comparative study of creative writing in the elementary school. *Journal of Research on Computing in Education, 29*(2), 159–166.

No Child Left Behind. (2002). Retrieved June 11, 2003, from www.ed.gov/legislation/ESEA02/pg34.html.

O'Neil, J. (1995, October). On technology and schools: A conversation with Chris Dede. *Educational Leadership, 53*(2), 6–12.

Oppenheimer, T. (1997, July). The computer delusion. *The Atlantic Monthly, 280,* 45–62.

Owston, R. D., & Wideman, H. H. (1997). Word processing and children's writing in a high computer access setting. *Journal of Research on Computing in Education, 30*(2), 202–220.

Owston, R. D., & Wideman, H. H. (2001). Computer access and student achievement in the early school years. *Journal of Computer Assisted Learning, 17*(4), 433–444.

Painter, D. D. (2000). Teacher as researcher. *Learning and Leading with Technology, 27*(7), 10–13, 27.

Panel on Educational Technology, President's Committee of Advisors on Science and Technology. (1997, March). *Report to the President on the use of technology to strengthen K–12 education in the United States.* Retrieved January 27, 2004, from www.whitehouse.gov/WH/EOP/OSTP/NSTC/PCAST/k-12ed.html.

Pflaum, B. (2001). How is technology impacting student performance? *School Planning & Management, 40*(12), 41–43.

Proctor, R. M., & Burnett, R. C. (1996). Computer attitude and classroom computers. *Computers in the Schools, 12*(3), 33–41.

Reed, W. M. (1996). Assessing the impact of computer-based writing instruction. *Journal of Research on Computing in Education, 28*(4), 418–437.

Rideout, D. (2002). Laptops on the range! *Education Canada, 42*(2), 20, 22–23.

Ringstaff, C., Sandholtz, J. H., & Dwyer, D.C. (1995). Trading places: When teachers utilize student expertise in technology-intensive classrooms. In *Apple education research reports* (pp. 35–37). Eugene, OR: International Society for Technology in Education.

Roblyer, M. D. (1996). The constructivist/objectivist debate: Implications for instructional technology research. *Learning and Leading with Technology, 24*(2), 12–16.

Roblyer, M. D. (1997). Predictions and realities: The impact of the Internet on K–12 education. *Learning and Leading with Technology, 25*(1), 54–56.

Rochowicz, J. A., Jr. (1996). The impact of using computers and calculators on calculus instruction: Various perceptions. *Journal of Computers in Mathematics and Science Teaching, 15*(4), 423–435.

Rockman et al. (no date). *A more complex picture: Laptop use and impact in the context of changing home and school access.* Retrieved January 27, 2004, from www.microsoft.com/education/aal/research3.asp.

Roschelle, J. M., Pea, R. D., Hoadley, C. M., Gordin, D. N., & Means, B. M. (2000). *Changing how and what children learn in school with computer-based technology.* Retrieved June 8, 2003, from www.futureofchildren.org/pubs-info2825/pubs-info.htm?doc_id=69787.

Sandholtz, J. H., Ringstaff, C., & Dwyer, D. C. (1995a). The relationship between technological innovation and collegial interaction. In *Apple education research reports* (pp. 37–38). Eugene, OR: International Society for Technology in Education.

Sandholtz, J. H., Ringstaff, C., & Dwyer, D. C. (1995b). Student engagement revisited: Views from technology-rich classrooms. In *Apple education research reports* (pp. 29–30). Eugene, OR: International Society for Technology in Education.

Sandholtz, J. H., Ringstaff, C., & Dwyer, D. C. (1997). *Teaching with technology: Creating student-centered classrooms.* New York: Teachers College Press.

Scardamalia, M., & Bereiter, C. (1996). Computer support for knowledge-building communities. In T. Koschmann (Ed.), *CSCL: Theory and practice of an emerging paradigm.* Mahwah, NJ: Lawrence Erlbaum.

Siegle, D., & Foster, T. (2001). Laptop computers and multimedia and presentation software: Their effects on student achievement in anatomy and physiology. *Journal of Research on Technology in Education, 34*(1), 29–37.

Sivin-Kachala, J. (1998). *Report on the effectiveness of technology in schools, 1990–1997.* Software Publisher's Association.

Solomon, G. (2002). Digital equity: It's not just about access anymore. *Technology and Learning, 22*(9), 18–20, 22–24, 26.

Stevenson, K. (1999). Learning by laptop. *School Administrator, 56*(4), 18–21.

Stolarchuk, E., & Fisher, D. (2001). An investigation of teacher–student interpersonal behavior in science classrooms using laptop computers. *Journal of Educational Computing Research, 24*(1), 41–55.

Stuebing, S., Celsi, J. G., & Cousineau, L. K. (1995). Environments that support new modes of learning. In *Apple education research reports* (pp. 27–28). Eugene, OR: International Society for Technology in Education.

Technology in education 2002. (2002). Retrieved April 9, 2003, from www.schooldata. com.

Tiene, D., & Luft, P. (2001). Teaching in a technology-rich classroom. *Educational Technology, 41*(4), 23–31.

Tierney, R. J., Kieffer, R., Stowell, L., Desai, L. E., Whalin, K., & Moss, A. G. (1995). Computer acquisition: A longitudinal study of the influence of high computer access on students' thinking, learning, and interactions. In *Apple education research reports* (pp. 31–32). Eugene, OR: International Society for Technology in Education.

U.S. Department of Education. (1996). *Getting America's students ready for the twenty-first century: Meeting the technology literacy challenge.* Retrieved January 27, 2004, from www.ed.gov/TechnologyPlan/NatTechPlan/title.html.

Valdez, G., McNabb, M., Foertsch, M., Anderson, M., Hawkes, M., & Raack, L. (1999). *Computer-based technology and learning: Evolving uses and expectations.* Oak Brook, IL: North Central Regional Educational Laboratory.

Walker, L., Rockman, S., & Chessler, M. (2000). *A more complex picture: Laptop use and impact in the context of changing home and school access.* Retrieved February 13, 2003, from http://rockman.com/projects/laptop/laptop3exec.htm.

Waxman, H., Connell, M., & Gray, J. (2002). *A quantitative synthesis of recent research on the effects of teaching and learning with technology on student outcomes.* Retrieved June 11, 2003, from www.ncrel.org/tech/effects.

Whitley, B. E., Jr. (1997). Gender differences in computer-related attitudes and behavior: A meta-analysis. *Computers in Human Behavior, 13*, 1–22.

Willis, E. M. (1996). Where in the world? Technology in social studies learning. *Learning and Leading with Technology, 23*(5), 7–9.

Yaghi, H. (1996). The role of the computer in the school as perceived by computer using teachers and school administrators. *Journal of Educational Computing Research, 15*(2), 137–155.

CHAPTER 6

Planning for Technology-Rich Instruction

FOCUS QUESTIONS

1. In what ways can technology be planned for in a lesson?

2. What different considerations are there in using technology to extend an existing lesson and drafting a technology-rich lesson from scratch?

3. In what ways can technology be used in each stage of a lesson?

The best way to maximize student learning in a technology-enhanced lesson is to engage in the same thoughtful planning that goes into preparing for any other quality lesson (Tomei, 1996). The myriad interrelated activities involved in teaching can be described as a three-step sequence of events that begins with *planning,* progresses through *implementation,* and concludes with *assessment.* Lessons not adequately planned, or planned only as a traditional lesson and assuming technology use will not considerably impact the instructional flow, run the risk of being unsuccessful, ineffective, and otherwise a waste of valuable instructional time. Although a glance at the sometimes brief and sketchy lesson plans of veteran teachers may give the impression that they plan very little, these experienced teachers typically have a much more fully developed plan in their minds. Their experience with teaching, knowledge of their students' abilities and needs, and familiarity with the resources available to them allow them to operationalize a lesson from a seemingly less detailed plan. This chapter examines the often ignored step of planning by detailing when, where, and how the role of technology in the classroom should be designed.

What Is Technology-Integrated Teaching and Learning?

An understanding of just what technology integration looks like is vital to planning for technology-integrated teaching. Effective technology-using teachers employ three unique types of knowledge: *content knowledge* about the specific topics that they teach; *pedagogical knowledge,* or the understanding of how to teach and manage students (Shulman, 1986); and *technological knowledge,* which involves an understanding of the unique characteristics of particular types of technologies that would lend themselves to particular aspects of the teaching and learning processes (Pierson, 2001). A technology-rich lesson requires teachers to draw on extensive content knowledge, to understand how best to use content-related technology resources, as well as pedagogical knowledge, to use the most appropriate methods to manage and organize technology use.

Discussion of the limitless classroom technology applications can be facilitated by describing them according to four types (Smith & Radigan, 2003). Note that these categories are flexible, and many activities can be described by more than one type.

1. *Technology as Business Resource.* It is as a resource for communication and information management that is often the first way that teachers new to using technology attempt a technology strategy. Before they are comfortable with using any technology with students, they can be attracted to the power of electronic tools for planning and management. (See Chapter 3 for coverage of communication and Chapter 13 for a discussion of classroom administration using technology.)

2. *Technology as Subject.* Technology is the subject when the software or hardware itself is the focus of learning. The aspect of technology that indeed poses unique challenges to teaching and learning is the levels of student skill. Diversity in student competency with technology is unavoidable, and the digital divide becomes evident quickly; some students in schools now have had regular computer access since they were toddlers, while others have had little. With any lesson, teachers must have ways to assess the prior knowledge of students about the material. Teachers have to make decisions about the technology skills that students need and when and how those skills should be taught. One school of thought maintains that all students must have basic instruction in the use of individual tools before actually using each tool. So, if a graphics software is to be used, students must engage in an introductory lesson during which they are guided to use the various functions of the software before they use it independently. Then, they can proceed to using the tool in the context of a learning activity. The opposite school of thought maintains that learning tools in isolation is ineffective; instead, learners need "just-in-time" instruction of what they need to know when they need to use it. Subscribing to this philosophy of learning about technology tools leads teachers to having students learn new tools as they are using them for real purposes, rather than up front. Most teachers fall somewhere between these two extremes; however, some thought must be given to how students will learn to use the technology needed to extend and demonstrate their learning. The best plan indeed is to have a plan. Be comfortable with experimenting with a variety of teaching methods, including direct instruction on the tools, having individuals or small groups of students learn and in turn teach others, and having students "play" with technology to discover new uses independently.

3. *Technology as Content Delivery.* Frequently the way technology is perceived as being an instructional tool is when it is used as the main lesson delivery, such as through an electronic presentation or web page on a specific topic. Used in these ways, technology comprises the majority of a lesson. To novice technology-using teachers, this large-scale use of electronic tools is often threatening and intimidating. Planning and designing activities in which technology tools will be the primary conveyor of information can be extremely time-consuming, and the greater the portion of a lesson in which technology plays a role, the greater the potential for change in teaching habits.

4. *Technology as Lesson Support.* An often overlooked genre of technology-enabled learning instances is the collection of strategies, from simple to complex, whereby technology can support learning opportunities. As lesson support, technology does not have to be a central component of a lesson; it can instead be "popped" in as just one among many other strategies. Thought of in this fourth way, technology does not have to represent a radical departure from established teaching methods. It instead becomes a flexible, as-needed, very approachable part of a teacher's instructional repertoire.

Before planning to use technology in a lesson, teachers should consider how this electronic tool will extend their abilities to teach. Technology can do things that traditional methods cannot: simulate dangerous or distance phenomena, easily connect multiple media formats to produce a sophisticated finished product, deliver obscure and timely resources to the desktop, or capture attention of otherwise uninspired students. Informed teachers armed with these tools enjoy a powerful advantage in reaching students with various learning modalities and styles. Informed teachers know that technology best serves its purpose in the classroom when it is combined with nontechnology resources so that a whole range of appropriate tools are used to help students reach each learning objective. Ill-informed teachers use technology because they know they are supposed to, and often the tools are used to do things that do not appreciably advance the learning opportunities of students. Teachers should ask themselves of each lesson, "Why *this* technology in *this* way at *this* time?" The questions in Table 6.1 are offered as starting points to the planning of using Internet-based resources; however, the questions are relevant to the planning for all technologies. If the answers speak to extending the teacher's abilities to meet the specific needs of students, to engage students in compelling content in accessible formats, to empower students to take a role in their own learning, then the use of technology may be warranted.

Planning Models

The structure of a technology-integrated lesson should be consistent with an individual teacher's teaching style and philosophy. If child-centered work is common in a particular classroom, for instance, then child-centered work should be considered for an Internet-based lesson. Of course, this should not discourage teachers from exploring new methods and letting the technology facilitate change in their teaching. It

TABLE 6.1	Questions to Consider When Planning for the Use of Internet Resources

1. What is the educational goal I want my students to achieve?
2. Is this a worthwhile educational goal, whether it be accomplished using electronic or traditional means?
3. Am I trying to make my educational goals conform to the available technology, or am I using these tools to more effectively meet my instructional goals?
4. When compared to other available tools, does this electronic tool effectively assist in achieving this goal?
5. Can this goal be reached just as effectively using more traditional methods?
6. Is this electronic medium an effective way to teach an educational goal, or is this activity just a skill-building exercise in the use of the tool?

Source: From Ross, P. (1995). Relevant telecomputing activities. *The Computing Teacher,* *22*(5), 28–30.

simply must be understood that any change that occurs is not the sole result of the use of any technologies. Technology can supply the resources to motivate teachers and students, but this will happen only with the conscious desire of teachers to embrace continuous growth in their teaching.

One practical consideration that arises as teachers contemplate ways to use technology in their teaching is whether it can be employed to enhance an existing lesson or whether teachers instead need to draft plans for completely new lessons. Both practices are acceptable and can lead to quality learning experiences. If a lesson has already proven successful, technology can be used simply to bring in fresh, timely resources. Based on the Lesson Support technology type (Smith & Radigan, 2003), technology tools can be "popped" into lessons without overly modifying the existing plan. This thoughtful placement of small uses of technology, however, should not be confused with a less advised tact toward technology use that is common among those new to using technology: taking a traditional lesson and just "tacking" technology onto the end of it. An example might be to have students participate in a book-based literature lesson and then, when they are done, to have them visit the website of the book's author. On the surface, this appears to be a related content-driven use of technology. However, if the visit to the website is an afterthought, it may not serve a real purpose, meaning in particular that it may not further students' opportunities to meet the stated learning objectives. The technology in this case is added *onto*, rather than integrated *into*, the lesson. A better way to think through the use of the website in this example, once the site was reviewed for quality and applicability, of course, is to consider how technology relates to the learning objectives. Which of the four types of technology is it? How will students use the tool in question to develop, advance, demonstrate, or enrich their learning? If the teacher determines that a technology strategy truly would benefit students, then that strategy should ideally be articulated as a part of the lesson objectives.

Oftentimes, however, it may be easier to start the planning completely fresh rather than trying to retool an existing lesson. The blank piece of paper may empower a teacher to try new teaching formats or learning procedures facilitated by the technology.

Lesson Plan Formats

There are countless lesson plan formats used by teachers, from those that are extremely structured to others with flexible parameters. Often school districts have a template they require teachers to use, yet frequently teachers settle into a shorthand sequence that is comfortable to them and reflective of their own teaching philosophies. Most lesson plan formats adhere to a predictable set of components, frequently resembling the classic steps of Madeline Hunter's *Essential Elements of Instruction* (Hunter & Russell, 1994). Considerations for technology use can be made at all stages of the planning process and are highlighted here as part of Hunter's basic model.

Anticipatory Set. This is a quick introductory activity that "hooks" students into the lesson from the very beginning, essentially preparing their minds to accept the new information. Teachers might show a relevant photograph found on the Internet, conduct a brainstorming session with a concept-mapping software, or check prior knowledge about the subject by posing a series of questions beamed to students' handheld computers.

Purpose. The teacher states the purpose of the lesson, or the objectives, based on content or technology standards, that will be met. Students hear a sense of why they would want to learn it and how they will know they have learned it. Understanding the place of a technology-based activity within the larger scope of a standards-based curriculum will help teachers to plan meaningful and effective learning experiences. (Chapter 1 introduces the NETS for Students; individual states all also have technology standards for students.) Teachers must make themselves aware of what their students are expected to know and be able to prepare them so that technology standards can be met at the same time as content standards. Using technology, teachers might project up for the whole class an electronic slide that states the purpose and then print the information for students to monitor their own progress.

Input. The input is the information, vocabulary, content, and skills—in other words, the "stuff"—that students need to learn in order to meet the objectives. Teachers have a variety of options for presenting this information in addition to the more traditional lecture, including educational websites, interactive electronic presentations, videos, teacher-produced documents, and digital photographs. Teachers may choose to present the material themselves with the assistance of technology, such as by using web-based content projected on a TV monitor or by guiding students through videos on a laser disc. Students may also be expected to grapple with new content independently. For this task, options include having students progress at their own pace through a teacher-produced electronic presentation that provides text, images, and perhaps audio, and even may feature assessment questions so students can check themselves. (See Chapter 14 for ideas on creating educational presentations.) Teachers might also develop activities that allow students to interact with online content in a collaborative, team-driven environment. WebQuests are a popular activity that follows a lesson formula (see the WebQuest site at **http://webquest.org**). Countless WebQuest examples exist online—a simple web search for "WebQuest" and the desired topic will result in those examples that other teachers have created and placed online. As with any lesson plan, teachers must preview all resources and consider in what ways the lessons might need to be modified to best serve the needs of their particular students. (For the most part, WebQuests placed online have been shared for the benefit of other teachers and students; any modifications made should include reference to the original source.)

Modeling. After the material is presented, the teacher demonstrates how students will be able to show that they have learned the information, especially showing examples or describing any products that they will be able to produce to exhibit their learning. Items in previous students' electronic portfolios might be used as examples, as might a live demonstration of any software that will be used.

Guided Practice. This is students' opportunity to interact with the material in a sheltered, assisted environment, often with the teacher leading the way through the necessary steps of an exercise. This is the teacher's best chance to make sure students are using the skills correctly. Having a computer that projects to a screen or monitor is helpful so that the teacher can walk through a procedure step-by-step. Students might also work independently through tutorials or sets of directions with screen captures.

Checking for Understanding. Before, during, and after Guided Practice, the teacher questions students to monitor and assess how well they understand the concepts before moving on. If students "have it," then the lesson can progress; if not, the teacher may need to back up and reteach the concepts. If working in the computer lab, teachers can walk around the lab and glance at students' computer monitors to assess progress as they work with a new piece of software. Students might be asked to come to the front of the class to lead peers through an electronic presentation. As teachers check for understanding, they can elect to jot down brief notes of student progress on a handheld or tablet computer.

Independent Practice. When the teacher is assured that students have mastered the content or skill enough to work on their own, they are ready to practice independently, in the form of in-class activities or homework. Practice homework activities might be listed on the class website, and product files can be either saved and submitted on disk, on the school server, or emailed directly to the teacher. Nonlinear "edugame" type activities, such as those created with PowerPoint templates, are effective practice activities because the game format attracts students' attention to repeatedly review the content.

Closure. The conclusion to the lesson is a chance for the teacher to cap off the learning experience with a few final examples or statements to help students make sense of what they have learned. Closure is often the part of the lesson that gets rushed as students run out the door when the bell rings, but allowing time for this important exclamation point in the learning process is an essential opportunity for students to reflect on what they have learned, solidifying this knowledge into a coherent understanding and improving the chance that this new information will indeed be used. Recording students' ideas of what they have learned on a word processing document or a quick electronic slide show projected up to the whole class can ensure everyone has input into the closure. Individual students might be asked to email the teacher with their own thoughts on their grasp of the material.

Alternatives to this classic directed lesson plan format exist; the *Unit of Practice* is one that was specifically developed to pay special attention to the natural use of technology. Developed by Apple Computers in collaboration with the National Science Foundation and the New American Schools Development Corporation, Units of Practice (UOPs) are structured curriculum frameworks for sharing lessons with other educators. UOPs emphasizes a holistic approach to technology, considering its inclusion as just one of many needed planning steps rather than including it as a tacked-on feature. Although the components of UOPs resemble those in more traditional lesson plans when viewed as a list, the UOP plan is conceived as a nonlinear, flexible plan (see Table 6.2).

Considerations beyond the Instructional Flow

The focus of the lesson plan steps in the previous section is on the discernable features of a lesson, those activities that would be noticeable if observing the lesson in action. Lesson plans typically consist of other information, those behind-the-scenes details that teachers either must attend to or risk dooming an otherwise well-conceived lesson to failure. Technology also commands thought for these areas.

TABLE 6.2 Unit of Practice Format

- **Invitation:** The curriculum question and project overview
- **Tasks:** The actions that students will be asked to undertake
- **Assessment:** The criteria by which students' work will be evaluated
- **Situations:** The places where the activity will take place, and the amount and specific periods of time that the students will have to work on the activity
- **Interactions:** The ways students will work, the ways the teacher will work with students, and the ways students will interact with others
- **Tools:** The materials that students will use to approach their tasks
- **Standards:** The frameworks developed by the school, district, or state as guidelines in the development and assessment of curricula

Source: http://ali.apple.com/ali_help/help_units.shtml.

Pedagogical Considerations

Just as with traditional learning activities, teachers must decide whether technology resources will be used as a demonstration with the whole class, with a small group, with partners, or even with students working individually. These determinations will depend on the concepts being taught and the strategy that will be the most effective with students. An effective teacher meters lessons with a tempo that mingles a variety of grouping options to move students through a choreographed and interesting array of experiences. Student boredom with the learning environment breeds inattention; frequent reshaping of the context encourages interest.

Identifying Resources

After lesson goals are solidified, locate the software, hardware, or Internet-based tools that will be necessary for where the lesson must be located. The time and effort involved at this stage can be significant, depending on a teacher's familiarity with locating web resources, the amount and quality of information available on the particular topic, and the ways and extent to which resources will be used in the instruction. Sometimes the time required to locate quality resources discourages teachers from using technology to teach. With regard to Internet resources, the best advice is to start with sites that have been recommended by others or with larger "portal" sites (see Chapter 8). The next steps can involve conducting a web search for information relating to your topic (see Chapter 3 for searching strategies). Because the quality and age appropriateness of websites vary, you will want to explore the entire site thoroughly prior to having students use all or parts of it.

The key to the effectiveness of any instructional tool lies partly in the tool's unique attributes, but also to a larger degree in how the tool is actually utilized. No matter how flashy or cute or seemingly educationally sound a website or piece of software, if time is not taken to carefully plan for its use as a part of an entire instructional sequence, the potential benefits to learners may be squandered. (Refer to the online resource evaluation information in Chapter 7.) Select several resources, including teacher background information, lesson plans, and student activities. At this point, you will also want to consider nonelectronic information sources to complement the online information. Finally, assess what tools you have available at the school and determine procedures to reserve and use those tools. A "scavenger hunt" of technology tools and policies available at a particular school should be an important part of any new teacher orientation.

Technology Tools for Lesson Planning

Thus far, technology has been addressed in this planning chapter as a resource to be worked into a lesson for the learning benefit of students. As is often the case, technology can serve a number of purposes if seen from different perspectives. Technology can also be a powerful tool that assists educators in the planning process itself.

- Software designed specifically to assist with the planning process provides lesson templates that can be customized, correlated to state standards, and printed in a variety of forms. Software exists in shareware versions that can be tried for a set period of time (see Lesson PlanIt at **www.lessonplanit.net** or LessonPlanZ at **www.unicornsoftware.com/windows.html**) as well as commercial software. In addition, many professional educator websites offer planning tools.

- Templates are a teacher's best technology friend. Templates for lesson planning mean teachers can save key lesson features, according to district requirements or personal preference, and then simply fill in pertinent information for particular lessons. (See Chapters 2 and 14 for discussion of templates and lesson planning.)
- Online resources are invaluable for acquiring background information as teachers prepare to teach unfamiliar subject matter. A little research before teaching a lesson can provide needed content, teaching strategies, and professional advice. (See Chapter 8 for content and professional web resources.)
- Productivity tools can be used in any number of ways to assist planning. Vicki Barrera, a teacher education student, suggested using a spreadsheet to keep track of when state standards are addressed (personal communication, October 17, 2003).

School- and District-Level Technology Planning

A chapter on planning for technology would not be complete without a section on technology planning on a scale larger than that of the classroom. Decisions that impact technology availability and policies for classroom teachers are made at the school and district levels. In fact, the "technology plan" will likely be located in a prominent location on the school or district website. Neglecting the planning process in favor of quick technology purchases risks wasting money for items that may not be used at all or may not be used effectively to further student learning.

Common downfalls of technology plans include a tendency to seek the most cost-effective way to purchase and organize computers, leading at times to underutilized machines; an absence of professional development for teachers; a need for a vision on what type of role technology can play in the classroom; and a surface-level sense of equity (such as doling out the same number of computers to each teacher) without consideration of how resources might best be allocated (Fishman & Pinkard, 2001). If the technology plan is the brainchild of one person, hastily written so as to simply have some kind of a plan in place, these downfalls will likely be endemic, and it may never enjoy the widespread support of those who must act to implement it and thus will ultimately not succeed.

Technology planning is accomplished best by a technology planning committee that invites input from all key players of the school community, including administrators, teachers, and parents. Novice teachers should seek opportunities to be involved in this type of planning, not only because it has the potential to impact their daily practices but also because their opinions and sometimes more recent technology experience would serve the planning process well. Regardless of its constitution, the committee should have the support of local and district administration and teachers; without such backing, any recommendations or policies emerging from the committee would face difficult implementation by those carrying out the work.

Planning for large-scale technology implementation is not a one-time occurrence; instead the planning and assessment of implementation is ongoing. Planning committees should begin by articulating a vision of technology use for the school. Based on that vision, the committee should then conduct a needs assessment to determine what technology purchases should be made to satisfy the vision and what policies need to be established to guide school community members to successful use of technology. Next, the committee must define an action plan and timetable for implementation (Valdez, 2003). It has been repeatedly shown that purchasing computers for no other reason that to merely have them, without consideration of how they will be used, is not a reliable plan (McNabb, 2003). Technology planning is most meaningful when use is based on curricular goals and intended learning results, as well as on the resources that schools have and can obtain. Seeking answers to the guiding questions in Table 6.3 will provide a planning committee with not only focus and direction at the outset but also benchmarks for ongoing evaluation efforts. Careful planning by an inclusive group of committed individuals will help prevent the plan from being solely budget driven, instead putting the emphasis on the learning vision and meeting the organizational, technological, and educational objectives (North Central Regional Technology in Education Consortium, 2001).

Data-Driven Decision Making

School leaders are transforming the way that they plan, from the district and school levels down to the classroom level, through the power of technology-managed and analyzed data (Olson, 2002). Data-driven decisions are based on an understanding of a wide collection of data, from student test scores to enrollment figures. Studying these data helps educators to know what methods and practices work and on what they need to focus additional attention. For example, if 35 percent of fourth-graders failed the end-of-the-year writing test, then fifth-grade teachers can use these data to guide their teaching during the next year. If significant numbers of middle school science teachers are not certified to teach science, this alerts the district to potential issues in teacher retention and student achievement in that content area. This type of data-informed thought also helps schools and districts demonstrate accountability with new federal regulations on reporting spelled out in the *No Child Left Behind Act* of 2001 (**www.nclb.gov**), which requires that districts measure success by an ap-

TABLE 6.3   Guiding Questions for Technology Planning
• What is your vision of learning?
• How will you use technology to support your vision of learning?
• How will you develop a supportive infrastructure?
• Do you understand the context of your technology planning process?
• How will you garner public support for your plan?
• How will you implement your plan?
• How will you evaluate the implementation of your technology plan?
Source: North Central Regional Technology in Education Consortium. (2001). Guiding questions for technology planning. *ERS Spectrum, 30*(1), 16–22.

praisal of student accomplishment. However, despite the research that shows that schools and districts that perform the highest rely on the use of data to inform their practices, most states and districts do not have the systems in place to collect, organize, and analyze data in meaningful ways. The challenge to educators is to create technology-rich learning environments not only for student learning but also for efficient school management (Fouts, 2000).

Schools with clearly articulated visions of technology integration were found to have more effective uses of technology (Hayes, Schuck, Dega, Dwyer, & McEwen, 2001). Vision statements should include the role of technology in teaching and learning activities, the extent of professional development for teachers, and the use of technology for the linking of teachers to their worldwide community of peers to ensure ready access to support and advice.

Summary

The best way to maximize student learning in a technology-enhanced lesson is to engage in the same thoughtful planning that goes into preparing for any other quality lesson. The interrelated activities involved in teaching can be described as a three-step sequence of events that begins with *planning,* progresses through *implementation,* and concludes with *assessment.* Lessons not adequately planned run the risk of being unsuccessful, ineffective, and otherwise a waste of valuable instructional time. A technology-rich lesson requires teachers to draw on extensive content knowledge to understand how to best use content-related technology resources, as well as pedagogical knowledge, to use the most appropriate methods to manage and organize technology use. Classroom technology applications can be described by four categories: Technology as Business Resource, Technology as Subject, Technology as Content Delivery, and Technology as Lesson Support. The structure of a technology-integrated lesson should be consistent with an individual teacher's teaching style and philosophy. Considerations for technology use can be made at all parts in the planning process of a basic lesson plan.

Technology can also be a powerful tool that assists educators in the planning process itself. Technology planning at the school and district levels results in decisions that impact technology availability and policies for classroom teachers, as well as providing data that inform decisions at all levels of school communities.

Worldwide Weather

DVD/VIDEO VIGNETTE

In an interview prior to a lesson on weather, the teacher describes expectations and objectives for the students and plans for obstacles that might occur while using technology. During the lesson, students use laptops to research weather and create a slide show using KidPix. Following the lesson, the teacher reflects on the strengths and weaknesses of the technology used in the lesson. How does the teacher's plan play out during lesson implementation, and how does her postinterview reflect that implementation?

DVD/VIDEO VIGNETTE

Navigating by Landmarks

This video is narrated by a number of educational specialists who critique this technology-integrated lesson. Is there more than one way to evaluate successful technology integration?

School Stories

When Patty Black wrote her weekly lesson plans on Friday afternoons, she typically jotted down a few page numbers and shorthand notes to herself, and that was plenty to jog her memory about the lesson when it came up the next week. During her sixth year of teaching, Patty had a student teacher for the first time. Carla Rivera's enthusiasm for her newly chosen career bubbled over, and she asked question after question throughout the day. When Carla asked Patty about why she never saw technology mentioned in Patty's lesson plan book, Patty thought she had a ready answer: There was really no need to write it down because they usually just worked on the computers if they had time, and if then, she had students either play an educational software game as a reward, or type up whatever they were working on using a word processor. But Carla's never-ending questions started Patty thinking . . . should she be putting more thought into what her students did with the computer? This novice teacher had caused her to rethink her reasons for using technology. Patty thought about the upcoming unit on state history. She sat down that evening and found four websites that had sections that seemed appropriate for her students. For the first time, she jotted down the websites in her plan book, drawing a line from the objective of the lesson to the website to show its connection. She even decided to try using a lesson planning software that the district had purchased and offered training on last year. Now, where was that email . . .

Challenge Yourself!

1. Find a lesson plan that includes no technology. Can you name three ways to support this lesson using technology?
2. Find a lesson plan that includes some technology. Can you classify the technology uses according to the four types of technology?
3. Take five minutes to brainstorm as many technology activities as you can think of. Then go through and identify which of the four types of technology categories each activity best fits into. Where do most fit? Why do you think that is?

4. Starting with a learning objective, write a new lesson plan based on the Hunter model that includes technology at every step. How realistic are your ideas for technology use? Are there other nontechnology methods that would also be effective?

5. Find a WebQuest of interest at **http://webquest.org** and identify the state content and technology standards that would be met with this activity.

6. Compare the traditional Hunter lesson plan model with the Unit of Practice. Where would "Situations" and "Interactions" of the Unit of Practice fit in with the traditional model?

7. Download either Lesson PlanIt at **www.lessonplanit.net** or LessonPlanZ at **www.unicornsoftware.com/windows.html** and use it to plan a lesson.

8. Review your school district's technology plan. What types of items are included? In what ways do these policies directly impact classroom teachers?

9. Review the DVD-Video Vignette Worldwide Weather. List three additional technology-rich activities that would support this lesson, along with any special considerations you would need to make to plan for those activities.

10. Review the DVD-Video Vignette Navigating by Landmarks. How do your thoughts on the lesson compare and contrast with the narrators' comments?

References

Fishman, B. J., & Pinkard, N. (2001). Bringing urban schools into the information age: Planning for technology vs. technology planning. *Journal of Educational Computing Research, 25*(1), 63–80.

Fouts, J. T. (2000). *Research on computers and education: Past, present and future.* Retrieved June 8, 2003, from www.esd189.org/tlp/images/TotalReport3.pdf.

Hayes, D., Schuck, S., Dega, G., Dwyer, J., & McEwen, C. (2001). *Net gain? The integration of computer-based learning in six NSW government schools, 2000.* Retrieved June 6, 2003, from www.curriculumsupport.nsw.edu.au/learningtechnologies/files/Lea_netgain.pdf.

Hunter, M., & Russell, D. (1994). Planning for effective instruction: Lesson design. In M. Hunter (Ed.), *Enhancing teaching* (pp. 87–97). New York: MacMillan College.

McNabb, M. L. (2003). *Conducting a needs assessment.* North Central Regional Educational Laboratory. Retrieved October 7, 2003, from www.ncrel.org/tandl/plan2.htm.

North Central Regional Technology in Education Consortium. (2001). Guiding questions for technology planning. *ERS Spectrum, 30*(1), 16–22.

Olson, L. (2002). *Schools discovering riches in data.* Retrieved February 11, 2003, from www.edweek.org/ew/newstory.cfm?slug=40data.h21.

Pierson, M. E. (2001). Technology integration practice as a function of pedagogical expertise. *Journal of Research on Computing in Education, 33*(4), 413–430.

Ross, P. (1995). Relevant telecomputing activities. *The Computing Teacher, 22*(5), 28–30.

Shulman, L. S. (1986). Those who understand: Knowledge growth in teaching. *Educational Researcher, 15*(2), 4–14.

Smith, D. O., & Radigan, J. (2003). Emerging themes in technology integration. *Technology and Teacher Education Annual 2003.* Charlottesville, VA: Association for the Advancement of Computing in Education.

Tomei, L. A. (1996). Preparing an instructional lesson using resources off the Internet. *T.H.E. Journal, 24*(2), 93–95.

Valdez, G. (2003). *Forming a technology implementation planning committee.* North Central Regional Educational Laboratory. Retrieved October 7, 2003, from www.ncrel.org/tandl/plan4.htm.

Selecting and Using Educational Software

CHAPTER 7

FOCUS QUESTIONS

1. What considerations must a district make when forming a plan for software or educational website review?

2. What are the defining characteristics of each type of software?

3. How can educational software be effectively integrated into a standards-based curriculum?

The number of educational software titles has topped 17,000 (ISTE, 2000). Therefore, educators must have effective, planned processes for the critical investigation and acceptance of software for use in their classrooms so as not to waste valuable teacher time and district money on advertising hype. Many times software publishers forsake strong instructional design for colorful graphics and packaging (Hoffman & Lyons, 1997). The lines between educational software and educational websites are blurring, as many new software titles include web interactivity and websites offer engaging student activities. This chapter presents strategies for making decisions about educational software, first highlighting considerations that must guide any resource choices, and then suggesting an assessment process that takes into account the intended uses. An example Software Review Form is offered, with extensive descriptions for use and adaptation, as is a guide for reviewing educational websites. The types of educational software are discussed, along with examples of how software can be integrated into the classroom. See Chapter 8 for guidance on evaluating and using educational websites.

Learning Resource Assessment Terminology

Distinctions must first be drawn among several similar and potentially confusing assessment terms. McDougall and Squires (1995) note the frequently interchangeable uses of the terms *evaluation, review,* and *selection* in the literature on educational electronic resources, and have, for clarity's sake, provided working definitions that distinguish the three. *Evaluation* is a specific process that occurs either during or immediately following the software development. *Review* refers to the more formal assessment of the performance and characteristics of a piece of software. Finally, *selection*, according to these authors, describes the informal decisions teachers make daily with regard to what learning materials they will use in their classrooms. Based on their own experience and teaching styles and on what they know about the abilities and needs of their students, but without actually performing any structured review, teachers select what they think will work best. Because the audience reading this book will be most interested in strategies they themselves can use to make informed decisions about what software will work best in their classrooms, this chapter will focus primarily on district review procedures and individual electronic resource selection.

Guiding Principles behind Developing a Resource Review and Selection Plan

Depending on the extent of its use in the classroom, electronic resources have the potential to make quite an impact on the delivery and even the interpretation of a school or district's curriculum. For this reason, districts must have a clear plan for reviewing and selecting educational resources for use with students.

At the outset of the entire selection process for electronic resources, it must be understood that merely sitting a child in front of a computer with an educational software title plugged into it does not constitute a sound educational plan. Doing this would allow a software publisher's goals and intentions to override those of the district and the classroom teacher, thus taking thoughtful control out of the hands of those closest to students. Resource use must be consistent with not only the goals and objectives of individual classrooms but also those of the school, the district, and the state. Not only should the content be compared to local scope and sequence guidelines, but also the instructional design and the way in which the material is presented should be considered. The learning theories that underpin the content of a resource should match what is accepted in current educational literature and should correspond to what is accepted in the local communities. Often, an implicit set of values are embedded into the structure and content of a piece of software or website, and these values must also be carefully examined to see whether they fit with the intended learning environment. In essence, electronic resources, like any other learning tool or activity, must match the purpose for which they will be used and must represent the best way to accomplish those particular educational goals. (See Figure 7.1.)

Some basic understanding of the idea of evaluation is also helpful from not only those involved with district review but also teachers who will be interpreting the reviews for classroom use. Evaluation is a highly subjective process, no matter how specific and criteria-based it aims to be. We make evaluations every day, such as whether we enjoyed a new restaurant or how well a tie looks with a shirt. Whoever is evaluating a software package is viewing it through the filter of his or her own unique perspective. The person's background experience, educational philosophy,

FIGURE 7.1 Merely sitting a child in front of a piece of software does not constitute a sound educational plan.

and even personal interests play a role in determining how he or she will rate the software. Because we are human, there is simply no way around this natural subjectivity. The important point to make is that anyone who reads a review of software, or hears of an opinion on anything for that matter, must always consider the source of the review and again filter it through his or her own perspective. Because one evaluator dislikes a program does not necessarily mean that it is completely unusable for all purposes.

A Software Review and Selection Process

With the regular influx of new software to educational markets, school districts must have an organized process for how new software will be assessed and how decisions regarding purchase and usage will be made. One of the first steps is to obtain software copies for review purposes. This can generally be done by contacting the software publishers directly. Many universities and regional education centers maintain review sites with software available for checkout.

The next part of the process that should be considered is who will actually have the first look at a new piece of software. Will curriculum policy administrators review software for the entire district? Will a committee of teachers representing their curricular areas or grade levels serve as reviewers? What role might parents or community members play in the process? Will students be observed using programs or will their opinions or comments be elicited? Although involving students in reviewing will add an extra step to the process, it promises the benefit of a very different rating than those that teachers or parents will provide (Reiser & Kegelmann, 1994). It is important for this flow of review information to be made clear to teachers so they have a clear understanding of how diligently and by whom a new software package has been reviewed. If there are comments available from district reviewers, a plan should be in place for disseminating the review information to teachers. If little local review has been performed, teachers should likewise be made aware of how much of the burden of selection and review falls to them.

Reviewers need some kind of a standard form on which review comments can be recorded and compared to comments about other programs. The easiest and most common method of assessing software is to use a checklist. The checklist form might contain any number of criteria to be examined and rated, sometimes with a simple yes or no and sometimes by choosing from a range of scores for each area. Forms can provide space to encourage longer answers regarding specific problem areas or ideas for integration of the program into curriculum. Later in this chapter, some objections to the checklist method of reviewing software will be raised, but it still remains the most straightforward way to compare results from several evaluators on several software titles.

Finally, a district software review plan needs to include some way of getting the review information into the hands of the teachers who will be using the software to teach. Teachers have a right to all information known about a program so they can make informed decisions about how to best use the program to facilitate student learning.

An Educational Software Review Form

This form is appropriate for district review purposes and allows software reviewers to assess the complete software package, including both content and technical considerations. It is easily modifiable so that districts can match it to their existing district goals and curriculum objectives. For the more informal software selection that classroom teachers perform, a form as detailed as this would most likely not be time-efficient; yet teachers should be familiar with the review categories and types of items that are considered here as they make those important decisions in selecting software.

Identifying Information

You will need the title, publisher, and price of the software to ensure that the most recent versions of software are being considered. Providing the reviewer's name becomes important when a number of different people are participating in the review process.

System Requirements. The list of system requirements is usually given on the software box or in the installation directions. Most districts have computers with a range of capabilities, so evaluators may want to try each software program on a number of different machines to get a complete performance picture.

Grade Levels. The grade level that is posted on the package documentation should be used only as a general guide for use. Reviewers, therefore, should always consider how each package might be used with students outside the stated grade-level range.

Subjects. Providing the evaluator with an entire list of subjects, as opposed to just a blank line on which to fill in the subjects, prompts the full consideration of the range of possible subject areas and allows consistent searching of reviews. Because many software packages cross curricular lines, check all the subject areas that apply.

Modes. The purpose for which the software was designed is described by the modes (ISTE, 2000). One piece of software can be classified under several modes because most software can be used in several different ways.

Program Description. Describe briefly the content that is covered by the program. This description is generic, omitting any evaluative opinions. It is useful if compiling a database of all of the software reviewed to give teachers some idea of what this program is about.

Content and Technical Information

Circle the number that best describes your rating of this program for each indicator. For each section, then circle the score that best summarizes the program's performance on all of the indicators to give a quick summation of a program's performance in each area.

Documentation and Supplementary Materials. Software is generally sold with some accompanying materials, including installation procedures, teacher's guides, student workbooks, and even the box itself. Were you able to install and operate the program successfully according to the supplied directions? Were educational objectives stated?

Program Content. The content is the heart of the program and determines in many ways just how useful the program will be. Does the way in which the instruction is presented reflect current research, allow for a variety of learners, and appear up-to-date and free from errors and stereotypes?

Presentation. Logical content with relevant examples and illustrations gives students have a better chance of making meaningful connections. Is information clear and shown with enough variety to keep the interest of the intended audience?

Effectiveness. What ultimately matters with any instructional tool or strategy is whether it leads to student learning. This category is best judged by incorporating student participation into the review process. Are students able to apply what they have learned, and does it seem that they are now interested in the topic?

Audience Appeal and Suitability. Rate whether the way the content is organized and presented will hold the interest of these students, and if once their interest is piqued, they will be able to read and respond as needed.

Practice/Assessment/Feedback. Good instructional design demands that the practice and the assessment be aligned with both the objectives and with the instruction. Is feedback related to student responses and does it occur immediately after a response in order to reinforce or remediate as needed?

Ease of Use. The most well-designed instruction is rendered meaningless if a student cannot access it easily. Are there directions and a Help screen available from every screen? Consider, also, how much control the user has to navigate freely and to move at a comfortable pace.

User Interface and Media Quality. Ideally, all of the media elements, such as graphics, audio, video, and animations, combine to create a virtual learning environment. Are these media elements used to heighten student interest and promote instruction, or are they merely decorative?

Evaluation Summary

Frequently, the only part of an evaluation that an end user sees is the final rating, so it is helpful to boil down the information to a more concise format. At the end of each section, you circled a summary score that best illustrated how the program performed on those particular indicators. Now, simply transfer those scores to the Section Summary Graph by shading in the score for each section. This creates a visual representation of the overall program rating, making it easy to see at a glance how the program rates and allowing for easy comparison of multiple programs. The Overall Evaluative Comments give you the chance to explain the strengths and weaknesses of the program, including any areas that might not have been represented by the indicators on the evaluation form.

The form in Figure 7.2 can be duplicated and modified for educational software review purposes.

Final Note on Software Review

New interactive multimedia programs that are becoming the norm in the software industry are so different from text-based learning materials and allow such a range of navigational freedom throughout a variety of media and information that teachers must recognize that they do not always fit neatly into review categories (Nicholls & Ridley, 1997). Students actually construct the learning experience as they go. Review checklists might need to be modified to include more consideration of the learning contexts and the specific types of media being evaluated.

FIGURE 7.2	Educational Software Review Form

Software Title:

Publisher:	Price:
Reviewer:	Review Date:

SYSTEM REQUIREMENTS:		GRADE LEVELS:
Platform:	☐	PreKindergarten
Processor:	☐	K–2
RAM:	☐	3–5
Hard Drive:	☐	6–8
CD:	☐	9–12
Other:	☐	Adult
	☐	Teacher Tool

SUBJECTS:

Art:
- ☐ Music
- ☐ Performing Arts
- ☐ Visual Arts
- ☐ Computer Science
- ☐ Cross Curricular
- ☐ Early Childhood/Preschool
- ☐ Health/Phys. Ed./Recreation
- ☐ Internet/WWW

Instructional Tools:
- ☐ Authoring Systems
- ☐ Class Management
- ☐ Comp. Assisted Drafting
- ☐ Computer Utilities
- ☐ Desktop Publishing
- ☐ Image Generator
- ☐ Personal Productivity

- ☐ Keyboarding
- ☐ Language Arts

Math:
- ☐ Advanced
- ☐ Algebra
- ☐ Geometry/Measurement
- ☐ Number
- ☐ Probability/Statistics
- ☐ Multimedia Production
- ☐ Problem Solving/Logic
- ☐ Reference Library
- ☐ School to Work

Science:
- ☐ Biology
- ☐ Chemistry
- ☐ Earth Science
- ☐ Environmental Ed./Ecology
- ☐ General Science
- ☐ Physics
- ☐ Scientific Method/Lab Equip.
- ☐ Space Science
- ☐ Social Studies
- ☐ Test & Testing
- ☐ World Languages (non-Eng.)

MODES:

- ☐ Authoring System
- ☐ Bilingual
- ☐ Computer Programming
- ☐ Creative Activity
- ☐ Demonstration/Presentation
- ☐ Drill & Practice

- ☐ Education Game
- ☐ Exploration
- ☐ Guided Practice
- ☐ Internet
- ☐ Limited English Proficient
- ☐ Multimedia

- ☐ Problem Solving
- ☐ Reference
- ☐ Simulation
- ☐ Tool
- ☐ Tutorial

(continued)

FIGURE 7.2   Continued

PROGRAM DESCRIPTION: (Briefly describe the content of the program.)

DOCUMENTATION & SUPPLEMENTARY MATERIALS:

Necessary technical documentation is included.	N/A	0	1	2	3	4	5
Objectives are clearly stated.	N/A	0	1	2	3	4	5
Learning activities that facilitate integration into curriculum are suggested.	N/A	0	1	2	3	4	5
Materials for enrichment and remedial activities are provided.	N/A	0	1	2	3	4	5
Section Summary:	**N/A**	**0**	**1**	**2**	**3**	**4**	**5**

PROGRAM CONTENT:

Instruction matches stated objectives.	N/A	0	1	2	3	4	5
Instructional strategies are based on current research.	N/A	0	1	2	3	4	5
Instruction addresses various learning styles and intelligences.	N/A	0	1	2	3	4	5
Information is current and accurate.	N/A	0	1	2	3	4	5
Program is free of stereotypes or bias.	N/A	0	1	2	3	4	5
Section Summary:	**N/A**	**0**	**1**	**2**	**3**	**4**	**5**

PRESENTATION:

Information is presented in a developmentally appropriate and logical way.	N/A	0	1	2	3	4	5
Illustrations and examples are relevant.	N/A	0	1	2	3	4	5
There is appropriate variety in screen displays.	N/A	0	1	2	3	4	5
Text is clear and printed in type suitable for target audience.	N/A	0	1	2	3	4	5
Spelling, punctuation, and grammar are correct.	N/A	0	1	2	3	4	5
Section Summary:	**N/A**	**0**	**1**	**2**	**3**	**4**	**5**

EFFECTIVENESS:

Students are able to recall/use information presented following program use.	N/A	0	1	2	3	4	5
Program prepares students for future real-world experiences.	N/A	0	1	2	3	4	5
Students develop further interest in topic from using program.	N/A	0	1	2	3	4	5
This is an appropriate use of instructional software.	N/A	0	1	2	3	4	5
Section Summary:	**N/A**	**0**	**1**	**2**	**3**	**4**	**5**

AUDIENCE APPEAL & SUITABILITY:

Program matches interest level of indicated audience.	N/A	0	1	2	3	4	5
Reading level is appropriate for indicated audience.	N/A	0	1	2	3	4	5
Examples and illustrations are suitable for indicated audience.	N/A	0	1	2	3	4	5
Required input is appropriate for indicated audience.	N/A	0	1	2	3	4	5
Necessary completion time is compatible with student attention.	N/A	0	1	2	3	4	5
Program supplies remediation or enrichment when appropriate.	N/A	0	1	2	3	4	5
Section Summary:	**N/A**	**0**	**1**	**2**	**3**	**4**	**5**

FIGURE 7.2   Continued

PRACTICE/ASSESSMENT/FEEDBACK:

Practice is provided to accomplish objectives.	N/A	0	1	2	3	4	5
Practice is appropriate for topic and audience.	N/A	0	1	2	3	4	5
Feedback corresponds to student responses.	N/A	0	1	2	3	4	5
Feedback is immediate.	N/A	0	1	2	3	4	5
Feedback is varied.	N/A	0	1	2	3	4	5
Feedback gives remediation and reinforcement.	N/A	0	1	2	3	4	5
Remediation and reinforcement is positive and dignified.	N/A	0	1	2	3	4	5
Assessment is aligned with objectives.	N/A	0	1	2	3	4	5
Open-ended responses and/or portfolio opportunities are promoted.	N/A	0	1	2	3	4	5
Collaborative learning experiences are provided for.	N/A	0	1	2	3	4	5
Section Summary:	**N/A**	**0**	**1**	**2**	**3**	**4**	**5**

EASE OF USE:

User can navigate through program without difficulty.	N/A	0	1	2	3	4	5
Screen directions are consistent and easy to follow.	N/A	0	1	2	3	4	5
Help options are comprehensive and readily available.	N/A	0	1	2	3	4	5
Program responds to input as indicated by directions.	N/A	0	1	2	3	4	5
Title sequence is brief and can be bypassed.	N/A	0	1	2	3	4	5
User can control pace and sequence.	N/A	0	1	2	3	4	5
User can exit from any screen.	N/A	0	1	2	3	4	5
Only one input is registered when key is held down.	N/A	0	1	2	3	4	5
Section Summary:	**N/A**	**0**	**1**	**2**	**3**	**4**	**5**

USER INTERFACE AND MEDIA QUALITY:

Interface provides user with an appropriate environment.	N/A	0	1	2	3	4	5
Graphics, audio, video, and/or animations enhance instruction.	N/A	0	1	2	3	4	5
Graphics, audio, video, and/or animations stimulate student interest.	N/A	0	1	2	3	4	5
Graphics, audio, video, and/or animations are of high quality.	N/A	0	1	2	3	4	5
Section Summary:	**N/A**	**0**	**1**	**2**	**3**	**4**	**5**

SECTION SUMMARIES:

⑤	⑤	⑤	⑤	⑤	⑤	⑤	⑤
④	④	④	④	④	④	④	④
③	③	③	③	③	③	③	③
②	②	②	②	②	②	②	②
①	①	①	①	①	①	①	①
⓪	⓪	⓪	⓪	⓪	⓪	⓪	⓪
Documents	Content	Presentation	Effectiveness	Appeal/ Suitability	Practice/ Assessment	Ease of Use	Interface/ Quality

OVERALL EVALUATIVE COMMENTS

Educational Software Types

With a varied assortment of educational software at hand, teachers are able to individualize instruction to enrich or remediate as is necessary for student success. A standards-based curriculum ensures students' continued growth according to identified standards, along with those strategies that will enable attainment of those outcomes. Teachers who understand how software might best be integrated into a standards-based curriculum will need to be aware of the different types of software that are available. This section defines and illustrates some of the common categories. In order to be an effective facilitator of software use in the classroom, however, it is not necessary for teachers to discern exact differences among the categories; in fact, most of the descriptors of the categories overlap and most software titles can be easily classified in a number of different software categories. In an attempt to provide full-service educational solutions, newer software includes components of most of the different software types grouped together in one integrated learning environment. Distinctions can be further blurred by the various terms used in the software industry to describe similar categories. The descriptions of software types provide a common vocabulary with which teachers can discuss software use.

Drill-and-Practice/Instructional Game Software

Category Description

In general, drill-and-practice software allows learners to come in contact with facts, relationships, problems, and vocabulary that they have previously learned until the material is committed to memory or until a particular skill has been refined. The best drill-and-practice software possesses an interesting format that encourages repeated use by students, thus establishing the stimulus–response association required for memorization of certain facts. Sequential learning tasks and immediate feedback assist the student in the mastery of the skill.

Drill-and-practice programs are available in a range of sophistication from simple programs that offer a flash-card-like series of items to study to more advanced programs that attempt to serve each student with questions that are at the appropriate level of difficulty. As the student answers questions correctly, the program automatically branches to more difficult subject matter, and students answering incorrectly are quickly brought to material at a lower level.

Quality drill-and-practice programs utilize brief, effective feedback, either giving students another chance for incorrect answers or giving positive, motivating reinforcement for correct responses. Students should be able to control the rate of the program, taking as long as they need to answer a question, and they should also have the ability to quit the program at any time and resume at the place they left off when they return.

Instructional games can be very similar to drill and practice, but have added increased motivation by having game rules, an entertaining environment, and competition to be the winner. Depending on the particular game, students can compete against the computer or against other students. Some instructional games take on the form of many traditional games, such as board games, logic games, adventure games, or word games, whereas others are originally created as software.

Practical Integration

Critics of classroom computer use often aim the brunt of their skeptical comments toward drill-and-practice software. Many of the early drill-and-practice programs were known as "drill and kill" because they presented the same isolated skills in the same way to every user, creating boring, impersonal learning environments. Because drill and practice was the first type of educational software brought into regular use by teachers, it was often used as a learning device rather than as a practice device by teachers unfamiliar with the potential of the media. As educational philosophy steers away from behaviorist principles toward more constructivist views of students constructing their own meaning, the practical use of all educational software must follow suit. Drill-and-practice software can be an effective tool if used as one of many educational tools, as appropriate, to meet specific educational goals.

Drill-and-practice software is ideal when students need to practice discrete skills. The electronic mode can be more motivating than a paper-and-pencil counterpart, and the feedback to student responses is immediate. It can be used repeatedly without the need for teachers to grade papers or keep direct track of progress.

School Stories

Carlos, Whitney, Tiffany, and Cari, kindergarten students in Mrs. Hassam's class, began the year well above other students in their mathematical abilities. By midyear, they could count by 1s, 2s, 5s, and 10s with fluency and could write numbers past 100.

To encourage their continued progress, Mrs. Hassam began introducing them to some basic place value concepts. She used base-10 blocks to illustrate the relationship between 1s, 10s, and 100s, and within a short amount of time the four were trading place value digits with confidence. Following the work with the concrete manipulatives, Mrs. Hassam connected what they were capable of with the blocks to numerical writing.

When the four students reached an independent level of familiarity with place value concepts, they began working with Mighty Math Carnival Countdown (Edmark). With the Bubble Band, they could trade 10 bubbles for one big tens bubble or trade 10 tens bubbles for a hundreds bubble. The students were able to practice place values at their own pace, allowing Mrs. Hassam to work with other students on other math instruction.

Drill and practice is usually thought of for aiding math skills because the largely unambiguous nature of basic math facts lends itself to the right or wrong format. It can also be effective in areas that take advantage of gamelike formats, contextual clues, rhymes, and riddles, such as vocabulary, historical dates, and scientific definitions. Although it is true that students may be more motivated to use instructional games, you must constantly evaluate whether the learning experience is purposeful. Students may have mastered the instructional objectives of a game long ago, but may still enjoy playing. Because many games may be violent or may tend to encourage aggressive playing behavior in the classroom, preview all content and monitor program use to see that it is serving a meaningful place in the instructional sequence of your classroom.

Integrated Learning Systems

Category Description

Integrated Learning Systems (ILSs) have offered schools comprehensive instructional and management features for decades. Largely traditional in methodology, the expensive ILSs are networked software compilations that address objectives in the core curriculum areas. Pretests, instruction, practice, and posttests are designed to be aligned with national or district curriculum goals. Students typically work independently, and their progress is tracked and reported automatically. When they have mastered a particular set of objectives, they advance to the next section. Teachers can monitor students' performance by examining reports printed out by the system and can choose to supplement the electronic instruction as necessary.

Practical Integration

The adoption of ILSs often makes the transition to using technology easier for schools because the curriculum is completely prepared. This packaged approach, however, may not always allow for easy integration into other outside curriculum. The software systems are generally intended to stand alone as the sole source of instruction. The systems follow a typically behaviorist approach to learning, funneling all students through a linear presentation of the curriculum. Some newer ILSs include real-world scenarios and projects to present skills in context (e.g., Waterford Early Reading Program by Pearson Digital Learning at **www.pearsondigital.com**). Some systems offer entire curriculum options designed to play a significant role in content delivery, with lesson management tools, proprietary software games, and multimedia elements updated regularly over the Internet. Systems like these (see, for example, Knowledge Box at **www.pearsondigital.com**, and Figure 7.3) are evolving into full-service options that recognize value in significant teacher participation, yet provide a great deal of support and resources for predetermined and standards-aligned topics.

The easy mistake many schools make is assuming that when technology is brought into their classrooms, these curriculum delivery systems will adequately replace their teachers. Another misconception is that the introduction of ILSs satisfac-

FIGURE 7.3 Knowledge Box delivers digital media in all content areas for PreK through sixth-grade students.

torily prepares students with technology skills. Just because students access lessons or assessments using the computer does not mean they are gaining important communication, information management, and problem-solving skills that broader technology use can help to develop.

Care must be taken to ensure that the instructional format and content provide the best learning opportunity for each student. Current beliefs about the variety of learning styles found in any group of students lead to the understanding that any one method will likely not be sufficiently individualized to be successful. The human teacher is needed to orchestrate ILS use so that the most instructional benefit can be derived by each student.

If your school has adopted an ILS, be prepared to assume the role of an instructional facilitator. Be aware of the content and format of the software so as to anticipate student needs and questions. Rather than relying solely on the automatic records of each student's progress, investigate further to be sure that students are getting the instruction they need.

Problem-Solving Software

Category Description

Problem-solving software requires students to apply higher-order strategies and synthesize knowledge from multiple curricular areas in order to solve problems. Students can test hypotheses, learn from mistakes, and refine skills as they gain mastery

School Stories

Ms. Brown always stresses problem-solving strategies to her upper elementary students and makes an effort to use word problems to illustrate real problem situations. Midway through the fall semester, she notices that although her students are largely successful with solving math problems on paper, they are not always able to describe in words how they solve the problems beyond pointing to the problems and saying the numbers. She decides to try some problem-solving software called Fizz & Martina's Math Adventures (Tom Snyder Productions) as another tool to provide a useful context for their learning (see Figure 7.4).

Over the course of two weeks, she introduces her class to Fizz and Martina and the other characters in Mr. Barney's math class. Mr. Barney loves to tell stories, which always involve some type of math problem. On the videos included in the program, Mr. Barney encourages students to take notes of any numbers they encounter during the stories. What intrigues Ms. Brown the most about the program is that not only does it help students to gain practice in team problem-solving skills but it also requires effective discussion techniques. Students have to be able to describe their problem-solving strategies without looking at their notes, so they learn to assist team members to verbalize their teams' thinking.

Ms. Brown soon sees students excited about the program and hears them talking about the Blue Falls Elementary characters well after they finish using the computer. Speaking with students individually over the next several weeks proves two things to Ms. Brown: Not only are the students demonstrating proficiency with problem-solving strategies, but also they are feeling confident about what they know. One student even offers to show students in another class how to use the software.

FIGURE 7.4 Fizz & Martina's Math Adventures.

of problem-solving techniques. Software of this type can provide practice in solving problems by modeling general critical thinking steps, by focusing on specific subject-area issues, or by creating an open environment in which students can discover their own strategies. Whatever the method, problem-solving software affords the user more freedom than does drill-and-practice or tutorial software, but may or may not present the real-world context that characterizes simulation software.

A useful framework for understanding the definition of problem-solving software classifies programs in terms of *learner control.* Some programs give little control to the user beyond the ability to make logical guesses, one at a time. Other programs provide for full learner control, with the user deciding exactly what he or she will do next and moving freely from one activity to another. Good problem-solving programs promote the development of logical, systematic thinking patterns and transcend the boundaries of simple tutorial or drill-and-practice software.

Practical Integration

Effective problem solving is built by continuous practice and experience in a variety of meaningful situations. This understanding must be clear in teachers' minds as they plan a place for problem-solving software in the daily workings of a classroom. No software can be used as the sole tool for developing students' critical thinking abilities. Instead, software should be seen as one effective component in a repertoire of activities that promote the acquisition of higher-order thinking skills.

Reference Software

Category Description

In years past, when students needed to conduct research, they were required to go down to the library to peruse heavy encyclopedic tomes. Technology has brought both the storage capabilities to gather volumes of facts onto one small CD-ROM and the media variety with which to effectively bring life to static reference material. Reference software can take the form of any traditional reference works, such as dictionaries, encyclopedias, and thesauri. Other reference software presents extensive collections of information on a focused topic.

Practical Integration

Electronic reference works can be utilized just as traditional reference material would be. Depending on the particular learning activity, students might refer to software as needed to answer specific questions. They also might openly explore a multimedia reference without specific goals to guide their learning. The multimedia components of reference software present information in graphic, audio, video, or other alternate formats that allow uniquely unlimited access to students who might not be developmentally able to contend with the text version of the information, thus changing our understanding forever of the form of reference materials (Johnson, 2003).

Simulation Software

Category Description

Educational simulations allow students to experience events or phenomena that they are not able to witness personally and that would be too difficult or too dangerous to duplicate in a classroom setting. Software can simulate manipulating objects, performing a set of procedures, or acting in a given situation. Real processes can be slowed down or speeded up to study the effects of artificially tinkering with the variables.

Simulations provide contexts rich for meaningful individual learning construction. Like life experiences, simulations require the synthesis of many skills and understandings, making for true cross-curricular learning. Students must use what they know in ways that force them to confirm and expand their understanding. Simulations allow students to make and be affected by their own decisions. Guided by data provided by the software, the student becomes an active player in the scenario, selecting certain options or taking risks, and then witnessing the results of his or her decisions. Their involvement in a simulated situation lets students experience some of the feelings and problems associated with participating in the actual situation. They see the reasons for developing good strategies and therefore begin to think in a more organized fashion. Good simulations build realistic, yet appropriately unpredictable environments. They combine text with a selection of media elements that create engaging, content-rich situations.

Practical Integration

Simulation software prompts active discussion and encourages cooperation toward common goals. Depending on the situation being simulated, the software can be effective with a variety of student groupings. Entire classes can work together, collaboratively making key decisions. Small groups of students can explore situations separately and then later compare notes to see how others performed under the same circumstances.

In science labs, students can pour and mix dangerous chemicals via simulation, so mistakes do not blow up the classroom. It is also possible to simulate experiments that are too expensive, complicated, or time-consuming to replicate in school laboratories, such as building models of the systems in the human body (Coleman, 1997). Simulations provide for more student involvement than is possible through a reading assignment or lecture.

Social studies simulations can help students reenact historical events, learn about other societies, or experience governmental procedures, such as elections and lawmaking. When running simulation software, students must first understand certain information and concepts so that they can then analyze situations and make wise decisions; therefore, learning becomes more relevant and useful to them.

Simulations can also be used to train students in the operation of tools and different types of equipment. Such training allows students to practice skills and procedures needed to operate the equipment safely and accurately—without danger to themselves or to the equipment.

School Stories

When he saw Decisions, Decisions: The Environment (Tom Snyder Productions) on the list of software the district had recently purchased, Omar Mahesh knew it was ideal for his seventh-grade government class. The software is a role-playing simulation of a small-town pollution crisis during a political campaign. Students use the briefing books provided with the software to represent four different expert viewpoints—including an environmentalist, an economist, a scientist, and a campaign manager—to advise the fictional candidate on environmental issues.

Mr. Mahesh divides students into groups of four so that the random number generator can control turn taking. With his students armed with their briefing books and gathered in teams around the television monitor at the front of the room, Mr. Mahesh begins the simulation introduction.

As students learn about the pond being polluted, the software prompts student groups, acting as the mayor of the town, to set goals in priority and then, acting as the advisers, to look up information in the briefing books. Based on this advice, groups decide how to act and evaluate consequences of those actions. Just as in real life, single decisions lead to new problems, and students continue with the simulation over several class periods. On an especially contested decision in the classroom, several students suggest further time to think and do some outside research. At students' suggestions, Mr. Mahesh broadens the activity to include parent interviews and Internet research before resuming the simulation. With amazing timing, a pollution issue appears in their own town newspaper just a couple of weeks after their study. Mr. Mahesh is pleasantly pleased when students demonstrate some of the same careful problem-solving habits developed during the simulation to debate the real environmental situation (see Figure 7.5).

FIGURE 7.5 Decisions, Decisions: The Environment.

Social studies, science, business, and vocational simulations can be valuable learning devices if their use is wisely integrated into the curriculum at appropriate times. Simulations do not serve as stand-alone units, but are most effective when used to illustrate and use skills, ideas, and experiences that have first been explored by other means. Students must be prepared with both knowledge of the content and an understanding of how to operate the simulation itself, preparation they would undoubtedly receive in advance of the corresponding real-life situation.

When having students work in a simulated environment, you must ensure that they understand the shortcomings of the software. No matter how realistic the representation of the life situation it remains merely a simulation and is thus not entirely accurate or sufficiently complex. Discussing decisions and consequences with others who have used the program can help students to connect the simulation with reality.

Tool Software

Category Description

Software tools help teachers and students become efficient and productive managers of textual, numerical, and graphical information. Because tools are not as content-specific as other software types, they can extend what humans are able to do in virtually any curricular or management area. Just as teachers and students use pencils, for example, as tools in innumerable daily activities, so, too, can the word processors, spreadsheets, databases, graphics, and authoring programs be used. Other tools lend themselves to a particular content area, but allow users of many different ages to create or do something unique. Tools such as these will be used by students all their lives in most professions. The general skills and habits they learn by using software for various learning tasks will be transferable to other software they will be required to use in their future.

Practical Integration

Software tools afford quite a bit of freedom to teachers in how technology can be integrated into various learning tasks. Whereas other content-specific software, such as drill and practice or tutorials, is appropriate only for a particular subject area or developmental level, productivity tools can be used across grade levels and across subjects. Children using this type of software are more in control of the operation of the program than they might be with other types of software. The processes and products can be more customized.

Your students might use word processors to record information they have researched or to write creatively. They may compose letters directly on the word processor or may type in field notes after having scribbled them down on paper. Tool software can guide students to correct grammar and language use, and thus improve writing skills (see Figure 7.6). With spreadsheet programs, students can study the relationships between amounts of money or can learn to schedule time. Students might organize research content using a database program. With graphics software, stu-

FIGURE 7.6 Perfect Copy software improves writing abilities by highlighting grammar, punctuation, and language errors.

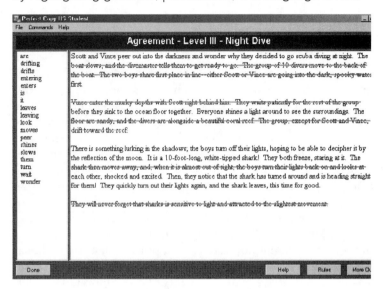

dents can explore geometric relationships, geographic features, and artistic representations. Concept-mapping tools facilitate brainstorming, process design and understanding of how concepts relate (see Figure 7.7).

Internet tools, such as HTML editors, are making up an increasing share of the tool software. The creative production versatility of authoring software is developed to a great extent in Chapter 14. Teachers should also be using productivity tools to support

FIGURE 7.7 Inspiration is a concept-mapping software that facilitates brainstorming, planning, and organizing of information.

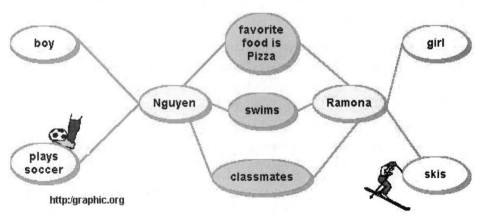

their efforts as teachers and managers of student information. Specific tips for using software as an aid to classroom administration can be found in Chapter 13.

Tutorial Software

Category Description

Tutorial software utilizes written explanations, descriptions, questions, problems, and graphic illustrations for concept development. Concepts are intended to be learned without any other instruction efforts, thus existing as a stand-alone form of instruction. This presentation of instruction differs from drill-and-practice software, which provides only practice and assessment. Students are given opportunities in tutorials to gain experience with new concepts much like they would when learning with a living and breathing teacher. After the tutorial portion of a lesson has been presented, drill-and-practice exercises are offered. Finally, a posttest for each objective or group of objectives determines mastery. Student scores may be displayed as the lesson ends, as well as suggestions for further study and practice.

Very basic tutorial programs present information and practice in a strictly linear fashion, similar to ways students would learn by themselves using a book. *Linear tutorials* present a series of screen displays to all users, regardless of individual differences among the students. There are very few reasons for these "page-turner" programs to be in electronic form because they utilize little of the technical capacity of computers. *Branching tutorials,* on the other hand, do not require all users to follow the same path, but direct students to certain lessons or parts of a lesson according to results of computerized pretests and posttests, or to student response to embedded questions within the program.

Tutorial programs that are designed to take full advantage of the medium should allow for students to interact with the programs continually as they practice new information. Good tutorials also allow individual students to work at their own pace, reviewing material as needed and moving ahead quickly when they fully understand a new concept. Adequate practice must be given following instruction, but prior to assessment. The program must respond intelligently to incorrect answers, predict the most common incorrect answers, and offer specially tailored explanations and learning experiences according to which incorrect answers were chosen by the student. In short, tutorial software requires the thorough instructional design that would be required of any good lesson a teacher would present in a traditional manner.

Practical Integration

In a busy classroom with dozens of different learning levels and styles, teachers can use tutorials to supplement their instructional efforts. Tutorial programs can teach students who require additional instruction on a topic or can allow more time to work through concepts at a slower pace. Instruction can be planned in a presentation style that complements what is available in a tutorial, so that students for which one style is not effective will have an alternative method to learn. Tutorials can open up learning opportunities to students in smaller or rural schools. If there are no teachers trained to provide instruction in higher-level math or science courses or certain languages, students can use tutorial software to learn what they would otherwise miss.

Web-Based Software

An increasingly viable resource for teachers is web-based software, made possible through the latest web technologies that provide the sophistication found on most CD-ROM-based software. The programs, available largely for free on an endless variety of content websites, are designed to be used entirely online. Web-based software generally requires the downloading of Internet plug-ins; however, the user typically is led to the download site automatically. Teachers are cautioned that this software is not necessarily designed for educational purposes. However, these *edutainment* games, part education and part entertainment, can be used effectively for specific purposes with clear planning. Depending on the purpose and provider of the software, teachers will find varying levels of supportive recommendations for classroom use.

Table 7.1 presents a selection of web-based software that may change by press time, so teachers are encouraged to search for the latest resources.

TABLE 7.1 Web-Based Software

Amazing-Space   http://amazing-space.stsci.edu
The Space Telescope Science Institute, operator of the Hubble Space Telescope, employs science teachers, scientists, and engineers to develop interactive web-based lessons based on a variety of space-related concepts.

Clicking Anastasia   www.lostsecrets.com
Students follow the story of Nicholas Romanov, former tsar of the Russian Empire, his wife Alexandra, and their five children, killed by communist revolutionaries. The mystery that remains is the location of the tsar's lost millions of diamonds and gems. Students can participate in interactive problem solving, receiving clues via email.

Funschool   www.funschool.com
Provides over 500 free online games based on educational concepts in a safe, interactive, and entertaining environment, organized by grade level and game type.

KidsPsych   www.kidspsych.org
This site was actually designed for parents to help children develop cognitive thinking skills and deductive reasoning, but it has great potential for the development of the same skills in the classroom.

Secrets at Sea   www.secretsatsea.org
Fourth- through seventh-grade students can participate in an online ocean adventure examining unusual behaviors by killer whales.

Spywatch   www.bbc.co.uk/education/lookandread
Spywatch is based on the popular BBC television series, set in a country village during World War II. Students develop phonics, spelling, and story-writing skills as they follow the adventures of a group of evacuees and investigate a range of spy suspects.

Educational Software for Handheld Computers

A software niche receiving plenty of attention in recent years is the market for educational software for handheld computers. Handheld computers (e.g., Palm or iPaq) allow teachers and students to write, create concept maps, draw pictures, collect data using probes, use spreadsheets, read documents, and take quizzes. Best of all, much of the educational software is free to the educational community (Topp & Hanquist, 2002). Software such as Quizzler, by Pocket Mobility (**www.pocketmobility.com/ quizzler/index.html**), allows teachers to create and access quizzes and educational games for handheld computers. The Center for Highly Interactive Computing in Education at the University of Michigan (**www.handheld.hice-dev.org**) has produced a whole range of free educational programs, and research on the effectiveness in classrooms is ongoing. Games such as Ayudame, a Spanish word processor, and Locker, a tool that helps students and teachers organize their schedules, are all available for free download during the beta testing period. Look for interest in and resources for handhelds to grow as the market develops and more schools discover the versatility of these tiny computers.

Future Directions for Educational Software

In looking back over the last few decades of educational software, noted educational software expert Judi Mathis Johnson (2003) has made some observations about where the industry currently stands. She has seen that educators move through a three-year progression in the way they interact with a new piece of software, from learning about it in the first year, to testing it in the second year, to finally initiating real integration in the third year. In fact, the promise of software tools encompasses more than what students can learn; teachers actually teach differently when they use quality programs.

The market for educational software has changed dramatically in the last couple of years (Johnson, 2003). Dozens of software titles over the past few decades are no longer available. So many were products of an overzealous industry trying to convince the educational community that glitzy new products were educationally sound. Not only are educators more savvy now about the role of technology for teaching and learning, demanding that software address important learning concerns, but with the requirements of the No Child Left Behind Act, software companies must now demonstrate how research has shown their products to be effective in order for federal money to be spent toward software purchases. Software companies will be looking to tie their product development closely to current research on software effectiveness, thus resulting in stronger products. An appealing direction advocated by some is to make the programs "open source," meaning that the actual software code would be able to be modified by teachers so that the content could be customized to meet student needs or local standards. This freedom to tinker with the design of a program is an element missing from most static, commercial software.

Summary

To ensure the purchase and effective use of quality educational resources, districts and schools need to formulate an established plan. Whether it is a committee reviewing the software at the district level or a teacher selecting the best website to fit with a particular lesson, it is imperative to consider the way the resource addresses the goals of classrooms, schools, districts, and states.

Everyone involved in the process of evaluating resources for educational purposes must understand that all evaluation rests to a large degree on subjective methods. Having a set process and a standard review form of which all participants are informed will help to make the results of reviews somewhat comparable across reviewers.

Checklists are the most common method for recording observations on software and website strengths and weaknesses. Generally, checklists require reviewers to respond to a range of questions from discrete yes-or-no items to longer narrative descriptions. Checklist review forms should be modified to fit the specific needs of the evaluation purpose.

Educational software allows teachers to use computers as versatile instructional aids to meet the individual needs of their students. Although knowledge of the software types is helpful for planning, teachers should know that the categories tend to overlap and many software pieces can be easily described by the descriptors of several of the categories. Drill-and-practice and instructional game software allow students to work with information they have previously learned, getting immediate feedback to assist in skill mastery. Integrated Learning Systems offer complete, networked instructional, assessment, and management packages. Problem-solving software requires logical thinking on the part of students and assumes that some previous concept development has taken place. The continuing development of logical thinking is an important goal for problem-solving software. Reference software brings together great amounts of facts and illustrates them with a variety of media elements, such as graphics, animations, video, and audio.

Computer simulations allow students to experience real-life events in the safety of the classroom. Software tools are not as content-specific as other types of software, meaning students and teachers can use them across the curriculum to manage all types of information. Tutorials attempt to aid concept development by carefully presenting instruction and feedback. New web-based educational software, available largely for free, can be used effectively for specific purposes with clear planning. Countless programs for handheld computers allow students and teachers to learn and teach. The software available to educators will continue to increase in quality as product development is tied more closely to research on effectiveness.

Challenge Yourself!

1. Have at least three people in different positions in the educational system (such as a student, parent, administrator, or community member) review the same piece of software. How do their reviews compare and contrast?

2. What modifications would be needed to use the Software Review Form in this chapter with students as the reviewers? Choose a target student audience, and list changes you would make to allow students to use the form to review software independently.

3. Write a complete review of a piece of educational software and submit it to the software editor of an educational technology journal.

4. Host an email forum with several peers or colleagues on the overall quality of educational software being produced today. Have participants send their responses to all in the "conversation" to keep everyone involved. Direct the ongoing discussion by sending questions soliciting perceived strengths and weaknesses of software that people have seen or used.

5. Is it possible to review one electronic resource for all audiences and purposes? Compose a position paper on the topic, discussing the problems with generic software reviews.

6. Look at some newspaper ads and make a list of the features that appear most desirable in the educational software that is advertised. Do these features appear educationally sound or does flashiness seem to be selling more software?

7. Identify all of the software currently available on the market that could be used for your intended teaching area or grade level. Comment on the selection available to learners in your area.

8. Choose one specific piece of software and write a lesson plan for how you would integrate it into a complete instructional sequence. Be sure to include the instruction or other preparation that would precede the software use and how your students would follow up their experiences with the software.

9. Summarize the advantages and disadvantages of teaching a particular concept with and without educational software.

10. Do an Internet search on "open source" software. Are there implications you can find for educational settings?

References

Coleman, F. M. (1997). Software simulation enhances science experiments. *T.H.E. Journal, 25*(2), 56–58.

Hoffman, J. L., & Lyons, D. J. (1997). Evaluating instructional software. *Learning and Leading with Technology, 25*(2), 52–56.

International Society for Technology in Education. (2000). Description of the *Educational software preview guide.* Retrieved January 27, 2004, from www.iste.org/ Bookstore.

Johnson, J. M. (2003). From lofty beginnings to the age of accountability: A look at the past 30 years of educational software. *Learning and Leading with Technology, 30*(7), 6–13.

McDougall, A., & Squires, D. (1995). A critical examination of the checklist approach in software selection. *Journal of Educational Computing Research, 12,* 263–274.

TABLE 8.1	Educational Website Review Guidelines

Documentation and Credibility

Site author information is clearly stated, including name and contact information.

Site author has provided credentials, if necessary.

Information sources are indicated, as necessary.

Date of latest site revision is provided.

New information is highlighted.

Fees or names are not requested to use site.

Content

Site title represents content.

Purpose of goals of site are clearly stated.

Content can be used for various learning styles and intelligences.

Site has links to other relevant sites.

Information is current and accurate.

Content is free of stereotypes or bias.

Audience Appeal and Suitability

General appearance of site is appealing to target audience.

Language is developmentally appropriate for target audience.

Text and graphics are appropriate for target audience.

Content of linked sites is appropriate for target audience.

Ease of Use, Navigation, and Accessibility

Users can navigate through site without difficulty.

Help features and site map are available and easy to access.

Information is well organized.

Links back to homepage are included on each succeeding page.

Links to other sites are relevant.

All links work.

Few large graphics increase download speed.

Directions given for downloading any needed plug-ins.

Site functions in variety of browsers.

Site is accessible to individuals with disabilities.

User Interface and Design

Navigation options are clearly marked and self-explanatory.

Spelling, punctuation, and grammar are correct.

Text is clear and in a font suitable for intended audience.

Media elements (e.g., graphics, audio, video, animation, databases, JavaScript) are used to enhance content, as appropriate.

Media elements (e.g., graphics, audio, video, animation, databases, JavaScript) are of high quality.

Design creates stimulating environment.

Design elements are consistent on all pages.

Advertising is either nonexistent or does not interfere with content.

A Framework of Educational Resources

The task of sifting through online resources can be a daunting one for teachers, who often have overwhelming professional responsibilities. Finding useful online information and understanding where it might be integrated into an established curriculum can best be accomplished by examining the sites according to a categorical framework. Berenfeld (1996) proposes comparing the scope of the information environment of the Internet to that of the natural environment of living things, commonly referred to as the "biosphere." Because the information environment grows and changes and is based on interdependence of its components, just as is the biosphere, he has coined the term *infosphere*. Based on this systemic view of the information environment, as well as on the proposed organizational models of both Berenfeld and Ellsworth (1997), this chapter presents examples of World Wide Web resources organized into a framework of infosphere processes: harvesting information, planting information, and cultivating information. The ideas for use suggested here should not be taken as comprehensive, but are meant only to spur thinking about integration.

Harvesting Information

Life is made possible in our biosphere because of the ability of each living thing to gather, or harvest, what is needed for survival. Educators using the Internet for educational purposes have at the click of a button the ability to harvest general educational information, content information, insights into what others have experienced, and research on an unlimited number of topics. Although examples are given to illustrate each category, most web resources could be classified in a number of categories.

Portal Sites

The vastness of the World Wide Web can be intimidating. Many times, teachers simply need a safe, informative place to get started. Portal, or "jumping off," sites provide links to a great variety of educational resources, from very general to topic-specific (Kirkman, Frady, & Walz, 2004). Someone at each sponsoring organization has done the searching "footwork," meaning that you can benefit from a convenient organized collection. Portal sites in turn link to the other resources.

The distinction should be made here between teacher tools and those meant to be used by students. Teacher tools, such as most of the portal sites in this section, contain lesson plans, teacher discussion boards, and links to other support materials, among a great deal of other information. For the most part, these resources are not designed for students. Just as with a nontechnology lesson, the lesson plan is a guide for the teacher to use in planning and implementing the lesson; the students never see the actual plan. These tools should be used by teachers to find lesson ideas, connect with other teachers, get advice on classroom management issues, and access professional development.

DISCOVERYSCHOOL.COM
http://school.discovery.com
One of the best places on the web to start for teachers, students, and parents, this site includes not only a searchable lesson plan database and downloadable teaching templates but also materials coordinated with Discovery Channel programs and a new Video Screening Room that allows you to preview and use brief video segments from its collection of video series.

EDUCATION WORLD
www.education-world.com
Education World boasts a searchable database of over 50,000 educational resource sites (see Figure 8.1). In addition, the site maintains current features on monthly lesson plans, timely education-related news items, administrator articles, curriculum ideas, educational books, and reviews of online educational resources.

FIGURE 8.1 Education World.

EDUPUPPY www.edupuppy.com
This is a very easy-to-use tool for early childhood educators to find age-specific information, tools, and resources.

KATHY SCHROCK'S GUIDE FOR EDUCATORS
http://school.discovery.com/schrockguide
Known by teachers since the World Wide Web was introduced, Kathy Schrock's Guide for Educators is a great starting point for teachers, students, and parents. Its vast array of web resources is logically categorized and well described.

MARCOPOLO www.marcopolo-education.org
The MarcoPolo program is a partnership between the MarcoPolo Education Foundation and national content organizations to produce content-specific educational websites. The sites present lessons, activities, and reviewed web resources for the K–12 classroom that have been developed by leading content experts. Select partner websites are described here under the appropriate content areas.

MICROSOFT CLASSROOM TEACHER NETWORK
www.microsoft.com/education/mctn/default.asp
From the dominant software producer comes a for-teachers website with a vast array of creative teaching ideas, tutorials on how to use productivity software, tips on integrating multiple tools, and a variety of timely professional development resources.

SCHOLASTIC http://teacher.scholastic.com
Of particular note on the Scholastic site are the extensive book-related tools, such as an A–Z author information index, featured online authors, writing

workshops, and Research Starters, with activity ideas and encyclopedia articles. There are professional resources for in-service, new, and future teachers, including advice from the experts and interviewing tips.

TEACHERVISION.COM www.teachervision.com

The TeacherVision site was created by teachers for teachers. Be sure to browse lesson plans in the Theme Library and download and print the Books on the Run.

TEACHNET.COM www.teachnet.com/index.html

The strength of this site comes through its organized list of lesson plans and Power Tools, including a wealth of practical advice on everything from Classroom Décor and advice for keeping students focused through the End of the Year, as well as dozens of Take 5 ideas, for when you need to keep students busy for just five more minutes, and an enormous bulletin board idea gallery.

TEACH-NOLOGY www.teach-nology.com

This comprehensive site touts 19,000 lesson plans, 5,600 printable worksheets, and links to over 200,000 reviewed websites, along with articles, rubrics, games, news, and advice.

U.S. DEPARTMENT OF EDUCATION www.ed.gov/index.jsp

The homepage of the U.S. Department of Education provides timely news regarding the state of education in our country, answers to frequently asked questions, links to related governmental officials, updates on legislation, application information for federal grants, and links to federally funded publications. There are hints for teachers and researchers who use the site, and a search feature allows you to search the expansive site for specific information. Up-to-date information on the No Child Left Behind legislation is highlighted.

WWW 4 TEACHERS www.4teachers.org

Billed as "The Online Space for Teachers Integrating Technology into the Curriculum," this site includes not only links to online sources, such as the Site of the Week, but also superb teacher tools, such as Casa Notes, Notable Pics, and the rubric maker Rubistar.

Educational materials, along with most other online information, have historically been available for free as part of the open spirit of the Internet. As the web matures, however, an increasing number of sites that were once free are being reconfigured as fee-based. For the added charges, teachers can often get more complete sets of resources that are aligned with standards and are better maintained and supported. The costs for these sites rarely fall to the individual teacher; school districts, and sometimes schools themselves, typically purchase subscriptions to these services for the benefit of all of their students. In order to get a flavor of what these fee-based portal sites offer, most allow you to register for a limited free-trial subscription. (See, for example, Classroom Connect at **www.classroom.com.**)

Kid-Friendly Portals, Reference Sites, and Search Engines. A recommended practice for teachers wanting students to examine online material is to preview and then bookmark websites that students are to use. However, there are times when students need to find answers to their spontaneous questions. A wonderful collection of websites have surfaced that present children of varying age ranges with safe places to begin information searches. Please note that these sites are not filters, thus not a guarantee that children starting at these kid-friendly sites might not end up stumbling into inappropriate material. As always, caution and careful monitoring are urged when students are on the Internet (Hodge & Herbert, 2003).

ASK JEEVES FOR KIDS www.ajkids.com
A partner site to the well-known Ask Jeeves site, this junior version is a kid-friendly way for kids to find answers to their questions. Kids can ask questions in natural question language and find child-appropriate answers online.

FACTMONSTER www.factmonster.com/index.html
Factmonster is a reference website for kids aged 8–14. Both entertainment and educational resources are indexed, and searching for an item taps into an *encyclopedia*, a *dictionary*, an *atlas*, and a number of *almanacs* of child-appropriate pieces of information.

KIDSCLICK! http://sunsite.berkeley.edu/KidsClick!
A reference site created by librarians has to be good! KidsClick! was developed to guide children to content-rich and age-appropriate websites.

WORDSMYTH www.wordsmyth.net
This is the first web-based dictionary designed for elementary-aged children.

YAHOOLIGANS! www.yahooligans.com
This directory of Internet sites for kids aged 7–12 is both browsable and searchable, and sites are reviewed by teachers. Try having your students take the Savvy Surfing Quiz to test their knowledge of safe web practices.

Content Resources

The largest category of educational resources on the World Wide Web, and those that are most easily incorporated into instructional plans, are those sites providing some type of content information. National organizations, research institutions, or even individual Internet users with a great interest in a particular topic might maintain these sites. The quality and extent of information will vary greatly between sites, necessitating thorough preview by teachers before students are asked to use them. These types of content sites can be used minimally as a supplemental or enrichment resource or can supply the backbone of a series of lessons.

Again, be cautious that websites you plan to use with your students are appropriate student material. You will know by such clues as the size of font, difficulty of reading, and even the color scheme or graphics used, whether this is a teacher or student tool. As with any learning resource, even if it is designated for students, make sure that it is appropriate for your particular students; information at the seventh-grade reading level, for example, will not be readable by your first-graders. However, portions of websites at easier or more difficult levels, or even teacher tools, could indeed have a place in a lesson if they help meet a particular learning goal. For instance, a site that a teacher might use to brush up on state history prior to teaching that unit might contain some clear photographs of historical sites that would be of interest to students. When the site is shown to a whole class using a projector and the difficult text paraphrased by the teacher, the photographs may be exactly the right choice to illustrate the lesson.

Language Arts

CHILDREN'S LITERATURE WEB GUIDE www.acs.ucalgary.ca/~dkbrown
This is a complete resource locator for those who teach literature to children. The site compiles an annual guide to newly published literature and points the user to annual award lists, such as Newbery and Caldecott. There are discussion areas, links to other children's literature online resources, a multitude of teaching ideas, and lists of current children's best-sellers. Still more links guide users to information on recommended books, authors, and movies based on books, as well as further resources for teachers, parents, and students.

Teaching Tip: Have book clubs in your class select their readings from a list you approve and join a discussion list about the author.

EDSITEMENT http://edsitement.neh.gov
This partnership of the National Endowment for the Humanities and Marco-Polo is the center for humanities resources, lesson plans, and activities on the web. Separate sections on literature, foreign language, arts, and history create a complete selection of information organized by grade level.

Teaching Tip: High school foreign-language teachers can begin with the provided resources and then branch out to related sites to bring to life the unique cultures students are learning about.

READWRITETHINK www.readwritethink.org
The newest of the MarcoPolo content partners, ReadWriteThink brings together the International Reading Association (IRA) and the National Council of Teachers of English (NCTE) to provide free Internet-based content for reading and language arts instruction. Dozens of lessons can be sorted by title, grade, or date.

Teaching Tip: Have early readers use the Word Wizard to practice vocabulary during and after a study of a book.

SHAKESPEARE WEB www.shakespeare.com
Whether used to enrich an established curriculum or to spur an individual interest, many gems of information can be found on Shakespeare Web. Itineraries on a traveling Shakespearean theater company and tidbits on Shakespeare history are highlights.

Teaching Tip: Use this site at the beginning of a middle school Shakespeare unit to research background history.

Mathematics

THE GEOMETRY CENTER www.geom.uiuc.edu

Funded by the National Science Foundation, the Geometry Center develops methods in which technology can be used to visualize and communicate mathematics and related sciences. Serving both academic and industrial fields, this site provides links to geometry references, software, course materials, and distance learning resources. Current projects include such areas as spacecraft design, solar system visualization, and satellite constellation visualization.

Teaching Tip: Have intermediate math students work together to design a space station using geometrical principles. Encourage them to check back with this site frequently to verify calculations and confirm hunches.

ILLUMINATIONS http://illuminations.nctm.org

Presented by the National Council of Teachers of Mathematics (NCTM) in partnership with MarcoPolo, Illuminations is a wealth of interactive multimedia lessons, video teaching vignettes, and innovative lesson plans centered on the NCTM standards.

Teaching Tip: Use the imath interactive figure for investigating triangles with the whole primary class. Then have students find triangles in your school.

MEGA-MATHEMATICS www.c3.lanl.gov/mega-math

Mega-Mathematics, a product of Los Alamos National Laboratory, brings very complex mathematical concepts to students in understandable, original ways. Lessons on such topics as colors, graphs, infinity, and algorithms are outlined completely so that teachers are prepared to facilitate the lessons. Lesson components include activities, vocabulary, background information, key concepts, evaluation ideas, relation to NCTM standards, preparation and materials, and indications for further study.

Teaching Tip: Have small groups of students work independently through the "A Usual Day at Unusual School" play. Encourage each group to record their thinking processes on paper. Have groups prepare charts to share their strategies with the rest of the class at the end of the activity. How do the strategies compare?

Science

EXPLORELEARNING.COM http://explorelearning.com

The ExploreLearning site features compelling multimedia activities called "gizmos." These allow students to simulate dozens of mathematical and scientific concepts, such as the Doppler Shift simulator that lets the user control the motion of a speaker to see how sound waves behave.

THE FRANKLIN INSTITUTE ONLINE http://sln.fi.edu/tfi/welcome.html

The Franklin Science Museum's online presence is a must-see resource that not only allows a glimpse into the real museum but also gives teachers and students rich learning activities. Content units, problem-solving opportunities,

FIGURE 8.2 The Franklin Institute Online.

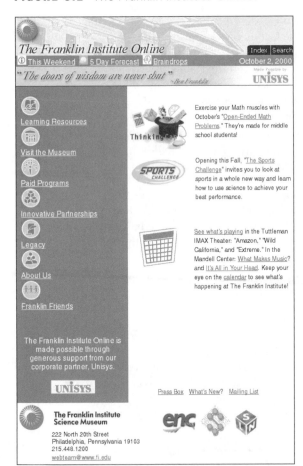

resource "hot lists," and multimedia enhancement are among the many learning resources (see Figure 8.2).

Teaching Tip: Use "The Heart: An Online Exploration," in the Learning Resources section, with younger students studying basic circulatory properties or with older students studying advanced human anatomy and physiololgy. Students can read the text of the units independently or with a partner. Consider projecting the photo slide shows in front of the whole class as discussion prompts.

OLOGY http://ology.amnh.org
The American Museum of Natural History presents Ology to demonstrate its belief that "everybody wants to know something." The Ology website tells children that if they are curious about something, they are "ologists." The highly interactive and informative resource links students with expert scientists in engaging content-based investigations.

Teaching Tip: Have students collect, sort, and compare "ology cards" to explore more about the specific content, such as the dinosaur varieties in the Paleontology exhibit.

SEAWORLD/BUSCH GARDENS ANIMAL INFORMATION DATABASE www.seaworld.org
Sea World and Busch Gardens maintain this vast website in order to provide an enthusiastic, imaginative, and intellectually stimulating atmosphere for students. Within the site, learners will encounter a list of animal information that spans animal rescue to zoological park careers, hitting sea turtles, penguins, and even Clydesdales along the way. Teachers can depend on numerous lesson resources and activities designed by the Sea World Education Department. Current animal-related news and Ask Shamu, a frequently asked questions area on animals, round out the resource.

Teaching Tip: Have PreK students choose an animal and work with older "buddy" classes to research their animals. Prereaders can illustrate using photos from the website as guides. Older students can synthesize factual information into a format their younger buddies can understand.

VOLCANOWORLD http://volcano.und.nodak.edu
Learn about volcanoes from the experts! This NASA-supported site is loaded with everything you have ever wanted to know about volcanoes (see Figure 8.3).

FIGURE 8.3 Volcano World.

You can find the latest information on currently erupting volcanoes, observatories, and monuments, and research on the topic. Learners can access pictures, videos, stories, games, and activities, and they can even send a message to a real volcanologist. Teachers have available extensive lesson plans, and anyone can arrange to be alerted through email of any new eruptions.

Teaching Tip: Use the email alert system to have your students embark on a yearlong project to track volcano eruptions. Locate eruptions on a map, use the web to research the countries in which the eruptions happen, and use details to construct detailed scenarios predicting how the eruptions will impact the affected communities.

Social Studies

THE AMERICAN CIVIL WAR HOMEPAGE
http://sunsite.utk.edu/civil-war/warweb.html

The American Civil War Homepage gathers together in one place hypertext links to the most useful electronic files about the American Civil War. The lengthy list of links points to resources on time lines, photographs, specific battles, original documents such as letters and diaries, information on state participation, reenactment groups, and other Civil War organizations.

Teaching Tip: Students can use the vast resources available from this site to plan the sequence of a Civil War unit. After a couple of hours exploring the information available, have students develop concept maps about what they know about the Civil War. Then encourage them to plan how best to "fill in" the gaps in their understanding.

CONGRESS.ORG http://congress.org

This federal site links learners with information on activity in the legislative branch of the government. There are a directory of members, a calendar of events, and a list of legislative committees (see Figure 8.4).

FIGURE 8.4 Congress.org.

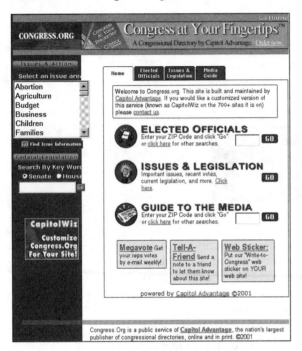

Teaching Tip: Secondary government students can compare information on this site with on-line news sources and state government sources to interpret different versions of the same events.

DIGITAL HISTORY
www.digitalhistory.uh.edu

The Digital History site supports the teaching of American history in K–12 schools and colleges. The resources on this impressive site include an interactive time line, multiple perspectives on history, such as Hollywood's America, and access to primary sources through the largest private collection of American history documents in the world. Special interactive features include Ask the HyperHistorian and History Day by Day (see Figure 8.5).

ECONEDLINK www.econedlink.org

EconEdLink, produced by the National Council on Economics Education, highlights the economics standards through real-world scenarios. The site provides lessons on authentic, up-to-date economics topics, real financial data, and economics-related news. This is a MarcoPolo partner site.

FIGURE 8.5 Digital History.

Teaching Tip: Use the lessons in EconomicsMinute to enrich weekly current events studies by encouraging students to think beyond the news to consider the economic implications of events.

NATIONALATLAS.GOV http://nationalatlas.gov

Composed from an enormous print-based collection of maps, this interactive tool promotes greater national geographic awareness. Users can create maps of the United States with a variety of environmental and sociocultural details, and with just a click can access relevant data according to geographic location.

NATIONAL GEOGRAPHIC XPEDITIONS
www.nationalgeographic.com/xpeditions

Xpeditions brings the National Geography Standards to life in innovative ways that make the most of emerging web technologies. Students can use the atlas to search for global locations and print detailed maps of any location in the world. They also can locate relevant websites to be used to meet the geography standards and explore at home with their families through readings, games, and virtual field trips. By visiting the stunning virtual world of the Expedition Hall, the geography standards come to life in compelling and intriguing ways. Xpeditions is a MarcoPolo partner site (see Figure 8.6).

Teaching Tip: As part of a unit on international relations, use the Culture Goggles feature with the whole class. Have students make predictions about how each of the cultures will respond.

Arts

ARTSEDGE: THE NATIONAL ARTS AND EDUCATION INFORMATION NETWORK
http://artsedge.kennedy-center.org

Operating under an agreement between the Kennedy Center for the Performing Arts and the National Endowment for the Arts, and supported by the U.S.

FIGURE 8.6 Xpeditions.

Department of Education and MarcoPolo, this massive site is designed to help artists, teachers, and students communicate to support the arts in the K–12 curriculum. The listed projects, performances, and study guides are given to further the stated mission: to connect people to people, to connect people to information and resources, and to build a new base of knowledge in arts and education (see Figure 8.7).

Teaching Tip: Rather than having art students create projects and simply hang them up in the hallway, have students communicate with other classes around the country who are working on similar projects. Comparisons among techniques of artists at different locations can be valuable in the development of artistic skills.

METROPOLITAN MUSEUM OF ART www.metmuseum.org

The Metropolitan Museum of Art, one of the largest and best-known art museums in the world, presents on this website collections of several hundred thousand exhibits at any given time. Exhibits cover world culture from prehistory to the present. The site features a calendar that details special exhibits, concerts, lectures, films, and other museum activities.

Teaching Tip: This is an excellent resource to study the art of presenting an exhibition. Students could be asked to look beyond the breathtaking museum content to focus on the professional presentation style, organization, resources, and other strategies in order to plan for their own school exhibits.

PLAY MUSIC www.playmusic.org

PlayMusic.org is produced by the American Symphony Orchestra League. The site allows students to learn about each family of instruments in an orchestra,

FIGURE 8.7 ArtsEdge: The National Arts and Education Information Network.

with specifics about each instrument. Students can meet composers and musicians and listen to classical selections from well-known composers. They also can meet individual mentors according to instrument.

Teaching Tip: Partner with music teachers to have students do research on specific instruments.

Experience Simulations

In these days of budget cutbacks, "frivolities" such as field trips are usually some of the first luxuries to go. Students, therefore, are not able to experience firsthand much of what their own community has to offer, let alone the richness and diversity that the world can show them. Through online communication, students can experience vicariously what they cannot see in person. Pictures and stories bring remote events and foreign parts of the world to vivid life through the computer screen.

GLOBAL ONLINE ADVENTURE LEARNING SITE (GOALS) www.goals.com
Through virtual field trips, GOALS lets students experience travel, adventure, science, technology, and nature (see Figure 8.8). Students can ride along with the first woman from the United States to sail around the world and the first transoceanic rowing expedition, among other adventures. Students can learn through reports, pictures, audio clips, and activities based on the actual exhibitions.

THE JASON PROJECT www.jasonproject.org
This multidisciplinary project allows students and teachers to do virtual fieldwork from the classroom with experts in distant locales such as oceans, rainforests, polar regions, and volcanoes. The JASON Project was initiated by Dr. Robert Ballard, the scientist who discovered the wreck of the *Titanic*.

NASA QUEST http://quest.arc.nasa.gov
The scientists and engineers at NASA let students virtually take part in training for space walks, flying the Shuttle, exploring distant planets, and building future

FIGURE 8.8 Global Online Adventure Learning Site (GOALS).

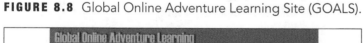

spacecraft. The site includes profiles of experts, live webcasts and chats, lesson plans, and searchable answers to student questions. Be sure to check the calendar for upcoming events.

THE QUEST CHANNEL http://quest.classroom.com
Join adventure teams as they solve mysteries around the world. Get to know experts, meet the adventure team members, and learn information needed to solve the mystery. Note that some features may require a Classroom Connect subscription.

Research Tools

ASKERIC http://ericir.syr.edu
The Educational Resources Information Center (ERIC) is a federally funded national information system that provides a variety of services and products on a broad range of education-related issues. The AskERIC website gives access to education information to teachers, librarians, counselors, administrators, parents, and others (see Figure 8.9). Abstracts of professional journal articles and other educational documents can be searched in order to conduct research on hundreds of search terms.

LIBRARY OF CONGRESS http://www.loc.gov
The heart of America's library is its collection of documents, photographs, movies, and audio selections that tell the story of our country. There are also links from this site to legislative information, special national exhibits, and tips and tools for librarians and researchers.

FIGURE 8.9 AskERIC homepage.

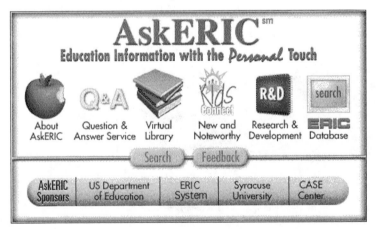

Planting Information

That which will eventually be harvested can be so only because it was once planted. The environment of the Internet was built on the spirit of free contribution of ideas, and even students can help in this regenerative process by planting their own seeds of information that will propagate the online resource supply.

Students crave authentic audiences for their work. When they have learned something, it only makes them understand it better to show someone else. With the World Wide Web, students are no longer limited to writing for classmates or family members to read. They can easily publish their work for the world audience. Reports, stories, poems, and school periodicals can be published easily on a server at the school or district (see Chapter 9 for information on creating educational websites).

There also exist websites dedicated to publishing the writing of students (see Figure 8.10). Because such sites are already created and require only following directions to submit a piece of writing, they are easy ways to let students see their work published.

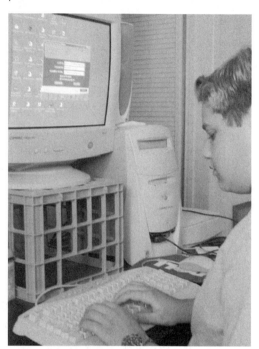

FIGURE 8.10 Websites dedicated to publishing the writing of students are easy ways to let students see their work published.

CRUNCH http://nces.ed.gov/nceskids/crunch
CRUNCH, a part of the NCES Students' Classroom, is an online magazine that accepts submissions in the form of feature articles, reviews, and creative writing from student writers.

CYBERKIDS www.cyberkids.com
The CyberKids site publishes original creative work by kids aged 7–12, including stories, articles, and poems.

FERN'S POETRY CLUB http://pbskids.org/arthur/games/poetry
This is an engaging place, hosted by Arthur's friend Fern on the PBSKids website, for kids to read poems from other children and contribute their own to. Students enter the text of their poetry directly on-screen.

KIDSCOM www.kidscom.com
The "Write Me a Story" feature allows students to submit stories using a given weekly character and setting. The site staff randomly selects five stories by kids 11 and younger and five by kids 12 and older; then site readers vote for the stories of the week. The winning works are showcased on the site the next week.

KID'S SPACE www.kids-space.org/story/story.html
Kids' Space is a safe place for kids to read and publish written works. Children can submit stories on their own and teachers can submit stories for their students.

MIDLINK MAGAZINE www.ncsu.edu/midlink
MidLink Magazine publishes original work from classrooms around the world. Teachers select thematic issues in which to participate, agree to edit their students' work, and publish it on their schools' websites for review.

TEENLIT.COM www.teenlit.com
TeenLit.com provides free online publishing of poetry, essays, short stories, and book reviews by teens. Teens can submit their writing and then discuss it with other readers.

THE VIRTUAL REFRIGERATOR DOOR www.educationindex.com/weaselworld/fridge.html
This site brings the kitchen gallery online, showing artwork from children aged 2–18. Artwork is organized by artist's name.

WEEKLY READER CLASSROOM PRESS www.iuniverse.com/weeklyreader
For a publishing fee, students can upload writing to the Weekly Reader Classroom Press site and it will be published in a bound trade-book format.

Cultivating Information

The harvesting and planting that keep the natural life cycle going are not always composed of separate one-sided efforts. The most exciting aspect of the Internet is the potential for collaborative work among learners. Students in different geographic locations can combine thoughts and talents to learn and discover together. Email is one way this collaboration might occur. (See Chapter 3 for more information on the educational applications of email.) A growing number of websites now offer the chance for classes to participate in organized online projects.

Many of these projects take place in real time using real data, so there are inclusive dates during which students can participate. There are usually different levels at which students can take part, from merely lurking, by reading the information that is posted, to being fully engaged, by reading, contributing, and communicating with peers around the world. Before getting their students involved, teachers should consider the size and duration of any project, along with expectations for student participation. The following sites present collections of individual projects that begin and end faster than can be listed here. Peek in on a few ongoing projects to get a sense of what it means to collaborate online.

- Center for Improved Engineering and Science Education (CIESE) Online Classroom Projects **http://k12science.ati.stevens-tech.edu/currichome.html**
- Education World's Collaborative Projects **www.education-world.com/projects/index.shtml**

- Global SchoolNet Internet Projects Directory **www.gsn.org/pr/_cfm/index.cfm**
- Houghton Mifflin's Education Place Project Center **www.eduplace.com/projects/index.html**
- I*EARN **www.iearn.org**
- KIDPROJ **www.kidlink.org/KIDPROJ**

Summary

The World Wide Web can be a source of unlimited resources that can bring exciting learning opportunities to students anywhere at any time. Categorizing available web resources according to a framework makes planning for their use a more realistic task. The Internet can be thought of as an information environment, similar in process to the biological world in which we live. Learners can participate in processes of harvesting, planting, and cultivating information on various websites with potential educational application. Considerable time and effort are required to find appropriate websites to match learning goals.

Challenge Yourself!

1. Using the guidelines in Table 8.1, review an educational website. Is it a site you would use?
2. Write a lesson plan that integrates information from at least two web resource sites.
3. Visit the content sites listed in this chapter. How are these sites set up? What level of involvement should a teacher have for your intended level of students to use each site successfully?
4. Do a web search for resources that would provide content information. How applicable are these types of sites to your area of teaching interest?
5. Look in the popular educational technology journals. What type of guidance do the articles supply for teachers? Are there complete lessons that you could use unaltered? How much customization will other ideas take to put them into practice?
6. Find an online interactive project for students at your level. How much participation does this project involve? How many suggestions are there for outside activities?
7. How can content resources from two different areas be integrated?
8. Should you start with planning a content lesson and add in World Wide Web resources, or start with the resource and plan the lesson around it? When would each strategy be appropriate?
9. What styles of teachers would not seem to lend themselves to easy integration of online resources? How might these teachers be convinced that such quality information is available on the web?
10. How can the infosphere metaphor be used to teach students about the Internet as a learning tool?

"How many of you have ever been to the ocean?" Mr. Pace asked his third-graders that morning. Five or six sure hands went up, along with a few other tentative ones, and the teacher proceeded to elicit stories from the experiences of these students. Other children said they had seen the ocean on TV and still others had read about it and seen pictures in books.

"Well, I have a way to take you to the beach, without even leaving our classroom." And as sounds of disbelief filled the classroom, Mr. Pace proceeded to explain their new project.

He told them about the teacher from California he had met at the conference he attended last month. She also teaches third-graders, and her school just happens to be very near the beach. The two teachers agreed to try a collaborative project to have their students teach each other about their respective climates—Mr. Pace's class about the mountain region in which its community was nestled and Ms. Garcia's class about its beach. He explained how each class would research the other environment, using information from the World Wide Web, as well as more traditional media such as books and videos, and report on what they think it would be like to live there. Then the classes would read each other's work and use their own personal experiences to help them edit for correctness.

Mr. Pace's class began that day with brainstorming a list of everything they knew about the beach and the ocean. They offered ideas on what they thought kids did for fun and even what kinds of clothes they probably wore. Based on these ideas, the teacher later spent the afternoon searching the Internet for beach-related informational sites and bookmarking those sites that were appropriate for his students' reading and understanding levels. Combined with the books he had already gathered from the library, and two videos that he had reserved from the district media center, he was ready to begin facilitating his students' exploration into life on the beach.

Over the next several weeks, students worked in pairs to investigate what the selected web pages had to offer. They took notes, and they discussed and argued over what the most important information was. Eventually, students wrote, individually and as a whole class, what their impression of living near the beach must be like. When their thoughts were complete, Mr. Pace posted their drafted text onto their class website.

While Mr. Pace's class had been researching life on the beach, Ms. Garcia's class had been doing the same regarding life in the mountains. Now, each class had an initial report posted on the web, and their jobs switched from researchers to editors. Students in each class spent time reviewing the other class's site in detail, writing up a list of comments and suggestions to send to their partner class. Each class also gathered pictures showing themselves in their surroundings to be scanned in and sent to the other class for its final website. The comments were emailed with the image files as attachments.

Mr. Pace's class eagerly listened as he read Ms. Garcia's class's comments about their research. They found that they were accurate about most of the facts, but needed to add some details regarding the specifics about the particular beach Ms. Garcia's class was most familiar with. They were surprised at how many things were similar even though they lived in such different places. Within several days, the class had amended its website and had developed a fairly complete vision about what it was like to live on the beach.

References

Berenfeld, B. (1996). Linking students to the infosphere. *T.H.E. Journal, 23*(9), 76–83.

Ellsworth, J. B. (1997). Curricular integration of the World Wide Web. *TechTrends, 42*(2), 24–30.

Hodge, L., & Herbert, L. (2003). A combined strategy for internet safety. *Our Children, 28*(6) 11–12.

Kirkman, C., Frady, A., & Walz, G. (2004). The internet, the hidden web, and useful web resources: ERIC, ERIC/CASS, and the virtual library. In CyberBytes: Highlighting Compelling Uses of Technology in Counseling. North Carolina: Couseling and Student Services. (ERIC Document Reproduction Service No. ED478217).

CHAPTER 9

Designing Online Instruction

FOCUS QUESTIONS

1. What planning is necessary prior to establishing web-based instruction?

2. What are some strategies for keeping the documents of a website organized?

3. Why is regular maintenance vital to a quality website?

Teachers at all levels are discovering the possibilities for facilitating meaningful learning with World Wide Web resources. Students working at a distance or at a different pace than others, as well as those in a more traditional learning environment, are able to use the web as the actual method of instruction. The more time educators spend working with this instructional and informational mode, the clearer it becomes what types of interactive lessons and communication are conceivable using the web. Once teachers know what can be done, it is only a matter of time before they become comfortable enough to want to start planting their own seeds of information in the web environment. This chapter introduces the reader to well-planned, meaningful web-based instructional or informational sites. Please note that this is only an introduction; the reader may want to consult other sources or even take a course in electronic document design in order to become a proficient web-based materials producer.

Types of Online Instruction

Online instructional materials span the range from supplemental—whereby the online materials are used as resources for a traditional face-to-face course—to distance education—in which case students are separated from the instructor and from each other by a distance and the entire course is delivered online. Most uses for online learning materials fall somewhere between these two extremes. However, teachers must carefully consider their instructional goals and intentions prior to investing the time and money to create online learning materials.

Online Instruction as a Supplement

Chapter 8 introduced the integration of web-based educational materials into an established curriculum. Recent software advances make it easier than ever for classroom teachers to create their own online materials, anything from study guides for students to information sites for parents. The degree to which student learning is dependent on these online materials rests on the instructional goals. A teacher might use a history outline on the class website to teach a lesson in class, have partners use a scavenger hunt created on literature resources, or require students to log on from home for homework information. In all of these instances, students attend school daily and use the online instructional materials as a supplement to other instructional materials. Reliance on an online format should be based on a pedagogically sound reason; teachers are cautioned not to feel pressured to post duplicate materials online if another nontechnical strategy is more appropriate.

One recently accepted and systematized form of online instruction is the Web-Quest. Dodge (1995) defines a WebQuest as "an inquiry-oriented activity in which some or all of the information that learners interact with comes from resources on the Internet. . . ." Rather than allowing students to endlessly "surf" through websites, these online lessons instead encourage learners to seek specific information from the web. They then analyze it, synthesize it, and use it for some end project. Teachers design WebQuests with the following components:

1. Introduction
2. Task
3. Information sources
4. Process
5. Guidance
6. Conclusion

WebQuests can be designed as either short-term knowledge acquisition tools for one to three class periods or longer-term knowledge refinement activities that can take up to a month. Students can be asked to use web resources solely or can integrate electronic, paper-based, and human resources. For examples, rubrics, and further information on the WebQuest process, see the WebQuest Page at **http://webquest.org,** or conduct a web search for WebQuests. Enough WebQuests exist online that teachers can frequently find a model lesson to either use or modify on a topic they are teaching.

Online District Information

Districts maintain informational websites to report everything from resources for new parents to updates on school board meetings to secure access to student grade reports. Such sites are a great convenience for parents with home computer access because parents can have their questions answered at any time from wherever they are. Mandatory web use is not yet typical of most school districts because home computer use cannot be guaranteed. Districts, then, offer such information as a supplement to more traditional parent resources.

Distance Education

As the availability of Internet resources ushers in changes in traditional forms of education, it simultaneously offers a new dimension to some alternative forms of education already moving past the four walls of a classroom. Distance education is literally defined as "the delivery of the educational process to receivers who are not in proximity to the person or persons managing or conducting the process" (Lewis, Whitaker, & Julian, 1995, p. 14). It has existed in some form for years, often serving students in rural areas who were not able to reach a school or students who for some health or behavior reasons could not attend traditional school.

The correspondence model of distance education, which has served as the defining model of the field, was usually built around the teacher sending out course materials via regular mail. Upon receiving the materials, the student worked independently to complete the assignments and then mailed them back to the teacher for grading. The technology that most aided this educational exchange was the telephone, giving students and teachers a chance to discuss necessary topics of concern. Although this arrangement allowed some school participation for large groups of students who otherwise would not receive education at all, it amounted essentially to a strict delivery of education, with a minimum of guidance aimed at actually inciting learning (Berge & Collins, 1995).

With the advent of a global network of telecommunications, distance education has had new life and possibilities breathed into it. No longer is learning away from a traditional classroom the exception, but rather it is becoming a learner-centered standard many educational models strive to replicate. Email and chat groups have provided a forum for relevant, content-rich, supportive online discussions between teachers and students as well as among students. Instead of sitting isolated at home working on assignments by himself, the distance learner can experience the feeling of being part of a collaborative group of learners, a member of a class that is right there in the room. This feeling is called "social presence" (Mason, 1994).

As students gain greater access to computer hardware and connections to the Internet, the chances for them to learn at a distance from one another increases. Students in small districts who would normally have a limited selection of courses available to them can learn from content experts anywhere in the world. Adults who desire additional education can fit the courses they need into a time schedule that fits with their work constraints. Parents who choose to teach their children at home have available a world full of content and the chance for social contacts that will enrich their children's learning environment.

The research on distance learning from the early twentieth century to the early twenty-first century clearly demonstrates that students who learn from a distance, whether it be the old correspondence method or modern-day web-based learning, achieve as well as students learning in traditional settings (Russell, 1999). This is good news, as virtual learning opportunities for high school students, and those even younger, abound. Seventeen states either have or are developing online high schools and about half of the 50 states have provisions for "cyber" charter schools (*E-Defining education,* 2002). Other states are examining ways to test students online.

Students taking courses from a distance include both those who also attend traditional public high schools as well as those who are home schooled (Doherty, 2002). The majority of students enroll in virtual courses so they can take courses that their schools do not offer, while others say that the flexibility of taking online courses helps them fit learning into busy extracurricular schedules. Programs report diversity in both ethnic and gender groups, as well as regarding technology skills of their students; not everyone taking an online course is a computer expert, an idea designers of online instruction need to remember as they design learning materials. In fact, a majority of students report some technical difficulties while trying to take online courses.

As many as 1,600 teachers taught online courses to K–12 students in 2002 (Blair, 2002). The 200 schools that participate in the Virtual High School agree to trade the time of one of their teachers teaching an online class of 20 students in return for 20 slots for their students to take other online courses (Trotter, 2002). The experience of teaching in virtual settings is clearly different from being faced with students in traditional classrooms. Whereas some teachers report stronger relationships with their students because of more frequent email dialogue, others say that quality "face time" with students is missing, even despite efforts to create community from a distance (Blair, 2002). Teachers feel isolated not only from students but also from colleagues. Making things tougher on teachers used to teaching in traditional environments is translating their teaching styles into the electronic environment. Many teachers do not realize how great a task it is to engage students in learning through often theatrical means that are not as easily replicable in online settings.

In the rush to install virtual programs, states must consider the reality of educating students from a distance. In order to maintain quality, the following questions are worthy of consideration:

- Are online courses aligned with state academic standards?
- Who is responsible for students' technological needs when they are taking online courses?
- Are online teachers trained effectively to teach via the Internet?
- Should parent approval be required before a child enrolls in an online course?
- Will students receive the same amount of credit for an online course as they would for a face-to-face class?
- And how will states ensure the quality of online courses, especially when students are taking them from teachers in other states or countries? (*E-Defining education,* 2002)

What a student can learn is no longer limited by the knowledge of individuals who are employed at one particular school building. As people experiment with the types of learning that are possible through the Internet to students at a distance, and as it becomes easier for educators to use and contribute to the online world, the structure of learning undoubtedly will change. Where now many distance courses are designed to closely resemble instruction that occurs face to face, new learning theories will be depended on to guide new forms of learning for the online world.

Getting a Mental Plan

Creating a website requires more than just the task of tagging it with the HTML code. The usefulness of countless websites accessible now in the online world is questionable. Some prove to be difficult to navigate through, others are visually confusing, and still others contain inaccurate or outdated information. Rushing out and posting just any old website for the sake of saying you or your school has one does not contribute to the cooperative information base of the web. Instead, it will ultimately serve as a waste of your valuable professional time. You will want to take care that the instructional site you are considering serves your intended purpose in a way that is appropriate for your anticipated audience.

Begin first by asking yourself some questions that will help to define your goals for this instructional site. Harris (1997) has suggested the following starting points:

1. Who will be interested in exploring the site?
2. What types of information should be available at the site to address the interests of different audiences?
3. How should this information be presented so that it is maximally helpful to identified project participants and/or to those just browsing through the site?

Audience

If you are designing a site that will provide content information for your students to use for instruction, it will be organized very differently than will a site meant to update parents or other outside community members on school announcements. If you are considering showcasing your students' writing, your site will have distinctive characteristics if the writing is done by kindergartners as compared to that done by sophomores. A website can serve many audiences by directing visitors to different sections. Think carefully about who will be accessing your site most often so that your planning can be efficient and audience-specific.

Types of Information

Primary to the planning of any website should be a consideration of the content the page is being designed to present. Without this forethought, the collection of pages you will be creating will resemble an art project more than the meaningful informative base it could be (Tennant, 1997). A classroom homepage will likely be viewed by parents or others interested in what students in the class are learning and doing. This type of page might include descriptions of projects, pictures of classroom events, or possible ways parents can extend the learning at home. A website meant to provide a thematic starting point for other classes would need to dedicate a certain amount of space to background information and facts pertaining to the project. If people find what they are looking for on your site, they will be more likely to come back to visit again. Inviting comments from visitors about the site and suggestions for what else they would like to see will help you to keep your site updated and relevant.

A word must be said here regarding the privacy of minor students. It is imperative that school districts adopt guidelines for posting student information online. Many districts deem it acceptable to include student first names but not last names on class websites. Photos showing students' faces might be allowed if parental permission has first been obtained. Other personal information about minor students is generally not acceptable except in special cases with parental permission or when the pages containing the personal information are password protected. Teachers are urged to become familiar with their districts' privacy policies prior to creating online classroom materials.

Presentation Strategies

There is an infinite number of ways to arrange the information on a website. Viewers may be required to scroll down the page through long chunks of text, or links can take viewers directly to other pages of information. Sometimes, your students might want to write the text of the page themselves. Other times, it might make more sense to provide a link to another established site that has already compiled an excellent treatment of the topic.

Based on your answers to these types of planning questions, you will begin to define the purpose of your proposed website. A website can take many forms in order for it to serve your identified purpose. One of the easier sites to begin with is a class homepage providing information to parents. Such a page might be organized, as would a newsletter that might be sent home, with such items as homework assignments and upcoming announcements.

In addition to these basic inclusions, website functions will also fall into the categories of web resources presented in Chapter 8. Written stories can be published for all to see and collaborative projects with other classes can be managed via your website. You might design an instructional site that provides content information your students need for class, or you might supply thematic information to keep parents apprised of what is happening in school. Field trips and other experiences can be documented through digital photographs and written reflections to share with other classes who may not have made the same trip or who may not be familiar with your area of the country. Unlimited amounts of online resources can be compiled by and for your students.

The Design Process

With a good mental plan for what your site needs to include, your next move is to plan how you want the site to appear to others who will view it. It would be easy to skip this planning step in favor of getting right to the web design, but your valuable time could be wasted trying to visualize what you want the site to look like at the same time you are creating the site documents. A small amount of planning time up front not only will save time later but also will make for a more organized and easy-to-use website.

Study

Begin by closely examining other websites you visit. Look at how the designer has laid out the text and graphics. Is it aesthetically pleasing or does it appear that page elements were just dropped in randomly? Are the graphics serving an obvious educational purpose or do they appear to be there for decoration only? Is the font size and style appropriate for the content and audience? As you move around from page to page, is the navigation intuitive and well-organized? Once you get to another page, is it easy to get back to where you started?

Sketch

When you have reviewed others' pages, sketch out what you envision for your page on a storyboard or a sequence of screen layouts. Your storyboard can be very rough or extremely detailed, as long as it gives you an idea of where text will be located, what size and other formatted text will be used, where graphics will be integrated, and how the navigational path is planned (see Figure 9.1). A simple, clean layout is the best place to start; more complexity can be added later if desired.

Use specially formatted text, such as **boldface** or *italics*, judiciously. An overly formatted page is difficult to read, and your user might spend more time concentrating on the abundance of special text rather than on the content of the page. Images should also be chosen carefully. Large graphics take a long time for the browser to load, which slows down the use of your website. Make sure that every picture serves a purpose in your layout and overall goals, rather than providing only meaningless clutter. Your page will appear even more organized if you plan all the pages to have a consistent look and feel, such as by using the same background color or coordinating graphics throughout the entire site.

FIGURE 9.1 Sketching a storyboard for a web page.

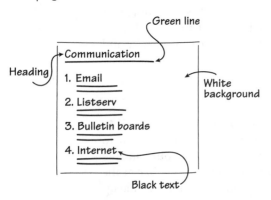

Plan Navigation

List in your storyboard the URLs for any hypertext links you would like to create. Good web design calls for fitting the link seamlessly into the text, rather than telling the user to "Click Here." Include links that enrich the information on your site, but not so many that the user is constantly thrown off-track. The linked resources should directly pertain to the goal of the lesson or informational piece.

Just as you create hyperlinks to other outside resources, you can also link your homepage to other pages in your own website. Connect pages within your storyboarded site with arrows showing the paths for how the user will be able to travel through the pages (see Figure 9.2). Plan a simple navigational path. You do not want people who visit your site to be lost wandering around between your pages. Make sure you include a link back to your homepage on every page in your site. Add to your storyboard any custom colors you plan on using to help you get an idea of whether the color scheme is visually pleasing and appropriate for your intended audience. The background color or image should be in high contrast to the text, such as light text on a dark background or dark text on a light background. Your students will be less likely to succeed in their web learning experience if they must struggle to make out what the page says. Finally, plan to place your name or school name and the date in a prominent place on the page so that people accessing your page will know how current the information is and how to contact you should they have comments or questions.

Plan Organization

To ensure an organized and easily modifiable website, it makes good sense to keep a record of the filenames of the HTML documents you create. Cafolla and Knee

FIGURE 9.2 A storyboard showing a navigational path for a website.

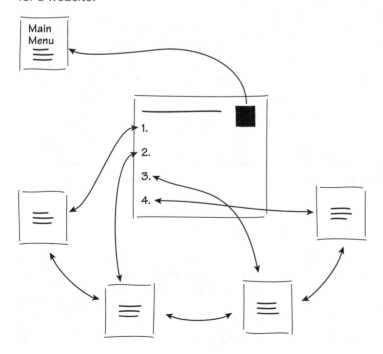

(1996–1997) recommend documenting the following information to create a complete record:

- Page titles
- Source of each link and the reasons it was selected
- Source of the graphics
- Size and type of graphics
- Width of horizontal lines

Even as you storyboard, jot down filenames you plan on giving to these pages. Keep to brief, logical filenames so you will remember what each page is by the name alone. Always use lowercase filenames to make it easier for your users to access your site with a browser. Web addresses are case-sensitive, so someone trying to find your site at "myhomepage.html" will not get there if it is actually named "MyHome-page.html." At this point in your planning, this record will serve as a checklist to guide your page creation. Later, when you are updating your site, it will streamline your job by reminding you of the filenames and the organization of the files.

Plan for Accessibility

One of the unique attributes of online learning is that everyone, regardless of appearance or abilities, can learn together. Thus, developers of online educational materials must now ensure that their websites are accessible to all potential learners, from students with disabilities to those with slower connection speeds. Most importantly, educational websites that are accessible "transform gracefully," meaning the information is accessible despite physical, sensory, and cognitive limitations, or technological barriers (Web Accessibility Initiative, 1999). Web materials should provide text equivalents to graphic, video, or audio elements so that alternative browsing devices (e.g., screen reading software) can interpret the content for the user who cannot see or hear. Web designers also must recognize that their content may be viewed on all sorts of hardware using a variety of input devices. The content should be easy to understand and to navigate; image maps or tables that may make a site's layout clear for those who can see or are using a large monitor may not be interpreted properly by screen reading software or compact screens. To scan your web page to test for compliance with accessibility guidelines, go to the Bobby site at **http://bobby. watchfire.com/bobby/html/en/index.jsp.**

Involve Students in Web Design

What better way to teach students about the Internet and instill some pride and confidence in their own work than to have them participate in the designing of a website? All of the aspects of website creation discussed in this chapter can be accomplished by students as well as by adults, and at times might even be handled better by students. The complete process can prove to be a valuable cross-curricular project. Depending on the abilities of the students, they can gain practice with written language and with measurement, such as with graphic sizes as they work with the page design and layout. They can do the background research, both on the content to be presented on the site and on websites to which links will be created. Participating in the process from the beginning through completion will teach students about follow-through and accomplishment. Some schools are even able to offer students their own individual homepages on which they can publish their writing for an authentic world audience.

The Development Process

Now that you are armed with both a mental concept and a visual plan, you are ready to begin creating the actual documents that will make up your instructional site. Remember from Chapter 3 that a web page is a text document that uses HTML tags to tell the browser software how to display the page (see Figure 9.3).

Web documents can be saved to either a disk, the hard drive, or some other location, using the document names you previously planned on your storyboard. Files saved with the proper ".html" extension can be viewed in a web browser when saved to your local drive during development. However, they must be uploaded using file transfer software (see Chapter 3) to a web server to be available for others to view online.

In the not-so-distant past, the only way to create web-based documents was to manually code the text document with the correct HTML tags. Although this is not a difficult process, the work can be tedious and prohibitively time-consuming. Even most web development purists now take advantage of new software solutions for creating web documents. All of these tools allow you some range of capabilities to format documents, paragraphs, and characters, as well as to insert hypertext links, multimedia elements, and more advanced scripting.

Web editing tools are to web-page creation as calculators are to computation, or even as electric mixers are to baking. The results are quicker and easier with the tools of convenience, although there are those who might say that those basic skills you learn doing it the "old-fashioned" way lead to a better end product. When HTML editors first hit the market, they were able to format with only the basic tags, but could not be counted on to produce some of the more advanced formatting. As is always the case with innovation and progress, however, the more recent editors are able to handle the more complex HTML programming, making web-page creation accessible to even those with no HTML knowledge whatsoever. This is good news for teachers who want to try their hand at designing web-based instruction, but fear their busy professional lives will prevent them from learning a complicated coding language.

HTML editors look and act very much like word processors. The ease of operation is based on a convention called WYSIWYG, the acronym for "What You See Is What You Get." Rather than seeing a mess of tags identifying various types of formatting, you see on the screen the actual formatted results. If you want a title to be centered, for example, the program shows it to you centered. Without your realizing it, the **<CENTER>,</CENTER>** tags are being added into the actual HTML document

FIGURE 9.3 The finished web page.

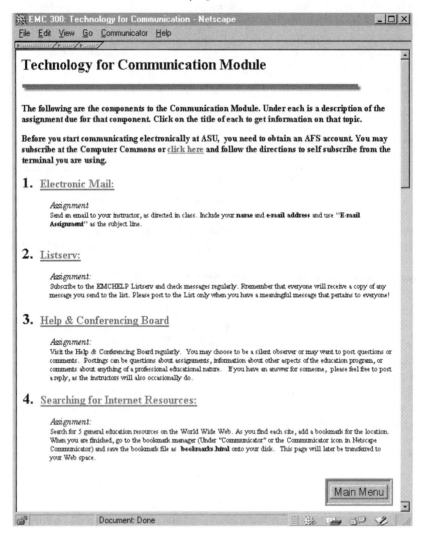

behind the scenes. Editors automatically insert the document formatting and allow you to choose any other of the paragraph and character formatting that is available by clicking on toolbar buttons for each of the procedures. Images can be easily inserted by clicking on the image button and identifying what image file you want. To create text that is hyperlinked, simply highlight the text, click on the link button, and type in the URL or other destination location. Whenever you want to view the actual HTML tags, you can usually click on a button to view the source of the document, and here you will notice all of the tags that have been inserted into the document (see Figure 9.4).

Web Editing Software

Editing software is now available in a range of stand-alone programs. The most basic offer a simple, intuitive tool that teachers and students can use with little training and a short learning curve (e.g., Page Composer, a free component of Netscape Communicator, at **www.netscape.com**). These programs allow for the construction of attractive and effective web pages complete with multimedia elements. More sophisticated software offers increased flexibility and a greater range of new web capabilities (e.g., Macromedia Dreamweaver, **www.macromedia.com**). Advanced features allow you to insert precoded objects such as frames, navigation bars, email links, and symbols. Some software uses layers so that objects and text can be moved freely in design, and many offer templates for preset coordinated color schemes. Site maps continue the good organization that was begun during the planning stage by automatically linking new files as the site is built. Other software focuses on site management, rather than individual page creation only (e.g., Microsoft FrontPage, **www.microsoft.com**). Sites are created and updated as a whole structure, making it easier for entire schools or districts to collaborate on consistent site creation (see Figures 9.5 and 9.6).

Productivity Software

Most new productivity tools (e.g., Microsoft Office) give you the option to save documents as web pages. This means that teachers can do two jobs at once: generating materials on a word processor for classroom use, for example, and then saving another version of the same materials to be placed on the class website. One distinct

FIGURE 9.4 A sample HTML document showing document, paragraph, character, and hypertext reference tags.

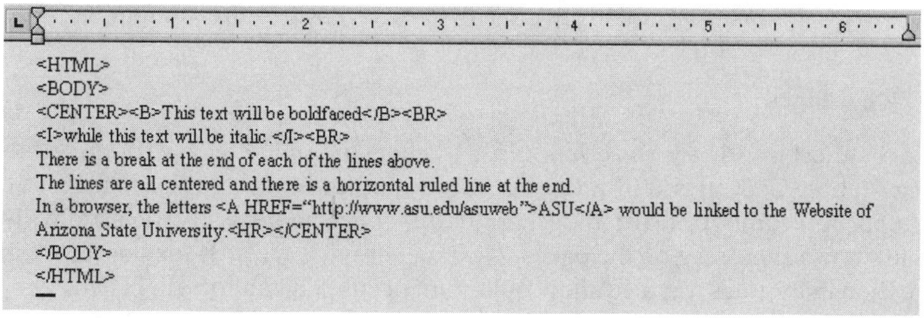

```
<HTML>
<BODY>
<CENTER><B>This text will be boldfaced</B><BR>
<I>while this text will be italic.</I><BR>
There is a break at the end of each of the lines above.
The lines are all centered and there is a horizontal ruled line at the end.
In a browser, the letters <A HREF="http://www.asu.edu/asuweb">ASU</A> would be linked to the Website of
Arizona State University.<HR></CENTER>
</BODY>
</HTML>
```

FIGURE 9.5 The sampler HTML document in Netscape Page Composer.

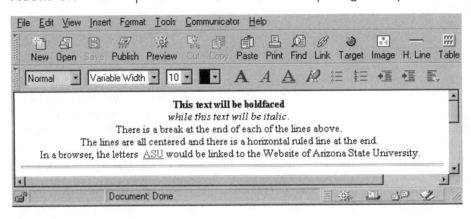

FIGURE 9.6 The way the tagged document would appear in a browser.

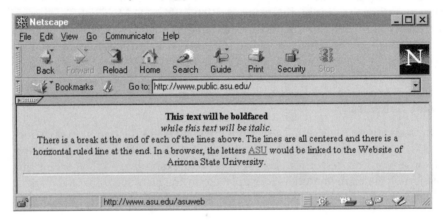

advantage is that teachers reluctant to learn new software can contribute to online learning environments using the software with which they are already familiar.

Online Web Editors

Some of the most exciting web advances for teachers are online web editors. These tools (e.g., Yahoo! GeoCities at **http://geocities.yahoo.com/home** and Filamentality at **www.kn.pacbell.com/wired/fil**) are generally free if teachers and districts are willing to see some advertising on the pages. The tools provide wizards for step-by-step page creation in minutes, yet also allow quite a lot of customization with HTML tags. Some even let you drag and drop objects, similar to the more advanced stand-alone software, and give plenty of interactive tools such as guest books, page counters, feedback forms, and streaming media. Finally, teachers can add and update favorite links and upload photos with little effort.

Course Management Software

The most sophisticated solution for creating online learning environments is course management software (e.g., WebCT at **www.webct.com** and Blackboard at **www.blackboard.com**). These software systems are not typically an option for the classroom teacher independently, not only because the cost would be prohibitive but also because these tools are designed to function as a larger system-wide effort. Course management software can be used either to create professional-quality course supplements or to convert entire courses to online format to be offered at a distance. Instructors are not required to invest a lot of time, resources, or technical expertise with this software. They are provided with design templates to present students with a consistent interface; a comprehensive set of communication tools, such as email and discussion boards; and administrative tools, such as online assessments, to help manage student grading and reporting. Students can customize their own homepages to access appropriate communication tools, course information and assignments, educational resources, and personal and school calendars.

Server Storage

Local Server Space

Your district or school likely already has a web presence and possibly even procedures for hosting individual classroom web materials. The procedure might entail your sending your files to a committee for review or to a server administrator to upload. Find out the policies prior to beginning your web design and development, because some districts have adopted web software and consistent procedures that may affect your capabilities.

Hosted Server Space

A number of public and educational websites offer free web pages (e.g., Yahoo! Geo-Cities at **http://geocities.yahoo.com/home**), while others offer subscription-based hosting (e.g., myschoolonline at **http://myschoolonline.com/golocal/0,1273,,00.html**). Although free hosting sounds attractive, the limited technical support and pop-up ads may frustrate teachers and students. Low-cost hosting alternatives offer better service and more user-friendly sites. Once registered, the sites allow you to have ample space on their servers to host multiple web pages with some multimedia elements. You will have your own URL that students and parents can use, as well as some ability to upload new documents and updates via FTP, sometimes with the assistance of an easy-to-use wizard.

Maintaining a Quality Website

If you are taking the time to design and create a website, you will want to be sure that you are posting a quality product and that the pages stay in good condition as time goes by. Make the time to check your site when you think you are finished constructing it, and then set a regular schedule of making updates and improvements.

Check Your Site

Just as you might have someone proofread something you have written, have someone who has not seen your website previously and who is able to provide candid comments navigate completely through the site. Have that person first check for basic spelling and grammatical errors. Putting a page on the Internet with these types of errors is reprehensible and reflects poorly both on you as a web designer and on your school as a quality educational institution. Have your test user also check all of the navigational paths to make sure that every link goes where it says it does and that the routes are intuitive and allow for easy return to the homepage. This way you will find any inactive or inaccurate URLs before your students or parents have the chance to become confused. It is important, also, to get an outside opinion on the page layout and color scheme. When you have worked with a page for quite a while, you may not even realize that the graphics make it hard to follow or that the font color is difficult to see on your chosen background.

Update Your Site

In the online world, information frequently changes, making it necessary for you to keep up or risk letting your site become antiquated. Skeletons of websites that are no longer functioning or current litter the Internet, slowing down search engines and proving endlessly frustrating to busy people looking for timely information (Tennant, 1997). Websites to which you have linked may be there one day and may vanish the next. If your links go nowhere, the learning goals you have for your students will not be achieved. Go through to check your links regularly, deleting or adding any as necessary. If your site contains content information, be on the lookout for any new developments in the field that should be included in your selection. New research or discoveries keep the site current and keep your audience motivated. As your class changes its thematic concentration, change your page to fit its studies. Any other timely data, such as announcements of upcoming events or homework calendars, must be kept up-to-date for the site to be fully functional.

Improve Your Site

As you browse through other websites, you may notice design features or instructional sequences that might add to your site's functionality or appearance. Do not be

School Stories

The fifth-graders from Mrs. Tabor's class are settling in on the floor next to their first-grade "buddies" in Miss Gomez's room. For five weeks, each of the classes has been studying "Habitats," both with age-appropriate assignments in their own rooms and integrated projects together. They are now preparing to go on their field trip to the museum next week. Mrs. Tabor and Miss Gomez have decided that a great way to share their trip experience with the other classes at school, as well as with the students' families, would be by putting up a website detailing what they have learned and what they see at the museum. They plan on taking the digital camera on the trip, so any pictures they take on the trip can be automatically inserted into the web page.

Prior to meeting together, each of the two classes separately has already brainstormed long lists of what they have learned so far in this habitat unit. Now, the two classes sit looking at both charts of data, ready to make some decisions on what they want to include in their website. The teachers lead the discussion, with students from both classes offering their ideas. Finally, through much discussion, a list of core learnings is decided on.

Now comes the job of designing their site. Using a projection system with her classroom computer, Miss Gomez shows several different websites she has found that are useful in pointing out to students layout features and color combinations. The classes talk about what types of pictures they will be able to use and how to best showcase student writing. Working with their buddies, the students then sketch out on chart paper their ideas for how their website might be arranged. It is too large of a job to finish in one sitting, but over the next couple of days before the field trip, the classes compare all of the proposed page designs to decide on a final layout. It is also decided that each student will contribute some of his or her writing for the project, and several students have artwork on habitats that will be scanned in using the scanner down in the media center.

Back in their own classroom following the field trip, the fifth-graders learn how to use an HTML editing program. Together with Mrs. Tabor, they make a class practice website to get the feel for how to use the program. Over the next several weeks, the fifth-grade students bring their first-grade buddies in to work on converting their writing to HTML and laying out their individual pages. When the website is finished, the two classes have a dynamic record of their trip and all that they have learned that can be viewed and used by other classes and even parents at home.

afraid to make changes, either subtle or drastic. Just because you liked that lime-green background when you originally designed the site does not mean it still serves your purposes today. Any good instruction must be flexible enough to accommodate new ideas. Changing the look and feel of your site will keep it fresh and keep regular visitors coming back.

Summary

Once teachers are familiar with integrating online resources into traditional instructional modes, they are ready to try exploring how to design web-based instruction. Planning ahead of time will ensure a site that serves your intended purpose for your anticipated audience. Sketching out a storyboard will help to visualize what the website will look like and how it will be organized.

Web documents are created using HTML code that gives directions to the web browser for how to display the page to the viewer. New software advances make it possible for users to create web pages without knowing HTML. Web editing software, productivity software, online web editors, and course management tools provide a range of features to develop online materials.

Completed websites must be maintained to ensure they remain quality learning and information tools. On a regular basis, inspect your site for accuracy and functionality. Replace outdated facts or linked sites and determine whether improvements are needed.

Challenge Yourself!

1. Create a simple storyboard of a lesson that incorporates at least two thematic online resources.
2. What schools in your area offer courses through distance education? Are there single courses available, and can entire degrees be completed from a distance?
3. Set up an account on a website that offers online web editing tools and free web-page hosting, such as Yahoo! GeoCities at **http://geocities.yahoo.com/home** or Filamentality at **www.kn.pacbell.com/wired/fil**.
4. Using an actual newsletter that a classroom teacher has sent home in printed form as a template, create an electronic newsletter website.
5. Find a classroom homepage on the World Wide Web. What types of items are included? How well is it organized? Is there quality instruction or mainly just informational items?
6. Find an educational website. Have two students from your level of interest go through the website following all of the instructions that are given. Record their progress and their comments. What improvements do you think would be warranted based on their results? What improvements do they suggest?
7. Survey a group of parents to see how many would make use of an informational class website if their children's classes had one available. Do this group's responses seem to fit with the impression the media give of parents' attitudes toward technology integration in the schools?
8. Familiarize yourself with your school's or district's adopted web software and procedures for web-page hosting.
9. Find out the procedures at your school for saving web documents to a web server.

10. Research what the experts recommend when designing web-based instruction. What considerations make for good instruction across grade levels and topics? What specific attributes are relevant to your chosen level or area?

References

Barkhouse, N. (1997). Grasping the thread: Web page development in the elementary classroom. *Emergency Librarian, 24*(3), 24–25.

Berge, A. Z., & Collins, M. P. (Eds.). (1995). *Computer mediated communication and the online classroom* (Vol. 3). Cresskill, NJ: Hampton Press.

Blair, J. (2002). *The virtual teaching life.* Retrieved February 11, 2003, from www.edweek.org/sreports/tc02/article.cfm?slug=35virtual.h21.

Burgstahler, S. (1997). Teaching on the Net: What's the difference? *T.H.E. Journal, 24*(9), 61–64.

Cafolla, R., & Knee, R. (1996). Creating World Wide Web sites. *Learning and Leading with Technology, 24*(3), 6–9.

Cafolla, R., & Knee, R. (1996–1997). Creating World Wide Web sites. Part 2: Implementing your site. *Learning and Leading with Technology, 24*(4), 36–39.

Cafolla, R., & Knee, R. (1997). Creating educational Web sites. Part 3: Refining and maintaining the site. *Learning and Leading with Technology, 24*(5), 13–16.

Descy, D. E. (1997a). Web page design. Part one. *TechTrends, 42*(1), 3–5.

Descy, D. E. (1997b). Web page design. Part two. *TechTrends, 42*(2), 3–5.

Descy, D. E. (1997c). Web page design. Part three. *TechTrends, 42*(3), 7–9.

Dodge, B. (1995). *Some thoughts about WebQuests.* Retrieved January 27, 2004, from http://edweb.sdsu.edu/courses/edtec596/about_webquests.html.

Doherty, K. M. (2002). *Students speak out.* Retrieved February 11, 2003, from www.edweek.org/sreports/tc02/article.cfm?slug=35florida.h21.

E-Defining education. (2002). Retrieved February 11, 2003, from www.edweek.org/sreports/tc02/article.cfm?slug=35execsum.h21.

Harris, J. (1997). Content and intent shape function: Designs for web-based educational telecomputing activities. *Learning and Leading with Technology, 24*(5), 17–20.

Hill, J. R., Tharp, D., Sindt, K., Jennings, M., & Tharp, M. (1997). Collaborative web site design from a distance: Challenges and rewards. *TechTrends, 42*(2), 31–37.

Lewis, J., Whitaker, J., & Julian, J. (1995). Distance education for the 21st century: The future of national and international telecomputing networks in distance education. In A. Z. Berge & M. P. Collins (Eds.), *Computer related communication and the online classroom* (Vol. 3, pp. 13–30). Cresskill, NJ: Hampton Press.

Mason, R. (1994). *Using communications media in open and flexible learning.* London: Korgan Page.

Monahan, B., & Tomko, S. (1996). How schools can create their own web pages. *Educational Leadership, 54*(3), 37–38.

Quinlan, L. A. (1997). Crafting a web-based lesson. Part two: Organizing the information and constructing the page. *TechTrends, 42*(1), 6–8.

Richardson, E. C. (1996). Site construction. *Internet World, 7*(4), 62–64, 66.

Russell, T. L. (1999). *The no significance difference phenomenon* (5th ed.). Raleigh, NC: North Carolina State University.

Tennant, R. (1997). Web sites by design: How to avoid a "pile of pages." *Syllabus, 11*(1), 49–50.

Trotter, A. (2002). *E-Learning goes to school*. Retrieved February 11, 2003, from www.edweek.org/sreports/tc02.

Web Accessibility Initiative. (1999). *Web content accessibility guidelines 1.0*. Retrieved June 16, 2003, from www.w3.org/TR/WCAG10/#content-structure.

CHAPTER 10

Technology Integration in the Content Area Including Multidisciplinary Units

1. How can teachers use technology in the content areas?

2. What factors must the teacher consider when planning to integrate technology?

3. What are the benefits of using technology across disciplines?

Chapter 1 presented profiles of technology-literate teachers and students. Of course, it is ideal when students are introduced to computer literacy topics and learning technologies in their earliest school experiences. The knowledge they gain then serves as a foundation for continued technology-based learning through high school and even into adulthood.

Perhaps the most important concept for students to grasp is that the computer is a powerful tool for getting work done. When computers are used across the curriculum, students begin to appreciate the vast range of tasks that computer power can accomplish. The computer no longer appears to be a technological enigma that can be understood only by science and math wizards. Students come to view the computer as a manageable and multifaceted tool for writing essays and stories, performing sociological and scientific research, solving mathematical problems, and learning more about any subject they wish to study.

Teachers of all content areas can foster this attitude in their students by designing instruction that integrates technology as a tool for learning rather than relying on technology as a delivery mechanism. This presents quite a challenge to teachers who are themselves novice technology integrators or who specialize in subjects that are not traditionally associated with technology-based learning activities. Remember, the emphasis is not on learning a software application such as PowerPoint, but on how to use the technology to solve problems. This chapter presents sample learning activities for five major content areas: mathematics, science, language arts, social studies, and special education. In addition four multidisciplinary lessons are outlined. It is our hope that teachers will use these activities as a springboard for their own creativity.

Formulating Learning Activities

Teachers will find that the process of designing learning activities that integrate technology is very similar to designing traditional lesson plans. Many of the same factors must be taken under consideration, whether students work with computers or with pencil and paper. In formulating learning activities, the teacher tries to answer a series of questions:

- For what ages or grade levels is this activity appropriate?
- What is the purpose of the activity?
- What will students know or be able to do after completing the activity? What materials are required to perform this activity?
- What preparation is required on the teacher's part? On the students' part? What knowledge, skills, and concepts are necessary for students to complete the activity successfully?
- What tasks are most effective in teaching the topic?
- How will student learning be assessed and at what points during the activity?
- What extensions might be useful in reinforcing or expanding knowledge gained through the activity?
- What comments will contribute to greater success of the activity?

Most teachers are accustomed to considering these factors in creating learning activities. There are additional factors that can make or break the technology-based learning experience. Other questions a teacher might address follow.

- How will my classroom change or adapt when I integrate technology?
- Which technology is best suited for meeting the learning purpose?
- How can technology be used to optimize learning?
- What aspect of the computer's capabilities make it the best tool to use? To a large extent, activities must be tailored according to the hardware and software resources available in the individual teacher's classroom, school, or district.
- How can an activity meet both curriculum standards and the National Educational Technology Standards for Students?
- What if there is limited access to the technology? Do students have access to computers in the classroom so that the only person controlling the amount of computer time is the classroom teacher?
- If so, how many computers are available?

- Can the entire class participate in the activity at the same time or will students need to work in shifts?
- Will students work individually, in pairs, or in larger groups?
- If computers are available in a central setting such as the media center, what constraints are placed on computer time for students?
- Will students work during normal class hours or will they schedule computer time outside of normal class hours?

These factors will determine how practical a given activity is for a particular class.

Most educational software is on CD-ROM. Usually, these programs are hybrid versions, meaning that the CD will run on a Macintosh or PC computer. Be sure to read machine requirements carefully before attempting to run the software on your computer. In addition, be sure to read the readme file; specific steps often are required to have the software sound, video, and printing work properly. One final note: Burning a backup copy of the CD is recommended as a safety precaution in case the original CD is lost or damaged.

The same precaution applies to software that requires students to store their work on disks. Have students save their work twice: first on their own disk and second to a shared network folder. Make it a habit to back up the shared network folder on a portable medium such as a zip disk or CD.

All the learning activities presented here have been designed for flexible use. That is, they can be tailored easily to meet the special needs of an individual teacher or class. Teachers can simplify a complex activity for younger or less experienced students by providing or even inputting data before the activity begins. On the other hand, a relatively simple activity becomes more challenging if students are required to research and key in data on their own. Teachers can also customize the activity by changing the topic. For example, the learning activity for researching scientists is also useful for researching writers, historical figures, athletes, and so forth.

Another feature of the learning activities in this chapter is that they are uniform in format following ISTE's *National Educational Technology Standards for Students: Connecting Curriculum and Technology* (2000). It is recommended that teachers decide on a standard format for designing learning activities. Doing so makes it easier to share learning activities with other teachers who want to integrate technology in their own classrooms.

The format of the learning activities incorporates the following subheads.

Activity Title: *Title of the Activity*

Grade-Level Range.   This is an indicator of the age or grade level for which the activity is considered appropriate. It should be used as a guideline only, not as a hard and fast rule. The level of difficulty of the activities can be adjusted for different grade levels or even different ability levels within the same class. Gifted students and those with prior computer experience will probably be quite successful with activities aimed at higher grade levels.

Purpose.   A simply stated goal or set of goals that the lesson should accomplish.

Description.   A summary of what students will do. Of course, in a very real sense, all technology-based lessons share an important objective: to help students become comfortable and competent in using technology as a tool.

Activity Preparation.   This section lists the preparation required before the activity is undertaken. The teacher needs to determine whether sufficient access to technology and learning resources exists to carry out the activity.

- Do computers have enough memory to run the learning technology?
- Is the software or digital media readily available, or must they be ordered externally?
- Does the activity require tools and resources such as textbooks, web pages, guest speakers, and so on? A critical consideration under this category is whether there is an available source of data that students will need to complete the activity.
- Do students have network access to a database, or will they be required to do library research before beginning computer work?

Activity Procedure.   This section is a step-by-step description of the activity in which students will participate. Sometimes the activity does not require hands-on work on the computer but instead calls for collaboration, research, discussion, and other activities that are part of the learning experience.

Tools and Resources.   Lists the identified software, hardware, websites, and other materials needed to support the learning activity.

Assessment.   This section presents ideas for assessing student learning.

Comments.   Provides additional information pertinent to the success of the activity or suggestions for varying the activity for use in another content area or with a different group or level of students. In addition, you may want to include special comments or notes that indicate potential problems and solutions.

Under each of the five content areas included—mathematics, science, language arts, social studies, and special education—two activities are given. The first is recommended for elementary classes, the second for secondary classes. Again, the teacher can adjust the level of difficulty of the activity to classroom needs. In some instances, commercial software has been identified, but alternatives have also been listed whenever possible.

Learning Activities for Mathematics

Because of its number-crunching ability, the computer is an excellent tool for use in teaching mathematics. Much of the educational software on the market today was written to teach mathematical principles. For that reason, the classroom teacher should have little difficulty in locating effective math packages. The activities in this section enable the teacher to use applications software—spreadsheet—to solve mathematical problems in much the same way a businessperson uses a spreadsheet to make predictions and plans.

Activity Title: *Avery's Skateboard*

Grade-Level Range: 3 to 6

Purpose.   In this activity students

- Explore a range of estimation strategies
- Problem solve with a spreadsheet application
- Create formulas to solve a linear equation
- Show different ways spreadsheets can be used
- Address the following National Educational Technology Standards (NETS) for Students Standards: 3—Technology productivity tools; 4—Technology communication tools; and 6—Technology problem-solving and decision-making tools

Description.   Students apply what they know about a spreadsheet application to solve a mathematical problem. Students use a spreadsheet to structure their problem-solution thinking. Students explore new uses for spreadsheets.

Activity Preparation

- Develop formulas for solving the problem.
- Create spreadsheet template.
- Gather examples of problem solving with spreadsheets.
- Prepare a handout with a clear statement of the problem.
- Invite a parent who is an accountant to talk to the class about his or her career and how he or she uses technology to solve problems.

Activity Procedure

1. As a class, review and discuss the spreadsheet concepts of row, column, and cell.
2. Have the invited speaker introduce the descriptive language appropriate to the problem and related to accounting: words and terms such as *cost, save, buy, spend, debit,* and *credit.* Speaker presents a sample problem from work and demonstrates how he or she thinks through a problem and the tools he or she uses.
3. Introduce the problem students will be working on:
   - Each week Avery receives an allowance of $5.
   - Avery wants to save part of her allowance to buy a skateboard, which will cost $60. She also wants to spend part of her allowance on candy and part on video games, which cost 25 cent a game.

- If Avery plays six video games each week and spends $1 for candy, how many weeks will she have to save in order to buy her skateboard?
- How many weeks if she stops buying candy and plays four video games each week?

4. As a class, discuss different computational tools (calculator, paper-and-pencil algorithm, or mental strategy) that could be used.
5. Working in groups of three or four, students estimate a solution set. Encourage them to explain their thinking frequently as they estimate.
6. Groups share with the whole class their computational estimation strategies.
7. Using a spreadsheet, small groups of students format the worksheet and input the problem data and formulas. Check their skills and understanding of how a spreadsheet works as they are doing the activity. Have your template ready for students who need assistance.
8. Groups share their spreadsheets with the whole class. Encourage them to explain their thinking as they present their findings and the formulas they used.
9. Compare and contrast their spreadsheet strategies with their estimation strategies.
10. Ask each student to create a similar problem and spreadsheet solution.
11. Students email the problem to another student and arrange a chat time to discuss the solution.
12. As a class, discuss alternative uses for spreadsheets. Share an example you found on the Internet and the search strategy you used. Ask students to find examples by asking their families and searching the Internet.
13. Keep a visible record of students' spreadsheet examples.

Tools and Resources

Software
- Spreadsheet, presentation

Websites
- Spreadsheets in the Math Class
  www.math.byu.edu/~lfrancis/readings302/Spreadsheets.html
- Spreadsheets for Images
  http://graphics.stanford.edu/papers/spreadsheets

Other
- Presentation equipment to display students' spreadsheets to the whole class (large-screen monitor, LCD panel, or classroom television connected to a computer)

Assessment.   Observe students working in groups and individually. Keep anecdotal notes on students explaining their thinking. Evaluate students on their ability to use spreadsheets, determine and explain solutions, and discuss alternative estimation strategies.

Comments.   An interesting variation of this lesson is to divide the class into two groups. One group will use the spreadsheet to solve the problem while the other group uses pencil and paper. This helps students appreciate the tremendous speed at which computers can perform mathematical calculations.

Activity Title: *Slippery Oil Prices*

Grade-Level Range: 7 to 12

Purpose.   In this activity students

- Use a variety of resources to gather information
- Use spreadsheets to organize data
- Explore data for patterns
- Represent data using graphs
- Make predictions of a future trend based on oil price data
- Discuss and defend their predictions with other students
- Address the following National Educational Technology Standards (NETS) for Students Standards: 3—Technology productivity tools; 4—Technology communication tools; 5—Technology research tools; and 6—Technology problem-solving and decision-making tools

Description.   Students access current information on oil prices from a variety of print and media sources including the Internet. Students enter the data into a spreadsheet and use the chart tool to graph the data. They then examine the graphs for patterns in oil prices and extrapolate the data to make predictions. Student groups present their predictions to the class using multimedia authoring software.

Activity Preparation

- Students need to be familiar with basic operations of a spreadsheet package.
- Invite a guest speaker to explain how he or she uses spreadsheet as a prediction and decision-making tool in his or her career field.
- Create a website with a History of the Spreadsheet time line and links to spreadsheet and data analysis tutorials.
- Create an email list of experts willing to answer questions and discuss students' findings.
- Develop a data collection worksheet.

Activity Procedure

1. As a review, introduce the activity with an historical overview of the spreadsheet from its invention in the 1970s as an accounting tool to its continually expanding applications as a prediction instrument and decision-making tool.
2. As a class, discuss the wide range of current uses of the spreadsheet in business, government, and research. Make connections to other curriculum areas as well.
3. Have the invited speaker explain how he or she uses a spreadsheet in business, government, or research.

4. Introduce the task with a discussion about trends and graphs. Invite the speaker to participate in the discussion.
5. Working in groups of three or four, students collect data about oil prices from the media center (library) and online resources on the Internet.
6. Groups share with the whole class the data and sources they have found.
7. Discuss the pattern of oil prices for a six-month period.
8. Students record their data findings on a spreadsheet.
9. Students research the pattern of oil prices for a prescribed period of time (e.g., six months, one year, five years). Using the spreadsheet's chart tool, students represent data in a variety of graphs.
10. Students assess the trend in oil prices.
11. Working in groups of three or four, students share their graphs and discuss possible reasons for patterns they detect. Encourage students to explain their reasoning. Groups email a question or a brief presentation of their analysis with a graph to an expert for feedback.
12. Students use the spreadsheet to predict future oil prices for a prescribed period of time and speculate how this trend might affect gasoline prices. Using the results, students generate line graphs of the pricing trend and write a prediction rationale.
13. Working in groups of three or four, students share and discuss their predictions and graphs.
14. Groups synthesize their findings to create a group prediction, rationale, and graph. Groups create a multimedia presentation for the class using software such as PowerPoint or HyperStudio, presenting their future trend and the rationale for their prediction.
15. As a class, discuss possible uses of the spreadsheet as a prediction and decision-making tool.

Tools and Resources

Software
- Spreadsheet, graphics, presentation, or multimedia authoring (PowerPoint, Hyper-Studio)

Websites
- Statistics—The Facts and Figures of Oil and Gas
  www.api-ec.api.org/newsplashpage/index.cfm
- Collection of PowerPoint slides by Jamie MacKenzie that identifies the trends in future supplies and consumption patterns of crude oil
  www.igc.org/wri/powerpoints/oil/index.htm
- Crude Oil and Natural Gas Prices
  www.bloomberg.com/energy
- Oil Price History and Analysis
  www.wtrg.com/prices.htm
- WTRG Economics
  www.wtrg.com/index.html

- Smithsonian Institution
  www.smithsonianeducation.org

Other
- Presentation equipment to display students' presentations and graphics to the whole class (large-screen monitor, LCD panel, or classroom television connected to a computer)
- Printer for generating hard copies of student graphs and charts
- Data collection worksheet

Assessment.   Evaluate students on their ability to graph data, explain and defend their predictions, and work productively in a group. Develop a rubric with students for scoring the independent spreadsheets and predictions and the group presentations.

Comments.   A WWW search can provide students with more information regarding oil sources that can be built into a spreadsheet file. This lesson can be adapted for a class in geography, political science, or economics as part of a study of major oil-producing nations.

Learning Activities for Science

There are many applications of technology in the science laboratory and classroom. In fact, some of our most innovative technological developments have come from computers that were designed for scientific applications. Therefore, it is appropriate that science teachers demonstrate to their students what a powerful tool the computer can be in furthering scientific investigation.

Activity Title: *The Weather Report*

Grade-Level Range: 2 to 5

Purpose.   In this activity students

- Plan and conduct a simple investigation
- Apply their understanding of data collection
- Generate bar graphs and pie charts
- Gather and analyze information
- Observe differences in weather conditions for different geographical locations
- Share their results with peers
- Address the following National Educational Technology Standards (NETS) for Students Standards: 3—Technology productivity tools and 5—Technology research tools

Description.   Students collect data on weather conditions. They observe, graph, and write about local weather for a month. Small groups synthesize their findings to demonstrate the relationship between weather and geographical location. Groups share their projects by creating a multimedia presentation.

Activity Preparation

- Students need to be familiar with the process of generating bar graphs or pie charts.
- Students understand the rudiments of systematic collection of data.
- Prepare a student worksheet listing the types of weather to be observed (sunshine, rain, clouds, snow, wind, and so on) and the days of the month during which weather will be observed.
- Gather resources (books, maps, CDs, weather videos, Internet sites). Invite a local climatologist to present and discuss weather concepts. Create a large outline of your state map. Create symbols for different types of weather (sunshine, rain, clouds, snow, wind, etc.) and different types of geographic features (mountains, lake, valley, river, grassland, plain, delta, desert, cape, rain forest, etc.).

Activity Procedure

1. Introduce the activity by placing a marker on a large state map indicating where the students live. Ask students to identify other cities or towns in the state. Hand out the weather worksheets and explain the project.
2. Begin each class by reminding students to observe the weather and record the data on their worksheets. Have a student select the appropriate weather symbol for the day and place it on the map.
3. Assign students to groups with three or four members, divided according to different state regions. On a weekly basis, have the groups locate weather sources to collect data on their assigned regions.
4. Encourage students to record weekend weather conditions at home and add these data to their worksheets as well.
5. Have students collect data for a prescribed period of time (e.g., one month).
6. After students complete data worksheets, assist them in entering the data into a graphing program as the basis for a pie chart or bar graph showing the number of sunny, rainy, cloudy, snowy, and windy days during the month.
7. Display students' graphs on a bulletin board for easy comparison.
8. Have each group complete its group worksheets and enter the data into a graphing program to create a pie chart or bar graph. Display group graphs.
9. As a class, discuss geographical differences of the state regions. Use Internet resources to locate landscape pictures. Have students place the appropriate geographic symbols on the state map.
10. Working in their region group, students discuss the differences between the region and local graphs and why they are different. Have each group reach a conclusion about the weather patterns for the month and prepare a short presentation for the class.
11. Following group presentations, discuss the conclusions and trends. Use weather sites on the Internet to show national and global weather patterns. Dis-

cuss how climatologists use computers to gather, calculate, and display weather data. Ask students to write a general description about weather patterns they observed.

12. Invite a local climatologist to speak to the class and bring samples of computer-generated displays of weather data.

13. Encourage students to continue collecting data over a longer period of time so that their body of data is larger. Have them select a city in another country to observe its weather pattern. The Internet is an excellent source for up-to-date information for class projects and research.

Tools and Resources

Software
- Graphics (or enter data into a spreadsheet and use the chart tool), presentation

Websites
- National Climatic Data Center
  www.ncdc.noaa.gov
- Climate Prediction Center
  www.cpc.ncep.noaa.gov
- National Weather Service Homepage
  www.nws.noaa.gov
- Weather Learning Resources
  www.exploratorium.edu/ti/resources/weather.html
- Weather Channel's website
  www.weather.com/homepage.html
- University of Michigan's Weather Cams
  http://cirrus.sprl.umich.edu/wxnet/wxcam.html
- Weather: What Forces Affect Our Weather?
  www.learner.org/exhibits/weather
- Smithsonian Institution
  www.smithsonianeducation.org

Other
- Presentation equipment to display students' graphics to the whole class (large-screen monitor, LCD panel, or classroom television connected to a computer)
- Printer for generating hard copies of student graphs and charts
- Data collection worksheet

Assessment.   Compare the students' graphs. Compare the group graphs. Are they similar? What accounts for differences between graphs? Use a rubric to score individual graphs, data collection worksheets, writing assignments, and group presentations and graphs.

Comments.   Older students may enjoy trying to predict the weather. Have students contact a website of your region of the National Weather Service for normal and record-setting weather conditions in your area within the past year. Students can use data to make weather predictions and then observe the actual weather to determine the reliability of their predictions. Check with your local television station for possible software. Using a weather radio and an LCD panel will allow students opportunities to be classroom meteorologists and give weather reports just like on television.

Activity Title: *Who's Who in Science*

Grade-Level Range: 6 to 12

Purpose.   In this activity students

- Explore individual contributions to the scientific field
- Gather and summarize information
- Apply their understanding of databases
- Address the following National Educational Technology Standards (NETS) for Students Standards: 2—Social, ethical, and human issues; 3—Technology productivity tools; 4—Technology communications tools; and 5—Technology research tools

Description.   Students collect information about a scientist using different types of resources. Students use a database to store and organize information about scientists. Students share with peers their information by creating a multimedia presentation. Students discuss the relationships among scientists and illustrate these relationships by creating a concept map and time line.

Activity Preparation

- Students are familiar with basic operations of database software.
- Vocabulary terms that must be presented are *template, record, field,* and *key.*
- With younger students, teachers may want to design a template including fields such as
  - Name
  - Nationality
  - Science field
  - Born
  - Died
  - Contribution
- Older students can benefit from designing their own templates; this will give them experience in naming fields and designating keys.

Activity Procedure

1. Have students research the library and the Internet for biographies of scientists.
2. Students should keep note cards with pertinent information to be keyed into the database later.

3. After records have been keyed in, students can access the database to share information they have uncovered or create trivia games.
4. Have students create brief multimedia presentations on the scientists they have researched.
5. As a class, discuss the relationships among scientists. Is there evidence that some of the scientists were influenced by others?
6. Using a concept-mapping tool such as Inspiration, create a concept map using terms from the contribution category.

Tools and Resources

Software
- Database, presentation, graphics, concept mapping (Inspiration)

Websites
- Internet History of Science Sourcebook
  www.fordham.edu/halsall/science/sciencesbook.html
- Women and Minorities in Science and Engineering
  www.mills.edu/ACAD_INFO/MCS/SPERTUS/Gender/wom_and_min.html
- A Science Odyssey **www.pbs.org/wgbh/aso** (especially the section on People,
  www.pbs.org/wgbh/aso/databank/bioindex.html)

Other
- Presentation equipment to display students' spreadsheets to the whole class (large-screen monitor, LCD panel, or classroom television connected to a computer)

Assessment.   How many records are contained in the database? By which keys can records be retrieved? Do students understand the sorting capabilities of the database? Score the project with rubric. The rubric can reflect not only the multimedia presentation and database competency but also the research methods used to search, collect, and organize information.

Comments.   Students may wish to make use of the database to generate a time line that illustrates the scientists' contributions as well as other major events.

Learning Activities for Language Arts

There may have been a time when teachers of language arts thought that the computer had nothing to offer their students. Fortunately, this is no longer the case. Many teachers and students have discovered that the computer is a wonderfully patient tutor of reading and writing skills. There is an abundance of word processing and desktop publishing software programs on the market for students of all ages. In addition, there are programs that assist with spelling, grammar, and word choice.

Activity Title: *Write a Story*

Grade-Level Range: PreK to 5

Purpose.   In this activity students

- Work cooperatively with others to produce a storybook
- Demonstrate their knowledge of short story elements
- Express their ideas using a variety of media and technological tools
- Address the following National Educational Technology Standards (NETS) for Students Standards: 1—Basic operations and concepts; 2—Social, ethical, and human issues; 3—Technology productivity tools; and 4—Technology communications tools

Description.   Students use basic functions of a word processing package or writing software program such as Pajama Sam's One-Stop Fun Shop to create a short story.

Activity Preparation

- Format a disk and create a document file with a story title.
- Students have had some practice with typing on a keyboard.
- Students understand the basic elements of a short story plot, setting, and characters.

Activity Procedure

1. Introduce the activity by reading a short story aloud and reviewing its basic elements.
2. Explain the short story writing project to the class.
3. To demonstrate the process, write a class story. Begin the story by typing the first sentence or simply an introductory phrase such as "Once upon a time. . . ."
4. After that, each student will add a sentence of his or her own.
5. Once all students have had an opportunity to add a sentence to the story, have everyone read aloud and in unison the finished story.
6. Students print the story (one to two sentences per page) and illustrate their sentence contribution. Have them take the story home to share with family members.
7. Discuss cooperating with others and sharing ideas.
8. Divide students into teams of three. Have them create a short story and illustrate it using a word processing, slide-show presentation, or story writing program.
9. Teams share their stories with the class.

Tools and Resources

Software
- Word processing, graphics, presentation, Pajama Sam's One-Stop Fun Shop, Kid-Pix Studio, Easy Book, Kid Works Deluxe

Other

- Presentation equipment to display students' stories to the whole class (large-screen monitor, LCD panel, or classroom television connected to a computer)

Assessment. Were students able to formulate and type in original sentences? Were they interested in the story? Did the story have basic elements such as plot, setting, and characters? Assess students on their ability to work cooperatively with others and their contribution to the short story. Before the project, develop a rubric with the students that addresses state writing standards and short story elements.

Comments. With very young children, it might be a good idea to provide illustrations that spark ideas and lend a coherent plot to the story. An interesting variation of this lesson is for the teacher to create a form in which students can fill in their own names and other information to create a story about themselves. Most major software companies have specific writing software programs that allow students to write and illustrate their own storybooks. The Key Caps accessory allows for foreign-language stories. Some programs are also available in a second language. Students should be encouraged to decorate their book covers further with their own artwork. This lends color and creativity to the book. Giant George and Ruby Robot, BIG and Little (Sunburst Communications) requires a Muppet Slate but also allows students to create and design various publications of differing sizes up to 5 feet tall. Clifford's Big Book Publisher (Scholastic New Media) provides graphics, clip art, and fonts for younger students to write their own big books. Other related programs are Print Shop Deluxe (Broderbund), Hyperstudio (Roger Wagner Publishing), Kids Works Deluxe (Davidson & Associates, Inc.), My Own Stories (The Learning Company), Children's Writing and Publishing Center (The Learning Company), and The Multimedia Workshop (Davidson & Associates, Inc.).

Activity Title: *Research Notes*

Grade-Level Range: 6 to 12

Purpose. In this activity students

- Conduct research on a topic
- Demonstrate their knowledge of search strategies
- Apply their understanding of databases
- Address the following National Educational Technology Standards (NETS) for Students Standards: 1—Basic operations and concepts; 2—Social, ethical, and human issues; 3—Technology productivity tools; and 5—Technology research tools

Description. Students use a database to store and organize research notes and format a bibliography.

Activity Preparation

- Students are familiar with basic operations and applications of databases.
- Students are familiar with the terms *template, record, field,* and *key.*
- Middle school teachers may want to design a database template including the following fields:
  - Author
  - Title
  - Publisher
  - City of publication
  - Year of publication
  - Topic(s)
  - Notes
- High school students may benefit from designing a template of their own and designating keys such as author, title, and topic.

Activity Procedure

1. Working with a common topic or with individual topics, students research the topics using library and Internet resources.
2. Students should keep note cards or word processing files with information to be keyed into the database. After all the records are keyed in, students can retrieve information or print listings of it.
3. Depending on the report formatting capabilities of the database, students format bibliographies with correct placement and punctuation of information.
4. Students use a standard style sheet to format their bibliographies.
5. Have students work in small editing groups to proofread and revise their bibliographies.
6. Discuss other ways databases simplify the research process; for example, allowing direct access to up-to-the-minute information.
7. Explore ways in which the computer is likely to change the way we do research. Discuss the advantages of formatting various reports of the same data for different purposes.

Tools and Resources

Software
- Database, presentation

Websites
- Electronic Reference Formats Recommended by the American Psychological Association
  www.apastyle.org/elecref.html
- Modern Language Association
  www.mla.org
- A Guide for Writing Research Papers Based on Modern Language Association (MLA) Documentation
  http://webster.commnet.edu/mla.htm

- Using Modern Language Association (MLA) Format
  http://owl.english.purdue.edu/handouts/research/r_mla.html
- Research Papers
  http://owl.english.purdue.edu/handouts/research/index.html
- Network Bibliography (Example of database bibliography)
  www.cs.columbia.edu/~hgs/netbib

Other
- Presentation equipment to display students' bibliographies to the whole class (large-screen monitor, LCD panel, or classroom television connected to a computer)
- Printer and bibliography style sheet such as the MLA's *Handbook for Writers of Theses and Dissertations*

Assessment.   Check the bibliographies for correctness and style. What have students learned about the process of research and the use of the computer to expedite research? How did students evaluate resources?

Comments.   This lesson can be used as an effective prelude to writing a research paper because students have created a working bibliography while completing the lesson. The WWW has access to most writing guidelines as well as step-by-step approaches for writing papers with projected time lines.

Learning Activities for Social Studies

Disciplines within the social studies area have benefited greatly from computer applications such as database and spreadsheet. Especially in fields such as psychology and sociology, in which large bodies of statistical data contribute to a greater understanding of human behavior, the computer has made life easier for both teachers and students. Simulation programs can bring history to life by placing students in the midst of historical situations. Social studies teachers can choose from a wide range of computer applications to challenge their students.

Activity Title: *You Want to Sell Me What? The Many Forms of Advertising*

Grade-Level Range: 3 to 5

Purpose.   Through this learning activity, students

- Understand advertising and the role it plays in the marketplace
- Discover the ways in which the attributes of various media contribute to the effectiveness of advertising for a particular audience
- Become discriminating consumers of advertising strategies
- Address the following National Educational Technology Standards (NETS) for Students Standards: 3—Technology productivity tools; 4—Technology communication tools; 5—Technology research tools; and 6—Technology problem-solving and decision-making tools

Description.   This learning activity takes place over an extended period of time and explores the purpose of advertising media. As a class, students examine advertisements using focus questions to determine their attributes, audience, and influences. In small groups organized by media type, students use focus questions to research a specific media type. Groups then present their findings to the whole class using presentation software. Small groups meet again to design and produce an advertisement in their researched medium. They also conduct a market analysis, including the cost of placing their ad. Finally, they present their ad to the whole class using the focus questions for discussion.

Activity Preparation

- Gather samples of advertisements in various media forms: newspapers, magazines, radio and television recordings, and websites.
- Preview relevant media-related websites. Assemble and troubleshoot necessary technology tools (see Tools and Resources).
- Schedule a guest speaker who either is involved in advertising or uses advertising extensively to promote his or her business.
- Schedule adult helpers or cross-age tutors to assist younger children with group activities.

Activity Procedure

1. As a class, discuss the purposes of advertising.
   - How do advertisements influence the way you act on needs and wants?
   - How do fact and opinion play a part in advertising?
2. As a class, study one advertisement from at least three media types (choose from newspaper, magazine, radio, television, and the web). Discuss the following focus questions:
   - How does the ad make you feel?
   - Were you persuaded to buy the product?
   - What do you think the purpose of the ad is?
   - Who do you think is the target audience?
   - What ad components were effective?
   - Was this a product that you need or that you want?
   - Why is this medium effective for this particular ad?
3. In small groups, students research advertisements found in various types of media. Each group works with one of the following: newspaper, magazine, radio, television, or the web.
4. Each group chooses a representative advertisement in its medium and discusses the attributes of the ad, using the list of focus questions.
5. Using presentation software, each group presents the results of its analysis to the class. As a class, discuss the similarities and differences among the media types, and their perceived strengths and weaknesses. Determine why a particular media type was used for a particular target audience.

6. Small groups meet again to design advertisements for a product of their choice, for the media they have been working with. The group chooses a particular audience to which it will advertise the product, focusing on how consumers in this particular group can best be reached by the attributes of this medium.

7. Small groups perform market research on their advertisements by soliciting opinions from their peers in a focus group setting. (Creating research questions that can be numerically analyzed is a valuable mathematics task.) How students ask questions about the product will define how the results are reported. (Use a rating scale? Comparison with other like products? Attributes of product? etc.) Market research begins by sharing ads with other groups in the class, other students at school, family members, or others in the local community. Students can then create graphs of their research results, using spreadsheet or graphing software.

8. After refining their advertisements, student groups use the web to find representative groups from their target audiences, experts in the advertising fields, and others with knowledge about their products. Students electronically send their advertisements to these groups for further comment.

9. Small groups investigate the cost of placing their advertisements in the media by contacting newspapers, magazines, and radio and television stations, or by researching the costs of advertising on the web. Discuss the impact of easy access to the web. Do a cost–benefit analysis comparing advertising costs with potential profits.

10. Small groups use electronic presentation software to present their final advertisements to the class, along with the results of their market research and cost-benefit analyses.

11. As a group, have the class reflect on the results of the small group work, discussing which media are most cost-effective for different audiences and purposes.

12. Further topics of discussion may include
    - Consumer spending habits of different population groups
    - How personal choices may affect the economy
    - How local advertisements compare with nationally run advertisements

Tools and Resources

Software
- Word processing, presentation, spreadsheet or graphing, video editing

Hardware
- Audiotape player, video camcorder

Websites
  Newspapers
- **www.denverpost.com**
- **www.nytimes.com**
- **www.latimes.com**

Magazines
- **www.time.com**
- **www.usnews.com/usnews/home.htm**
- **http://pathfinder.com/people**
- **www.zdnet.com**

Radio stations
- **www.web-radio.fm**

TV commercials
- **www.usatvads.com**
- **www.clipland.net/index_tvc.shtml**

Other
- Newspapers, magazines, recordings of radio and television advertisements, World Wide Web advertisements (found on almost any commercial website)

Assessment.   Develop a scoring rubric to evaluate each group advertisement. As the assignment develops, share the rubric with the class. Be sure to adjust the rubric based on appropriate student suggestions. Students use the rubric to evaluate their group advertisements. Give samples of advertisements in various media and have students discuss the ads in terms of the beginning focus questions.

Comments.   Many teachers have found that the combination of group and individual work in this learning activity works well in meeting the needs of all students. This is especially true for classrooms in which there are second-language learners. Nuances in the words used in advertising can be deceiving to second-language learners. The group work helps take care of finding the many grammatical and spelling errors that used to show up in final projects. The use of the new technology has made this project much more successful than when conventional tools were used. Students are always pleased with the professional-looking results.

Activity Title: *Career Decisions*

Grade-Level Range: 8 to 12

Purpose.   Through this learning activity, students

- Access multiple sources to a research topic
- Formulate a decision based on prioritizing strategies and data comparison
- Apply understanding of databases
- Address the following National Educational Technology Standards (NETS) for Students Standards: 3—Technology productivity tools; 4—Technology communication tools; 5—Technology research tools; and 6—Technology problem-solving and decision-making tools

Description.   Students make career decisions after researching several major U.S. cities.

Activity Preparation

- Students are familiar with basic database operations and terminology, particularly *template, record, field,* and *key.*
- Middle school teachers may want to design a template that includes fields such as
  - City
  - State
  - Population
  - Population under 35
  - Per capita income
  - Unemployment rate
  - Average temperature
  - Average rainfall
  - Number of colleges
  - Number of hospitals
  - Popular sports
  - Number of churches
- Older students can benefit from designing their own templates to include factors they consider important in making career decisions.

Activity Procedure

1. Tell the students to imagine that they have completed their education and are ready to enter their chosen career fields. They have received three job offers in three different cities. Before making decisions about which offers to accept, they are to conduct research about the three cities.
2. Either have the class choose three cities for research or have individual students select three cities that appeal to them.
3. Encourage students to select major cities so that current data will be readily available.
4. After students have conducted research on three cities, assist them in entering the data into the database. Students can then print a listing of their data for easy comparison.
5. After students have had an opportunity to review their listings, ask them to choose one of the job offers based on their findings.
6. Have them list the factors that most influenced their decisions and prepare brief presentations. Suggest that they use tables to show data comparisons.
7. Have students write essays explaining their decisions and the factors on which they are based.
8. Discuss the different factors people consider in relocating and how these factors are prioritized differently by different people.

Tools and Resources

Software
- Database, presentation

Websites
- USA City Information **www.pe.net/~rksnow**
- The USA CityLink Project **www.usacitylink.com**
- Maps **http://mapquest.com**
- Weather maps **www.weather.com/weather/maps**
- The Travel Site **www.randmcnally.com/rmc/home.jsp**
- Understanding the USA **www.understandingusa.com**
- Hoovers Online: The Business Network **www.hoovers.com**

Other
- Presentation equipment to display students' spreadsheets to the whole class (large-screen monitor, LCD panel, or classroom television connected to a computer)

Assessment.   Were the students able to locate all of the information called for in the database? Did the students suggest additional characteristics that could be included? Were students able to reach decisions with which they felt comfortable?

Comments.   The Carmen Sandiego series by Broderbund may be used to build a classroom database on countries, states, and cities. Several commercial software programs and some WWW sites provide maps as well as related information.

Learning Activities for Special Education

The computer is an extremely effective tool in the special education classroom because it is infinitely patient. Students can work at their own pace without feeling threatened or rushed. Also, the computer seems to motivate many students to repeat lessons and exercises, thereby reinforcing the knowledge they have gained. In effect, the computer provides the student with limitless individual attention that the special education teacher cannot always provide. Although there is limited educational software on the market that has been designed specifically for use in special education, most educational programs can be adapted to the unique needs of the special education classroom. It is especially easy to tailor educational software that includes authoring components so that the teacher may create questions or problems that relate specifically to the subject area under consideration. The lesson plans that follow present educational software that adapts well to use with exceptional students.

Activity Title: *Logic Builders*

Grade-Level Range: Because Logic Builders (Scholastic New Media) allows the student to choose from three levels of difficulty, the game can be adapted to a wide range of skill levels.

Purpose.   Through this learning activity, students

- Improve their ability to follow directions by re-creating spider webs according to computer-generated patterns
- Address the following National Educational Technology Standards (NETS) for Students Standards: 1—Basic operations and concepts; 2—Social, ethical, and human issues; and 4—Technology communication tools

Description.   Students use the software gaming program, Logic Builders, to create a graphic image.

Activity Preparation

- Students understand basic operations of the computer and have minimal typing skills.
- Teachers should be familiar with loading the programs and selecting the appropriate games from the main menu.

Activity Procedure

1. Students select DRAW A WEB from the main menu of Logic Builders. This game enables students to experiment with the process of drawing a spider web with the help of on-screen spiders.
2. Students play MATCH A WEB in which they are required to re-create a master design displayed on the right side of the screen.
3. Still more challenging is RECALL A WEB, which requires students to re-create the master web from memory. Students achieve high scores for re-creating webs in as few moves as possible.
4. As students earn points, they receive promotions to the level of Big Boss.
5. Have students share their thoughts about the game using a synchronous communication tool (CHAT program).

Tools and Resources

Software
- Logic Builders (Scholastic New Media), synchronous communication tool

Assessment.   The score maintained by the computer can be used as an indicator of student success in redrawing patterns. Do students select higher levels of challenge after gaining experience with the program? Do they demonstrate positive social and ethical behaviors when using technology?

Comments.   Factory (Sunburst), The Oregon Trail 2 (The Learning Company), Lego TC Logo (LCSI), Carmen Sandiego series (Broderbund), and the Sim series (Maxis) of programs are alternative software approaches to this lesson. Students can do screen captures to cut and paste their webs into a paint program to color them or even use them as screen savers.

Activity Title: *Recreation and Leisure*

Grade-Level Range: 8 to 12

Purpose. Through this learning activity, students

- Locate and participate in recreational and leisure activities in the community
- Address the following National Educational Technology Standards (NETS) for Students Standards: 1—Basic operations and concepts; 2—Social, ethical, and human issues; 3—Technology productivity tools; 4—Technology communication tools; and 5—Technology research tools

Description. Students use a database to store and organize their research findings.

Activity Preparation

- Students are familiar with databases and have minimal typing skills.
- Students are familiar with collecting data from the Internet.
- Design a template to include the following fields: Activity, Organization, Address, Cost, Services, Hours, and Eligibility.
- Develop a bookmark folder with local websites.
- Format a data disk in advance of the lesson.

Activity Procedure

1. Students create lists of recreational and leisure activities that they enjoy.
2. As a class, discuss what opportunities are available in the local community.
3. Students search online resources, contact public agencies, and conduct research to discover other leisure activities offered in the community.
4. After students have completed their research, have them key their data into the database. This is an excellent opportunity to teach students about retrieving and sorting records in the database.
5. Have students print a copy of their databases for a referral list.
6. Have students email friends, key pals, or relatives their listings of available community activities.

Tools and Resources

Software
- Database (ClarisWorks, Filemaker, Microsoft Access, Inc.)

Other
- Reference materials on local recreational and leisure activities

Assessment. Have students uncovered valuable information about leisure activities available to them? Are students able to enter and access their information quickly and easily? Do some of the students participate in any of the activities included in the database?

Comments. As an ongoing class project, ask students to bring in information about new activities, schedule changes, and so forth to keep the database up-to-date. Students who participate in community activities can report their experiences to the class. Have students plan a class trip using their database information. The previous lessons presented a number of suggestions for introducing students to common computer applications such as word processing, database, graphics, spreadsheet, as well as the Internet and educational software. Teachers can adapt learning technologies easily to fit into virtually all areas of the curriculum.

Multidisciplinary Units

The following lessons will demonstrate how technology can be integrated into multidisciplinary units. When creating multidisciplinary units that integrate technology, the teacher needs to consider the same factors as the previous content lesson plans. The availability and location of computer hardware certainly affect the way activities will be presented and whether students will work individually or in groups.

When using educational software, read the product's suggestions for maximizing the learning experience. It is a good idea to review these suggestions carefully before presenting activities.

Teachers may also benefit from talking with other teachers about their technology integration experiences. For example, teachers who have used educational software before can judge how much knowledge—both of computer usage and of the subject being presented—is required for the student to operate the program effectively. Are there bugs in the program that may hinder learning? Are some activities in the program more interesting, more useful, or more challenging to students than others? Experienced software users can answer these and other questions that the new user may have. Schools could build a resource bank of technology-based learning activities that includes teacher comments.

Planning is the key to integrating technology. For example, ordinary software may take several weeks to order and receive if it is not available at a local software or teaching supply store. Teachers may face limited choices if their districts have not set aside sufficient funds for the purchase of software. In some cases, it is possible to rent software for a short period of time at much less expense than the purchase price of the package. But rental also requires planning and lead time. Teachers are strongly urged to do some research of their own to see what other learning technologies are available for teaching all areas of the curriculum.

The sample multidisciplinary units follow the ISTE (Thomas & Bitter, 2000) *National Educational Technology Standards for Students: Connecting Curriculum and Technology* format for multidisciplinary resource units incorporating the following subheadings:

- Title of Unit
- Activities
- Tools and Resources

These units provide a powerful theme on which to build multidisciplinary learning activities. Each unit addresses content standards from two or more discipline areas as well as the National Educational Technology Standards for Students.

Multidisciplinary Unit for Primary Grades (PreK–2)

Title of Unit: *Helping Hands*

Helping Hands examines the theme of cooperation and community. This unit provides students with hands-on experience working with peers, family members, and other community members. Students learn how to work as a team and interact with others.

In this unit students address the following National Educational Technology Standards (NETS) for Students Standards: 1—Basic operations and concepts; 2—Social, ethical, and human issues; 3—Technology productivity tools; and 4—Technology communication tools.

Activities

1. Students use drawing or painting software to make a banner entitled Helping Hands. Assign each letter to a group of two or three students. Display the banner on a wall or bulletin board.
2. Have each student trace his or her hand on paper. Use a scanner to digitize the tracing. Use drawing or painting software to decorate the hand, and use the text tool to write the student's name anywhere on the hand. Print the hand pictures, cut them out, and decorate the banner with them.
3. Students use a digital camera to create group pictures (pictures of students working cooperatively).
4. Students use interactive CDs to explore and learn about community helpers.
5. Have students use Big Book software (e.g., Big Book, Scholastic SuperPrint Deluxe) to create and print a story based on a group picture.
6. Students use painting or drawing software to make a picture dictionary that describes and illustrates cooperation.
7. Use a video camera to document classroom activities. As a class, check the video for examples of cooperative and uncooperative behavior.
8. At the end of each day, determine the classroom cooperation level. Record cooperation levels on a large graph posted on a wall.
9. Have students use a spreadsheet program or graphing software to draw, tabulate, or graph the information for use in a class discussion.
10. Have students work with an adult family member to learn about neighborhood watches or other types of community activities designed to help neighbors meet each other and look out for each other. Use a digital camera to take pictures of your neighborhood. Use slide-show software such as Kid Pix Studio to create a neighborhood watch presentation.

11. Students visit Mr. Rogers' Neighborhood website to learn about families and their neighborhoods.
12. From a list of I-statements, have students select one to role-play cooperative behavior with a partner.
13. Go on a field trip to the local police station. Have students send the station a thank-you email.
14. Work with the local fire department to develop a home safety chart. Have students use the chart to investigate the safety level of their homes.

Tools and Resources

Software
- Kid Pix Studio
- ClarisWorks for Kids
- Easy Book
- SuperPrint
- HyperStudio
- Kid Works Delux
- GraphPower
- Graph Club
- Richard Scarry's Busytown
- Multimedia encyclopedia

Hardware
- Color inkjet printer
- Video camcorder
- Digital camera
- Scanner
- Large-screen monitor, LCD panel, or classroom TV connected to a computer
- VCR

Website
- Mr. Rogers' Neighborhood
  http://pbskids.org/rogers

Multidisciplinary Unit for Intermediate Grades (3–5)

Title of Unit: *Eco Busters*

Eco Busters emphasizes the causal link between the United States' tremendous consumption of natural resources and the resulting effect of that consumption on the rest of the planet. Students will learn about the impact fossil fuels and other wastes have on Earth.

In this unit students address the following National Educational Technology Standards (NETS) for Students Standards: 1—Basic operations and concepts; 2—Social, ethical, and human issues; 3—Technology productivity tools; 4—Technology communication tools; 5—Technology research tools; and 6—Technology problem-solving and decision-making tools.

Activities

1. Students form small groups and list the items found in the garbage in their homes and in their classroom.
2. Have students research the impact unchecked consumerism has on the world's natural resources, as well as its effect on the rain forests, the coral reefs, and the Earth's atmosphere.
3. Students investigate means by which they can educate parents, relatives, and each other on how to reduce the damage done to our world.
4. Students publish their findings on a website as well as send an email or letter to all news media reporting their findings.
5. Go on a field trip to the sewage plant. Discuss modern technology's impact on waste disposal. Take digital pictures to record observations on how sewage is treated to become effluent. Working with an adult or older student, develop a small multimedia project that reports the observed water treatment processes. Send the sewage plant an email thanking the personnel there for the visit.
6. Go on a field trip to the recycling plant. Take digital pictures to record observations on the recycling process. Working with an adult or older student, develop a small multimedia project that reports the observed recycling processes. Send the plant an email thanking the personnel for the visit.
7. Students explore the environmental impact of landfills. Have students learn about landfills in their area, regulations imposed on them, and their expected ecological impact over time.
8. Have students create pieces of art constructed entirely of recyclable materials.
9. Students use the Internet to research different advocacy groups that campaign against vinyl plastics. Email one of these groups a question.
10. Have students chart statistics from the past 10 years regarding recycling, landfill size, and monies involved in recycling.
11. Have small groups of students create charts examining the amount of time it takes for different products to biodegrade. Students share their findings by preparing a multimedia presentation.
12. Students working with a partner create recycling posters aimed toward motivating other students to recycle. Try to include statistics and other facts in each poster.
13. Working in small groups, students brainstorm solutions on how to make recycling a part of daily life.
14. Have small groups of students develop a slide-show or multimedia presentation illustrating what happens to a plastic bottle or styrofoam cup sent to be recycled contrasted with one sent to the landfill, including the environmental effects of these processes and their results.

Tools and Resources

Software
- Word processing
- Spreadsheet
- Graphics
- HyperStudio
- Presentation
- GraphPower
- Graph Club
- Web-page creation
- Multimedia encyclopedia

Hardware
- Color inkjet printer
- Video camcorder
- Digital camera
- Scanner
- Large-screen monitor, LCD panel, or classroom TV connected to a computer
- VCR

Websites
- National Environmental Trust
  www.envirotrust.org
- Greenpeace
  www.greenpeaceusa.org

Educational Videos

Available through Disney Educational Productions
- Bill Nye the Science Guy shows (Pollution Solutions, Garbage and the Water Cycle)
- Recycle Rex (stars animated recycling dinosaur)
- The Energy Savers (stars Donald Duck, Mickey Mouse, and Goofy)
- Zort Sorts: A Story about Recycling
- The Great Search—Man's Need for Power and Energy

Multidisciplinary Unit for Middle Grades (6–8)

Title of Unit: *Attitude Shapers*

Recognizing that "a picture is worth a thousand words," it is important that students understand how businesses and governments seek to shape our thoughts and opinions on everyday occurrences through the careful selection and dissemination of photographs and sound bites.

Students will analyze photographs, sound bites, advertisements, and any other media sources they encounter and investigate whether the published material accurately reflects the truth. Students will state whether the published material accurately reflects the actual events or advertised products, and they will state how the published material was used to shape the attitudes and opinions of a specified audience.

In this unit students address the following National Educational Technology Standards (NETS) for Students Standards: 1—Basic operations and concepts; 2—Social, ethical, and human issues; 3—Technology productivity tools; 4—Technology communication tools; 5—Technology research tools; and 6—Technology problem-solving and decision-making tools.

Activities

1. Students form small groups and select photographs, sound bites, advertisements, and any other media sources encountered that they believe misrepresent the truth.
2. Students investigate the selected media sources and research the background issues involved and compile their findings in a group multimedia presentation and written report.
3. Students explore Civil War–picture manipulations. As a class, discuss reasons for the inaccuracies and what benefits, if any, were obtained by the publisher of the inaccurate media.
4. Demonstrate various technologies showing how easily businesses and governments can manipulate media sources for their own purposes.
5. Working with a partner, have students select an inaccurate media source and compose a letter or email to the publisher of the information expressing their concerns about the inaccuracies found.
6. Have students write using a quote from George Orwell's *1984* as a prompt: "There were the huge printing shops with their sub-editors, their typography experts, and their elaborately equipped studios for the faking of photographs" (p. 43). Have students discuss their responses using a discussion board or classroom listserv.
7. Have students investigate the economics of "sensational" journalism. Do publications that misrepresent the truth make a profit? Have students create charts demonstrating the differences in earnings for several types of publications and news shows.
8. Have students investigate how media shape our attitudes about war. Divide students into small groups and have each group select a war. Groups create multimedia or slide-show presentations to report findings.
9. Discuss heroic qualities. Have students select one of the following heroes to investigate the qualities of heroism their selection represents and the historical circumstances in which their selection emerged. Students determine the historical accuracy or plausibility of the heroic action attributed to their selections. Class develops a website to publish findings.
   - Ellen Ripley/Sarah Connor
   - T. E. Lawrence (Lawrence of Arabia)
   - Joan of Arc
   - Ho Chi Minh

- Luke Skywalker
- David and Goliath
- Homeric heroes—Achilles

10. Discuss Jean Bethke Elshtain's claim that our "attitudes to war are determined by the traditional stories and histories of war we hear and read" (see her book *Women and War*, p. 32).

Tools and Resources

Software
- Word processing
- Presentation
- HyperStudio
- Spreadsheet
- Image manipulating
- Web-page creation

Hardware
- Color inkjet printer
- Scanner
- Large-screen monitor, LCD panel, or classroom TV connected to a computer
- VCR
- Film projector

Websites
- The ABCs of Web Site Evaluation: Teaching Media Literacy in the Age of the Internet
  www.connectedteacher.com/newsletter/abcs.asp
- Critical Evaluation Information by Kathy Schrock
  http://school.discovery.com/schrockguide/eval.html
- The Gallup Organization
  www.gallup.com
- Center for Media and Public Affairs
  www.cmpa.com
- The Pew Research Center: For the People and the Press
  www.people-press.org
- American Society of Newspaper Editors
  www.asne.org
- On Shrinking Soundbites by Mitchell Stephens
  www.cjr.org/year/96/5/soundbites.asp
- Project for Excellence in Journalism
  www.journalism.org
- American Memory Collection: Does the Camera Ever Lie?
  memory.loc.gov/ammem/cwphtml/cwpcam/cwcam1.html
- Photojournalism Ethics: Chapter Six
  http://commfaculty.fullerton.edu/lester/writings/chapter6.html

- Visual Literacy Bibliography
  http://tc.eserver.org/15237.html
- Photographic Evidence, Naked Children, and Dead Celebrities:
  Digital Forgery and the Law
  www.thirdamendment.com/digital.html
- DIGITAL PHOTOGRAPHY: A Question of Ethics by Bonnie Meltzer
  www.fno.org/may97/digital.html

Books
- *The Eyes of Time: Photojournalism in America* by Estelle Jussim (Boston: Little, Brown, 1989)
- *Photography and the American Scene* by Robert Taft (New York: MacMillan Co., 1938)
- *Fallen Soldiers: Reshaping the Memory of the World Wars* by George L. Mosse (New York: Oxford University Press, 1990)
- *Women and War* by Jean Bethke Elshtain (New York: Basic Books, 1987)
- *1984* by George Orwell (New York: Harcourt, Brace, 1949)

Film
- Thomas Doherty, *Projections of War: Hollywood, American Culture, and World War Two* (New York: Columbia University Press, 1993)

Multidisciplinary Unit for Secondary Grades (9–12)

Title of Unit: *Know Your Propositions*

Every year people seek to place new laws on election ballots. The need for new laws arises from concerns, political agendas, mistakes, and historical events. Using a current local proposition, students examine the arguments for and against the proposition and consequences if enacted or not enacted. Students take a position for or against the proposition, supporting their decision with arguments and facts. Students predict the proposition outcomes and follow the election returns.

No specific websites are provided for several reasons. First, searching for information about propositions is considered a valuable part of the learning process. Second, new-proposition websites arise and fall with each new election. Hence, any suggested site will likely be defunct by the time this reaches publication. Third, Internet searches can be tailored to fit any political region around the world.

In this unit students address the following National Educational Technology Standards (NETS) for Students Standards: 1—Basic operations and concepts; 2—Social, ethical, and human issues; 3—Technology productivity tools; 4—Technology communication tools; 5—Technology research tools; and 6—Technology problem-solving and decision-making tools.

Activities

1. Students research pending ballot propositions on the Internet and through other sources and list them according to election date and topic.

2. Working in small groups, have students investigate the sponsors of the propositions, specific interests of the sponsors, and the potential benefits to the sponsors should the propositions be enacted into law. Create a database to store this information.
3. Have students collect copies of the official propositions, along with the official position statements, including officially published arguments for and against the propositions.
4. Working with a partner, have students research the published arguments.
5. Have a chat session with government officials and interest groups about their positions on a proposition.
6. Students take a position, supporting their decision with arguments and facts, and present their findings using a slide show.
7. Discuss the language selected by the government to describe the propositions to see whether there exists an attempt to conceal the true effect of a vote, for or against the propositions.
8. Students draft separate reports of their findings that will be incorporated into a single group report, which will be delivered to the news media for publication.
9. In small groups, students calculate the amount of money, both public and private, expended by both proponents and opponents of the various propositions. Have students write their own proposition listing better uses for the funds spent on the propositions. Create a website to publish the student-generated proposition.
10. Publish class findings and conclusions on a website. Suggested format for displaying database information of the proposition's analysis follows.

Proposition Number
    Title:
    Sponsor:
    Major Provisions:
    Background:
    Policy Considerations:
    Fiscal Impact:
    State Government:
    Local Government:
    Taxpayers:
    Support Arguments:
    Opposition Arguments:

- Have students email the media, interested businesses, and government officials a summary of their findings plus a request to visit their website.
- Working in small groups, have students create a WebQuest for another grade level.
- Have students predict proposition outcomes and follow election returns. Discuss prediction reasoning. Have them calculate the accuracy of their prediction.

Tools and Resources

Software
- HyperStudio
- Presentation
- Database
- Spreadsheet
- Web-page creation

Hardware
- Color inkjet printer
- Scanner
- Large-screen monitor, LCD panel, or classroom TV connected to a computer

Summary

Teachers of all content areas can incorporate technology-based learning activities into their traditional curricula. This increases the number of students who have experience with technology when they finish school. It also increases the amount of technology in use in the classroom and serves as a bridge to the future when technology-based learning activities will be the rule rather than the exception. The first step in incorporating technology into the curriculum is being able to develop effective technology-based learning activities.

In general, technology-based learning activities must account for the same factors that all learning activities depend on:

Grade-Level Range
Purpose
Description
Activity Preparation
Activity Procedure
Tools and Resources
Assessment

The learning activities presented in this chapter follow a format that includes all these features and may also include an activity description and comments.

With technology-based learning activities, additional factors must be taken into consideration. Most of these factors have to do with availability of software and hardware. Will students have unlimited access to several computers with network connectivity? This situation allows the teacher to plan more extensive use of technology than a situation in which students must go in pairs to a media center where they can use the computer for no more than half an hour. Are there programs available to handle the activities planned?

This chapter presented sample learning activities. There are two learning activities for each of the five content areas—mathematics, science, language arts, social studies, and special education. Under each content area, the first learning activity is for use by elementary teachers, the second by secondary teachers. It is the authors' hope that teachers will use these learning activities as a springboard for creating their own innovative and effective technology-based learning activities.

Also in this chapter four multidisciplinary units based on a powerful theme were presented. Learning through the use of multidisciplinary, student-centered activities has been shown to be effective. The multidisciplinary units follow a format similar to ISTE's publication *National Educational Technology Standards for Students: Connecting Curriculum and Technology* (Thomas & Bitter, 2000). The format design facilitates teachers in planning, carrying out, and evaluating units effectively. Teachers are encouraged to discuss with other teachers their technology integration experiences.

These units are intended to serve as guidelines for the teacher who is in the process of integrating technology. Each unit provides a variety of activities, related technology, thematically relevant information, tools, and resources. In addition, each unit addresses content standards from two or more discipline areas while also addressing the National Educational Technology Standards for Students. When designing multidisciplinary units, and lesson activities, teachers should reflect on how technology enables them to teach content at greater depth and how their use of technology enhances instruction.

Bird Rap

Students make use of various technologies to research, gather data, and report on specific elements of ornithology. How does the teacher use these technologies to support the learning of the content?

DVD/VIDEO VIGNETTE

Challenge Yourself!

1. Present one of the activities in this chapter to your peers and report on the results.
2. Review the DVD Video Vignette for this chapter. Identify and list the NETS Student Standards that are covered in the lesson. List the strengths and weaknesses of the lesson. Compare your results with those of your classmates.
3. Write a technology-based learning activity for your content area following the format suggested in this chapter.
4. Research the Internet, books, and periodicals that include technology-based learning activities. Develop a web-based bibliography of these resources.
5. Adapt one of the learning activities in this chapter for use with a specific software package.
6. Adapt one of the learning activities in this chapter for a higher or lower grade level.
7. Write a learning activity that develops a thematic learning environment and integrates several content areas.
8. Write a learning activity that includes the WWW for data collection.

9. Integrate cooperative learning into one of the learning activities. Try the activity with a class.
10. Modify one of the learning activities to include portfolio-assessment procedures.
11. Compare and contrast the following terms: *interdisciplinary*, *multidisciplinary*, and *transdisciplinary*. Share your findings with the class by creating a multimedia presentation.
12. Prepare a multidisciplinary unit for a grade-level range following the sample format.
13. Develop a plan for storing software, manuals, and student diskettes in the classroom.
14. Adapt one of the multidisciplinary units in this chapter for a higher or lower grade level.
15. Create a new lesson plan for software not included in this chapter. Follow the same format as the lessons in this chapter do.
16. The National Council of Teachers of Mathematics (**www.nctm.org**), the National Academy of Sciences (**www.nas.edu**), the National Council for the Social Studies (**www.socialstudies.org/standards**), and the National Council of Teachers of English and the International Reading Association (**www.ncte.org/about/over/standards**) have established curriculum standards. Develop a multidisciplinary unit addressing these curriculum standards and integrating appropriate technology.
17. Select a multidisciplinary unit from this chapter and integrate new methods of assessment such as portfolios.
18. Write a multidisciplinary lesson plan based on the Smithsonian Education website **www.smithsonianeducation.org**.
19. Connect to the EDUCAST site at **www.educast.com** and research the resources available through this website. Download several lesson plans for class discussion.
20. Write a lesson plan for the DVD Video Vignette: Bird Rap.

References

Albrecht, B., & Davis, P. (2000). Measurement and modeling. *Learning and Leading with Technology, 28*(2), 32–35, 39–41.

Albritton, D. (September, 2002), LOGO. *PC Teach It,* 46–47.

Allen, D. (1994a). A spring software sampler. Teaching with technology. *Teaching PreK–8, 24*(8), 20–22.

Allen, D. (1994b). Teaching with technology: Byte into math. *Teaching PreK–8, 24*(4), 22–27.

Allen, D. (1995). Teaching with technology. Software that's right for you. *Teaching PreK–8, 25*(8), 14–17.

Anderson-Inman, L. (1987). The reading–writing connection: Classroom applications for the computer, Part II. *The Computing Teacher, 14*(6), 15–18.

Anderson-Inman, L. (1990–1991). Enabling students with learning disabilities: Insights from research. *The Computing Teacher, 18*(4), 26–29.

Balajthy, E. (1988). Keyboarding, language arts, and the elementary school child. *The Computing Teacher, 15*(5), 40–43.

Barnes, S., & Michalowiczs, K. D. (1994). Now and then: From cashier to scan coordinator; from stones to bones to PC clones. *Mathematics Teaching in the Middle School, 1*(1), 59–65.

Bayliffe, J., et al. (1994). Tech time: Using technology to enhance "my travels with Gulliver." *Teaching Children Mathematics, 1*(3), 188–191.

Beck, J., (2002). Emerging literacy through assistive technology. *Teaching Exceptional Children, 35*(2), 44–48.

Berlin, D. F., & White, A. L. (1995). Using technology in assessing integrated science and mathematics learning. *Journal of Science Education and Technology, 4*(1), 47–56.

Bitter, G. G., & Frederick, H. (1989). Techniques and technology in secondary school mathematics. *NASSP Bulletin, 73*(519), 22–28.

Braun, J. A., Jr., & Kuseske, T. (Eds.). (1994). A teacher's perspective on what's ahead for technology. Media corner. *Social Studies and the Young Learner, 6*(3), 26–28.

Bristor, V. J., & Drake, S. V. (1994). Linking the language arts and content areas through visual technology. *T.H.E. Journal, 22*(2), 74–77.

Browning, R., & Nave, G. (1983). Computer technology for the handicapped: A literature profile. *The Computing Teacher, 10*(6), 56–59.

Brush, T., & Bitter, G. G. (2000). An innovative approach to high-tech learning. *Learning and Leading with Technology, 28*(1), 23–30.

Bull, G., et al. (2002). Learner-based tools revisited. *Learning and Leading with Technology, 30*(1), 10–17.

Cappo, M., & Osterman, G. (1991). Teach students to communicate mathematically. *The Computing Teacher, 18*(5), 34–39.

Carrol, J., Kelly, M. G., & Witherspoon, T. (Eds.). (2003). *NETS•S curriculum series—Multidisciplinary units for prekindergarten through grade 2.* Eugene, OR: International Society for Technology in Education.

Cerrito, P. B. (1994). Writing, technology, and experimentation to explore the concepts of elementary statistics. *Mathematics and Computer Education, 28*(2), 141–153.

Connelly, M. G., & Wiebe, J. H. (1994). Teaching mathematics with technology: Mining mathematics on the Internet. *Arithmetic Teacher, 41*(5), 276–281.

Cradler, J. (2003). Technology's impact on teaching and learning. *Learning and Leading with Technology, 30*(7), 54–57.

Cuoco, A. A., et al. (Eds.). (1994a). Technology tips: A potpourri. *Mathematics Teacher, 87*(7), 566–569.

Cuoco, A. A., et al. (Eds.). (1994b). Technology tips: Technology in perspective. *Mathematics Teacher, 87*(6), 450–452.

Cuoco, A. A., et al. (1995). Technology tips: Technology and the mathematics curriculum: Some new initiatives. *Mathematics Teacher, 88*(3), 236–240.

Decker, G. (2003). Creating a framework to make data-driven instruction a reality. *Multimedia Schools, 10*(2), 22–25.

Dickens, R. A. (1991–1992). Success with writing and the concept formation model. *The Computing Teacher, 19*(4), 27–29.

Faltis, C. J., & Devillar, R. A. (Eds.). (1990). *Language minority students and computers.* New York: Haworth Press.

Finegan, C., & Austin, N. (2002). Developmentally appropriate technology for young children. *Information Technology in Childhood Education Annual* (2002), 87–102.

Gagne, R. M. (1987). *Instructional technology: Foundations.* Hillsdale, NJ: Lawrence Erlbaum.

Gardner, H. (2000). The complete tutor. *TECHNOS, 9*(3), 10–13.

Gardner, J. (2003). Learning about learning. *Learning and Leading with Technology, 30*(6), 36–39.

Glasser, L. (2000). Information technology in educational science: Chemistry teaching by computer. *South African Journal of Science, 96*(4), 155–160.

Goldberg, K. P. (1994). Applications: Using technology to understand the jury decision-making process. *Mathematics Teacher, 87*(2), 110–114.

Hannah, L. (Ed.). (2002). *NETS•S curriculum series—Multidisciplinary units for grades 3–5.* Eugene, OR: International Society for Technology in Education.

Hardwick, S. W. (2000). Humanizing the technology landscape through a collaborative pedagogy. *Journal of Geography in Higher Education, 24*(1), 123–130.

Harvey, J. G., et al. (1995). The influence of technology on the teaching and learning of algebra. *Journal of Mathematical Behavior, 14*(1), 75–109.

Heid, M. (1995). Impact of technology, mathematical modeling, and meaning on the content, learning, and teaching of secondary school algebra. *Journal of Mathematical Behavior, 14*(1), 121–137.

Hooper, S., & Rieber, L. P. (1995). Teaching with technology. In A. C. Ornstein (Ed.), *Teaching: Theory into practice* (pp. 154–170). Boston: Allyn and Bacon.

Hoyles, C., et al. (1994). Learning mathematics in groups with computers: Reflections on a research study. *British Educational Research Journal, 20*(4), 465–483.

Hsu, L., & Lee, G. D. (1991–1992). Providing access for students who are visually impaired. *The Computing Teacher, 19*(4), 8–9.

Hunt, N., & Afford, L. (1991–1992). Involving students in computer-based cooperative lessons. *The Computing Teacher, 19*(4), 34–37.

Hussey, W. (2000). Technology and teaching music. *Computer Music Journal, 24*(2), 92–95.

International Society for Technology in Education. (1998, June). *National Educational Technology Standards for Students.* Eugene, OR: Author.

James, R. K., & Lamb, C. E. (2000). Integrating science, mathematics, and technology in middle school technology-rich environments: A study of implementation and change. *School Science and Mathematics, 100*(1), 27–35.

Johnson, D. C., et al. (1994). Evaluating the impact of IT on pupils' achievements. *Journal of Computer Assisted Learning, 10*(3), 138–156.

Johnson, D. L., Maddux, C. D., & Candler, A. C. (Eds.). (1986). *Computers in the special education classroom.* New York: Haworth Press.

Johnson, J. M. (2000). *The 2000 educational software preview guide.* Eugene, OR: International Society for Technology in Education.

Kader, G., & Perry, M. (1994). Power on! Learning statistics with technology. *Mathematics Teaching in the Middle School, 1*(2), 130–136.

Kapisosky, R. M. (1990). Math and science: Vitality through technology. *Media and Methods, 26*(4), 59–61.

Kaput, J. J., & Thompson, P. W. (1994). Technology in mathematics education research: The first 25 years in the JRME. *Journal for Research in Mathematics Education, 25*(6), 667–684.

Kelly, R. (2000). Working with WebQuests. *Teaching Exceptional Children, 32*(6), 4–13.

Kemp, J. E. (2000). John Dewey never said it would be easy: Designing education in the 21st century. *TECHNOS, 9*(3), 25–29.

Kuechle, N. (1990). Computers and first grade writing: A learning center approach. *The Computing Teacher, 18*(1), 39–41.

Lach, C., et al. (2003). Weaving technology and multiple intelligences into science and art. *Learning and Leading with Technology, 30*(6), 32–35, 59.

Lampert, M., et al. (1994). Using technology to support a new pedagogy of mathematics teacher education. *Journal of Special Education Technology, 12*(3), 276–289.

Layton, T. G. (2000). Why tomorrow's schools must learn to let go of the past. *Electronic School, 187*(9), 23–24.

Lehman, J. R. (1994). Technology use in the teaching of mathematics and science in elementary schools. *School Science and Mathematics, 94*(4), 194–202.

Leu, D. J., Jr., & Kinzer, C. K. (2000). The convergence of literacy instruction with networked technologies for information and communication. *Reading Research Quarterly, 35*(1), 108–129.

Lewis, P. (2002). Getting started with project-based learning. *Learning and Leading with Technology, 30*(3), 42–45.

MacArthur, C. A. (2000). New tools for writing: Assistive technology for students with writing difficulties. *Topics-in-Language-Disorders, 20*(4), 85–100.

Manes, M. A. (1994). Technology tips: A global electronic community. *Mathematics Teacher, 87*(8), 650–651.

Mason, M. (1983). Special education: A time of opportunity. *Electronic Learning, 2*(8), 54–55.

McClain, K., Cobb, P., & Gravemeijer, K. (2000). Supporting students' ways of reasoning about data. In M. J. Burke & F. R. Curcio (Eds.), *Learning Mathematics for a New Century: 2000 Yearbook* (pp. 174–187). Reston, VA: National Council of Teachers of Mathematics.

McKenzie, W. (2002). *Multiple intelligences and instructional technology.* Eugene, OR: International Society for Technology in Education.

McMurdo, K. (2004). *Structured Writing II—Using inspiration software to teach essay development.* Eugene, OR: International Society for Technology in Education.

Milone, M. N., Jr. (1990). Painless grammar: Revising with the help of a grammar checker. *Classroom Computer Learning, 10*(6), 18–23.

Miltenoff, P., & Rodgers, J. (2003). Teaching with technology: Multimedia and interactivity in social science education. *Multimedia Schools, 10*(2), 34–36.

Moni, K. B., & Jobling, A. (2000). LATCH-ON: A program to develop literacy in young adults with Down syndrome. *Journal of Adolescent and Adult Literacy, 44*(1), 40–50.

Moursund, D. (2003). *Project-based learning.* Eugene, OR: International Society for Technology in Education.

Nelson, T. B., & Rogel, J. (1995). Operation Sluggie and other software products from the fourth grade. *The Computing Teacher, 22*(5), 39–41.

NETS Project. (2003). *National Educational Technology Standards for Teachers—Resources for assessment.* Eugene, OR: International Society for Technology in Education.

O'Connor, J., & Brie, R. (1994a). Mathematics and science partnerships: Products, people, performance, and multimedia. *The Computing Teacher, 22*(1), 27–30.

O'Connor, J., & Brie, R. (1994b). The effects of technology infusion on the mathematics and science curriculum. *Journal of Computing in Teacher Education, 10*(4), 15–18.

O'Hara, S., & McMahon, M. (2003). *NETS•S curriculum series—Multidisciplinary units for grades 6–8.* Eugene, OR: International Society for Technology in Education.

Orwell, G. (1949). *1984.* New York: Harcourt Brace.

Parr, J. M. (1999). Extending educational computing: A case of extensive teacher development and support. *Journal of Research on Computing in Education, 31*(3), 280–292.

Pastorek, M. J., & Craig, L. (2000). Technical frience: Integrating science, foreign language, and social studies. *Learning and Leading with Technology, 28*(2), 18–21.

Pedersen, S. (2003). Motivational orientation in a problem-based learning environment. *Journal of Interactive Learning Research, 14*(1), 51–77.

Pert, T. (1990). Manipulatives and the computer: A powerful partnership for learners of all ages. *Classroom Computer Learning, 10*(6), 20–29.

Phelps, M. V. (1994). The federal role in educational technology. *Educational Media and Technology Yearbook, 20*, 142–150.

Phillips, R. J., & Pead, D. (1994). Multimedia resources in the mathematics classroom. *Journal of Computer Assisted Learning, 10*(4), 216–228.

Phillips, R. J., et al. (1995). Evolving strategies for using interactive video resources in mathematics classrooms. *Educational Studies in Mathematics, 28*(2), 133–154.

Reinking, D., & Watkins, J. (2000). A formative experiment investigating the use of multimedia book reviews to increase elementary students' independent reading. *Reading Research Quarterly, 35*(3), 384–420.

Resources on computer-based reading and writing instruction. (1988). *The Computing Teacher, 16*(1), 24–27.

Rice, M. (1995). Issues surrounding the integration of technology into the K-12 classroom. *Interpersonal Computing and Technology Journal, 3*(1), 67–81.

Riddle, B. (1988). Computer-based astronomy: The opposition of Mars. *The Computing Teacher, 16*(3), 20–23.

Risinger, C. F. (2000). Social studies portals: More than just a web page. *Social Education, 64*(3), 150–152.

Rowland, K. L., & Scott, D. (1992). Promoting language and literacy for young children through computers. *Journal of Computing in Childhood Education, 3*(1), 55–61.

Schack, M. B. (2000). The judicious use of instructional technology in science education. *Science Activities, 37*(1), 3–5.

Schipper, D. (1991). Practical ideas: Literature, computers, and students with special needs. *The Computing Teacher, 19*(2), 33–37.

Selby, L., et al. (1994). Teachers' perceptions of learning with information technology in mathematics and science education: A report on Project Prometheus. *Journal of Computing in Teacher Education, 10*(3), 24–30.

Smerdon, B., Cronen, S., Lanahan, L., Anderson, J., Iannotti, N., and Angeles, J. (2000). *Teacher's tools for the 21st century: A report on teachers' use of technology.* (NCES 2000–102). Washington, DC: U.S. Department of Education. National Center for Education Statistics.

Solomon, G. (1989). Computers help students see art in a different hue. *Electronic Learning, 9*(2), 16–18.

Solomon, G. (1990). Learning social studies in a one-computer classroom. *Electronic Learning, 9*(7), 18–20.

Solomon, G. (2003). Project-based learning: A primer. *Technology and Learning, 23*(6), 20–30.

Stahl, G., et al. (1995). Share globally, adapt locally: Software assistance to locate and tailor curriculum posted to the Internet. *Computers and Education, 24*(3), 237–246.

Suddath, C., & Susnik, J. (1991). *Augmentative communication devices.* Reston, VA: Office for Special Education Technology.

Symington, L., & Stanger, C. (2000). Math = success. *Teaching Exceptional Children, 32*(4), 28–32.

Tankersley, J. (2003). Using technology to promote reading. *Multimedia Schools, 10*(3), 40–41.

Thomas, L. (Ed.). (2002). *National Educational Technology Standards for Teachers: Preparing teachers to use technology.* Eugene, OR: International Society for Technology in Education.

Thomas, L., & Bitter, G. G. (Eds.) (2000). *National Educational Technology Standards for Students: Connecting curriculum and technology.* Eugene, OR: International Society for Technology in Education.

Thompson, E. O. (1989). Using the geometric supposer: Triangles. *The Computing Teacher, 17*(1), 30–34.

Waring, B. (1998). The 1998 New Media Hyper Awards. *New Media, 8*(3), 36–49.

Watkins, M. W., & Abran, S. (1985). Reading CAI with first grade students. *The Computing Teacher, 12*(7), 43–45.

Wepner, S. B. (1990). Computers and whole language: A "novel" frontier. *The Computing Teacher, 17*(5), 24–28.

Wicklein, R. C., & Schell, J. W. (1995). Case studies of multidisciplinary approaches to integrating mathematics, science and technology education. *Journal of Technology Education, 6*(2), 59–76.

Widmer, C. C., & Sheffield, L. J. (1994). Putting the fun into functions through the use of manipulatives, computers, and calculators. *School Science and Mathematics, 94*(7), 350–355.

Widmer, C. C., & Sheffield, L. (1998). Modeling mathematics concepts: Using physical, calculator, and computer models to teach area and perimeter. *Learning and Leading with Technology, 25*(5), 32–35.

Wilson, E. K., & Rice, M. L. (2000). Virtual field trips and newsrooms: Integrating technology into the classroom. *Social Education, 64*(3), 152–155.

Wissick, C. A., & Gardner, J. E. (2000). Multimedia or not to multimedia? That is the question for students with learning disabilities. *Teaching Exceptional Children, 32*(4), 34–44.

Wresch, W. (1990). Collaborative writing projects: Lesson plans for the computer age. *The Computing Teacher, 17*(8), 19–21.

Young, M. (1995). Assessment of situated learning using computer environments. *Journal of Science Education and Technology, 4*(1), 89–96.

Zola, J., & Ioannidou, A. (2000). Learning and teaching with interactive simulations. *Social Education, 64*(3), 142–146.

Data Analysis and Simulations

FOCUS QUESTIONS

1. How can teachers develop data analysis skills in their students?

2. What factors must teachers consider when planning data analysis activities?

3. What are the benefits of using computer simulations?

Chapter 10 presented several learning activities involving data analysis. With the influx of information, skill development in using data to reason and to make statistical-based decisions is necessary for students to become informed citizens and intelligent consumers (NCTM, 2000). However, teachers are reluctant to teach data analysis for several reasons: lack of time, skill, and motivation (Goodman Research Group, 1998; Russell, 1990). Employing the use of simulations may help reduce this reluctance. Simulations facilitate exploring and understanding problem solving, especially in the field of mathematics. As far back as 1972, cognitive scientists used simulations to help develop and validate learning theories (Newell & Simon, 1972). This chapter takes a closer look at data analysis and simulations, and offers suggestions and resources to support teachers' integration of these technology-based inquiry and problem-solving approaches.

Data Analysis

The technological discipline of data analysis emerged from the union of statistics, computer science, pattern recognition, artificial intelligence, and machine learning. Data analysis is the process of transforming data into information. Similarly, information evolves from data in the process of answering a question. Therefore, the question is the key part of the process. Computers have made it possible to aggregate several data sets into huge databases. Although problems arise—for instance, storage—when attempting to manage and make sense of large data sets, the time invested leads to the development of new software tools, with the expectation that the mined data will lead to better decision making.

In 1970 statisticians began to question the traditional paradigm of data analysis. The traditional process began by formulating a hypothesis, followed by collecting data, and ended by testing the hypothesis. To address their questioning of the traditional data analysis process, statisticians began to use open-ended data exploration methods. John W. Tukey of Princeton University and AT&T Bell Labs established a new approach called "exploratory data analysis." Tukey (1977) suggested investigating data as a detective investigates a crime scene with an open mind and few, if any, assumptions. Tukey saw data analysis as a mixture of science and art. The process of analyzing data includes the creative search for meaning as well as a systematic method for guiding the search. The goal of exploratory data analysis (EDA) is quite different from the traditional paradigm of hypothesis testing also known as confirmatory data analysis. EDA seeks to find "patterns in data for hypothesis generation and refinement" (Behrens & Smith, 1996, p. 952).

Computers are problem-solving tools that help implement a systematic method of exploration. Certain valuable cognitive skills warrant special emphasis for PreK–12 students:

- The ability to analyze a variety of problems and understand how to select and use productivity tools to find solutions
- The ability to understand the theoretical background to use software programs to solve different types of problems encountered in both personal and professional activities

Problem-solving activities help students learn how to collect, interpret, and represent data. In the long run, these computer-assisted activities help students deepen their understanding of using data analysis to answer questions, solve problems, and make decisions in business, politics, and research.

The National Council of Teachers of Mathematics (NCTM) advocates having students generate questions that require collecting and exploring data. The NCTM Data Analysis and Probability Standard (2000) for PreK–12 students has four goals:

1. Formulate questions that can be addressed with data; and collect, organize, and display relevant data to answer them.
2. Select and use appropriate statistical methods to analyze data.
3. Develop and evaluate inferences and predictions that are based on data.
4. Understand and apply basic concepts of probability.

The NCTM recommends a strong emphasis on developing data analysis skills in all grades as well as progressively increasing the sophistication of the concepts and procedures. This ensures that by the end of high school students have a strong statistical background and knowledge of using computers as a problem-solving tool.

Simulations

A *simulation* is the process of imitating a real situation or object with a set of mathematical formulas. Computer simulations can imitate weather conditions, chemical reactions, nuclear accidents, medical techniques, costs required to produce a particular design, biological processes, cockpit and spacecraft systems, and product safety testing, to name just a few. Some situations or objects are more problematic to create than others relative to their ability to be reduced to mathematical data and equations. An important factor when creating simulations is to clearly define the situation or object and determine the most important factors. Simulations are used to test theories of causal relationships.

How can teachers effectively incorporate simulations into the curriculum? The critical task is to coherently integrate the simulation software as a vital part of the curriculum, not as an add-on. This means students use the simulation for an extended time period and should be engaged in extension activities based on the thinking skills embedded in the simulation (Henderson, Klemes, & Eshet, 2000). Computer simulations can be used but are not limited to

1. Visualize the invisible
2. Manipulate variables, observe results, and draw conclusions
3. Facilitate role playing

Simulations can be created with web pages (HTML), the scripting language of Javascript, authoring environments such as Director, animation environments such as Flash, and the programming language of Java. Commercial software programs such as KidSim and Microworlds allow students to create their own simulations. The simulated worlds students create have characters who have rules, appearances, and properties.

Statistics

Simulation software and data analysis activities help develop the central elements of statistics. *Statistics* is defined as a set of methods used to collect, analyze, present, and interpret data. Whereas a computer assists in summarizing data, statistical methods focus on the interpretation of the output in order to make inferences and predictions. Young students start off working with simple classroom census data. At this age, the teacher may elect to generate the question at first. For example, the problem of deciding on a breakfast menu for an elementary school could begin with the question "What do kids like to eat for breakfast?" Students collect data to answer the question. The notion of sampling is difficult to develop. However, upper elementary and middle school students start to acquire an understanding about statistical inference. Before students leave high school, they should know that statistical techniques are used daily in work settings to solve problems and make informed decisions (NCTM, 2000).

Software programs as well as the websites that follow may be used as resources for the creation of curriculum units, educational resources, and learning activities. Yeo and Tan (1999) recommend designing simulations to "provide dynamic problem situations for learners," which foster a "theoretical understanding of the interactions in the simulated environment through direct feedback from their actions" (p. 70). This can be done by encouraging three types of feedback: self, peer, and teacher. Time should be provided for students to (1) reflect and write about their simulated experience and (2) share their reactions (Tomlinson, 2000). Students need to understand that computer systems and software programs are designed to perform specific jobs. This helps them acquire the skill and knowledge of selecting the best tools to accomplish a task, solve a problem, and/or make a decision based on available data.

When using simulations and other problem-solving programs, remember never to rely on the software to teach higher-order thinking skills. Students need teachers to help them make connections. Encourage students to explain their thinking frequently when working collaboratively. Brainstorming tools such as Inspiration help students structure a strategy needed to solve a problem by flowcharting or explore the problem domain by creating concept maps.

Simulation Websites and Data Resources

Free Simulations

Chemistry Simulations
http://ir.chem.cmu.edu/irProject
The IrbYdium Project at Carnegie Mellon University funded by the National Science Foundation to create simulation-based chemistry learning environments

Computer Traffic Simulation: Graphical Version
www.math.toronto.edu/mathnet/carcompet/simulation.html
Provides a simple model of traffic flow

Physics Java Applets
www.walter-fendt.de/ph11e
Many applets available for download covering buoyancy, optics, and the theory of relativity to name just a few

SimScience
http://www.simscience.org
Devoted to areas of science in which computer simulations are at the forefront of discovery; provides access to four simulations: membranes, fluid flow, cracking dams, and crackling noise

SimSurface
http://storm.shodor.org/simsurf/simsurfinfo.html
A simulation designed to solve the problem of minimization of potential energy using the computational technique of simulated annealing and the relaxation method

Statistics
www.ruf.rice.edu/~lane/rvls.html
Virtual site that includes simulations and demonstrations on various topics and formulas on statistics

ThinkQuest
www.thinkquest.org/library
Archived site of student-generated ThinkQuest Contest entries. Enter "simulation" in search box to locate simulation entries

United Nations Simulation—The Electronic United Nations
www.simulations.com/cont1.htm
A United Nations simulation in which classrooms become "classroom countries" and interact with other "classroom countries"

Activity Examples

The Chaos Game
http://math.bu.edu./DYSYS/applets/chaos-game.html
An online game designed to improve students' geometric intuition and algorithmic thinking

Easy Fibonacci puzzles
www.mcs.surrey.ac.uk/Personal/R.Knott/Fibonacci/fibpuzzles.html
Provides puzzles that have Fibonacci numbers as their answers
NCTM electronic example of using data sets available on the Internet
http://standards.nctm.org/document/eexamples/chap5/5.4

NCTM simulation example
http://standards.nctm.org/document/eexamples/chap5/5.2
Grades 3–5 understanding distance, speed, and time relationships using simulation software

Statiscope by Mikael Bonnier
www.df.lth.se/~mikaelb/statiscope/statiscope-enu.shtml
Interactive environment (Java applet) for summarizing data and descriptive statistical charts

Statistical Teaching Activities
www.statcan.ca/english/kits/teach.htm
Categorized by grade bands; provides interactive exercises focusing on data analysis and survey skills maintained and developed by Statistics Canada

The WebWinds
http://asds.stsci.edu/packages/graphics/WebWinds.html
An interactive data system for collecting, representing, and analyzing data, and statistical decision making

Other Online Resources and Data Sets

Bureau of Census data—Population data set
http://factfinder.census.gov/servlet/BasicFactsServlet
www.census.gov/main/www/access.html
Comprehensive sites to locate population, housing, economic, and geographic data

Forbes.com
http://www.forbes.com
Source for business data; for example, a comparison of health benefits and 401(k) plans

Liberty Library of Constitutional Classics
http://www.constitution.org/liberlib.htm
Online collection of classic books and other works on constitutional governments ranging from antiquity to the present

Mathematics Archives
http://archives.math.utk.edu/software.html
A collection of software, abstracts, and reviews

National Center for Health Statistics
www.cdc.gov/nchs
Federal government agency provides statistical information to guide actions and policies for the purpose of improving the health of the American people; see its data warehouse at **www.cdc.gov/nchs/datawh.htm**

U.S. Federal Election Commission
www.fec.gov
Comprehensive information on the voting process

Problem Activity 1: Business

This activity gives students experience in real-world business operations. Students develop decision-making skills by scaling up a simulated business. Have students use the Lemonade Stand simulation at **www.coolmath4kids.com/lemonade** or use a search engine (e.g. Google, Yahoo, Lycos, etc.) and search on *lemonade stand simulation* for alternative versions. Provide students sufficient time to interact with the simulation and reflect on their experiences. Then ask them to conceptualize and define a problem resulting from the experience that they would like to analyze. Help them, if necessary, to formulate a question based on their problem spaces. Have them explore the solution by increasing the size and scope of their lemonade businesses. Challenge students to increase business profits and incorporate standard business operations, including inventory, sales, marketing, taxes, payroll, employee benefits, and personnel issues such as training. Have students explore purchasing and labor expenditures, and analyze consumer behavior and economic trends to assist their decision making about operational procedures and policies. Compare results and discuss their solution strategies. Determine which practices result in higher profits and why. Challenge students to form corporations and stage hostile takeovers. Have students work in small groups (perhaps the corporate groups they formed) through a stock market simulation. Have them use a search engine (e.g. Google, Yahoo, Lycos, etc.) to find a *stock market simulation* that interests them. Challenge student corporations to offer stock options to their employees. Have them appoint board members and hold board meetings to discuss business operations. Plan a field trip to visit a local hospital's or utility holding company's board meeting. Have students create a profit-and-loss statement as a culminating activity. For closure, discuss their responses to the experience.

Problem Activity 2: Politics

This activity gives students experience in real-world sampling and polling situations. Students develop skills in techniques of sampling and predicting from a sample as well as developing strategies for organizing and managing the data.

Create an election simulation based on Kids Voting results based on either the last general election or any current issue before the U.S. Senate or other legislative body. Have students do an internet search (e.g., Google, Yahoo, Lycos, etc.) on *kids voting results* for ideas. Have pairs of students use the simulation for a designated period of time. Students should reflect on their experience and identify a problem to investigate, for instance, voter irregularity. They formulate questions such as "Does ballot design affect voting patterns?" Students divide according to the current U.S. registration ratios between the two major parties and any third-party "wannabes." Students campaign for their candidates and/or issues for a specified period of time and create supporting propaganda, which will be displayed in the classroom. Throughout the specified period, selected students in support of each candidate or issue will make speeches and hold press conferences. At the end of the selected time, an election will occur. If students are voting for candidates only, students will vote only to elect "electors," who will then gather later to actually elect the candidates of their choice. Students create their own ballot box and secure the ballots. Students create a program to automate the voting process on a computer. Following the voting students will compare, contrast, and critique results and procedures. The teacher or elected committee will rule on challenges to any requested procedure. Students learn about issues relevant to any modern election, the effect of third-party vote dilution, as well as the need for coalitions to further their parties' interests.

Summary

This chapter took a closer look at data analysis and simulations with suggested resources to support teachers' integration of these technology-based inquiry and problem-solving approaches. Skill development in using data to reason and to make statistically based decisions is necessary for students to become informed citizens and intelligent consumers (NCTM, 2000). A brief history of data analysis highlighted a new approach called "exploratory data analysis." The next section introduced the use of computers as problem-solving tools, the NCTM Data Analysis and Probability Standard, and the NCTM recommendation to develop data analysis skills in all grades. To help teachers teach data analysis, the use of simulations is recommended.

A simulation is the process of imitating a real situation or object with a set of mathematical formulas. Simulations should be integrated as a vital part of the curriculum rather than as an add-on. Simulations can be used but are not limited to:

1. Visualize the invisible
2. Manipulate variables, observe results, and draw conclusions
3. Facilitate role playing

Simulation software and data analysis activities help develop the central elements of statistics. Statistics is a set of methods used to collect, analyze, present, and interpret data. Two problem activities were provided as examples of using simulations and data analysis. A listing of free web-based simulations and data sets will help teachers develop learning activities and materials for classroom use.

DVD/VIDEO VIGNETTE

Solving a Logical Reasoning Problem

Observe students solving a logical reasoning problem using calculators and then demonstrate their solutions by using a SMART Board and a document camera. Would this lesson have been possible without these technologies?

Challenge Yourself!

1. Use the Lemonade Stand simulation. Create activities that extend the simulation and deepen students' understanding of data analysis. Reflect on how the computer simulation will influence students' thinking and behavior. Describe in detail how you plan to scaffold their learning.

2. Go to the NCTM site at **http://standards.nctm.org/document/eexamples/ chap5/5.2/index.htm#APPLET.** Select a grade level and a task of your choice. Complete the task as directed. Scroll down the page to the section entitled Additional Tasks and Questions. Select one of the three tasks to complete as directed. As suggested, reflect on this question: What important ideas about functions and representing change over time can students learn while working on this activity?

3. Incorporate a data analysis activity into a unit or learning activity for your content area.

4. Integrate collaborative learning into one of the exploration activities. Try the activity with and without collaboration. Determine the best practice providing details on the context, grade level, and other relevant variables.

5. Create a web-based simulation to explore a problem in your content domain. Field-test your simulation. Use appropriate data analytic tools and statistical methods to formatively evaluate your simulation and refine the process based on your results.

6. After a thorough exploration of the simulation and data resources, post a question on your class discussion board or appropriate listserv to prompt a discussion of the theoretical principles underlying software programs and computer systems.

7. Review the DVD Video Vignette for this chapter. Identify and list the NETS Student Standards that are covered in the lesson. List the strengths and weaknesses of the lesson. Compare your results with those of your classmates.

8. Write a lesson plan for the DVD Video Vignette: Solving a Logical Reasoning Problem.

References

Behrens, J. T., & Smith, M. L. (1996). Data and data analysis. In D. C. Berliner & R. C. Calfee (Eds.), *Handbook of educational psychology* (pp. 945–989). New York: Simon & Schuster Macmillan.

Bryan, V. (2002). Increased productivity, staff development, and community collaboration using handheld PDAs, portals and exchange servers. *Journal of Interactive Instruction Development, 15*(2), 3–5.

Garofalo, J., & Sharp, B. (2003). Teaching fractions using a simulated sharing activity. *Learning and Leading with Technology, 30*(7), 36–41.

Goodman Research Group, Inc. (1998). *An evaluation of the testbed for telecollaboration.* Cambridge, MA: Author.

Hartley, K. (2000). Online simulations: Tools for inquiry-based science classrooms. *Learning and Leading with Technology, 28*(3), 32–35.

Henderson, L., Klemes, J., & Eshet, Y. (2000). Just playing a game? Educational simulation software and cognitive outcomes. *Journal of Educational Computing Research, 22*(1), 105–129.

Konold, C., Coulter, B., & Feldman, A. (2000). Engaging students with data. *Learning and Leading with Technology, 28*(3), 50–55.

National Council of Teachers of Mathematics. (2000). *Principles and standards for school mathematics.* Reston, VA: Author.

Newell, A., & Simon, H. (1972). *Human problem-solving.* Englewood Cliffs, NJ: Prentice-Hall.

Russell, S. J. (1990). Issues in training teachers to teach statistics in the elementary school: A world of uncertainty. In A. Hawkins (Ed.), *Training teachers to teach statistics. Proceedings of the International Statistical Institute Round Table Conference* (pp. 59–71). Voorburg, The Netherlands: International Statistical Institute.

Russell, S. J., Schifter, D., & Bastable, V. (2001). *Developing mathematical ideas: Collecting, representing and analyzing data.* Parsippany, NJ: Dale Seymour Publications.

Shaw, T. (2003). Technology, algorithms, and the creativity conundrum. *Multimedia Schools, 10*(4), 45–46.

ThinkQuest Student Journalists. (2002). Exploring the future of learning at ThinkQuest live. *Multimedia Schools, 9*(5), 11–14.

Tomlinson, B. (2000). Using simulations on materials development courses. *Simulation and Gaming, 31*(2), 152–170.

Tukey, J. W. (1977). *Exploratory data analysis.* Reading, MA: Addison-Wesley.

White, W. (2003). The essential fairness of a mortgage loan: Developing financial literacy. *Mathematics Teacher, 96*(7), 486–492.

Yeo, G. K., & Tan, S. T. (1999). Toward a multilingual, experiential environment for learning decision technology. *Simulation and Gaming, 30*(1), 70–82.

CHAPTER 12

Mathematical Modeling

FOCUS QUESTIONS

1. How are simulation and modeling activities different? Under what conditions is one approach more effective than the other?

2. How should a spreadsheet activity be structured?

3. What are the benefits to using modeling activities?

This chapter extends the introduction to data analysis and problem solving in Chapter 11 by discussing the use of mathematical modeling, spreadsheets, and a programming language. With the emergence of new data analysis tools and new types of data problems, novel types of models are consequently required to deal with them. Examples of these models include rule-based knowledge representations as used in expert systems, neural networks, genetic algorithms, multivariate adaptive regression splines, computer-intensive estimation methods such as the Markov chain, Monte Carlo methods, and statistical databases, which need operations such as datacube.

The modeling process is evolutionary. There are always other influences or factors, not anticipated in the first model or prototype, that interfere with prediction accuracy. Reiterating steps in the modeling process, making improvements to define the problem, constructing the model, and improving data collection techniques improve not only the product but also the conceptualizing process. The refinement of a model may progress ad infinitum if using a trial-and-error approach and still achieve only an arbitrary degree of accuracy. However, in the context of data analysis, an extremely sophisticated data analytic technique can data mine the information and achieve more predictive power.

A strategy for data analysis descriptively plans the steps, decisions, and procedures to follow when analyzing data to build a model or answer a question. Generally stated, the steps are

1. Define the problem.
2. Extract and identify the most important factors.
3. Construct a model to describe the shape of the reduced data.

Effective procedures are called algorithms. Flowcharts are used to graphically represent algorithms, which are detailed sequences of simple steps needed to solve a problem. A problem is unsolvable if no algorithm can solve it and, if a decision problem, undecidable if no algorithm can decide it.

Mathematical Modeling

There are different types of models. For instance, a miniature replica of a spacecraft used to study design features is a physical model. Examples of this model type can be found at science fair exhibits in which students represent the solar system using a box with balls of various colors and sizes hanging from strings. Another, and perhaps the most useful, type is a conceptual model. For instance, a diagram of the water cycle is used to describe the behavior of the system, in this case water. When the language of mathematics is utilized to describe the system's behavior, a mathematical model is created. For example, representing the shape of the Earth as a sphere provides a mathematical model. In this case, elementary geometry is used to describe the system.

Models, both physical and conceptual, are problem-solving tools because they are easily manipulated and changed as needed. Models assist experimentation, which aims to achieve an understanding and generate new information about the modeled system. Some systems may be too complex or too inaccessible to explore in their original settings. In many business and scientific situations, the design and use of models in planning and production processes are critical. The process of modeling follows these steps:

1. Observing a system or problem
2. Constructing a mental image or model
3. Identifying important variables and constants (parameters)
4. Determining relationships
5. Developing equation(s) to express relationships
6. Testing
7. Revising

Modeling is used when simulations are not a feasible approach. Modeling activities can be used to demonstrate change. Additionally, modeling is a technique of expression and explanation. For an excellent learning activity for the secondary grade level, see "Chaos and Beyond" in ISTE's *National Educational Technology Standards for Students* (Thomas & Bitter, 2000).

Problem Activity 1

Mathematical modeling can occur in nonmathematical contexts. Develop a mathematical model of how you plan to read this textbook. Share your model in a small group (no more than four). Work together to create a group model. Diagram or make a flowchart of your group process. How did your group achieve consensus?

Problem Activity 2

Consider the following real-world problem:

> What is the cost of illiteracy to a community? In groups of three or four, brainstorm the possible cost areas using a brainstorming tool such as Inspiration to develop a concept map. Identify the important variables and parameters. Decide on a data collection plan. After the data are collected and graphically represented, construct a mathematical model by developing an equation representing the relationships between variables and parameters. Test using what-if questions and refine your model. Would using a different definition of illiteracy change your model?

Mathematical modeling can be applied to additional real-world problems. Some examples are predicting wildlife populations, costs of long-distance phone calls, irrigation flow rates, and deciding on the fastest checkout line at a grocery store.

Modeling is effective in education. Due to changes and shifts in population, it is important for educational institutions to assess their immediate future needs, as well as long-term ones. By asking what-if questions based on census information and other known statistics, school districts, colleges, and universities can be better prepared to offer quality education. In the classroom, probability situations can be modeled with a computerized framework such as a spreadsheet. A spreadsheet model is created and its figure displayed; the user then asks the computer "what if" a specific value were to be changed. The value can be a change in actual numbers or an increase or decrease by a specified percentage rate. By experimenting with various probabilities, students can examine the basic theory of probability.

Spreadsheets

Spreadsheets are very useful for modeling activities (Scaife & Wellington, 1993) and are fast becoming programming environments (Carson, 1997). As explained earlier in Chapter 2, the spreadsheet's array of rows and columns may be organized in such a way as to be easily understandable to the reader. Because each piece of data entered into the spreadsheet is considered as it relates to the other data, any change made in one part affects the whole spreadsheet. Subsequently, information can be manipulated to reflect potential change or what-if questions in any or all sections of the spreadsheet. This capability makes spreadsheets a useful tool to detect mathematical change. Having students graph and chart using spreadsheets helps them visualize change and learn the advantages and disadvantages of different graphical representations.

More on Spreadsheets: Their History and Use

The electronic spreadsheet made its debut in 1979, a creation of two Harvard Business School graduate students, Daniel Bricklin and Robert Frankston. They named their program VisiCalc, and it became the prototype for many other software programs that formed the first generation of electronic spreadsheets.

The second generation came on the scene with the introduction of Lotus 1-2-3 in 1982. This program was unique in being the first integrated software program. An integrated software program blends several different programs so that information can be presented in various forms. For example, a graphics option allows the user to create visual aids, such as line graphs, vertical and horizontal bar graphs, and pie charts. In this way, the figures from the spreadsheet can be converted into graphs that show at a glance what the user wishes to communicate about the financial picture.

Another option contained in Lotus 1–2-3 is database management. A *database* is an electronic filing system in which large volumes of data (information) can be stored and organized. For instance, names, addresses, phone numbers, and account numbers entered into a database can then be sorted alphabetically, numerically, or in any other way that will be helpful to the user. In an integrated program, any of the needed stored information can be retrieved from the database and inserted into the spreadsheet. The time saved in locating and adding data to a spreadsheet made this new generation of software a welcome addition to the electronic spreadsheet family.

The most recent addition to this family, and the beginning of the third generation, is the integrated software program with extended capabilities. It adds word processing, expanded spreadsheet size, and communications between computers. Word processing allows text to be added to the report. In this way, an explanation of the spreadsheet figures or the graphic pictures can complete a financial report.

Another improvement is the potential size of spreadsheets. Spreadsheet programs vary in the numbers of rows and columns available, but average size is much larger now than what was originally offered. Any number of these columns and rows may be used, depending on the needs of the user and the memory capacity of the computer. Although only a small portion of this total picture appears on the computer screen at one time, the user may move around within the spreadsheet to display any part of it.

Yet another improvement in this latest generation of spreadsheet programs is the ability of computers to communicate with each other. Through the new technology of telecommunications, computers in different locations can communicate by telephone lines and exchange data as needed. Examples of programs combining all of the preceding options are AppleWorks and Microsoft Office. Chapter 2 discussed the use of spreadsheets in education. The following section presents additional practical applications related to problem solving and data analysis.

Analysis and Projection

Spreadsheet information is essential in analyzing the financial condition of any organization. Spreadsheets also make analysis of statistical information more manageable and much faster. Analysis, then, is one of the more important uses of electronic spreadsheets. A natural outcome of analysis is projection for the future. Let's look now at the value of spreadsheets in these two areas.

In business and other organizations, analysis is the examination and evaluation of data to measure their impact on the particular organization for which it is being performed. Spreadsheets are an excellent way to compare data. To accomplish this, spreadsheets can be combined, both in part and in total. By defining a range of cells, rows, or columns, any part of a spreadsheet may be retrieved and made a part of others. In this way, very complicated data can be displayed for comparison. Windowing, discussed earlier, is most helpful for these operations.

As in education, planning for other public and social programs is dependent on knowing what will happen if certain changes take place within society. Changes in the political climate, for instance, have an impact on almost every area of life. The educational community will obviously benefit quite as much as private business and industry by using the analytic properties of electronic spreadsheets.

By combining the information gained from analysis of a spreadsheet with expectations for the future, it is possible to project what may happen. Projection is the predicting, or forecasting, of what may be logically expected to occur in the future based on what we know about the past. There are three basic types of planning for the future: operational, tactical, and strategic. There are also two basic areas wherein planning is necessary—expense and income.

In the area of expense, operational planning is the simplest and covers a period of only a few months at a time. It deals with day-to-day operations. Usually done by lower-level managers, this type of planning obviously is short-term and therefore requires less complex spreadsheet information than do other types. An example of operational planning is the adjustment of teaching staff and classroom space.

Tactical planning is for an intermediate period, perhaps covering a time span of one to three years. This includes planned stages of development working toward long-term goals. An example of this type of planning is the revision of school budgets in response to projected increased enrollment.

Strategic planning occurs at the highest level of management and addresses the overall long-range welfare of the organization. Examples of this level of planning are direction of growth, curriculum development, and expansion of school districts.

Future income also requires planning and projection on the part of school administrators. For instance, expected changes in income due to school bond issues can be included in planning.

For higher-level educational institutions, administrators must predict potential changes in student population and project income based on tuition and fees. For instance, funds allotted from other agencies may change from time to time. For this and other reasons, planning for the future is essential to a smooth operation.

Government agencies have a similar need to make projections based on changes in population, income, and societal needs. One of the most obvious areas of public service is transportation. How many freeways to build? What is the projected need for public transportation? This is only one of many services provided by local, state, and national government agencies that may be better analyzed through the use of electronic spreadsheets.

Problem Activity 3

In small groups look at census data from your state. (Visit **http://factfinder.census. gov/java_prod/dads.ui.homePage.HomePage** for Bureau of Census data or **www. census.gov** for data sets.) Look at the available spreadsheet data files from the Crime

& Justice Electronic Data Abstracts' website (**www.ojp.usdoj.gov/bjs/dtdata.htm**). Select a data set to download. Create a spreadsheet to compare the downloaded files. Look for a mathematical change to detect a pattern. Try out different types of representations such as maps or graphs. Based on exploratory data analysis, develop a question to explore using this sentence stem: Is there a relationship between *xxx* and *yyy*? Write a formula that represents the relationship. Test the formula. What happens numerically? Graph the change. Create what-if questions to further explore the changes. Present your findings to the class and discuss the results.

Logo as a Learning Tool

As noted earlier, an important part of computer literacy is to familiarize students with the process of programming computers to perform specific functions. With the advent of languages such as Logo, programming skills can be taught to even the youngest students. The use of computer programming need no longer be limited to specialized secondary courses.

Many people have found that they can learn a great deal about programming by simply typing into the computer a Logo program that has been written by another person. This technique can be quite effective in the classroom. The student gains a sense of control over the computer by entering a set of program instructions and then observing the computer carrying out the instructions. Students come to understand some of the fundamentals in this manner. For example, they see that the computer can do only that which it has been programmed to do. They see the need for very accurate and concise instructions to avoid errors. They begin to understand that the computer can work for them once they learn to communicate with it.

For this reason, it is a good idea to begin exploring programming with user-friendly languages such as Logo. Students need to see that the computer can understand commands in plain English and that programming languages are not overwhelmingly complicated sets of numbers and esoteric symbols. Designing activities using Logo as the programming language is a good starting place because Logo is relatively accessible and understandable to students. Other options are Microworlds or Geo Logo.

A number of books have been published with public domain programs that students can key into the computer for practice. Some perform basic calculations to solve problems or track numerical data and others play games. The programs range from very simple to very complex, providing practice for students of all grade and skill levels. A word of caution is necessary, however. Not all the programs to be found have been debugged carefully. Students may be frustrated if they spend hours typing and correcting their typed instructions only to find that the program does not work as promised even when the instructions are typed correctly. Teachers who possess strong programming skills can help their students out of such difficulties. Teachers with less experience in this area may do well to read reviews of the materials before using them in the classroom.

Another good source of programs for students to use is popular Logo computer periodicals. Some of these periodicals feature program instructions (also called code) and documentation on a regular basis. Many school libraries subscribe to these periodicals, so the materials are often readily available to teachers and students.

The following Logo activity focuses on the area of mathematics. Gifted or highly motivated students can be encouraged to venture out on their own by tailoring the programs to perform additional functions as well. The activity focuses on using the computer as a tool for problem solving, which is really the forte of the computer. The authors suggest that teachers introduce programming early and in a nonthreatening way by integrating programming skills into subject areas across the curriculum. Specifically, because the computer is an excellent mathematical tool, it makes good sense to integrate the use of Logo to teach and explore mathematics. Students can learn programming skills with relative ease while they are mastering mathematical concepts. Teachers who want to introduce Logo to explore mathematics in their classrooms can use the following activity.

Teachers should use their own judgment in adapting the activity for their grade levels and use with their own students. How well students perform in programming depends on a number of factors, including previous experience, attitudes toward computers, and perceived value of programming skills. Class discussions conducted before programming activities are presented can aid the teacher in discovering and exploring these crucial factors.

Activity Title: *Problem Solving with Logo*

Grade-Level Range: 4 to 6

Purpose.   In this activity students

- Use Logo to solve mathematical and geometrical problems
- Explore the concept of symmetry
- Address the following National Educational Technology Standards (NETS) for Students Standards: 3—Technology productivity tools and 6—Technology problem-solving and decision-making tools

Activity Preparation

- Students need to be familiar with Logo commands used to draw shapes.
- Prepare and copy activity sheets.
- Draw several simple shapes on paper. Then using the mirror, introduce the students to the concept of mirror images.

Activity Procedure

1. Have students write Logo programs that will produce mirror images of the shapes displayed on the activity sheet.
2. Students test their programs to see how well they run.
3. Assist students in performing any debugging that may be required in order for the programs to recreate the shapes accurately.

Tools and Resources

- Computer
- Compatible Logo software
- Activity sheet
- Mirror

Assessment.   Do the students' programs draw mirror images of the shapes on the activity sheet? Have students been successful in locating and correcting errors in their programs?

Comments.   Another interesting experience would be to give students only one half of a shape so that the mirror images they create would complete the picture. Simple shapes such as houses or faces can be used effectively.

Summary

Computers have been used by business, education, government, and individuals to organize and analyze all kinds of information. Mathematical modeling is an effective problem-solving approach used to represent systems. The spreadsheet is a useful tool for managing financial and statistical information in data analysis contexts. Called an electronic spreadsheet when done by a computer, this technique has become one of the most effective time-savers of our new technology.

From the prototype created by two Harvard students in 1979, to the latest sophisticated integrated software packages, electronic spreadsheets have grown from a useful tool to an indispensable fact of life. All areas of daily existence have been influenced by this development.

In education, spreadsheets are used in various ways. These include teaching (e.g., accounting, math, and science classes), maintaining student records, budgeting for both the entire school and various groups within it, and management of data by research groups.

Government agencies are also big users of electronic spreadsheets. They manage and manipulate vast amounts of data, analyze changes in all areas of society, and plan for the future needs of communities and the nation.

We as individuals benefit from this new tool as well. We use electronic spreadsheets for personal banking, household management, tax records, and budgeting. Each of us is influenced either directly or indirectly by the widespread use of spreadsheets in the real world. For this reason, the practical application of spreadsheets has been stressed in this chapter. To implement a spreadsheet, a user must be familiar with the terms, modes, commands, formulas, and functions presented here.

Once a spreadsheet has been created and data entered, it may be used to analyze the data it contains and to make projections for the future based on that data and other knowledge and expectations. What-if statements may be used to set up theoretical conditions; the spreadsheet then calculates the potential results. The instant answers given by this method save many hours of tedious labor, without mathematical error.

Spreadsheets serve us all in many ways. In some cases, we use them to make our individual tasks easier. In other instances, we benefit from their use in business, government, and education.

This chapter presented two problem activities and one learning activity to assist teachers in using the computer to teach mathematical skills. As has been noted, even the youngest students can begin acquiring skills that are necessary in writing instructions for computers to follow.

The activities can be adapted to the various grade levels with minor modifications. All of the activities are aimed to develop problem-solving and data analysis skills. Numerous resources are available to teachers of all subject areas who want to use modeling, spreadsheets, or Logo in their learning activities. Students can learn a great deal about programming by typing into the computer the programs found in these resources and experimenting with them. Students also learn by modifying simple Logo programs to fit their own needs. Teachers should check their school media centers as well as local libraries for availability of computer periodicals that feature Logo activities.

Using modeling, spreadsheets, and Logo as problem-solving–decision-making tools prompts class discussions or avenues for further research. Students are also a valuable source of inspiration in the use of Logo. It is a good idea to encourage students to look for ways of enhancing programs or expanding applications of programs. After all, the more creative our future programmers are, the brighter the future for all of us.

DVD/VIDEO VIGNETTE

Million $ Project

Real-world problems are solved through the use of spreadsheets, the Internet, and presentation software. How does the authentic context improve learning over simply teaching students how to use these technology tools in isolation?

Challenge Yourself!

1. Interview a student taking a computer programming class in a local high school or college. Write a summary about his or her experiences and expectations.
2. Review the DVD Video Vignette for this chapter. Identify and list the NETS student Standards that are covered in the lesson. List the strengths and weaknesses of the lesson. Compare your results with those of your classmates.
3. Present one of the activities in this chapter to your class and write a report on the results, include appropriate data analysis.
4. Locate a spreadsheet tutorial and follow several lessons. Evaluate its effectiveness in terms of utility, ease of use, time, and achievement.
5. Create a poster showing common commands in Logo.
6. Find a Math Modeling Exercise website. Select an exercise and work with a partner to complete the exercise and present your model to the class. Adapt one of the exercises for your content area.

7. Locate a data analysis activity using spreadsheets from an online resource. Write a review of the activity outlining its strengths and weaknesses and provide empirical support.
8. Create a learning activity using Logo to teach geometry concepts.
9. Plan a sequence of activities utilizing mathematical modeling, spreadsheets, or Logo to teach mathematical concepts aligned with the National Council of Teachers of Mathematics Standards.
10. Does Logo have a future use in education? Why or why not? Support your position with classroom scenarios.

References

Branzburg, J. (2000). Spreadsheets. *Technology and Learning, 21*(3), 67.

Carson, S. R. (1997). The use of spreadsheets in science—an overview. *School Science Review, 79*(287), 69–80.

Doerr, H. (2003). A modeling perspective on students' mathematical reasoning about data. *Journal for Research in Mathematics Education, 34*(2), 110–136.

Drier, H. S. (1999). Do vampires exist: Using spreadsheets to investigate a common folktale. *Learning and Leading with Technology 27*(1), 22–25.

Fortunato, J. (2002). Selling your students on spreadsheets. *Learning and Leading with Technology, 30*(2), 28–31.

Golshan, B. (1997). *Problem solving with Microsoft Excel.* Williamsport, PA: Lycoming College.

Kosko, T. (1985). Some projects for your programming classes. *The Computing Teacher, 12*(6), 24.

Lewis, P. (2002). Spreadsheet magic. *Learning and Leading with Technology, 30*(3), 36–41.

Maddux, C. D. (1985). *Logo in the schools.* New York: Haworth Press.

Maddux, C. D., & Johnson, D. L. (1988). *Logo: Methods and curriculum for teachers.* New York: Haworth Press.

Niess, M. (2002). Exploring linear equations with technology. *Learning and Leading with Technology, 30*(2), 32–35.

Ostler, E., & Grandgenett, N. (1999). *Mathematical modeling activities: A primer for grades 5–12.* Omaha, NE: Midwest Educational Technology Services.

Papert, S. (1980). *Mindstorms: Children, computers and powerful ideas.* New York: Basic Books.

Resnick, M. (1994). *Turtles, termites and traffic jams.* Cambridge, MA: MIT Press.

Scaife, J., & Wellington, J. (1993). *Information technology in science and technology education.* Buckingham, UK: Open University Press.

Shimabukuro, G. (1989). A class act: Junior high students, Lego and Logo. *The Computing Teacher, 17*(5), 37–39.

Smith, D. N. (1997). Independent mathematical modeling. *Teaching Mathematics and Its Applications, 16*(3), 101–106.

Staudt, C. (2002). Understanding algebra through handhelds. *Learning and Leading with Technology, 30*(2), 36–38.

Thomas, L., & Bitter, G. G. (2000). (Eds.). *National Educational Technology Standards for Students: Connecting curriculum and technology.* Eugene, OR: International Society for Technology in Education, 122–125.

Watt, D. (1989). Research on Logo learning as a path to professional teacher development. *Electronic Learning, 8*(5), 22–24.

Wiburg, K. M. (1989). Does programming deserve a place in the school curriculum? *The Computing Teacher, 17*(1), 8–11.

Websites

Bureau of Justice—Crime & Justice Electronic Data Abstracts **www.ojp.usdoj.gov/bjs/**

Fractal Modeling Tools **http://scan.shodor.org/master/fractal**

Instructional Resources **http://scan.shodor.org/master/fractal/curriculum**

Live Access to Pacific Marine Environmental Laboratory Data **http://ferret.pmel.noaa.gov/Ferret**

Logo for Kids **www.kidsandcomputers.com/SiteToc.cfm**

Logo Programming **http://el.media.mit.edu/logo-foundation/logo/programming.html**

Mathematical Modeling of Evolution **http://pespmc1.vub.ac.be/:/MATHME.html**

Mathematics: Modeling Our World—Teacher Support Web Site **www.comap.com/highschool/projects/mmow**

Math Numeracy **www.gainsborough.school.cheshire.org.uk/Numeracy_Sites.htm**

MSWLogo—free download **www.softronix.com/logo.html**

Some Simple Population Models **www.krellinst.org/AiS/textbook/unit2/pop.html**

Spreadsheet Lesson Plan for Eighth-Graders **www.dpi.state.nc.us/Curriculum/Computer.skills/lssnplns/SSlesson.G8.3.2.1.html**

CHAPTER 13

Organizing and Managing

FOCUS QUESTIONS

1. What are some considerations behind the choice to group computers together into labs versus putting them into individual classrooms?

2. How can collaboration with colleagues lead to more student opportunities to use technology?

3. How might the physical conditions of a classroom and educational philosophy of a teacher affect how computers are placed?

Some would say that in a perfect world, every student would have his or her own computer. Students could work whenever they wanted or needed, they could gather together to learn collaboratively, and they could use computers as easily as they now use other learning tools, such as pencils or books. Because this dream is not yet a reality for the majority of schools, the question of how student learning can be organized in any given technology situation needs to be addressed. How can teachers make the most of what they have available, ensuring that students get experience with the types of skills that will be indispensable in their future academic and professional pursuits? Unfortunately, the simple logistics that are explained in teacher in-service trainings or in professional journals and books do not always prove simple when put into practical use.

Classroom Computers versus Computer Labs

In order to devise a workable plan for both student and teacher computer use, you need to begin with an understanding of how computers are distributed in your school. There is an ongoing debate among educators as to how computers can best be arranged to offer students the most equitable and effective access to technology. One school of thought values a distributed model that breaks apart the traditional computer labs and distributes the machines out among the classrooms. It stresses that in order for technology to be truly integrated into the learning process, it must be immediately accessible to learners. If computers are located in a lab, that may mean that students place their hands on the equipment only once a week and then in only an artificial, disconnected way. Having a set "computer time" gives the impression that computers are some separate entity, a "field trip" on which students get to embark just once each week. This contrasts with the idea that the machines are viable learning tools that can provide endless research and production possibilities each day.

Educators on the other side of the debate see advantages in placing all of the computers into one computer lab, generally located in an extra classroom or other free space at the school (see Figure 13.1). This layout was the common practice during the early years when computers were still gaining an accepted place in our schools. It still makes the most sense to many technology planners today. It is cost-effective in that it gives all students in all grade levels a chance to use the machines, and it means that the expensive machines are used virtually all day. Each class typically schedules a weekly computer time when students can go to the lab together to work. If a school is fortunate, it may have a full- or part-time computer teacher to instruct with or about technology or to assist the classroom teacher with ideas and technical support.

Of course, lab advocates are quick to point out that a plan that involves sending all of the computers into the classrooms creates problems of its own. Although a small group of students can work on a timely activity in the classroom, the whole class cannot learn the same thing at the same time (Huffman et al., 2003). Teachers may be forced to explain the same concept a number of times, as each group comes to the class computer. Not having computers in one location also may preclude a designated technology teacher from presenting lessons. It instead might require the classroom teachers to assume the majority of technology instruction.

FIGURE 13.1 A school computer lab.

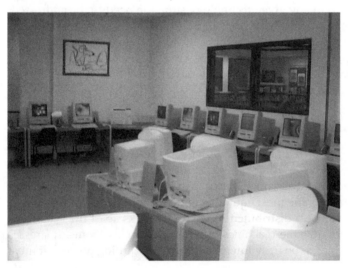

There are countless variations of computer distributions that fall somewhere in between these two extremes. Sometimes new computers are arranged together into labs so that all students have access to them, and the older computers are doled out to individual classrooms. Many schools are now experimenting with distributed computers in classrooms with the addition of "minilabs" of a small number of computers located in groupings around the school, possibly shared by two or three grade levels. Understanding the issues, and then considering which path your school has chosen to take and the thinking that went into making that choice, will help you plan for the smartest computer use possible for your class.

Organizing Learning in a Classroom Setting

A great deal of thought must go into how you plan on utilizing your classroom computers, whether you have one or are fortunate enough to have several. The use of the computer in your classroom should reflect your personal style and educational philosophies just as the use of any other learning tools do. Your very attitude about the computer's place in your instructional plan goes a long way in determining how your students will view its usefulness. If the computer sits in the corner under an inch of dust or if computer time is spent only "playing games," students will naturally fail to see its potential importance in their learning. If, on the other hand, students see your enthusiasm for technology, if they see you using it as a tool to accomplish real goals despite your fear of learning something new, they will be drawn to learn and experiment with skills they must have to be successful in the future. For simplicity's sake, these recommendations will be directed primarily to the multiple-computer classroom, but they can be easily modified to fit the technology available to you as well as to fit the particular needs of your students.

Room Arrangement

How you arrange your classroom is an expression of the way you view the learning process, and how you integrate technical equipment into the physical space of your classrooms is an extension of these beliefs. Instead of pushing your classroom computers into the nearest corner, thoughtfully consider how they will be used by you and your students (Anderson, 1996).

If you plan to have individuals or partners use computers while the rest of the class engages in other activities, you may want to put the computers off to one side of the room. Because what is seen on a computer monitor can be distracting to students working elsewhere, resist pushing the computers up against the wall, and instead turn them so that the monitors face away from the majority of the class. Bookshelves or other furniture can also be moved to create a more private computer area, if desired. This, of course, makes it more difficult for you to view the computer screens to see how students are progressing, so be prepared to adjust your supervision habits.

If small groups will be using the computers, be sure there is enough room for several chairs to be pulled up and that there is easy access to other group work areas. If you plan to use the computer as one station in a series of learning centers to which students will be rotating, plan ahead for traffic patterns. Be sure students can easily get around the work area, even if others are sitting at the computer (Waddick, 1997).

You might like to try using your classroom computer as a presentation aid for the whole class (see Chapter 14 for more information on producing and presenting with your classroom computer). In that case, you will want to be sure the computer is located so that it is easy to connect to a projection device or can be easily moved.

As important as the learning purpose is to deciding how to arrange computers, what also must be considered is the reality of the physical situation of your classroom. Computers must be within reach of electrical outlets, for example. Care should be taken so that the glare from windows does not make seeing the screen impossible. The actual furniture on which the computer is placed should also be given some thought. Some schools purchase specially designed computer furniture. Others have gone as far as to ingeniously build the computer monitor right into the desk itself, allowing students to see it through a sturdy, waterproof glass top, but leaving a flat work space across which students can easily see and be seen (Bozzone, 1997). If your school has not acquired any special furniture, you may be forced to creatively craft a computer workstation by pushing together existing desks and tables. Take the time to make this workstation as ergonomically appropriate for your students as possible, such as by raising or lowering the table legs. These preparations will make for a more functional technology classroom (see Figure 13.2).

Technical Procedures

When computers are distributed into classrooms, teachers must assume much of the responsibility for the day-to-day technical operation of the equipment. There

FIGURE 13.2 A classroom computer workstation.

may be a school or district technology specialist available, but you will want to be familiar with enough of the basic troubleshooting strategies to prevent long interruptions of student productivity. You will want to take time to study how the wires are connected to the computer and to other peripherals, such as a monitor and a printer. Organize software on the desktop with icons so that students will be able to quickly and easily find applications they need without disturbing other directories or programs.

Model appropriate care and use of the machine and software to prevent some potential problems. Dust the computer and the monitor weekly, for example. Keep floppy disks away from magnetic devices and excess heat or cold. Depending on students' ages or capabilities, they can be taught to handle many common operational and maintenance procedures, such as loading a new CD-ROM or replacing paper into the printer. When technical or other problems arise, think aloud to students as you consider your options, and demonstrate how you would solve them, thus providing a real problem-solving model. The more independently students can operate classroom computers, the more confident they will be in using them.

Scheduling Computer Use

Students should be made aware of the expectations you have for their computer use just as they are aware of expectations for other academic and behavioral habits. Make it clear when it is appropriate to go to the computer and when other work should be focused on. This will prevent congregation around a computer every time a new sound is heard or when your students enter the room at the beginning of the period.

Whether you have six or thirty computers in your classroom, you can design efficient use strategies by scheduling time for students to work on the computers. Your students will need time to use the computers in two different ways. It is first essential to provide time for students to explore and learn how to use computer hardware and software. This may be an informal discovery time or may be structured so that students work with one particular skill or program. Students also must have time to use what they have learned for productive purposes. These personal work times should allow students to use technology to work on class assignments or to pursue individual projects, but should be organized around an ultimate goal of a finished product.

A number of different strategies can be used to introduce new computer skills. To demonstrate some basic operational skills, such as manipulating text in a word processor or saving files to the school network, you may choose to show the entire class at once using a projection device. If you have received new software, you might decide to show it to a couple of students, and let them teach the next couple of students, and so on. You can also write some simple, developmentally appropriate directions and let students discover how to use a graphics program on their own using the directions as a guide. With any method, students must be allowed time to practice these ideas before they are required to use them for real purposes. Once students are confident with the basics, they can apply what they know to achieving other academic goals.

A sign-up sheet for computer time is one way teachers organize student computer use. Unfortunately, if students can sign up for time only when they have finished their other work, only a select few students will ever get regular computer experience. Creating a set weekly schedule for computer use can help to ensure equity in opportunities for students in á high student–computer ratio classroom. Look at all of the available time when your students are in the room, and divide this time into workable blocks of perhaps thirty minutes each. Slot in students' names so that each has time for both practicing new skills and authentic technology use, ideally scheduled in two separate work times to give them the best chance for quality learning. Schedule students for times during the day when they can work on the computers without missing instruction that they need. Depending on your students' experience levels and specific needs, having them work in pairs could be more beneficial than working by themselves. Post the schedule so that students know when their weekly times are and when there are open slots (see Figure 13.3). This allows them to plan when they will be working on the computers and also shows open times that are available for spontaneous technology use. Students must feel that they have opportunity to word process a story or create graphics when they need to without necessarily having to wait for their slot once or twice a week. The posted schedule also encourages student monitoring of computer use. When a student's computer time is over, he or she can alert the next person on the list, relieving you to work with students in other capacities.

Assistance

Successful facilitation of a technology-rich classroom requires the coordination of help from a number of sources. Parent volunteers with computer experience can provide needed technical support, and those who are computer novices can encourage and supervise as they learn along with the students. Older students who are able to donate time can teach younger students the finer points of a new piece of software

FIGURE 13.3 Weekly schedule of classroom computer use.

	Monday	Tuesday	Wednesday	Thursday	Friday
8:00-8:30	Raymond	Jenny	Maura	Mary	Donna
8:30-9:00	Jonathon			Gene	Jeffrey
9:00-9:30		Ally	Tonya	Winston	
9:30-10:00	Rachel	John	Robin		
10:00-10:30		David			
10:30-11:00	Alex	Elaine		Harmony	Vonny
11:00-11:30			LUNCH		
11:30-12:00			RECESS		
12:00-12:30	Tricia	Joshua		Greg	Tommy
12:30-1:00			Gina	James	Shawna
1:00-1:30			Troy		
1:30-2:00	Marisa	Gwen		Jimmy	
2:00-2:30	Whitney		Travis		
2:30-3:00					

or can help with some of the manual work that sometimes slows down little hands, such as typing text into a word processor. Peers can also serve as teachers to one another, sharing special skills or teaming to work out a problem. They often can fill in where teachers may lack the technical expertise.

Make your students aware of their options for assistance so that they learn not to depend on you alone. This is a difficult lesson, especially considering the inherent technical problems that come with regular use of computers. A simple paper jam in the printer or a malfunctioning CD-ROM can bring to a standstill the immediate continued use of the computer. Students' first reaction is to think that you alone will be able to remedy the situation, and, indeed, many teachers new to using technology fall into the trap of running to solve every technical glitch that springs up. If this habit continues, being the sole technical problem solver will monopolize your time. An independent, problem-solving atmosphere established in your classroom will help students to troubleshoot technical problems themselves and with those who are there for them.

Teamwork

As talented at scheduling the use of limited computers as a teacher may be, there remain considerable limitations to having only a few machines. This is an excellent time when teamwork among your colleagues can be invaluable to your students. One easy way to make the most of the computers in classrooms is to work out a schedule with other teachers so that your students can go to use the computers when their students are not using them and vice versa. When schools have such a low ratio of computers to students, the time computer keys are sitting idle should be minimized.

Organizing Learning in a Single-Computer Setting

A single-computer setting is not the ideal situation. However, with careful planning and a pioneering, creative spirit, the recommendations discussed can be modified to fit the one-computer classroom (Banaszerski, 1997). If students use the computer regularly, placing the computer on your desk gives the impression that it is your computer and students are merely borrowing time on it.

A more drastic, yet potentially more beneficial, act is to consider teaming with other teachers to pool your single computers together to create a minilab. One teacher can volunteer to house the lab in a corner of the classroom, and a schedule can be worked out so that small groups of students from all the classes involved can come together to work on projects or content software. As teachers everywhere strive to effectively integrate technology into everyday learning experiences, they must all be open to the creative possibilities that happen when they work together.

Organizing Learning in a Lab Setting

If the majority of your students' time with computers will be spent in a computer lab setting, some forethought and well-planned procedures can make for successful utilization of the technology. Many of the planning and operational procedures parallel those that have been discussed for classroom use, but the differences lie with the decreased freedom you have in room arrangement and scheduling. Trooping your entire class down to the computer lab without any plan as to what will happen will only waste your students' valuable time with computers and cause undue frustration for everyone involved. Consider each of the following areas as they relate to the real situation at your school (Wodarz, 2003).

Equipment

Being prepared is a motto teachers live by, but when it comes to technology, that motto becomes a rule that simply cannot be broken. You need to be familiar with the equipment your students will be using so that you will be able to effectively facilitate their learning. Although this does not mean you need to be a technology expert, you must be at least familiar enough with the operation to facilitate your students' learning experiences.

Skill with computers is a unique area that is leading teachers to reconsider the notion that they must be knowledgeable about everything that they teach in the classroom. Students may in fact know more about a particular piece of software or hardware, and may have less fear of exploring the unknown than many of their teachers. Although there are a multitude of ways teachers can encourage and capitalize on these individual strengths and desires to experiment, they should at the same time be making an effort to acquire a personal level of familiarity with the present technology. A learning experience in the computer lab will be more closely integrated into the ongoing curriculum and be therefore of greater educational benefit to students if you have taken the time to walk down to the computer lab to become comfortable with how the computers are configured prior to bringing your entire class down for a lesson.

Preplanning and Preinstructing

To make the most out of a brief weekly computer lab experience, students must be primed for what they will be doing and what will be expected of them. Valuable time will be wasted if the class must wait until they are seated in the lab to receive instructions for how their time will be spent. A lesson that fits well into a curriculum sequence will be planned in advance. Any materials students will need should be brought along with them. If groups will need to do any note taking, for example, they should have paper and pencils available. If students will be using a productivity tool to finish a piece of work, such as a word processor to type stories they have written, that work should be out and ready to go when you leave for the lab. If possible and appropriate, instructions can be given and work strategies discussed prior to arrival in the lab. This not only will maximize available lab time and prepare students with a productive mind-set for the work period but also will stress to students the continuity between what they learn in the computer lab and what they are learning in class. This strategy reflects the view that technology is just another tool in your instructional arsenal, rather than a special, disconnected activity.

Assistance

One important consideration when planning class use of a computer lab is the extent to which you can depend on supplemental assistance. If your school or district employs a designated technology teacher, find out how often this teacher is available to help you. Depending on other responsibilities, some technology specialists may offer to plan with you for technology integration, may co-teach an activity with you, or may even teach entire technology-rich lessons. Sometimes several schools are forced to share a technology teacher, meaning that the teacher's time available for each individual teacher is limited. Unfortunately, other districts, whether due to lack of funds or insufficient teacher interest, do not have additional technology help available. A situation like this puts the onus on teachers to plan and implement lessons with technology on their own. An enormous number of educational journals now address technology issues, providing current and very practical suggestions for lessons and projects. Subscriptions to a few of these will encourage meaningful discussion about effective technology integration within the school. In any case, knowing what type of assistance you can expect will allow you to plan accordingly (see Figure 13.4).

Teamwork and Creative Scheduling

In the absence of additional assistance, or with the intention of capitalizing on the benefits of collaboration, teachers must seek out opportunities to team with colleagues at their school. Collaborating with peers leads to the expansion of ideas and more concise use of time with any teaching endeavor, but even more so with the new

FIGURE 13.4 A parent assisting students with work on computers.

and potentially time-consuming possibilities presented by technology. There is no need to "reinvent the wheel" each time you plan a lesson that takes advantage of a computer. Talking about successes and challenges with other teachers will motivate you to grow and explore more than you might be moved to on your own.

Working closely with peer teachers also allows for creative scheduling of time in the computer lab. If each class is allotted only one time slot per week, two classes working together could conceivably get twice as much time in the lab. Working with a partner on the computer is often a great way to learn, and at the same time students benefit from having the combined teaching expertise of two teachers. If just one or two students are not able to go to the lab with the rest of your class, or if they require more time to work on a project, a cooperative plan with another teacher could allow them to join the other class during its time. The newness of technology in the school setting has the potential to prove the many benefits of collaboration to teachers who would not otherwise consider opening themselves to the idea.

Basic Lab Procedures

Just as your class lives by a set of basic classroom rules, so should students have some key understandings to help their time in the computer lab operate smoothly. Although most of your regular classroom procedures will apply, teaching in a computer lab is unique because of the sheer addition of a room full of machines. Depending on how the furniture in the lab is arranged, moving around the room might be challenging and even potentially dangerous, with the multitude of connection cables and power cords protruding from the backs of computers. Many labs push the computer tables around the perimeter walls of the room, meaning students can see and talk to other students sitting directly on either side of them but must get up to speak to others. Labs with tables arranged in long rows may make it difficult to get from one point in the room to another just a few rows back. Small groupings of four computers pushed together have been shown to allow for good student communication and room navigation. Unfortunately, although the "best" arrangement might depend on your students' needs and your own teaching philosophy, these types of room arrangement decisions will likely not be left up to you. Teachers using a communal school lab are generally at the mercy of those who originally set up the lab.

Large monitors sitting on top of the tables tend to hide students' faces, making it difficult to make eye contact with a student or gain the attention of the whole group when you need to make a general announcement. The quiet hum of one computer does not seem at all intrusive to normal conversation, but an entire room full of computers can sound something like a roar when you are trying to get the attention of someone across the room. In addition, many educational software programs rely heavily on auditory effects, which can turn the room into a circus of beeps and bells. Finally, students simply might just be so intensely engaged in the interactive work they are doing that they may not even be paying attention to what is going on around them. The introduction of a number of simple behavior habits adjusted to fit the students you teach and your own personal management style can facilitate a more productive atmosphere in the computer lab. Explaining and modeling these habits to students before the computers are even turned on will encourage their adoption and continued use.

Traffic and Communication Patterns. Establish clear traffic and communication patterns with students. Consider the layout of the room, including where wires are located and the amount of space surrounding student work areas. You want students to be able to move through the lab safely and with a minimum of distraction to others who are working. Decide if it is best to have students be able to get up and move freely around the room when needed or if they need to speak only with those sitting directly next to them. Have a plan for where students can go during class to help ensure both their safety and the order of the classroom.

Help Signals. It is sometimes difficult to see a small hand raised for help between all of the computer monitors, so another way for students to attract attention is needed. Some labs have signs or other objects that students can place on top of their monitors so that you can see at a distance when someone needs help. Reminding students to use this method rather than raising their hands sometimes seems to counteract the hand-raising habit they have in the regular classroom, but it generally works better than having them yell out when they need you. In addition, it allows other helpers, such as parents or older students, to respond to the request for help.

Group Attention Signals. Because of the difficulty in attracting student attention in the lab setting, it is vital to have a highly visual signal to let students know you need their attention. Flickering the lights on and off works well. Having a set place for students to look to find you once you have given the attention signal can also help you focus their attention more quickly.

Time to Exit. The time spent in the lab often seems to pass very quickly, but the time needed to prepare to leave can be great. Students not only need to reach a good stopping point in their work, but they also need to save their files, close the programs they were using, and possibly shut down the systems. Give students ample warning before it is time to leave so that they will have time to prepare. This will save the rest of the class from waiting too long at the door and prevent conflicts when the next scheduled class enters the lab.

Volunteer Helpers. To give your students the best chance for success while using the computer lab and to decrease the time they have to sit idly waiting for you to help them, solicit extra help during lab time. In addition to content instruction, students will need help operating new software programs and assistance with the ever-present technical problems. Many parents have experience with computers or are willing to volunteer despite their lack of computer knowledge. They can gain some computer familiarity of their own and at the same time can offer another set of hands to help students. Other invaluable help can come from older students who have some time between their own classes or can arrange to get away from class during your lab time. These students can reinforce their own skills and confidence by helping those younger than them. You might even have students in your own class take turns serving in the role of technical monitor, collaborating with peers on some problems and alerting you when your help is needed. Make sure that whoever is helping is introduced to the class so students know who is available to assist them. If you normally do not utilize outside helpers in your class, your students may need to develop a trust in the helpers before they stop waiting for help only from you. The combination of assistance can create a productive atmosphere in the computer lab.

File Storage

Encouraging students to use technology for authentic productive purposes often requires giving them the means to work on one project over the course of several class periods. Students therefore will need the ability to save their work for the next time through a number of storage methods.

If students will be sitting at the same computer each time they are in the lab, one storage solution is to have them save their work to a designated directory on that particular computer's hard drive. In this case, all teachers with students using the lab throughout the day would need to agree on a common directory structure. Directories can be made for each student on the machines they use, meaning directories for students in many classes could be found on any one computer. Students would need instruction on exactly where and how to save their work so as not to damage anyone else's files or any other application programs on the hard drive.

If a school is wired for a local area network, student work may be saved into the network drive, making it accessible from other school computers. Students would then be able to sit in a different location each time in the lab or could also edit their work from a computer elsewhere on campus. An organized directory structure should be planned for a network, such as making directories for all students in one class under their teacher's name.

If no network exists or if saving work to the hard drive of a computer in the lab restricts future work on projects, students can also save work on disks. Each student should be taught how to insert and remove disks, how to save to them, and how best to care for them. Because of the somewhat fragile nature of disks, you may want to develop a system for group storage of the disks, such as keeping all students' labeled disks in one basket that can be brought to the lab each time. Older students may be able to keep and care for their own disks, but should be introduced to the concept of always saving a backup copy of any important files (see Figure 13.5).

The Role of the Library Media Center

Becoming information managers and assisting students in becoming knowledge workers are new roles for teachers and media specialists. Learning with multimedia technology maximizes the time available for discussion, thinking, and creating knowledgeable responses to the data, issues, and problems.

Storytelling as an instructional strategy is both timeless and effective. Elementary school library media centers often take full advantage of this strategy and offer special areas for book talks, dramatic productions, story time, student-authored works, and independent free browsing, viewing, and reading. Electronic storybooks on CD-ROM, books on tape, videotaped readings of popular big books, books and stories presented in other languages, pop-ups, and flip animations may all be available for enjoyment.

Living in a global village has diminished the distance between the world's countries, while simultaneously illuminating the differences among cultures. Library media centers may provide materials and resources in a variety of formats that learners may access (Hauser, 2003). General reference material such as an encyclopedia (e.g., The New Grolier Multimedia Encyclopedia by Grolier Electronic Publishing), almanac, dictionary, thesaurus, maps, globes, and charts are all available in the digital formats of CD-ROMs and DVDs or accessible through CD-ROM networks, proprietary Internet indices, and web servers. A library management system of digital and traditional resources may also include posters, multimedia kits, audiocassette recordings, films, videotapes, models, and microforms.

FIGURE 13.5 Student disks organized together.

Having a shared production area available within the library media center allows both faculty and students to create and publish instructional and learning materials. Ideally, there might be two or three production areas for students, faculty, and the library media specialists. A production area might provide a scanner, digitizer, copier, printer, project templates that integrate the Internet, website creation tools, VCR, video and digital cameras, audio equipment, CD burners, web server, and computers. Software would include desktop publishing; spelling and grammar editing programs; clip art; font, graphics, and art programs; and multimedia and publishing tools such as Multimedia and Publishing and Teacher Productivity Tools (Teacher Street), HyperStudio (Knowledge Adventure), and mPower (Tom Snyder Productions). Fully outfitted production areas might also include a darkroom facility, a multistation computer lab, and a video/audio studio with editing equipment.

The reference area should include both CD-ROM and DVD players to facilitate the many informational resources available in these formats. It should be a large, flexible space to accommodate both large- and small-group presentations and for individual research. Online electronic networks and database services might be available as well as videoconferencing capabilities. A computer with large-screen display capabilities using media source switching should be available for instructional presentations. Some reference areas include display space for student-produced work as well as realia. In addition to CD-ROM–DVD players, the reference area might contain equipment that facilitates video and screen capture, scanning, and viewing as well as docking stations for handheld devices (Ferguson, 2000).

Many new library media centers are being built to include either an adjacent computer laboratory and/or an area within the center for hands-on mathematics and science activities, including robotics such as *Robolab;* computer-based microscopes like the *Intel Play QX3* computer; bar-code weather-gathering equipment that may include an online database and simulation materials; educational software; as well as computers, printers, scanners, digital cameras, and graphing calculators with display capabilities. The instructional practice of using real-life models, patterns, data, and problems as the basis for learning activities is catching hold.

Having the library center's collection available through media management systems and computer terminals, which may be housed in other parts of the school as well as on site, provides faculty and learners with immediate means and the capability of enhancing and/or remediating the instruction through the availability of other resources and materials. If the school library media center is a participant in a resource-sharing project with other libraries, the quantity of resources is even greater.

Flexible use of space and the ability to electronically access information outside the center and school are the two key factors when designing or re-creating school library media centers (Maxwell, 2000). The library media center must house, circulate, and distribute information in all formats to hundreds of users on a daily, hourly, and minute-by-minute basis. Reading, viewing, accessing information, and learning are all encouraged to become pleasurable lifelong activities within the library media center of the twenty-first century.

Summary

Because budget shortages in school districts preclude the purchase of a computer for each and every child, choices must be made regarding the best placement of the available machines. Schools can opt for distributing them to individual classrooms, grouping them together into a computer lab, or some variation between those two extremes. The debate between supporters of each end of the spectrum wages on, but teachers must be prepared with some strategies for teaching with technology no matter where it is located.

With computers distributed in the classroom or only a single computer in a classroom, students use the electronic tool in a spontaneous, integrated manner. With a single computer, though, only small groups of students can work at any one time. Teachers may be forced to reteach a concept a number of times so that everyone gets a chance to learn. With computers installed in a lab, students can all work on the same thing at the same time, and all students in a school can get their hands on a computer every week. The drawback to the lab setting, however, is that each student in the school might get a chance to use a computer only once a week, turning technology into a special activity disconnected from other learning.

Educators must have strategies in place to make the most of teaching with either several or only one computer in their classrooms or in a computer lab away from

School Stories

Charonda and Adam sat together in front of the computer by the door in their classroom. This was their "Exploration Time" for the week, and this week's assignment was to explore the new software Mrs. Jaworska had shown them last week, PowerPoint (Microsoft Corporation). She had said that they could use PowerPoint to make presentations, possibly for their history projects that were coming up.

Charonda took the laminated page of activities called "Try This" that Mrs. Jaworska had left next to the computer for them to work with during their 30 minutes. She read the first activity out loud to Adam: "Make a new slide."

The two continued working through the page of activities, creating a sample slide show. They reminded each other of how Mrs. Jaworska had demonstrated the program and worked together to figure out how to do the couple of things she had not shown. The last item on the Try This page required them to think of ways that they might be able to use this program in a real way.

"I think we could make some slides to show what we learned in history," began Adam. "Maybe we could put the words we want to say on the screen and then we could just read the screen when we are talking in front of the parents. Then if we forget what to say, we could just look up there at the screen."

"Yeah," said Charonda. "And maybe we could put some pictures in so it looks good. My project is on the colonists, so maybe I could find some picture of the *Mayflower* or of what the people looked like then. But I don't want to wait that long to try it. I think I'm going to make a slide show tomorrow during my 'Production Time' or maybe when we're in the computer lab."

The two practiced showing their sample slide show for the rest of their time, trying to speak without looking at the screen just as Mrs. Jaworska had shown them.

their classrooms. Teachers with classroom computers should plan the machines' location carefully to reflect its intended uses. A schedule can ensure equity in student access to computers. Modeling of basic technical procedures can make it possible for students to solve many simple technical problems. To keep work in a lab relevant and efficient, teachers need to be prepared and informed. Giving students the information they need on what the goal is for a lab session prior to setting foot in the lab allows them to have a proper mind-set. It emphasizes the connectivity between what they work on in the lab with other learning processes. The unique attributes of working in a room with multiple computers humming away demand that students be taught specific procedures for getting help, giving their attention, moving safely around the room, and storing their work files.

Soliciting help from parents or older students provides for smoothly operating computer work in either setting. Creative collaboration with colleagues can create even more opportunities for students to use computers as a tool in authentic learning endeavors.

Challenge Yourself!

1. Visit several elementary, middle, or secondary schools, or speak with several teachers. How are the computers at these schools organized? How successful do the teachers appear to be at making the arrangement into an effective learning environment?
2. Using a weekly teaching schedule from an actual classroom as a guide, create a weekly computer use schedule for students at your intended level. Without having any student miss a required activity, how much time per week can each use one classroom computer? How much free space in the schedule is there available for spontaneous use?
3. List the pros and cons of both lab and classroom placement of computers.
4. Prepare a budget proposal for purchasing a computer for every student at a school near you. Include in your plan the number of students, the approximate price of computers based on current retail prices, and any furniture that would be necessary.
5. Write a lesson plan that effectively incorporates a trip to the computer lab. Include related preparation ahead of time and follow-up work afterward, so that the uses of the technology tools are framed in context.
6. Write a letter to convince parents to volunteer their time to help students with using technology.
7. Visit a computer lab at a local school. Based on the specifics of the room layout, make a list of procedures you think would be necessary for safe and organized use of the lab. How does your list compare with any procedures that are actually used in the lab?
8. Design a floor plan that would facilitate effective computer use in a one-computer or six-computer classroom.
9. Write a unit of practice that effectively incorporates computer use in either a one- or six-computer classroom. Include related preparation ahead of time and follow-up work afterward, so that the uses of the technology tools are framed in context.
10. What are ways to propose team collaboration on computer use? How can cooperation be encouraged among new teams?
11. How do you envision classrooms of the future? How many of these procedures will still apply?

References

Anderson, G. (1996). Setting up computer workstations in classrooms and libraries. *Media and Methods, 32*(5), 14–16.

Banaszerski, R. (1997). Strategies for the one computer classroom. *Learning and Leading with Technology, 25*(1), 32–33.

Bozzone, M. A. (1997). Technology for kids' desktops. *Electronic Learning, 16*(5), 47–49.

Ferguson, D. B. (2000). Change is good: The new face of the library media center. *Curriculum Administrator, 36*(1), 30–37.

Hauser, J. (2003). Media specialists—targeted for TechTrends! *TechTrends, 47*(1), 29–32.

Huffman, H., Jernstedt, G., Reed, V., Reber, E., Burns, M., Oostenink, R., et al. (2003). Optimizing the design of computer classrooms: The physical environment. *Educational Technology, 43*(4), 9–13.

Maxwell, D. J. (2000). Making libraries mobile: Innovative means to give information services. *Education, 120*(4), 722–732.

Waddick, J. (1997). Physical considerations in the development of a computer learning environment. *British Journal of Educational Technology, 28*, 69–71.

Wodarz, N. (2003). Computer lab configuation. *School Business Affairs, 69*(2), 53–54.

CHAPTER 14

Producing and Presenting

FOCUS QUESTIONS

1. In what ways might the specific purpose for a multimedia production guide the planning?

2. What forms of media can be used to enhance instructional presentations?

3. What preparations must be made in advance of giving a technology-aided presentation?

As current educational research lauds the advantages of authentic, project-based instruction and assessment, it becomes apparent that educators and students alike can use the capabilities of technology to make these new goals a practical reality. Technology presents some amazing opportunities to compile varied, quality informational products and effectively present those products to groups of people in meaningful ways.

Multimedia productions are so named because they are designed by integrating different media of information, such as text, graphics, video, audio, and animation elements. As opposed to a traditional lesson or presentation, in which the user sits passively and receives the information in only the one way it is presented, multimedia can cater to a whole range of learning and teaching styles. At one end of the spectrum, multimedia can enhance somewhat traditional presentations in which the control for the sequence of the presentation of information lies primarily with the presenter. On the opposite end of the range, multimedia can form hypermedia environments, whereby the user has the freedom to make decisions as to how or in which direction to explore. A hypermedia structure creates an environment without the linear restrictions associated with many paper-based learning materials. These hypermedia environments let the user access information in any order he or she wishes. This access simulates the natural, nonlinear ways in which humans learn and allows for individual construction of knowledge. The flexibility and interactivity that can be achieved by synthesizing information with these multimedia elements can create a sensory experience that matches individual thinking patterns of both presenters and learners.

The process of creating multimedia products ideally reflects the philosophy that teachers and students are at times both the experts and the learners in the classroom. Both groups can use technology to prepare and present cohesive lessons or to demonstrate what has been learned in a unit of study. As with any use of technology, multimedia projects should be seen as a natural part of the teaching, learning, and evaluating processes that occur regularly in classrooms rather than as some separate, added-on requirement. This chapter will outline a practical process both teachers and students can follow when using technology to author informative products and present them to others.

Planning and Research Preparation

Defining the Purpose

Creating a multimedia production can provide not only for real acquisition and use of technology skills but also for the practice of visioning, planning, and making purposeful choices. Just as with any lesson, you and your students can make the most of the preparation process and the unique attributes of the technology if you understand the distinctive purpose of each project from the beginning. For what audience will it be prepared? To what extent will technology play a role in the creation and presentation of the production? Putting together a quick lesson for your class on the differences between warm- and cold-blooded animals in your area of the country will require different preparation than a research project undertaken to convince the school board to purchase new, safer playground equipment. The following is a sample of types of multimedia projects teachers and students can design:

Lessons. Whether taught by teachers or peer students, new concepts can be presented to others with the variety of media required to ensure all learners have the chance to learn in ways that make sense to them. Lessons can be prepared for whole groups to view at once, for small groups, or even for individual tutorial purposes.

Research projects or book reports. Resources can be collected and reports written as usual, but they can then be compiled with relevant media about the topic or author. These projects can be used as the sole form of holistic evaluation or as a comprehensive review for another, more traditional assessment.

Stories or games. A simple story written by a student can be transformed into an interactive project by infusing media elements and giving the user some decision-making ability. This gives an alternative to simply word processing a story and drawing pictures to accompany it.

Parent or community informational works. Both text and media elements can co-operate nicely to inform others of rules, current events, and policy. This type of project could be realized as continuously running slide shows as participants enter a room or even stand-alone, kiosk-type, self-guided tours.

Electronic portfolios. Just as artists collect samples of what they have produced, students can bring together choice bits of written work, scanned images, photos, and videos of events and explain the importance of each in their own voices by recording a voice-over narration. Students can choose work they most want to include and may even be required to defend their choices in front of a group of teachers, parents, and peers. Electronic portfolios reflect the current educational philosophy that places value on what students can actively do rather than relying only on static scores they receive on a test to tell the story of what they have learned. Teachers might also maintain portfolios, documenting instructional and professional growth and providing some proof of accountability. (See Chapter 15 for more on portfolio assessment.)

Background Research

Multimedia projects, like traditional projects, require strong, accurate content. Students and teachers should never make the mistake of thinking that audio clips and pretty pictures can make up for flimsy descriptions or missing facts. If you are teaching a lesson to students, make sure you have solid objectives and examples. Students should follow whatever research techniques and writing processes they normally do, making use of both text-based and electronic resources. Notes and other text can be word processed during this stage or simply handwritten. It is helpful for later procedures if this text is proofread and ready to be made into a final draft form.

Storyboarding

The importance of visually planning for the organization of a project was stressed in Chapter 9 with regard to the design of websites, but it is as equally vital to the successful creation of other electronic projects. You and your students should list the titles of the final drafts of the written forms of projects and transfer them to storyboard form, such as onto 5" × 7" index cards. These cards can be easily arranged and rearranged in order to arrive at a visual, logical flow of information. Storyboards can be created with varying amounts of detail, from sketches only to full graphic plans. This detail will be determined, again, by your purpose, time constraints, and the developmental levels of the audience.

Screen Design

Considering some basic design features at this stage in the planning will help ensure clear presentations. Model examples and nonexamples of these recommendations to even very young students so they can make personal judgments about what guidelines would make for the clearest presentations. Always temper each of these general recommendations with an understanding of the audience for the presentation or instruction. If an instructional presentation would benefit from an unorthodox use of text or color, make the best call for the purpose. Whatever design choices you make, remember that consistency is key. Random design features will make for a busy, distracting presentation. (See Table 14.1 for additional design tips.)

TABLE 14.1	Multimedia Design Issues

1. Limit the amount of text on each screen. Different audiences of students can handle varying amounts of text, but leave some space around the text or use graphics to break up large text pieces.
2. Choose a font that will be legible to learners. Some fonts prove easier to read when viewed on a computer screen or when projected up on the wall. A sans serif font, one without any decorative letter features, in a size of between 18 to 24 points is the easiest to read from a distance.
3. Use phrases or just keywords rather than complete statements.
4. Words written in all capital letters are difficult to read. Underlined text should be reserved for hypertext links only.
5. Use colors appropriate for the topic and audience. Be sure text color contrasts with the background color, such as light text on a dark background or dark text on a light background.
6. Use graphics or other media elements for a real purpose rather than for mere decoration.

Producing Multimedia Elements

Once the content of the presentation is mapped out, you and your students can begin to consider what media elements might lend themselves to creating a complete learning experience. Inclusion of these elements will depend on the extent and quality of the equipment available to you at your school, but as with any teaching endeavor, resourcefulness and creativity will take you past many of the technical limitations.

Text

Text can include multimedia menus, navigation elements such as site maps, and content. Text files are prepared using a word processing program such as Corel WordPerfect or Microsoft Word. When creating text for multimedia, determine how much information will appear on one screen and how the related pages or links will fit together. Text in presentations, such as a slide show using Corel Presentations or Microsoft PowerPoint, should be key phrases and limited to small chunks of information. To format information effectively, keep the following techniques in mind:

Place text next to a graphic.
Convert sentences with serial items to lists.
Use white space to separate points.
Use headings as content summarizers.
Place complex information into tables.

Fonts. Millions of fonts are available from free shareware, CD-ROMs, and application software such as Corel DRAW. There are five basic font styles:

> *Serif.* Small points called serifs cap the ends of most strokes. Times New Roman is the most common serif font.
>
> *Sans serif.* Sans means "without," so no points cap the strokes. Helvetica and Arial are the most common sans serif fonts.
>
> *Script.* Fonts that mimic handwriting. Kaufman and Lucida Handwriting are examples.
>
> *Novelty.* Fun and frivolous fonts not designed for large amounts of text. This type of font is used for logos and commonly appears in advertisements, especially billboards. Font collections offer many novelty fonts, especially ones for the holidays such as Bones or Snowcaps.
>
> *Special purpose.* Fonts that fill a specific need, such as the set of numbers printed at the bottom of your bank checks. They are primarily used for technical purposes.

When selecting a font color make sure there is a high contrast between text and the background. For example, use dark text on a light background or light text on a dark background. If the presentation will be projected, use light text and dark background. Projected colors tend to wash out.

Selecting a font size also depends on viewing distance. For individuals viewing a desktop monitor, use a font size of 12 or 14, but for younger children use a larger font size. For a group viewing a large screen from a distance, use font size 22 or 28, depending on the distance.

Graphics

Graphics can include any visual component, even the artful representation of text. Graphics in a presentation should serve an instructional purpose rather than merely providing aesthetic decoration or clutter. A picture can show concepts that words can only hint at, illustrating relationships that might remain unclear with mere descriptions. Graphics can come from a number of sources and can include drawings, paintings, graphs, and photographs.

Clipping. Premade clip art graphics can be "clipped" from a CD collection or a sample from another program and placed into your program. Although clip art is often a good place to start, especially for those who are hesitant to try their hand at creating their own artwork, clip art can provide only a generic illustrative component. When using clip art read the copyright information. If using a CD collection, this information appears in the front of the image catalog. Some collections are copyright-free without restrictions and others state restrictions and prohibitions.

Drawing and Painting. Most integrated software suites contain some sort of a graphics program that allows you to create your own graphics. Painting programs provide a selection of tools that allow you to create pictures by assigning color attributes to the actual pixels that comprise the screen, similar to how you would use paint to create a picture on a canvas. Drawing tools allow you to create illustrations by combining different line-based objects. These objects can be selected individually and moved around to be placed in any desired position (see Figure 14.1).

More advanced computer-aided design (CAD) software has carried the design of jet engines, automobile parts, circuit boards, tools, bridges, and homes to new heights of sophistication. Three-dimensional (3-D) graphics programs allow you to create 3-D images. Many 3-D tools are available that will create 3-D text and animate the image as well. 3-D modeling tools allow you to place two-dimensional (2-D) objects into a "virtual" scene. Mathematica is an integrated technical computing system, which combines interactive calculation (both numeric and symbolic), visualization tools, and a complete programming environment. Mathematica allows you to create 2-D and 3-D graphics.

Screen Capture. Screen capture programs are utility tools. They allow you to capture any text or picture you see on a screen and save it as another file format. The captured image can very easily be cropped and edited. Some capture programs let you edit the image in various ways. You can add drop shadows, create a button, and even feather the edges.

Scanning. Scanning allows project designers to customize their presentation with a range of graphical elements. By using a flatbed scanner, you can convert any graphic into digital form that can be added to a multimedia presentation (see Figure 14.2). Traditional artwork, such as sketches and paintings, paper creations, magazine pictures, and even photographs, can be scanned in. If copyrighted graphics are used for

FIGURE 14.1 Paint, available with Microsoft Windows.

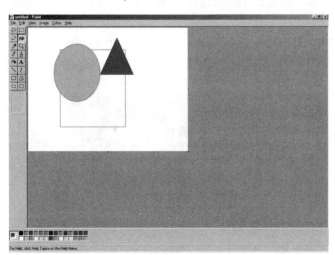

FIGURE 14.2 Viviscan DeskSaver Scanner.

a student learning opportunity, proper credit should be given to the original source, and if your presentation will have a potentially wide audience, obtain permission to use copyrighted material first.

Taking Digital Pictures. Digital cameras can be used to take pictures just like traditional cameras, but instead of recording the image on film, they save the image electronically (see Figure 14.3). These cameras can then be plugged directly into a computer and the images can be downloaded right onto the hard drive. Some cameras store the images on a removable disk. Pictures can be taken of students, families, surroundings, special events, or anything else of particular interest. An excellent digital photography resource is located at **www.shortcourses.com.** This website offers tutorials and accurate information on selecting and using digital cameras.

Video

The proliferation of camcorders has made novice video producers out of many families. Video segments can illustrate an event or a procedure so that learners feel as though they were actually there. With the help of some special equipment, videos can easily be inserted into multimedia presentations.

Using Video Clips. Like clip art in still graphics, prerecorded video is available for purchase on disk or CD-ROM. In addition, search portals at **http://Realguide. real.com, http://windowsmedia.com,** and **http://broadcast.com** help you find videos

FIGURE 14.3 (a) Samsung SSC-410N digital still camera. (b) Casio QV-300 digital camera.

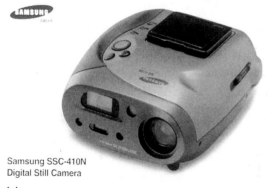

Samsung SSC-410N
Digital Still Camera

(a)

(b)

on the web. The quality of these clips is often high because they are professionally produced. They are often copyright-free and so can be used for educational purposes. These types of premade clips are ideal for presentations on topics that you would have no way of viewing personally, such as of exotic wildlife or historical events.

Digitizing Prerecorded Video. Once a video clip is chosen from a videotape using a standard VCR or a camcorder, it must be transformed into digital form in order to be incorporated into a multimedia program. Digitizing applications can be used to perform this process and to produce as a result a movie in one of several formats, including QuickTime movies and AVI files (see Figure 14.4). The platform operating system you have will dictate what movie format is required. Once the video is digitized, it can be edited and saved using digital video editing equipment. The ability to digitize video allows personal experiences, such as a family trip or a school event, to become part of a presentation.

Recording Digitally. Digital video cameras record directly into digital form. Although these cameras remain relatively expensive, they allow the video segments to be dropped directly into a multimedia presentation without the need for other preparation.

Audio

From voice-overs to sound effects to background music, the addition of audio elements has the potential to create any learning atmosphere you or your students can imagine.

Using Sound Effects and Music. Digitally recorded sound effects, such as nature or other environmental sounds, are readily available on CD-ROM or as part of many authoring programs. Regular music that is digitally recorded on CD can also be used. Simple sound-mixing programs, some that come packaged on computers and others available as part of CD-ROM sound effects packages, allow you to easily record and edit clips of the music as you play it through the computer's CD-ROM drive. Experimenting with the combinations of lifelike sounds can help ensure a learner-friendly environment.

FIGURE 14.4 Computer Eyes frame grabber.

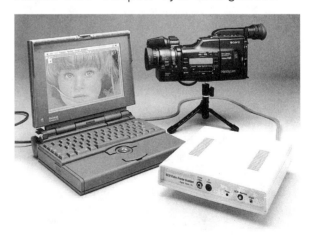

Recording Sounds. Simple recording applications let you use a microphone to record voice-over narration or the reading of a favorite story. What is recorded can be saved and then manipulated using a sound-mixing program (see Figure 14.5). Adding your own

FIGURE 14.5 Sound Recorder recording application, available with Microsoft Windows.

voice to a presentation personalizes it as well as allows complete customization of what is being said.

Creating Sounds. Computer music synthesizers combine a pianolike keyboard with a music synthesizer and computer software. When using a synthesizer to create music, musical issues such as pitch, amplitude, special effects, tempo, note sequence and duration, and other important elements of music can be considered. During and after the composition process, music can be played back through the computer and, in some cases, through stereo speakers. Compositions can be stored on diskettes and played and retrieved at any time.

Animation

Animation shows a series of slightly different still graphics in quick succession to give the impression of action and movement, similar to the idea of flipping the pages of a pad of paper quickly to see the sketched figures appear to move. Animation can illustrate something happening that video may not be able to ideally portray, such as the completion of the water cycle or the activity of the inside of a volcano.

Using Premade Animations. Like the other media mentioned, collections of premade animations that can be dropped right into a multimedia presentation are available on CD-ROM. Animations can be extremely time-consuming to create because of the many numbers of drawings it might take to effectively simulate an action. Therefore, finding a ready-made animation that illustrates a desired effect will save time and allow those with little experience with the animation process to benefit from the usage of this medium.

Animating. Many sophisticated authoring and presentation programs now offer tools to facilitate animation. Flash by Macromedia is a very popular animation program. Still images can be made to appear to move without requiring the user to have extensive animation skills. Still images can easily be animated with simple animated GIF programs. Many of these programs are available free from the WWW (see websites at **www.tucows.com** or **http://download.com.com/2001-20-0.html?legacy=cnet**). The capabilities of these programs can only be expected to improve, allowing novice multimedia designers to incorporate quality effects with minimal effort.

Authoring Multimedia Productions

With the content planned and the media elements selected and prepared, the next step in the production process is actually to drop the text and media into a program that serves as a "shell" that comprises the final product. Although some programs work best in creating multimedia-enhanced presentations and others result in full nonlinear hypermedia programs, all share some basic properties that are important to understand. The procedures outlined here are general but are applicable to whatever software tools to which you will have access.

Building Blocks

What we are capable of doing with technology is often difficult for us to comprehend, so analogies to other things with which we are familiar are frequently used as a way of explanation. Multimedia programs are often built on basic units called "cards" or "slides." The analogy to index cards or transparency slides is deliberate. You can write pieces of information or notes for a presentation on index cards and put all the cards together into a stack. These index cards can then be moved around, arranged in any order, and rearranged as needed to fit the purpose of the presentation and the meaningful flow of the content. So, too, can the electronic cards and slides be ordered and reordered within the electronic "stack," thus providing a very editable presentation format.

Each card or slide has a background, which can be made to be a color or a design. Authoring and presentation programs offer a selection of premade backgrounds or you can use one of your own graphics. These backgrounds are generally designed to remain constant throughout the presentation, although the designer may choose to change the background color or graphic to fit the purpose of the content of each card. Any text that needs to be seen on every card or slide, such as the date or a school logo, can be placed on the background.

Objects

Onto each card or slide can be placed any number of objects. Objects can be text fields, graphics, or other media items in the form of buttons. Placing these objects on the cards or slides is like writing information on traditional index cards, except that the objects on these cards can be moved around easily to make for effortless layout editing. When the card or slide appears in the presentation, those objects appear superimposed on the background (see Figure 14.6).

Text Fields. In order to place text onto a card or slide, you must first create a text field. A text field is a rectangular tablet onto which text can be typed or imported from a word processing program and then edited as needed. The field can be moved anywhere on the card or slide and can be resized and reformatted. Text can be arranged within multiple text fields on each card or slide.

Graphics. Prepared graphic items, including clip art, scanned images, and digitally produced pictures, can be placed anywhere on a card or slide. They can be moved, resized, and overlapped.

Media Buttons. Other media items, such as audio, video, and animations, can be placed on any card or slide. These types of objects can be accessed during a presentation by clicking on an icon or button or can even be set to play automatically.

FIGURE 14.6 Objects inserted onto a PowerPoint slide.

Transitions

The way in which a user moves from one card or slide to another in a multimedia program is the defining difference between presentation slide programs and hypermedia programs and is one reason why an author might choose one type of production software over the other. Presentation programs that are composed of a series of slides are typically intended for the sequential presentation of information. The presenter or user can view slides in ascending order by clicking the mouse button or can view the slides in order passively by using an automatic timed advance feature. A previous slide can be reviewed, and particular slides can be brought up by number from a navigational menu. You and your students may choose to use a slide program when designing an information product or a more traditional instructional lesson.

Hypermedia authoring programs capitalize on the concept of nonlinear movement among slides. Just as buttons can be added to a slide in order to utilize media elements, buttons can also be used to offer the user options for movement to other information. The project author adds a button to a card and assigns an action to the button. Some actions define media usage and others function as transitions to other specific cards. Rather than require a user to know a specific slide number in order to go directly to that slide, the author can make the button a direct avenue to any card in the stack. Depending on the complexity of the authoring program and the sophistication of the author, these buttons can be chosen from a selection of predefined actions or can be customized with special scripting languages. Hypermedia authoring programs offer unlimited interactive design for any type of research project, story, or portfolio. Table 14.2 lists several popular presentation and hypermedia programs.

TABLE 14.2	Example Presentation and Hypermedia Software Tools
Presentation/Slide Software	**Hypermedia Authoring Systems**
KidPix (Learning Co.)	HyperStudio (Knowledge Adventure)
PowerPoint (Microsoft Corporation)	Digital Chisel (Pierian Spring Software)
AppleWorks (Apple Computer, Inc.)	Authorware (Macromedia)

Presenting with Multimedia Technology

Regardless of whether your audience of learners fills an auditorium or fills one chair, or whether your presentation is intended to prompt a live presenter or is meant to function as a stand-alone product, computer hardware and software facilitate clear, effective presentation of ideas. Understanding the differences in possibilities technology presents over traditional presentation methods will make you and your students confident presenters of all types of information.

Hardware

The hardware that is needed to present information using a computer depends on the purpose of the presentation. If an individual or small group of students will be working through a hypermedia lesson, a standard computer monitor may be sufficient for all to see. Make sure the computer is located in an area with room to pull up enough chairs for all learners and other aspects of the setting, such as lighting, are such that everything on the screen can be seen without problem.

If your audience, however, is an entire class or even a larger crowd, you will need a compatible projection device. Some rooms are equipped with television monitors that can be interfaced with a computer so that the screen display can be displayed on the monitors. An AverKey (**www.aver.com**) is an inexpensive and durable projection device that attaches between the computer and television monitor to display the computer screen. Liquid crystal display (LCD) panels are lightweight, flat devices that can be placed onto an overhead projector and attached to a computer to project an image of the computer screen. The clearest images are produced with projection devices that connect to a computer and shine the display directly up onto a wall screen in either a small room or a large auditorium. Become familiar with what is available to you at your school or district. Practice connecting the computer with the projection devices, becoming familiar with the physical layout of the cables and adapters. Note any adjustments that are needed to the screen resolution to make the image viewable on the larger screen. Connect and disconnect the peripherals several times with your students, if appropriate, so that they see what kind of preparation is necessary to pull off a successful presentation. Many preferences need to be set correctly for a computer to cooperate with a projection device to project its image onto a larger screen, so do not leave these types of preparations to the last minute (see Figure 14.7).

FIGURE 14.7 Practice connecting and adjusting to pull off a successful presentation.

Software

Each presentation or hypermedia program has specific procedures for showing the final product. Become familiar with these procedures, and use them to do a "dry run," advancing through every card or slide in a presentation using the mouse or keyboard as will be required in actual usage. When giving a lesson or presentation in front of a group, rehearse what you will say to accompany the program content. When students are using a program to learn independently, check all buttons to make sure they perform the planned action.

Preparation

The best advice you and your students could follow when planning to use your computers for presentations is always to have a backup plan. Even a thoroughly planned presentation can be thwarted by unforeseen technical problems. Something as simple as a missing cable adapter or an incompatible version of software can stand in your way of making a successful presentation. If it is essential that the instruction be carried off at a certain time, make transparencies of the slides so that you can make do with an overhead projector if necessary. If the instruction can be handled in another method or at another time, be ready to make an instructional switch at the last minute. Although we always hope our plans can be carried out smoothly, modeling this kind of quick thinking will teach your students invaluable, real-world problem-solving skills.

Summary

The capabilities of technology can be used to support authentic instruction and assessment by both teachers and students. Presentations for a variety of purposes can be created by combining different media with instructional or informational ideas.

A quality multimedia production must first begin with careful background research and planning. Consideration of details such as consistent screen layout and design will contribute to ease of learning. Accurate, comprehensive facts and examples will complete the presentation.

Text, graphics, video, audio, and animation are multimedia elements that can be used to frame the learning environment. There are a range of file formats that are acceptable for use in multimedia design. Any of these files can be adopted from pre-made media collections or originally created using a number of methods.

These media elements are then placed, along with any text, into an authoring or presentation program. Presentation applications are comprised of individual slides that can be shown in order, whereas authoring applications let the author create non-

School Stories

Clayton and Ellie's kindergarten class has just finished learning about dinosaurs, but none of them is going to be sitting down to take a test to assess what they have learned. Instead, each student will design one slide in a class multimedia presentation, highlighting facts and illustrations about his or her favorite dinosaur. The slide show will be presented to students' parents at this semester's Open House, so everyone wants to do his or her best.

Clayton chooses to draw a picture of a Stegosaurus. He uses the drawing program to outline the dinosaur from a picture in a book his teacher had read to them. He has trouble drawing the tail, so he erases it and redraws it. When the picture is complete, he adds a text field to type in all the dinosaur words he knows. He finds the microphone on the computer shelf above the monitor, plugs it into the computer, and records his slide narration: "This is my Stegosaurus. He's as big as the whole page and he just stepped on a little tree." When he is done with his slide, he saves it to his personal folder because his teacher said she would put all the slides together when everyone was done.

That afternoon, Ellie starts her dinosaur slide. She has trouble deciding which dinosaur to choose, so she decides to split her slide in half and show the differences and similarities between carnivores and herbivores. She draws a detailed illustration of two dinosaurs she remembers from a CD-ROM her class used last week. She finds a book that tells about carnivores and herbivores, and because she does not know all the words herself, she slowly copies some of the sentences into two text boxes. When she hears that it is time to go to lunch, and she still has not finished the slide to her liking, she saves it to her folder so that she can complete it tomorrow.

When the night of the Open House comes, Clayton and Ellie walk excitedly through the door of the classroom, knowing that right inside is the computer on which the slide show is playing over and over, or "looping" as their teacher had called it. She had put all of the students' slides into one show and programmed it with an automatic timing option so that when parents entered, they could watch the entire show at their leisure. Parents commented on how good all of the slides looked. When Mrs. Guidia, the principal, looked in to check on the progress of Open House, she was able to see very quickly what students had learned and how technology was facilitating the instruction and assessment of students at all levels.

linear productions of information and media placed on individual cards. Choosing which type of production is most appropriate requires considering both the intended purpose and the needs of the audience.

Either type of production can be presented in a number of ways using technology, from using a regular computer screen for teaching to a small group to projecting the program images onto a larger screen for many to see at once. Computers must be configured to work with projection devices. Checking connections and setting preferences ahead of the scheduled time for a class or presentation will help ensure a working presentation system. Being prepared with a backup plan, such as skipping ahead to another lesson or using transparencies of the slides to give the presentation, is vital to establishing the flexibility necessary to be proficient in the skills of technology-enhanced presentations.

DVD/VIDEO VIGNETTE

Navigating by Landmarks

In this video excerpt, students develop multimedia maps of their neighborhood by inserting video and audio files into electronic presentation software. How effective was the use of technology in this lesson?

Challenge Yourself!

1. Find out what authoring applications are available on your school's computer systems. Familiarize yourself with one of the programs by creating a sample multimedia production.
2. Write simple directions for creating a production using the authoring software. Include specific references that would be appropriate for students who are new to the concept of authoring.
3. Use a presentation slide application to create a simple slide show. Experiment with the colors and transition effects to arrive at an effective presentation environment.
4. Make a list of instructional or informational situations that would require a nonlinear presentation and those that would best be accomplished using a slide-type presentation.
5. Review the DVD Video Vignette for this chapter. Identify and list the NETS Student Standards that are covered in the lesson. List the strengths and weaknesses of the lesson. Compare your results with those of your classmates.
6. List the technology support preparation required to teach the lesson presented in the DVD Video Vignette. Prepare an alternative plan if the technology fails.
7. How might a multimedia project be used to assess a student's understanding of a concept in your area of interest? Give specific examples and criteria that could be used in making a judgment of understanding.
8. A series of steps necessary to creating a multimedia product is outlined in this chapter. Adapt this list to a more specific step-by-step plan that could be followed with students at the level you are interested in teaching.
9. Design three example screen layouts for presentations with three very different end purposes. Include color, font size and placement, and graphics that would be appropriate for both the topics and the audiences.

10. Find a commercial collection of clip art or video segments. How extensive is the collection? When would it be appropriate to use these premade media elements, and when would original creations be more suitable?
11. Borrow a digital camera or digital video camera. Record an event using the equipment and choose several pictures or video segments that would be useful in illustrating an informative presentation on the event. How does having the pictures or video already in digital form affect the job of compiling the product? What types of considerations would need to be made when using such equipment with students at the level you plan to teach?
12. Obtain a projection device that is compatible with an available computer. Learn how to connect the cables and configure the computer preferences in order to make it work. Practice projecting in different-sized rooms and in various conditions. How long does it take you to set up in preparation for a presentation? Make a list of the types of technical problems you think you could possibly run into.

References

Allen, D. (1995). Teaching with technology: Enhancing student projects. *Teaching PreK–8, 26*(30), 20–23.

Barron, T. (1996). Getting friendly with authoring tools. *Training and Development, 50*(5), 36–46.

Branzburg, J. (2003). How to create PDF files. *Technology and Learning, 23*(10), 41.

Chen, P., & McGrath, D. (2003). Knowledge construction and knowledge representation in high school students' design of hypermedia documents. *Journal of Educational Multimedia and Hypermedia, 12*(1), 33–61.

Clark, J. H. (1996). Bells and whistles . . . but where are the references? Setting standards for hypermedia projects. *Learning and Leading with Technology, 23*(5), 22–24.

Cross, L. (1995). Preparing students for the future with project presentations. *Learning and Leading with Technology, 23*(2), 24–26.

D'Ignazio, F. (1996). A multimedia publishing center from scratch (and scavenge). *Book Report, 15*(3), 19–22.

Downs, E., & Clark, K. (1997). Guidelines for effective multimedia design. *Technology Connection, 4*(1), 8–9.

Dunham, K. (1995). Helping students design hypercard stacks. *Learning and Leading with Technology, 23*(2), 6–7, 61.

Elin, L. (2001). *Designing and developing multimedia: A practical guide for the producer, director, and writer.* Boston: Allyn and Bacon.

Ennis, W., & Ennis, D. (1996). Ten tips to aid teachers creating multimedia presentations. *Journal of Computing in Teacher Education, 13*(1), 14–20.

Farmer, L. S. J. (1995). Multimedia: Multi-learning tool. *Technology Connection, 2*(3), 30–31.

Florio, C., & Murie, M. (1996). Authoritative authoring: Software that makes multimedia happen. *NewMedia, 6*(12), 67–70, 72–75.

Freed, G., Rothberg, M., & Wlodkowski, T. (2003). *Making educational software titles and web sites accessible: Design guidelines including math and science solutions.* Boston: The Media Access Group at WGBH.

Gribas, C. (1996). Creating great overheads with computers. *College Teaching, 44,* 66–68.

Jordahl, G. (1995). School-grown videos. *Technology and Learning, 15*(8), 26–27, 30, 32.

LeCrone, N. L. (1997). Integrating multimedia into the curriculum. *Technology Connection, 4*(1), 14–15.

Lewis, S. (1995). Student-created virtual tours. *Learning and Leading with Technology, 23*(2), 35–39.

Mauldin, M. (1996). The development of computer-based multimedia: Is a rain forest the same place as a jungle? *TechTrends, 41*(3), 15–19.

McGrath, D. (2003). Designing to learn. *Learning and Leading with Technology, 30*(6), 50–53.

Milone, M. N., Jr. (1995). Electronic portfolios: Who's doing them and how? *Technology and Learning, 14*(2), 28–29, 32, 34, 36.

Milone, M. N., Jr. (1996). Kids as multimedia authors. *Technology and Learning, 14*(2), 22, 24, 27–28.

Milton, K., & Spradley, P. (1996). A renaissance of the Renaissance: Using Hyper-Studio for research projects. *Learning and Leading with Technology, 23*(6), 20–22.

Monahan, S., & Susong, D. (1996). Author slide shows and Texas wildlife: Thematic multimedia projects. *Learning and Leading with Technology, 24*(2), 6–11.

Reese, S. (1995). MIDI-assisted composing in your classroom. *Music Educators Journal, 81*(4), 37–40.

Reinking, D., & Watkins, J. (2000). A formative experiment investigating the use of multimedia book reviews to increase elementary students' independent reading. *Reading Research Quarterly, 35*(3), 384–419.

Roblyer, M. D. (1997). Videoconferencing. *Learning and Leading with Technology, 24*(5), 58–61.

Sammons, M. C. (1995). Using in-house CD-ROM publishing to store and present classroom materials. *Educational Technology Review, 4,* 26–32.

Schuler, M. (September, 2002). Digital Photography. *PC Teach It,* p. 41.

Stafford, D. J. (1997). PowerPointing the way. *Technology Connection, 4*(1), 14–17.

Strasser, D. (1996). Tips for good electronic presentations. Online, *20*(1), 78–81.

Taylor, H. G., & Stuhlmann, J. M. (1995). Creating slide show book reports. *Learning and Leading with Technology, 23*(1), 8–10.

Thorp, C. (1995). Choices and consequences. *Teaching PreK–8, 26*(2), 58–60.

Troutner, J. (1996). Yes, they put on quite a show, but what did they learn? *Technology Connection, 3*(1), 15–17.

Troxclair, D. (1996). Teaching technology: Multimedia presentations in the classroom. *Gifted Child Today Magazine, 19*(5), 34–36, 47.

Tuttle, H. G. (1997). *Electronic portfolios tell a personal story. MultiMedia Schools, 4*(1), 32–37.

Wang, J., & Hartley, K. (2003). Video technology as a support for teacher education reform. *Journal of Technology and Teacher Education, 11*(1), 105–138.

Welsh, T. (1997). From multimedia to multiple-media: Designing computer-based course materials for the Information Age. *TechTrends, 42*(1), 17–23.

Wolinsky, A. (2003). Beyond multimedia production and web publishing to 3-D writing. *Multimedia Schools, 10*(3), 42–45.

Woodward, M. (1997). Developing a multimedia product. *English in Education, 31*(1), 48–54.

CHAPTER 15

Assessing and Evaluating

FOCUS QUESTIONS

1. What roles does technology play in the assessment of student learning?

2. How can technology resources assist with data collection and analysis?

3. What methods of assessment determine appropriate student use of technology?

Understanding your students' grasp of the content and their ability to apply what they have learned completes the final step of the instructional sequence of planning, teaching, and assessing. The power of technology can make the assessment process more efficient, but is most effective when the following questions are considered:

- Why and in what ways are you looking to make judgments about students' work?
- What skills and abilities are you attempting to measure?
- How might technology assist your efforts to collect, record, analyze, and communicate measurement data?

This chapter will begin by defining some basic assessment and evaluation terms. Then it will draw distinctions about the focus of measurement and finally will explore specific strategies for the use of technology for understanding the progress of students.

Measurement Definitions

To understand the role that technology might play in measuring student progress, it is first helpful to understand what types of measurement you would like to make. Although the terms *assessment* and *evaluation* are frequently used interchangeably, the two can be distinguished by the nature of the processes. *Assessments* are collections of written, oral, observational, and performance measures that provide information to determine student abilities and progress toward reaching intended objectives. Assessments can take the form of (1) quantitative, numerical measures, such as quiz scores; or (2) qualitative records, such as informal teacher observations, anecdotal notes, or reflective comments that recognize learning and performance in complex, authentic situations. *Evaluation* is the use of a combination of assessments to make judgments about a student's ability and informed decisions about continued instruction.

Teachers make assessments and evaluations continuously and for a variety of purposes. *Formative* evaluations are measurements made throughout the instructional sequence to attempt to answer the question "How are we doing?" The information gained through formative assessments is key to informing and redirecting the learning process. *Summative* assessments typically occur at the end of an instructional segment to answer the question "How have we done?" These measurements are intended to examine the outcomes of instruction by indicating an end mastery of objectives or demonstration of competency. The distinctions among these definitions will help you to consider the most effective ways in which technology can assist in understanding students' progress.

Technology as the Focus

Measurement choices regarding technology depend both on how the role of technology is perceived and on what types of assessment information are desired. The following section will deal with the prevailing opinion in the educational technology community that technology is an instructional and assessment tool with the focus of assessment on the content that students learn. First, however, teachers should be aware of other types of assessments of technology in educational settings that focus on technology itself. A brief introduction to these perspectives will help to clarify the participation of classroom teachers.

Technology is frequently the focus of assessment on the large national, state, or district scale to determine whether the purchase of computers has been a good investment. To measure the effect technology has had on student learning, lawmakers, district administration, and taxpayers look to assessments that might include counting the number of computers in classrooms, the number of "contact hours" teachers and students spend using computers on a regular basis, the attitudes teachers and students have toward technology, teacher and student skill levels, and perhaps the contexts in which technology is being used. These assessments are most meaningful when school and community stakeholders determine the performance indicators necessary to define success (Sun, 2000) and when these indicators are built into a comprehensive technology plan. Findings of such evaluations are ultimately reported to the appropriate stakeholders and then ideally used to plan future goals, such as customizing professional development training to meet teachers' skill needs.

Data to answer these questions of technology use are often collected by surveying technology directors, principals, or teachers. Local assessments can be informed by nationally recognized assessment tools such as the CEO Forum's StaRChart (**www.ceoforum.org/starchart.cfm**) and by the Milken Exchange's Seven Dimensions for Gauging Progress of Technology (**www.mff.org/edtech**). Other data collected from individual students may further describe technology use habits, such as from achievement tests or attendance records (Barnett, 2000). However, these individual data are generally used only to compile school or district profiles rather than to assess individual competence (Sun, 2000).

To measure a student's ability to operate a computer or use a software tool, teachers often use checklists based on national, state, and local standards of what students should be able to do with computers to efficiently note abilities and deficiencies. These assessments might be handled in an informal observational manner or in more deliberate performance tasks. Classroom teachers are closest to the learning contexts and understand best the abilities of students, meaning they are in the best position to report a true picture of classroom technology use.

Content as the Focus

When technology is seen as the tool for instructional delivery, communication, or information seeking, student learning is measured on mastery of content objectives rather than on mastery of technology use itself. Strategies for assessing student learning through technology-assisted processes and technology-produced products should be consistent with strategies used for assessing learning through more traditional means. This is especially true if the existing strategies already address the student-centered, problem-based, interdisciplinary learning that is characteristic of constructivist learning environments. *Constructivist learning* integrates disciplines, skills, and strategies so that students can develop their own understandings. It challenges teachers to assess student learning in a format that most closely matches how the information was learned, as well as with formative methods that will provide students feedback with which to inform further learning.

Student learning through collaborative team projects, often culminated with products that have been produced using technology tools such as multimedia presentations, cannot adequately be assessed using traditional methods. More appropriate strategies for assessing growth in content knowledge within project-based, integrated learning activities include conferences with students, anecdotal records, and observation (Kumar & Bristor, 1999). *Rubrics* can strengthen these assessments. Simkins (1999) defines rubrics as "sets of formal guidelines we use to rate examples of student work . . . usually presented in the form of a matrix with performance levels in the top row and performance dimensions along the left column" (p. 23).

Well-constructed rubrics assist teachers in making decisions about student skills, competencies, abilities, and attitudes within complex learning processes and products (see Table 15.1). Students can be introduced to rubrics, and even those students with learning disabilities can more precisely focus on learning when they know ahead of time what will be expected of them in an activity (Jackson & Larkin, 2002). Student teams can broaden their understanding by assessing peer projects according to rubric criteria. Simkins (1999) provides these tips for constructing effective assessment rubrics:

- Construct rubrics that are not too task-specific—more general rubrics can be used again for other projects.

TABLE 15.1	Assessment Rubric Example			
	Exemplary	**Expected**	**Adequate**	**Inadequate**
Content	Information is in a logical, intuitive sequence; information is clear, appropriate, and accurate.	Information is in a logical sequence; information is largely clear, appropriate, and accurate.	Information is in some logical sequence; some information is confusing, inappropriate, or inaccurate.	Information is not in a logical sequence and is confusing, inappropriate, or inaccurate.
Written work	Maintains clear focus and logical organization; establishes a tone appropriate to the intended audience; clearly conveys complex ideas with ample supportive details; has no misspellings or grammatical errors.	Maintains focus and displays organization; conveys complex ideas with supportive details; has fewer than two misspellings and/or grammatical errors.	Attempts to maintain focus and organization, but occasionally is not clear; simple ideas are conveyed well, but more complex notions are not developed and supported with details; has multiple misspellings and/or grammatical errors.	Frequently loses focus and organization; ideas are not conveyed clearly or supported with details; has significant spelling errors and/or grammatical errors.

- Construct rubrics that are not too general because they will lack the specificity required to make appropriate distinctions.
- Avoid highly detailed criteria that become more of a checklist than a rubric.
- Use a limited number of dimensions, or main areas of focus, in order to decide where to look for the main learning priorities of the project.
- Use key criteria that matter the most about each dimension of the project.
- Use measurable criteria that can be counted or ranked.
- Select descriptors that clearly describe traits that should be present in work.
- Use four performance levels that make fine enough discrimination, yet are not too divisive.
- Maintain an equal interval distance between levels so that the highest and next highest are an equal distance to the lowest and next lowest.
- Involve students in creating rubrics so they will clearly understand what the expectations are and "buy in" to using them.

Numerous rubric examples can also be found on the web (e.g., Kathy Schrock's Guide for Educators at **http://school.discovery.com/schrockguide/assess.html**). Practical assessment strategies using technology tools are described in the final section of this chapter.

Technology as a Data Collection Tool

The jury is still out on how two powerful educational trends—the rise of constructivist teaching practices and the increased demand for accountability as expressed through high-stakes testing—will find ways to coexist in education practice. For now, society still expects student progress to be translated into numerical form for easier understanding and comparison. Standardized tests are required not only of those students desiring to pursue postsecondary study but also of students every year in most K–12 classrooms. While we know that learner-centered and problem-solving activities help students to make sense of the world, local standards and curriculum still place great value on memorization of discrete data and demonstration of other lower-order skills. It is therefore important that educators comprehend how the power of technology can contribute to the organization and accuracy of test taking, from sophisticated college entrance exams to simpler tests and quizzes that teachers can create themselves and use in their classrooms with all ages of students.

Objective tests assess knowledge that can be responded to with right or wrong answers. Other assessment tasks, such as mathematical computational problems or longer written works, do not lend themselves as well to electronic assessment. Using a computer to deliver a test offers testing on demand, the inclusion of multimedia elements to create real-life testing scenarios, and fast, accurate scoring and reporting of results (Straetmans & Eggen, 1998). Teachers can use this information to make immediate adjustments in instruction, and test questions can be edited and updated at any time to reflect instructional variation (Bushweller, 2000).

The most sophisticated computerized tests, *computer adaptive* tests, are "smart" enough to actually change their form in response to a test taker's input. More traditional paper-and-pencil tests assess all students at the same level, meaning all students must take a longer test consisting of all levels of test items, some too difficult and some too easy. Computer adaptive tests attempt to mimic a human examiner by adjusting to a level of difficulty appropriate to each individual user (Straetmans & Eggen, 1998). During examination, the computer selects an item from a large item bank and presents it to the user. If the user responds correctly, a more difficult item is presented next; if incorrectly, the computer presents an easier item. The goal is to assess student knowledge accurately in the quickest sequence of test items. An additional benefit of computer adaptive testing is that each test taker is essentially given a unique test, decreasing the potential for cheating (Center of Advanced Research on Language Acquisition, 1999). Computer adaptive formats are now being offered for the Graduate Record Exam (see GRE at **www.gre.com**), and computerized versions of the SAT and ACT are being considered. Software is also available for districts to create computer adaptive exams based on local standards (e.g., Northwest Evaluation Association, **www.nwea.org/cat-int.htm**).

Computer-based tests are direct electronic versions of their paper-and-pencil counterparts. The computerized format is attractive because of the ease and accuracy of scoring large quantities of tests, leaving teachers time for more academic tasks, such as planning and instruction. Students have a motivating test format, can focus on one item at a time (Kingsbury, 2002), can take the tests when and where they want, can receive individual and immediate feedback, and can return to previous answers for further deliberation.

Results on the effectiveness of computer-based tests are mixed, with some studies demonstrating increased student accuracy on computer-based exams than on the same paper versions (e.g., Bocij & Greasley, 1999) and others showing computerized and standard formats to be equivalent (e.g., Haaf, Duncan, Skarakis-Doyle, Carew, & Kapitan, 1999). Results on computer-based tests may favor African American and Hispanic students (Gallagher, Bridgeman, & Cahalan, 2002). Results for computerized assessment of more subjective responses, such as essay writing, are even more inconclusive. Essay grading software matches scores of human graders 50 percent of the time on the Graduate Management Admission Test (GMAT) (Bushweller, 2000). This type of software assesses items such as passage length, redundancy, and spelling, but is less effective at assessing cleverness or organization of a written piece (see, for example, the Intelligent Essay Assessor, **www.knowledge-technologies.com**).

Teachers also find computers a useful tool in creating their own informal electronic exams and quizzes, either for grading or review purposes in the classroom. Electronic tests can be created by entering questions and answers into test-creation software (e.g., HotPotatoes, **http://web.uvic.ca/hrd/halfbaked**). Some websites (e.g., WebAssign, **www.webassign.net**) allow teachers to take advantage of ready-made tests or to create exams based on item banks that can be given and scored online. Other sites give teachers freedom to easily create exams and quizzes in a variety of formats, such as multiple choice or essay, and have student results emailed directly to them (e.g., FunBrain's Quiz Lab, **www.funbrain.com,** and Quia, **www.quia.com**). These sites also feature databases of ready-made quizzes searchable by content area or grade level (see Figure 15.1). Some advise attention to security to protect the integrity of test data collected or stored through the Internet (Shermis & Averitt, 2002).

FIGURE 15.1 FunBrain.com.

Technology as a Recording, Analysis, and Communication Tool

Instructional effort is undertaken by both the instructor and the learner with the hope that the learning of something new will be the end result. Almost continuously, teachers arrive at various forms of evaluative conclusions that shape and guide plans for future instruction. The recorded products of evaluative activity can take a number of forms but can generally be discussed in two chief categories: quantitative and quali-tative data. Classroom technology can assist teachers with both types of record keep-ing, making the tedious, potentially error-prone activities quick and accurate, thus facilitating the straightforward report of progress to parents. Further, technology tools can be invaluable in the ongoing presentation of student learning.

Quantitative Record Keeping

Traditionally, students have been assessed according to standard, established criteria. Their achievement has been compared either to each other as in *norm-referenced* as-sessments or according to their mastery of the objectives themselves as is the case with *criteria-referenced* conclusions. In either case, scores received on assessments must be recorded and compiled so that a longer-term evaluation of an individual can be accomplished. A teacher's grade book has always been thought to hold all the an-swers regarding a child's progress. The story was told in the neat columns and rows of handwritten names and numbers.

Educational record keeping has received a helping hand from spreadsheet soft-ware. Now, instead of entering student names by hand, names can be easily typed in. Records for new students can be inserted into the alphabetically correct position, rather than being tacked on to the bottom of the list out of order. Grades that are en-tered can be modified if assignments are resubmitted without creating a mess of eras-ings and blobs of correction fluid.

The most powerful advantage of using a spreadsheet to keep track of student grades is the software's ability to perform computational functions on numbers. No longer does a teacher need to take time to enter each grade for a student into a calcu-lator to calculate an average grade. With a drag to highlight a row of grades, and a click on a shortcut button, a simple average computation can be placed into a target spreadsheet cell. Formulas can also be easily written to perform more complicated calculations, such as applying different weights to the scores received on different as-signments. Keeping grades using spreadsheet software allows teachers to represent scores graphically as graphs and charts to present student achievement in ways that are readily understandable and comparable. Visually tracking student performance is an ideal way to involve students in assessing and understanding their own progress.

Numerous programs are designed expressly for the purposes of recording and cal-culating grades, planning seating charts, and keeping attendance, and it is likely that your school district will give you access to one (e.g., 1st Class Gradebook, Grade Ma-chine, and Making the Grade [see Figure 15.2]). Formulas most useful in calculating grades are already written and made easily accessible in these programs, and graph-ical outputs are created especially for student progress reporting purposes. Web-based grade book management systems allow teachers to manage grades from any computer connected to the Internet and email students when grades are updated (see, for example, Excelsior Pinnacle at **www.gradebook.com** or experiment with a free trial of ThinkWave Educator at **www.thinkwave.com**). Parents can input their child's student identification number and a PIN code to access real-time progress, grade, and attendance reports.

FIGURE 15.2 Making the Grade grade book software.

ASSIGNMENT NUMBERS→	7	8	9	10	11	12	13	14	15	16	17	18	19	20	21	22	23	24	25	26	27	28	29	30	31	32	33	34	35	36	CURRENT STUDENT TOTALS
ASSIGNMENT CATEGORIES→	SPL	SPL	LIT	SPL	SPL	LIT	SPL	PAR	SPL	LIT	MAT	SPL	SPL	LIT	MAT	SPL	SPL	LIT	MAT	SPL	SPL	LIT	PAR	SPL	QFT	ORL	LIT	LIT	WRT	QFT	
ASSIGNMENT VALUES→	50	36	84	50	28	54	51	25	31	10	50	34	88	10	54	28	78	10	54	30	58	25	30	182	50	100		✓	100	200	
1 Archer, Dennis E.	43	27	69	43	24	34	39	25	26	10	36	17	72	10	41	24	70	10	36	27	44	25	23	121	DRP	76	✓	B-	92		76.4=C
2 Bowles, Charles A.	36	30	63	34	25	19	33		26		DRP	33	22	51	10	34	0	44	10	40	24	19		20	100	30	70	✓	C	120		61.5=D
3 Chancellor, James L.	48	25	79	49		45	50	25	29	10	44	27	68	10	52	27	70	10	49	24	42	DRP	23	168	40	86	✓+	C+	164		86.0=B
4 Dickerson Michael R.	46	32	66	42	27	46	44	DRP	26	10	44	29	53	10		24	63	10	50	26	35	27	156	45	78	✓	B	120		82.6=B
5 Garcia, Eugene F.	43	33	71	37	26	24	36	25	27	10	40	22	51	DRP	47		50	0	46	26	24	25	29	107	40	72	✓	B-	164		75.7=C
6 Glenn, Helen B.	EXC	EXC	EXC	EXC	EXC	EXC	EXC	EXC	EXC	EXC	EXC	EXC	EXC	EXC	EXC	EXC	EXC	EXC	EXC	EXC	EXC	EXC	EXC	29	164	DRP	86	✓+	A	172		90.9=A
7 Gray, Kathleen R.	35	36	72	37	26	34	43	DRP	31	10	40	34	63	10	41	26	58	10	45	30	39	25	30	93	35	72	✓	C+	92		70.5=C-
8 Howard, Stacey E.	49	35	68	41	28	44	44		31	10	43	31	58	10	52	0	67	10	52		DRP		18	152	40	80	✓+	B+	156		79.5=C+
9 Huntington, Susan L.	49	36	74	41	28	41	47	DRP	25	10	45	30	88	10	51	22	76	10	48	30	41	25	26	168	50	90	✓	A	196		92.1=A
10 Huston, Stephen B.	48	34	80	48	28	36	56	20	31	10		30	40	10	49	24	67	10	54	24	53	DRP	28	182	40	82	✓	B+	196		88.1=B
11 Ingram, Thomas L.	40	36	57		24	35	35	25	26	10	35	31	51	DRP	21	26	57	10	22	26	22	25	26	119	35	72	✓	C	92		69.8=C-
12 Jansen, Beverly H.	46	36	80	48	28	49	50	25	30	10	45	30	46			50	28	22	10	53	30	55	DRP	28	177	40	84	✓	A	172		88.4=B
13 Jenkins, Lynn T.	34	26	61	46	28	43	47		31	10	36	31	52	10	38	0	47	DRP		30	21		24	112	30	72	✓	D+	104		63.1=D
14 Knight, Rebecca J.	33	CHT			28	26	29		31	10	32						24		10	39	13	22	27	72	DRP	66	✓-	D-	104		45.1=F-
15 Kosterman, Jason D.	42	36	68	46	26	37	49	25	31	10	46	28	12	10	48	26	50	10	46		DRP	29	117	40	74	✓	B-	162		78.7=C+
16 Lee, Tamara C.	30	36	82	32	26	41	32	20	26	10	36	30	66	10	26	18	60	10	DRP	30	42	25	25	112	35	90	✓	C+	88		73.1=C
17 Lewis, Jeffrey P.	28	32	74	36	22	38	32	25	30	10	31	25	TRU	TRU		21	TRU	TRU	22	27		DRP	19	64	30	60	✓	C	62		56.8=F
18 Mc_Cann, Molly M.	39	33	84	42	28	38	46	15	26	10	30	32	66	10	45	0	77	10	38		45	DRP	22	158	40	94	✓	B	92		78.7=C+
19 Morgan, Donald T.	49	35	68	42	28	44	44	DRP	31	10	41	31	58	10	52		68	10	52	27	20	25	26	152	40	80	✓	C	154		81.8=B
20 Nuss, Timothy A.	47	35	61	42	28	26	45	25	31	10	46		DRP	10	43	28	47	10	53	30	28	25	29	124	40	68	✓	C-	136		76.5=C
21 Ogden, Kristi N.	26	36	64	36	26	33	35		0	10	28	30	48	DRP	35	28	54	10	47	30	47		25	105	35	82	✓	C	76		64.4=D
22 O'Grady, Shelli N.	DRP	34	66	40	28	40	35	25	31	10	37	32	45	10	47	26	49	10	46	30	36	25	27	122	40	84	✓	B	152		80.7=B-
23 Powell, Jr., John C.		35	DRP	42	25	22	48	25	30	10	46	28	73	10	42	25	51	10	50	28	44	25	29	135	45	94	✓	B-	120		81.2=B-
24 Raymond, Carie S.	27	34	58	35	28	DRP	32	25	24	10	36	24	53	10	43	26	54	10	46	30	35	25	27	102	35	82	✓	C-	116		71.6=C
25 Rutledge, Michael S.	DRP	36	71	40	27	42	39	20	23	10	42	29	66	10	46	21	66	10	44	28	51	25	28	130	45	94	✓	D	104		77.0=C
26 Sampson, Eugene J.	41	36	68	38	26	40	41	25	25	10	34	27	54	10	31	23	54	10	36	26	10	DRP	25	124	35	76	✓	C+	103		74.5=C
27 Smith, Vickie R.		36	75	44	26	46	43	25	30	10	41	32	81	DRP	37	28	77	10	45	29	41	25	29	180	45	90	✓	A	192		93.2=A
28 St._James, Lester L.		36	52	29	28	46	40	25	29	10	41	30	DRP	10	42	23	61	10	47	25	27	25	27	80	35	68	✓	B-	103		73.5=C
29 Torrence, Jeremy D.	EXC	EXC	EXC	EXC	EXC	EXC	EXC	EXC	EXC	EXC	EXC	EXC	EXC	EXC	EXC	EXC	EXC	EXC	EXC	25	27	156	DRP	78	✓	B	156		84.5=B		
30 Winston, Kristin R.	35	11	81	36	28	47	44	25	30	10	41	29	74	0	36	24	79	10	41	30	62	DRP		161	40	88		C+	112		80.3=B-
31 Yoder, Jeremy D.	39		72	36	27	33	42	25	31	10	42	29	DRP	10	37	24	55	10	42	30	58	25	25	92	35	90	✓	C	60		71.1=C-

	ASSIGNMENT TITLES	POINTS	ITEMS	X-FACTORS
34	COMPOSITION 1: The Nature of Man [10/28]	100	100	1.000
35	QUARTER I: Spelling Final Test [10/28]	200	100	2.000
36				

Qualitative Record Keeping

As educational philosophy demands that students have authentic opportunities to demonstrate their unique understandings and capabilities, views of what type of information provides adequate indication of learning are changing. The steadfast belief that numbers can tell the complete story of a learner is giving way to a recognition that what a teacher observes in daily interactions with students is in fact very telling of the growth of those students. Indeed, as educators embrace this new anecdotal method of assessment, at the same time they scramble to find ways to consistently and comparably report student progress in words instead of numbers. This challenge can be made more manageable, and perhaps more meaningful, with the help of classroom technology.

By creating or adding to an existing database record for each child, teachers can record observations in a central, organized location. Even word-processed notes can provide handy reminders of progress when reporting to parents (see Figure 15.3). Both options allow a teacher opportunity to scroll back up through a student's record to track patterns or make predictions. Although this type of recording could, in essence, be done with paper and pencil, handwritten notes are static documents. The text of anecdotal records recorded in a database can be searched by keywords to see, for example, how frequently a student has offered an answer in class or has had a problem behaving with another student. These records can additionally be merged into word-processed documents to create instant parent reports of student progress.

FIGURE 15.3 Anecdotal records kept on a word processor.

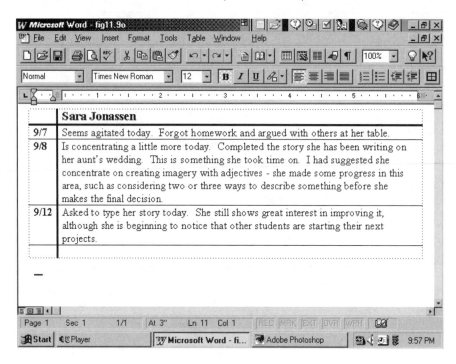

Because it is not practical to run over to the computer to access the database whenever a student says or does something of note, teachers can develop note-taking practices that work with the technology-based record keeping. Keeping a notepad handy allows teachers to quickly jot down the names of the students and what indication of progress they notice. At a later time, just as a teacher would need to take time to record quantitative grades, a teacher can sit with the database application open and enter the observations. Voice recognition technology can expedite this observation process by allowing teachers to record their verbal comments and translate them automatically into digitized text format.

Portfolio Assessment

Portfolios are alternative assessment forms that have been described frequently as the intersection between instruction and assessment. The Northwest Regional Educational Laboratory defines a portfolio as "a purposeful collection of student work that tells the story of student achievement or growth" (Arter, 1995). Barrett (2000) adds the concept of the portfolio as a "reflective tool." Whereas answers given on tests can indicate only a student's response to a given stimulus (Kennedy, 1999) at a given time, a portfolio can function as a window into that student's head, as well as a broad time line of learning. A powerful portfolio should:

- Demonstrate that a student has engaged in self-reflection so that he may learn about and assume ownership for his own learning.
- Involve the student in the selection of the pieces to be included in the portfolio.
- Convey the rationale, intents, contents, standards, and judgments of the student's work.
- Show growth.
- Serve a different purpose in progress than it serves at the end (Paulson, Paulson, & Meyer, 1991).

The distinct advantage of portfolio assessment over more traditional tests is that the ownership of learning and product production shifts away from the teacher (Wiggins, 1989). Instead, portfolio development reflects a jointly negotiated process, reached by the teacher and the student, which entails complex discussions and customized evaluation of learning. Educators should strive for a balance between student-centered portfolios and teacher-centered portfolios. In the former, students collect, select, and compile items to illustrate personal learning. In the latter, portfolios are created and maintained by teachers with items that demonstrate learning in accordance with program goals (Barrett, 1998). Students must be carefully introduced to the concept of portfolios and to the methods of selecting items and reflecting on learning relevance (Stone, 1998). However, prescribing too structured of a portfolio format eliminates student creativity (Mills, 1997).

Traditional educational portfolios are collected in notebooks, binders, and even boxes, filling shelves and file cabinets. As artifacts of learning are increasingly represented with digital products, electronic portfolios provide a natural solution to representing student learning. Electronic portfolios can include word-processed writing examples, spreadsheets, scanned writing or drawing, digital photos, videos of performances or actions, audiotaped narration reading, or multimedia projects. Years' worth of work can be efficiently stored on CD-ROM, making work much more portable than large binders of pages.

Educational portfolios serve purposes distinct from other professional portfolios; not a collection of every single item, as is the case with stock portfolios, yet not solely the best of the best examples that constitute artistic portfolios. Carlson (1998) suggests two distinct types of portfolios: *process* and *product*. Process portfolios collect students' work throughout a period of time in order to show growth in ability and attitude. Product portfolios exhibit a selection of a student's best work.

Niguidula (1997) suggests that all stakeholders ask a series of questions to guide the creation of a portfolio-based assessment system:

1. *Vision.* What should a student know and be able to do?
2. *Assessment.* How can students demonstrate the school vision? Why do we collect student work? What audiences are most important to us? How do we know what's good?
3. *Technology.* What hardware, software, and networking will we need? Who are the primary users of the equipment? Who will support the system?
4. *Logistics.* When will information be digitized? Who will do it? Who will select the work? Who will reflect on the work?
5. *Culture.* Is the school used to discussing student work? (pp. 27–28).

Once these areas have been considered, Barrett (2000) identifies the following stages of electronic portfolio development.

Stage 1: Defining the Portfolio Context and Goals. Educators should consider why the assessment is occurring, what standards students should be able to meet, what resources are available, what skill levels teachers and students possess, and who the audiences for the portfolios are.

Stage 2: The Working Portfolio. The main concerns of this stage are the types of items to select for the portfolio, determined by the goals set in the first stage. Storage and software options should also be considered as work is collected.

Stage 3: The Reflective Portfolio. Criteria for selecting and judging learning artifacts can be managed with a rubric. Student self-reflections on artifacts and goals for future learning are key to determining the quality of the portfolio.

Stage 4: The Connected Portfolio. Learning artifacts can be organized and linked so that they can be navigated to demonstrate that the learner has met the learning goals. Such connecting also aids evaluation and planning for future instruction.

Stage 5: The Presentation Portfolio. Final storage options must be considered here so that work can be preserved, and students will share their portfolios in some manner, as in student-led conferences.

Electronic Portfolio Formats. Electronic portfolios might take a number of formats depending on available technology and skill levels. The most basic collections can be created with slide-show software (e.g., PowerPoint), which can present information in both linear and nonlinear structures. Easy-to-use multimedia software (e.g., HyperStudio) can allow for the linking and presentation of work samples, and more advanced authoring software (e.g., Macromedia Authorware) allows for the creation of more sophisticated portfolio interfaces. Electronic portfolios can also involve the use of relational databases (e.g., Access) to organize student work samples so that they can be sorted, clustered, and compared over time.

Web-based portfolio formats further encourage individuality by allowing students to demonstrate creativity in presentation and organization, to create multiple design formats for multiple audiences (Watkins, 1996), and to establish connections easily among related portfolio components (McKinney, 1998). The web, as both a technology and an interface, enables students ultimate control in assembling and ease of reorganizing, as well as the ability to integrate narrative captions among the learning evidence to emphasize the interrelated nature of the learning (Watkins, 1996). The web environment permits students the flexibility to maintain their portfolios in either a protected intranet environment or on a web space that can be remotely accessed from anywhere at any time, by the student, faculty, peers, scholarship review committees, and potential employers. Finally, web-based portfolios promote seamless access to student work by eliminating software and platform incompatibilities encountered when viewing electronic portfolios created with multiple authoring tools (Mills, 1997). As a caveat, online web-based portfolios will require password protection to protect student privacy on the Internet. They will further necessitate some local consideration of the types of photos or videos of students that are appropriate to post. Other drawbacks of using portfolio assessment on a large scale: Portfolios are less efficient than numerical scores, more difficult to administer, more time-consuming, not as easily standardized, and ultimately, more costly (Madaus & O'Dwyer, 1999).

Technology as a Plagiarism Detector

Unfortunately, the enormous benefits of the Internet as a rich information source for student writers are tempered by the vast potential the technology presents for using information inappropriately. Student Internet users have become adept at pasting whole pages of text into their writing without even reading or paraphrasing. It is just so tempting—they have the writing of experts already in digital form, and how would their teachers ever know? In a more active show of cheating, students can access complete essays online from "paper mills," some that offer essays for free and others for a charge, on virtually any topic a teacher would assign (see, for example, **http:// Cheathouse.com, www.planetpapers.com,** or **www.coastal.edu/library/mills2.htm**).

Teachers must develop conscious strategies to battle this Internet-assisted plagiarism. First, teachers should let students know that they are aware of the possibilities the Internet presents for the misuse of information. Many students will be deterred from stealing online text simply by knowing their teachers are aware that it can be done. Informing students about correct citation of online information is also vital. Frequently, students simply are not aware of the seriousness of the act of copying text, or they think that if they change a word or two, they are in the clear. Other times, students justify cheating because they are facing an assignment deadline.

Teachers who suspect a piece of writing has been plagiarized can employ some specific strategies, from basic to more advanced. At the basic end of the spectrum is some good old-fashioned detective work. Teachers should first look for clues that a piece of writing may not have been written by the student who turned it in. Are the references current? Are there any formatting changes that would signal pasted chunks of text? Is the topic appropriate to the assignment? Is the writing style compatible with that of other writing from that student?

Harris (2002) recommends these further strategies for remaining ever-vigilant in holding Internet-assisted plagiarism in check: (1) Compare writing with in-class writing assignments; (2) require specific components or sources that prewritten essays may not contain; (3) stress process over product; (4) structure assignments with smaller parts due at regular intervals, thus putting less emphasis on the final project; (5) include topics of real interest to students; (6) educate students about plagiarism; and (7) demonstrate the poor quality of online papers (many are contributions from site users, so there is no real guarantee that even a purchased paper will be of quality).

If still unsure about the source of the work, teachers can paste or retype a phrase from the text directly into a search engine such as Google (**http://google.com**) or Alta-Vista (**http://altavista.com**). If the original source is among the countless websites indexed by these popular search engines, it should turn up in the search results. Finally, if there is still no clear answer, many districts now subscribe to specific plagiarism detection sites, such as TurnItIn (**www.turnitin.com**), which require students to directly upload their assignments to the website. Such sites then match the essay text to their databases of other papers online, as well as other papers submitted by students in that teacher's previous courses, and return color-coded results showing the pieces of the text that have been plagiarized.

Summary

Technology can make the assessment process more efficient if the role of technology and the types of assessment information desired is considered. Technology can be either (1) the focus of assessment on large scales to justify the purchase of computers or (2) the tool for instructional delivery, communication, or information finding, basing student learning on mastery of content rather than technology use. Learning

---

School Stories

The French culture multimedia projects were nearly finished. Some students in Cassie Lichtner's eleventh-grade French class were putting in a last few minutes of rehearsal before the parent presentations that evening. Others were completing the Project Reflections necessary to submit with their projects to their electronic portfolios.

Students write reflections to accompany all major projects, listing strengths they perceive of the assignments, as well as those aspects they would do differently next time. This was a difficult process for many students at the beginning of the year, because they had never been asked to think about their own learning before. At first, some students only described the assignment, rather than considering their own effort and learning. Ms. Lichtner often meets with students individually to ask them questions before they write their reflections so students will better be able to elicit thought and self-reflection.

Ms. Lichtner reads her students' reflections for a better understanding of each one's learning habits, but does not grade them. The purpose of the reflections is to record personal understandings at the time of the assignments. At the end of each nine weeks, students will spend extensive time reviewing their entire portfolios to assess their learning and set goals for the next quarter. If students waited several weeks to look back at each assignment, they would not recall the detail and relevance as meaningfully.

through integrated activities is best assessed using alternative methods such as student conferences, anecdotal records, and observation, guided by rubrics.

Educators should understand how the power of technology could contribute to the organization and accuracy of test taking. Computerized formats make scoring large quantities easier and more accurate so that teachers can attend to academic tasks. Sophisticated computer adaptive tests change form in response to a test taker's input. Other computer-based tests directly mimic their paper-and-pencil counterparts. Educators must also be vigilant in identifying text that has been plagiarized from online sources.

Quantitative record keeping can be more efficient with the use of spreadsheet software, and qualitative anecdotal assessment methods are made more manageable through the use of database records or word-processed notes. Electronic portfolios can incorporate various electronic learning formats and can be stored easily on disk or CD-ROM. Web portfolios enable students' control in assembling, reorganizing, narrating, and maintaining learning artifacts, while also allowing remote access and viewing by multiple audiences.

Challenge Yourself!

1. Research your state or district's technology resources for assessment.
2. Search the web using such keywords as *portfolios* and *technology*. What types of portfolio examples do you find?
3. Design a four-level rubric for a course activity you have recently been asked to complete. How might your grade on that assignment have changed with a rubric-driven assessment?
4. How can a classroom that already uses portfolios transition toward using electronic portfolios? Write a short plan consisting of easy to more advanced strategies.
5. Rate your school's technology preparedness using the CEO Forum's StaRChart (**www.ceoforum.org**).
6. Research technology skills checklists for students found online. Are there other skills that should be included? How do you imagine using such a checklist to assess your students' technology proficiency?
7. Using a spreadsheet application, design a simple grade book for a fictitious class. Include scores for several assignments and formulas to calculate the final grades.
8. What does the research say about the use of anecdotal records? What are some methods that experienced teachers use to keep track of these types of observations?
9. Design an electronic form on which to record qualitative, anecdotal records on individual students. What will be the best way to keep these records updated?
10. Design an online quiz using FunBrain's Quiz Lab (**www.funbrain.com**). Have three friends take the quiz and email the results to you. How long does this whole process take from start to finish? Could it have been accomplished as easily without technology?

References

Arter, J. A. (1995). *Portfolios for assessment and instruction.* ERIC Clearinghouse on Counseling and Student Services (Report No. EDO-CG-95-10). Greensboro, NC: ERIC Clearinghouse on Counseling and Student Services. (ERIC Document Reproduction Service No. ED 388890.)

Barnett, H. (2000). Assessing the effects of technology. *Learning and Leading with Technology, 27*(7), 28–31, 63.

Barrett, H. C. (1998). Strategic questions: What to consider when planning for electronic portfolios. *Learning and Leading with Technology, 26*(2), 6–13.

Barrett, H. C. (2000). Create your own electronic portfolio: Using off-the-shelf software to showcase your own or student work. *Learning and Leading with Technology, 27*(7), 15–21.

Bocij, P., & Greasley, A. (1999). Can computer-based testing achieve quality and efficiency in assessment? *International Journal of Educational Technology, 1*(1). Retrieved June 2000 from www.outreach.uiuc.edu/ijet/v1n1/bocij/index.html.

Bushweller, K. (2000). Electronic exams. *Electronic School.* Retrieved June 20, 2000, from www.electonic-school.com.

Carlson, R. D. (1998). Portfolio assessment of instructional technology. *Journal of Educational Technology Systems, 27*(1), 81–92.

Center for Advanced Research on Language Acquisition. (1999). *Frequently asked questions about computer adaptive tests.* Retrieved April 22, 2003, from http://carla.acad.umn.edu/CATFAO.html.

Gallagher, A., Bridgeman, B., & Cahalan, C. (2002). The effect of computer-based tests on racial-ethnic and gender groups. *Journal of Educational Measurement, 39*(2),133–147.

Haaf, R., Duncan, B., Skarakis-Doyle, E., Carew, M., & Kapitan, P. (1999). Computer-based language assessment software: The effects of presentation and response format. *Language, Speech, and Hearing Services in Schools, 30*(1), 68–74.

Harris, R. (2002). Anti-plagiarism strategies for research papers. Retrieved April 22, 2003, from www.virtualsalt.com/antiplag.htm.

Jackson, C. W., & Larkin, M. J. (2002). Rubric: Teaching students to use grading rubrics. *Teaching Exceptional Children, 35*(1), 40–45.

Kennedy, D. (1999). Assessing true academic success: The next frontier of reform. *The Mathematics Teacher, 92*(6), 462–466.

Kingsbury, G. G. (2002). *An empirical comparison of achievement level estimates from adaptive tests and paper-and pencil tests.* Paper presented at the Annual Meeting of the American Educational Research Association, New Orleans, LA.

Kumar, D., & Bristor, V. J. (1999). Integrating science and language arts through technology-based macrocontexts. *Educational Review, 51*(1), 41–53.

Madaus, G. F., & O'Dwyer, L. M. (1999). A short history of performance assessment: Lessons learned. *Phi Delta Kappan, 80*(9), 688–695.

McKinney, M. (1998). Preservice teachers' electronic portfolios: Integrating technology, self-assessment, and reflection. *Teacher Education Quarterly, 25*(1), 85–103.

Mills, E. (1997). Portfolios: A challenge for technology. *International Journal of Instructional Media, 24*(1), 23–29.

Niguidula, D. (1997). Picturing performance with digital portfolios. *Educational Leadership, 55*(3), 26–29.

Painter, D. D. (2000). Teacher as researcher: A means to assess the effectiveness of technology in the classroom. *Learning and Leading with Technology, 27*(7), 10–13, 27.

Paulson, F. L., Paulson, P. R., & Meyer, C. A. (1991). What makes a portfolio a portfolio? *Educational Leadership, 48*(5), 60–63.

Shermis, M. D., & Averitt, J. (2002). Where did all the data go? Internet security for web-based assessments. *Educational Measurement: Issues and Practice, 21*(2), 20–25.

Simkins, M. (1999). Designing great rubrics. *Technology and Learning, 20*(1), 23–24, 28–29.

Stone, B. A. (1998). Problems, pitfalls, and benefits of portfolios. *Teacher Education Quarterly, 25*(1), 105–114.

Straetmans, G. J. J. M., & Eggen, T. J. H. M. (1998). Computerized adaptive testing: What it is and how it works. *Educational Technology, 38*(1), 45–52.

Sun, J. (2000). How do we know it's working? *Learning and Leading with Technology, 27*(7), 32–35, 41, 49.

Watkins, S. (1996). World Wide Web authoring in the portfolio-assessed, (inter)networked composition course. *Computers and Composition, 13*(2), 219–230.

Wiggins, G. (1989). A true test: Toward more authentic and equitable assessment. *Phi Delta Kappan,* 703–713.

CHAPTER 16

Productivity and Classroom Administration

FOCUS QUESTIONS

1. How can basic software tools be used to facilitate print-based communication?

2. What types of planning and scheduling can be aided with the use of technology?

3. What specific-purpose software aids teacher productivity?

The aspect of a teacher's job description that rarely makes it into most discussions in college teacher preparation programs is that of being a classroom administrator. Many new teachers arrive in their first classrooms ready to get on with the job of "teaching" and instead discover that they are poorly prepared to manage the day-to-day operation that a bustling classroom community requires. It is unrealistic to see modern teachers solely in the role of instructors. In fact, their necessary administrative duties require them to wear many of the hats that most leaders in the professional world must also don. Noninstructional activities make up a large segment of a teacher's typical day, and those daily responsibilities could easily infringe on the time allocated for actual instruction. Although teachers are often open to consider ways in which students can benefit from learning with technology, they sometimes are not aware of how technology can help them in accomplishing administrative duties (Office of Technology Assessment, 1995). Technology can aid greatly in making time spent in these routine administrative tasks effective and efficient, and this undoubtedly can lead to more minutes available for meaningful contact with an educator's clients, the young learners.

Because computerizing these basic administrative affairs can make for more consistent and accurate management systems as compared to the handwritten and figured approach, more democratic leadership patterns can emerge in the classroom. Teachers are finding that students of all ages are capable of some degree of responsibility for the routine tasks that surround and make possible the learning environment of the classroom. This shift in power necessarily accompanies the general shift from teacher-directed learning situations to productive, child-centered learning contexts. Technology facilitates greater student participation by providing secure, predictable organizational systems.

By reflecting and modeling this shift in pedagogical and organizational focus, this chapter will serve to provoke thought and experimentation on the part of teachers in how they might best use technology to ensure their daily efforts are faster and more efficient. The ideas here should not be construed as comprehensive nor should every idea be assumed to be vital to successful classroom management in the Information Age. A teacher's individual management style and the unique composition of each individual class will determine the extent to which technology might streamline administrative tasks.

Step-by-step instructions will not be given in this chapter on the operation of software tools, such as how to create a document using a word processor or how to write a formula in a spreadsheet; proficiency with common productivity tools is now considered a baseline skill for employment in any professional field. (See Chapter 2 for an overview on using word processors, spreadsheets, and databases for educational purposes.) The purpose of this chapter, rather, is to suggest beginning points for implementing a technologically organized plan of action. The chapter is arranged according to administrative purpose, with ideas for those software choices that might best be used for each task. Uses for productivity software tools that come packaged on most computers are primarily discussed because teachers are more likely to have access to these basic programs in their classroom computers. Features of some specific-purpose tools that are applicable to particular administrative responsibilities are also described.

Communicating

Inherent to the role of a classroom teacher is the need to act as a liaison among many groups of people: parents, administrators, students, other teachers, students from other classes, and community members. Strong, organized strategies are a must to pull off communication that often rivals corporate public relations campaigns. Email, as discussed in Chapter 3, is the communication mode of choice for many educators; however, paper-based communication forms remain a necessary component to a teacher's communication arsenal. Teachers cannot assume that all stakeholders that make up a classroom community have the capabilities to communicate electronically, and many items, such as those giving parent permission, require handwritten signatures. Basic productivity tools to which most teachers have access can prevent the job from becoming a correspondence nightmare. The suggestions that follow may seem like obvious uses of computer technology, but will serve as basics on which to build a strong communication platform.

Student Contact Information

Keeping in touch with your students' families is made easier by keeping up-to-date student records. Schools often provide teachers with printed lists of student information, but these pages represent a static form of keeping this information. If a family changes phone numbers, or a parent gets a new job with different hours, a printed list can be modified only by hand, leaving a messy record-keeping system.

Creating a database record for each student in class allows for a neat, easy-to-update filing system. The fields in a database can be customized to allow for information specific to particular students and situations. A database for a class in which most students ride the school bus may need to include a field identifying the bus number in order to be complete, whereas a database on secondary students might include students' after-school work numbers. Larger text fields can be used to add anecdotal comments. Databases not only provide for a convenient, consistent compilation of information about students, but that information can also be searched and sorted. If, for example, all of the students who have other siblings attending the same school need to be contacted, students with completed "sibling" fields can be sorted. Student information can be entered into a database by teachers, or the data may be available through the school's central system. Having the database open on the computer screen, along with an example of a student record, as parents come in for a "Meet-Your-Teacher" night at the beginning of the school year can serve as an invitation for parents to fill in their own child's data. Not only does this spread the workload, but it also introduces parents to some of the many ways technology is being used in the classroom.

Letters

Whether it is a lengthy summary of a semester's work or a brief response acknowledging a note received, writing letters to parents is a requirement of most teachers' jobs at the K–12 level. With teachers having little time in the daily routine to sit and compose an intelligible letter, a word processor can prove invaluable. Letters can be generally typed faster than they can be handwritten, especially if a computer is available in the classroom. Time can further be saved by beginning with a previously written letter as a template and modifying it to fit the current purpose. Most word processing programs include ready-made templates or wizards to assist with composing letters.

Letters that are sent home can be saved in case a parent does not receive it or there are questions regarding what was said. Spelling and grammar can be checked, formatting adjusted, and personal touches, such as a class or school logo, can be inserted to design a professional-looking letter. Parents will appreciate the legibility of a typed letter and therefore may actually be more likely to respond to it. As with any typed letter, always be sure to sign it by hand; a letter with a typed signature implies that little care was taken to elevate it past the status of a mere form letter, lowering the letter's importance in parents' eyes to that of junk mail. Word processors can also be used to create thank-you notes and solicitations for help or information to other teachers, community members, and content experts.

The merge function greatly streamlines the process of sending out letters to multiple families. The *merge* function allows you to insert information automatically from another document, such as your student contacts database, into the letter, creating a letter customized with names and other information for each family in the time it takes to write one letter. The merge function can also be used to print address labels to further assist the process.

Newsletters

Keeping parents up-to-date on classroom and school occurrences is vital to the maintenance of a strong parent–school network, and the job can easily be done by publishing a weekly newsletter. Publishing a professional-looking newspaper-type document right on the classroom computer is possible with word processing or document layout software.

Depending on the ages and abilities of students, class "reporters" can actually write much of the text of the newsletter. This gives students an authentic writing purpose with a real audience, and the student participation guarantees a newsletter with the appeal of personality and variety. Many classrooms come up with a catchy title for their weekly publication and find or create relevant graphics with which to personalize the final product. The basic layout can be saved as a template to be used week after week, minimizing time spent to simplify what it takes to insert the new information each week.

Official Correspondence

Parent permission is frequently required for participation in anything from field trips to Internet usage. Creating, printing, and copying these types of releases to send home makes for consistent, professional-looking records of parent responses. Although most schools, or even districts, have standard forms for these purposes, occasions may arise for which there is no set form in place, such as requesting permission to take home a class pet, for example, or notifying families of an end-of-semester recital. Teachers should make sure any forms that are sent home are easy to understand and provide ample writing space for parents.

Planning

Regardless of the personal teaching style and philosophy of each teacher, most create some sort of plans to reach both long- and short-term objectives. Plans that are sketched out on paper may grow messy and unreadable through subsequent modifications. Productivity software can aid in planning activities by saving teachers' time and making quality, functional, final products.

Lesson Plans

When a newly certified teacher heads to the teaching supply store, the first item placed in the shopping cart is usually a "Teacher's Plan Book." These books contain blank weekly calendars, with the days identified down the left side of the page and half-hour increments clearly marked across the top. As schedules of special activities and class times are mapped out, changed, and finalized throughout the weeks before the start of the school year, and sometimes well into the first days of school, the neat order of most plan books begins to suffer. Handwritten schedules get crossed out, erased, and modified. Even when weekly plans do settle down into routine schedules, daily activities must still be handwritten into the book. Regularly scheduled activities must be repeatedly entered week after week. Many times activities take longer than the time planned and must be carried over into other time slots. All in all, handwritten plan books are messy, redundant, and generally not an effective utilization of a teacher's time.

Word processing or spreadsheet software can make some of this hassle more manageable. Teachers can easily map out a generic weekly or daily schedule. If activities change, they can simply be deleted or moved. Classes that occur predictably at the same time every day or week can easily be copied over to the next cells. Teachers who require more space to plan for lessons can format their planning pages to allow for large blocks of planning space. Tentative plans can be printed out on a daily, weekly, or longer basis, or plan templates, with recurring activities blocked in but learning time left blank, can be printed out to allow for handwritten adjustments (see Figure 16.1).

Planning for days when a substitute teacher will be in is also simplified. Typed plans supply the substitute teacher with accurate information on all necessary special student and schedule considerations and can be prepared ahead of time to lessen the busy work of preparing to be absent for a day. The planning options are as endless as the variety of teaching styles and circumstances.

Longer-term planning can be accomplished using software tools as well. Monthly calendars can be created manually using a spreadsheet, with help from templates or wizards that come packaged with most word processing software or even by using software especially intended to create calendars. An entire school year can be mapped out ahead of time, making it possible to see how thematic units might interrelate or how required curriculum elements can be coordinated into the allotted school days. As plans change, calendars can be easily modified accordingly. Online tools allow teachers to post assignments to web-based calenders so students can view them from anywhere (e.g., "Assign-A-Day" at **http//assignaday.4teachers.org**).

Visually aided planning can also be facilitated with the use of technology. It is common for teachers to plan for various related curriculum areas at the same time often with student input, using a web-type graphical representation so connections between topics or activities can easily be seen. Using a simple drawing program, teachers can map out thematic units or entire semester plans, making it possible with one glance to see how learning might be structured. Specific concept-mapping software (e.g., Inspiration at **www.inspiration.com**) can simplify the planning process with premade symbols and relational indicators.

New lesson plan software that is now available is designed to assist educators of all teaching levels in planning, editing, and organizing lessons for multiple classes (e.g., Lesson Manager Professional at **www.isdsoftwaredesign.com/edu.htm**). Such software provides word processing and database tools, standardized lesson formats, drag-and-drop capabilities among lessons and units, project time lines for a graphical overview of a lesson, and calendar and agenda tools (see Figure 16.2). Most websites offer free trial downloads and versions now exist for handheld computers.

FIGURE 16.1 A simple, word-processed lesson-planning page.

	Monday
8:00-8:15	Opening (Attendance, Lunch Count, Calendar)
8:15-9:30	Language (Literature, Writing)
9:30-10:00	Music
10:00-11:30	Math
11:30-12:15	Lunch
12:15-1:30	Science/Social Studies
1:30-1:50	Recess
1:50-2:30	Group Work
2:30-3:00	Journals, Storytime

Planning for Individual Student Needs

As teachers make plans for reaching both long- and short-term goals, customizing those plans to meet the educational needs of individual students can be facilitated by referring to a database of individual student concerns. Whether added to a main database of student information, or created as a separate file of learning characteristics, comments on everything from student learning modalities to special classes required can be recorded, simplifying the planning to meet the needs of students. If, for instance, three students leave to go to work with a speech pathologist every Tuesday at 1:00, a guest speaker can be scheduled around that time so that the students would still be able to participate. Whereas scheduling around one or two students' special

FIGURE 16.2 Lesson Manager Professional.

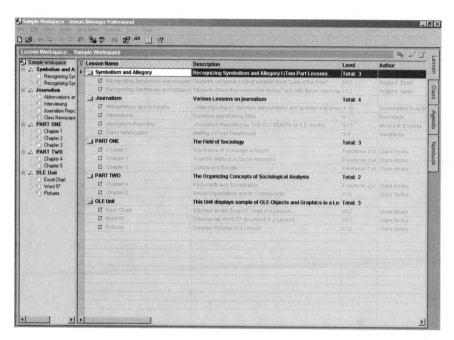

schedules or planning for ways in which they will learn best might be possible without any help from a computer, effectively planning based on the needs of 30 students or close to 200 teachers who see a series of different classes throughout the day could become problematic. A database created for this purpose will maximize planning and teaching time by helping to manage the specific characteristics a teacher must remember about every student.

Designing a Classroom Layout

How the furniture in a classroom is physically arranged reflects both the personal style and the teaching style of a teacher. Not only does the placement of desks or bookshelves contribute to the aesthetic atmosphere, but it also determines the functional traffic patterns of the room. Desks pushed into groups are more conducive to different learning experiences than are desks organized into measured rows. Regardless of the desired learning atmosphere, graphics software can be of great assistance. Available furniture can be mapped out and moved. Student names can be assigned to desks or tables and shuffled to achieve a workable mix of personalities and learning styles. These types of modifiable seating charts are especially helpful for substitute teachers to become familiar with students (see Figure 16.3).

FIGURE 16.3 Using a graphics program to design a classroom floor plan.

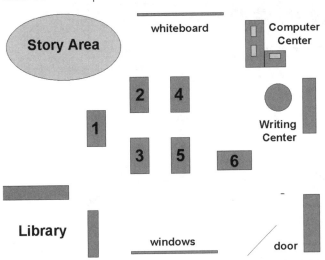

Scheduling

Along with the educational planning necessary in quality learning environments, much attention must also be paid to the fundamental scheduling of activities and other arrangements. Budgeting money, booking guest speakers, and making arrangements for field trips can all be simplified with the use of classroom technology.

Budgeting Money

Operating a classroom frequently involves the planning, collecting, accounting, and distributing of money. Money might be collected to pay for a field trip, raised by having a school candy sale, or saved to reach a class goal. When students begin bringing in wrinkled dollar bills and handfuls of coins, an orderly system of money management is vital. The features of a spreadsheet are best designed for the purpose of budgeting money. Columns can be organized to account for who has brought in what amount, and functions can calculate the total amounts. Time estimated to reach monetary goals can be planned, relying on calculations based on an anticipated income from a money-raising event; this makes a good, relevant learning activity for students. A legible spreadsheet accounting for every penny is a much superior method of tracking classroom expenses than a handwritten list of names and amounts scrawled on the back of an envelope full of dollars and change (see Figure 16.4).

Booking Classroom Guests

Despite the perception of isolation that four walls give to most classrooms, there are, in reality, often enough visitors moving in and out of classrooms to give teachers

FIGURE 16.4 Budgeting classroom expenses with a spreadsheet.

Total Cost for Field Trip to Mexico			
Cost per student X	# of Students =		Total Cost
$900.00	27		$24,300.00
Candy Sale			$14,000.00
Car Washes			$2,500.00
Bake Sales			$800.00
Remaining Personal Contributions			$7,000.00

plenty of practice in the role of talent-booking agents. Guests may range from parent helpers to community experts, but the appearances of all visitors must be carefully choreographed to fit in seamlessly with the natural flow of classroom learning. Teachers and students can use word processors to compose initial letters inviting guests to come to the class. These letters might even be based on generic letter templates written to include all of the basic information about the class that a visitor might need to know. Scheduling visitors can be done with either a spreadsheet or a calendar program, making accurate work of keeping track of who can be expected each day of school. Consulting online schedules regularly will remind teachers of upcoming visits so that if any unexpected schedule changes occur, guests can be contacted and rescheduled in a timely manner. Guest contact information should be carefully recorded into a database, so that it can be quickly accessed. Finally, word processors and possibly even graphics programs can be utilized to write thank-you notes.

Generating

Teachers generate learning documents every day, no matter the subject or age of students taught. Even teachers who adhere closely to packaged curricula have frequent cause to supplement commercial materials with those that are teacher made. Working from what is known about individual and collective abilities of students, as well as on the pace and climate of learning, work pages, recording sheets, quizzes, tests, dictated stories, and an unlimited number of other materials need to be created. Many teachers have scribbled down a handwritten quiz at the last minute only to have students run into problems trying to read the handwriting. When students are faced with a handwritten page with which to work, they may not put forth their best effort because it does not appear as though a great effort was shown in the creation of the assignment itself. Word-processed documents are professional, neat, and customizable. Topics that come up on the spur of the moment can be quickly added to an existing document, and an appropriate amount of space on the page can be left for students to write depending on the size of handwriting of which students of that particular age are capable. Any special grading practices employed by a class can be accommodated by creating custom documents.

The web now offers teachers a great number of easy ways to generate fun, appropriate, and free activities to use with all ages of students. For example, Quia (**www.quia.com**) has online game creation with a seemingly limitless selection that includes matching, flash card, concentration, word search, pop-ups, jumbled words, hangman, and scavenger hunt games. Microsoft in Education (**www.microsoft. com/education/?ID=ClassCorner**) offers a whole host of ready-to-use activities and ideas that utilize its productivity tools, including the Certificate of the Month Club with printable certificates according to monthly and current events. As with anything on the web, these offerings tend to change frequently. Teachers can quickly locate other learning tools, already made and ready to use, with a web search.

Another strength of using technology in generating learning materials for the classroom is that it facilitates sharing of ideas among teachers. So often, a teacher who wants to use a page that another teacher has created is left to merely copying the document, making do with any portions that do not directly pertain to the class, or attempting to cut and paste to customize it to fit a unique purpose. Word-processed documents are superior because they can be shared either on disk or through a network and can be easily modified to reflect class needs.

Conclusion

The few ideas presented here are only beginning thoughts of how technology can aid in the administrative duties of a teacher. Once teachers conquer initial fears that technology will only give them more work to do, they can start to understand how truly liberating technology tools can be (Sandholtz, Ringstaff, & Dwyer, 1997). Software is continually being improved, adding automatic features that perform functions that now must be done manually. Teachers should be aware of what software is available to them through their schools and must always be ready to consider new ways that technology can make their jobs easier and more organized.

Summary

Along with their instructing responsibilities, teachers must serve as administrators of the day-to-day operations of their classrooms. Basic software tools can make it easy for teachers to create consistent, professional, and accurate products for communicating, planning, scheduling, and generating management tasks.

In addition to electronic communication such as email, teachers still have many occasions when print-based communication is necessary. Word processing applications can be used to quickly send all kinds of letters, from newsletters to thank-you notes. Teachers can begin with a template form and can then save finished products for future use. Contact information on students' families and other community members

School Stories

Margaret Anderson unlocked the door to the sixth-grade class in which she would be substitute teaching today. As a regular substitute teacher for the district, she had seen all types of teaching situations and worked with all levels of preparation left by the classroom teacher. It was always a mystery as to how much information would be given to her when she walked into each new day of substituting.

Margaret could see that the day's plans, as usual, were left on the teacher's desk. Right away, she knew the outlook for a successful day was good! The plans were word-processed and very explicit. It appeared as though these were the regular teacher's plans, but they had been modified to include notes especially for someone not familiar with the regular class routine. For example, typed next to where the day's plan listed the day's starting time as 8:00 A.M. was "You will find students lined up outside next to the large tree."

Such helpful details were sprinkled throughout the plans:

- "Remember to send Jason to speech class at 10:35."
- "Pick up students from lunch at the west side of the cafeteria."
- "A guest speaker, Mrs. Hernandez, will be coming at 2:10 to speak about her job at the county courthouse. She is aware that you will be here, and she will bring everything she needs."

Margaret got the impression that not only was this teacher organized but also she was smart. Rather than having to handwrite directions thorough enough for a stranger to keep the class moving throughout the day, she had had to modify her existing plans with only a few pertinent notes. It left Margaret feeling confident that she had enough information to make the day a good experience for both the students and herself.

Her impression of this teacher's ability to use technology to keep a well-managed classroom was furthered when the students entered the classroom. The first girl to walk in turned on the computer by the doorway and launched a database application. She found her name, signed herself in, and entered her lunch order. One by one these jostling, active sixth-graders made their way through the door and independently used the computer to take their own attendance and lunch count. All that was left for Margaret to do was glance at the list to make sure it was complete and send it to the office via email. It appeared that more teachers than just this one were using technology to their advantage to make this school run more smoothly and efficiently.

with whom teachers and students need to communicate can be stored and organized in a database application.

Planning for both short-term lessons and longer-term curriculum maps can be done by using a word processor or a spreadsheet. Regular, predictable activities can be automatically scheduled, and individual student schedules can be planned. Seating charts designed with a graphic program can keep the classroom layout functional and can serve to inform guest teachers.

Teachers have a need to schedule a number of different items, and a spreadsheet application is ideal for keeping accurate records. Money for special activities or trips must be counted and accounted for. Classroom guests and helpers must be booked into the set schedule and then planned around it.

Regardless of the topic being taught, there are frequently teacher-made materials, including practice pages and quizzes, that are required. Word processing programs and graphics applications allow for nearly spontaneous generation of all types of professional-looking print materials. Documents are easy to share among colleagues and to modify to fit individual needs.

Challenge Yourself

1. Look for the templates that are included in the word processing software you generally use, and be sure to examine any templates available online. What possibilities does the program present for the administrative tasks of teachers?
2. Locate a website that offers printable teaching tools, such as flash cards or games. Customize and print a learning tool that corresponds to a topic with which you have experience. How long does it take and how does the quality compare with something you could have created yourself without the tool?
3. Make a list of ways in which the students you plan to teach can participate in administrative duties of their classroom.
4. Open a database program and experiment with creating a student database of information. What types of categories might be required to keep complete records of your students?
5. Using a template or beginning with a blank page, design a weekly newsletter for your class. Include a catchy title, any necessary graphics, and all formatting to create a finished product. What types of information will you include on a regular basis? How much of the writing and compilation of the letter can realistically be done by your students?
6. Obtain a teacher's plan book after it has been used for several months. Study the types of activities that are written, as well as how much space is used and how many lessons appear to be moved around or otherwise altered after being planned. Based on this teacher's planning habits, how would you design a custom lesson-planning page using a software application?
7. Create a calendar for scheduling classroom guests and other long-term special activities. Brainstorm a list of all possible visitors to your classroom, including those who will help on a regular basis as well as the types of people who might come only once.
8. Use a graphics program to design a classroom floor plan. Visit a classroom at the level you will teach to see the type of furniture that is used and in what ways it can be organized. Plan for smooth traffic patterns and varying size group work areas.

9. Create a small contacts file with a database, and write a form letter to parents. Use the mail merge function of your word processor to create custom letters.
10. Download a trial version of concept-mapping software and use it to plan a content-based curriculum project.

References

Office of Technology Assessment. (1995). *Teachers and technology: Making the connection.* OTA-CHR-616. Washington, DC: U.S. Government Printing Office.
Sandholtz, J. H., Ringstaff, C., & Dwyer, D. C. (1997). *Teaching with technology: Creating student-centered classrooms.* New York: Teachers College Press.

The Professional Educator

FOCUS QUESTIONS

1. How can teachers use technology to develop and maintain collegial relation-ships from a distance?

2. What information about funding opportunities is available online?

3. In what ways can technology assist teachers to remain lifelong learners?

The notorious image of the teachers' lounge brings to mind educators escaping for brief minutes between responsibilities to vent frustrations about students, parents, and administrators. In the old model of teacher communication, these stolen moments were often the only adult contact during otherwise isolated days within the four walls of the classroom. This isolation perpetuated stagnant teaching models, as teachers did not have consistent opportunities to share with and learn from each other.

Technology allows teachers to break that mold by giving them convenient access to remote resources, colleagues, and experts not previously as available. Teachers can access on the web everything from traditional resources, such as information on print-based journal subscriptions, to entirely electronic resources, such as listservs. At the same time that this professional information is so widely available, a concerted effort is being made to develop and maintain teachers' professional skills. Ongoing training in both content and pedagogy is advocated by professional organizations, school districts, and society, as more than ever, teachers are being perceived as pro-fessionals who must be lifelong learners.

This chapter will introduce the broad categories of web-based professional infor-mation for teachers. It begins with a discussion of the resources and strategies for on-line collegial communication, followed by information about contacting national professional organizations. An overview is given of the types of online funding sources for the support of classroom projects, and the chapter concludes with online professional development sources.

Collegial Communication

The most prominent professional education websites now offer virtual communication areas where teachers can discuss educational trends, share innovations in specialty fields, and get advice for challenging situations. (See Table 17.1 for example sites. Please note that many sites now require that users join as members. For some sites, membership is free and simply requires filling out an online form. Other sites may require a subscription for more robust resources.) Teachers can post favorite lesson plans or air frustrations they have with students or colleagues. Some websites match teachers with partner classrooms for email collaborations, whereas others invite experts to participate through "guest appearances." "Host" teachers, representative of a particular content area or grade level, moderate some of these online conversations, whereas other dialogues are open for free discussion. Teachers can communicate about both traditional and technology-assisted activities, so those "tried-and-true" strategies that prior to the Internet lived only in the minds of our expert teachers can now be widely shared with others for the ultimate benefit of students.

Electronic discussion areas offer a convenient avenue for collegial sharing, allowing teachers access to colleagues any time of the day or night. A teacher might need to post an online query during his only planning break at 2:45 in the afternoon to see whether anyone else is experiencing the same behavior issue. Or another might want to log on late at night after a school board meeting to see whether others are facing similar challenges with administrative relations. Some sites offer conversation threads for first-year teachers to seek advice from the more seasoned, as well as to commiserate with others at their own level during that frequently overwhelming initial year of teaching.

The power of these electronic conversations can be found at opposite ends of the spectrum. From the global perspective, the advice and viewpoints reflect teaching traditions around the country and even the world. No longer do teachers have only

TABLE 17.1	Online Teacher Collaboration Sites

Classroom Connect   http://connectedteacher.classroom.com/home.asp
Education World   www.education-world.com/boards/wwwthreads.pl
English Language Teachers' Forum   www.eltforum.com/home.html
ESL Teacher Forum   http://teachers.englishclub.com/forum
Math Forum's Teacher2Teacher   http://mathforum.org/t2t
Microsoft Classroom Teacher Network New Teacher's Corner
    www.microsoft.com/education/?ID=TeacherDiaryArchive
TAPPED IN's After School Online (ASO)   www.tappedin.org
Teacher Focus   www.teacherfocus.com/phpBB2/faq.php
Teacher Talk   www.teaching.com/ttalk
Teachnet.com's Teacher-2-Teacher   www.teachnet.com/t2t

the individuals in their own school to rely on for advice. On the other hand, teachers are often surprised to find colleagues who actually live quite near to them, in their own state or even district. These local perspectives are insightful in sorting through new state standards or regional events. The ease and flexibility with which teachers can access these electronic forums match the professional needs of classroom teachers while catering to the unique nature of teaching. For additional online teacher resources, please see Portal Sites in Chapter 8.

Professional Associations

Professional associations provide the glue that binds a whole range of diverse educators who share very important common interests, and the web provides the ideal communication medium to bring those educators together at any time from any location. With a by-the-people, for-the-people spirit, professional associations introduce like minds, from experts to novices, and prolific scholars to reluctant observers. Educators at all levels, from early childhood to secondary, from researcher to practitioner, join in the conversations. Teachers who work in relative isolation among their immediate peers, such as the one German teacher in the foreign-language department or the only reading specialist in the school, can find solace with colleagues with similar concerns in professional associations. Teachers negotiating the practical day-to-day activities can learn of theoretical advances and research connections that complement their individual endeavors, while at the same time help researchers stay in touch with the reality of classrooms. Even if teachers cannot personally attend the national conferences sponsored by their professional associations, concerns and common interests shared online help them to experience virtually these face-to-face gatherings. New teachers are encouraged to participate in their professional associations from the beginning of their careers; the satisfaction from contributing to a growing body of professional knowledge sustains a career. See Table 17.2 for example professional association websites, and conduct a web search for new sites not listed.

Educational Funding Opportunities

The financial hardships of school districts are well documented. Teachers are often motivated to spend their own money to provide the supplies they feel are necessary for their students' learning. Many teachers go through their entire teaching careers without recognizing that there are a great number of organizations, foundations, and agencies that aim to fund exceptional and innovative education programs. Thus, the web serves as a vital information source. Federal and state programs set aside funds to provide assistance on the broad scale. Professional associations finance projects related to their missions and goals. Private foundations contribute to district and classroom projects in accordance with stated objectives and beliefs. In addition, both national and local corporate donors sponsor educational initiatives. Along with good teaching, good teachers must now also take an active role in seeking a share of these outside financial resources for the benefit of their students.

TABLE 17.2	Professional Association Websites

American Association for the Advancement of Science (AAAS)   www.aaas.org
American String Teachers' Association (ASTA)   www.astaweb.com
International Reading Association (IRA)   www.reading.org
International Society for Technology in Education (ISTE)   www.iste.org
National Association for Bilingual Education (NABE)   www.nabe.org
National Association of Biology Teachers (NABT)   www.nabt.org
National Center on Education and the Economy (NCEE)   www.ncee.org
National Council for Teachers of English (NCTE)   www.ncte.org
National Council of Social Studies (NCSS)   www.ncss.org
National Council of Teachers of Mathematics (NCTM)   www.nctm.org
National Education Association (NEA)   www.nea.org
National Endowment for the Humanities (NEH)   www.neh.gov
National PTA   www.pta.org
National School Boards Association (NSBA)   www.nsba.org
National Science Teacher Association (NSTA)   www.nsta.org

Most money available for education is awarded in the form of competitive grants, and it is in this area that web-based information can be the most helpful. The writing of grant proposals is both a time- and resource-intensive process. Websites for granting organizations give proposal writers easy access to announcements of new grants, proposal guidelines, application forms, and information for new grantees. Table 17.3 lists a small selection of web-based fund-raising resources; others are announced daily.

Recent web-based innovations offer new ways for educators to raise much-needed funds. One group of e-commerce websites designates a percentage of all sales to selected schools. (See, for example, FundingFactory.com at **www.fundingfactory.com**

TABLE 17.3	Educational Fund-Raising Resources

The Foundation Center Grantmaker Information
   http://fdncenter.org/grantmaker/index.html
National Educational Association's Foundation for Educational Improvement
- www.nfie.org
National Endowment for the Humanities   http://www.neh.gov
TeacherGrants.org   www.teachergrants.org/bulletins/current.html
U.S. Department of Education Grants Information   www.ed.gov/fund

and Schoolcash.com at **http://schoolcash.com**). It seems that the public's interest in seeing education succeed matches its love affair with the web; expect such innovative corporate–educational alliances to continue.

Professional Development

School districts make substantial ongoing commitments to develop and maintain their teachers' professional skills and inspire fresh and innovative teaching practice. Good professional development transcends the "one-shot" standard to include continuous practice, reflection, and classroom application based on individual goals and prior experience. The difficulty with providing effective professional development lies with individualizing training to meet the needs of teachers. Should beginners be overwhelmed with advanced procedures? Should more experienced teachers be forced to sit through the basics? With traditional training methods, the answer to both questions is often yes. However, web-based training offers teachers who are open to the unique online learning format up-to-date instructional options that can be customized to fit their needs.

Many districts are experimenting with developing their own online workshops and training modules for their teachers and staff, on topics from content standards to cafeteria training. Some districts that have been early leaders in this professional development process have packaged their efforts for other districts to purchase. For-profit professional development sites provide a wider range of specialized instruction at a greater number of proficiency levels. The realization that educators need to continually improve their abilities makes even fee-based web training appealing. In addition to these commercial sites, most universities are offering courses, certificate programs, and even full advanced degrees online. Table 17.4 lists a sample of web-based professional development choices, although, as with all web resources, this selection will constantly change. A simple web search will turn up both local and distant colleges and universities with online offerings.

TABLE 17.4	Online Professional Development Sites

Apple Learning Interchange   http://ali.apple.com

Connected University from Classroom Connect   http://cu.classroom.com/info.asp

Disney Learning Partnership   http://disney.go.com/disneylearning

Pearson Skylight Professional Development   www.skylightedu.com

Survival Guide for New Teachers   www.ed.gov/teachers/become/about/survivalguide

Teacher Talk   http://education.indiana.edu/cas/tt/tthmpg.html

Teacher Tap   www.eduscapes.com/tap

Teacher Universe   www.riverdeep.net/teacheruniverse

T.H.E. Institute   www.thejournal.com/institute

Summary

Technology provides teachers with convenient access to remote professional resources, colleagues, and experts not readily accessible otherwise. Professional education websites offer virtual communication areas wherein teachers can discuss educational trends, share innovations, and get advice for challenging situations at any time of the day or night. The advice and viewpoints reflect teaching traditions around the world or around the state. Professional associations bring together diverse educators who share common interests, and most now have a web presence. As professional educators' responsibilities expand to include financial procurement duties, web-based information and tools for competitive grants for education can be invaluable. Finally, web-based training offers teachers up-to-date instructional options that fit their individual needs.

Challenge Yourself!

1. Inquire into the interest groups available in your district. If there is not a group that matches your interests, research the possibilities of starting a listserv for other teachers in the district with the same interests.
2. Scan the communication areas of at least two of the websites listed in this chapter. Which do you find easier to use? In which is the dialogue the most active?
3. Visit the website of a professional association in your content or interest area. Subscribe either for online access or for print publications, or see whether your school has money available for a school subscription.
4. Obtain an online application and guidelines for a local or national grant for which a project you are involved with or want to develop would qualify.
5. Gather a team of colleagues who are interested in writing a grant proposal. Find an online tutorial on writing grant proposals, and work through it together, perhaps collaborating via email.
6. Investigate whether your district has any existing funding relationships with local corporations. Then, use company websites to learn about the company, its mission, and its corporate giving policies. Locate contact information and see whether sources will consider funding a class project.
7. Compare the prospect of taking an online course to taking a course at a local university. How do the price, selection of courses, and overall quality seem to compare?
8. How does your district or a district in which you are interested in teaching offer professional development? Are there online training opportunities?
9. Explore the U.S. Department of Education website for funding opportunities. Bookmark the pages that show promise for future grants.
10. Use one of the websites listed in this chapter to find another class across the country that your students can be key pals with.

Social, Ethical, Legal, and Human Issues

FOCUS QUESTIONS

1. How does technology use contribute to social and equity issues in schools?

2. What are the ethical issues presented by technology in education?

3. In what ways can education overcome the ethical, equity, and social concerns about technology in the schools?

Computers are now so pervasive in our society that the question of how they can be used most wisely, efficiently, and ethically is a human issue that demands the attention of anyone interested in computer use. Although many of the purposes for which computers are used are extremely beneficial to the individual and to society, there is a wide range of misuse as well. For the past several decades, science fiction writers, philosophers, educators, and many others have been warning us about dramatic changes that computers will cause in our lives. What will these changes be? How will we adapt to such drastic reorganization of our routines?

Implementation of these changes and adaptations requires that we act responsibly with our new technologies. How do we, as pioneers and educators, encourage ethical behavior on the technological frontier? We must grapple with these issues now if we are to shape a productive and humane future. Computer fraud, invasion of individual privacy, and freedom of speech are issues impacting our lives. This chapter will examine the contemporary social and human issues of computer crimes, security, privacy, and the ethical, legal, and equity concerns in education.

Computer Fraud and Misuse

Hundreds of thousands of large mainframe computers are used in the United States. People involved with these systems number in the millions. Many others have access to mainframes through personal computers. These figures add up to an alarming increase in incidents of computer abuse, especially computer-related crime, a trend that will likely continue into the future.

There are a variety of ways in which computers can be used to defraud others in our society. Theft of *money* can occur through criminal programming or intentionally inaccurate accounting transactions and rounded amounts. Stealing information from a computer and using a computer to market stolen information illegally are not uncommon practices. Many private companies and government agencies maintain computerized lists of their customers and clients. Once unauthorized personnel access these lists, the information can be sold to others for various uses. Theft of *information* is a serious concern to school personnel who store student records on computers. With access to a computer and the determination to break into confidential records, students have been known to alter the grades of their friends and enemies. The theft of *computer time* is another computer-related crime on the increase. People who invade computer systems without authorization are called hackers, and their escapades are not always innocent.

Software piracy, or bootlegging, is the theft of *computer programs.* Software piracy occurs whenever a person purchases a computer program and then copies it for friends or resale. This is a violation of state and federal law, and those engaged in the practice are criminals. Software theft occurs on such a large scale that it costs an estimated $2.5 million each month—$1.0 million in actual losses and $1.5 million in lost sales opportunities. It is easy to copy computer programs, and for that reason the victimless practice may appear harmless and practical. Unfortunately, piracy also occurs in the classroom. Many teachers are caught in a bind: They have a class full of students who want to use the same software at the same time, but there is not enough software to go around. Given the ease with which software can be pirated, it is tempting to make unauthorized copies. Although the act of piracy takes only a few minutes, the ramifications are long-term. First, piracy sets a poor example for students, who are, after all, the computer users of the future. Second, it ultimately results in higher software prices because publishers must raise prices to compensate for losses through piracy. See **www.spa.org** for copying guidelines and other policies on software use. Piracy results in fewer legitimate customers and, consequently, higher-priced software packages.

Theft of *identity* is the fastest-growing white-collar crime. Victims' identities are assumed through stolen social security numbers, drivers' licenses, ATM cards, credit card information, and employee data theft. While impersonating their victims, criminals quickly spend as much money as possible before moving on to another stolen identity. Thieves can also use computer databases and the Internet to access large amounts of personal data. They steal passwords, social security numbers, and banking information from websites and employer databases. With this information, identity thieves apply for loans and make purchases over the Internet. Sometimes thieves "spam" or send unsolicited email offers requesting identification data. Naive email recipients provide the requested information, unaware of the fraud. Identity thieves create websites with links to legitimate sites to acquire passwords and credit card numbers. Some websites display forms and run scripts that provide unscrupulous webmasters with any information a person is foolish enough to post on an online form. Other information is directly mined from website visitors' computers while they browse a site. Workers with access to company data can also steal employee and customer information to either use themselves or sell to others for fraudulent purposes.

Today the social security and driver's license numbers of others, as well as business credit reports, individual credit reports, criminal records, civil records, bankruptcies, license verifications, marriage licenses, divorce records, death records, driving records, property records, utility records, and social security number verifications can all be accessed online (see **www.infoseekers.com** and **www.fastbreakbail.com**). Self-policing by the information broker industry has not restricted the sale of sensitive personal information to the general public. The federal government estimated 500,000 to 700,000 persons were victims of theft of identity in 2000. On average, victims of identity theft believe it took an average of 175 hours to remedy the theft of their identities, with average out-of-pocket expenses of $808 per victim (Benner, Givens, & Mierzwinski, 2000). Charp (2003) reported that identity theft increased nearly 80% in the past year (2002).

New forms of secure technologies should minimize the risks of stealing an identity (see Maintaining Security in this chapter).

Computer Viruses and Spam

Viruses also attack computers. Viruses are destructive programs that wreak havoc on computer data. Saboteur computer hackers bury virus programs within other harmless data. The delivery method evolves daily. No longer are viruses confined to executable files. Viruses can now invade all forms of media and data. Only through constant upgrades of antivirus programs can users be relatively safe from infection.

Computer viruses might not be immediately noticed. Some are designed to lie dormant until triggered by a sequence of keystrokes or a date. On November 1, 1988, a person entered a virus that was intended to live innocently and undetected in ARPANET, a U.S. Department of Defense computer network, the original "Internet." A design error in the virus caused it to replicate out of control. It jammed more than 6,000 computers nationwide, including computers at the Rand Corporation, SRI International, Lawrence Livermore Laboratories, the Massachusetts Institute of Technology, and military bases all over the United States. The virus spread by "mailing" itself to other computers under the auspices of a legitimate user. Because it continued to replicate, all infected computers slowed down and eventually shut down. In the past few years we have experienced viruses by the names of Klez, Melissa, W32, Blaster, and Michelangelo. The Sobig-F email worm created millions of copies of itself and spread worldwide more rapidly than earlier viruses. (See **www.pcworld.com/news/article/0,aid,112411,00.asp.**)

Trotter (2003)summarized the cyber virus software intruders as follows:

> *Backdoor.* A secret computer program that gives its creator a method of gaining access without a password to a computer system or computer network, often allowing the infected system to be used in later attacks.
>
> *Trojan horse.* A program that evades security and masquerades as something harmless. Unlike viruses, Trojan horses do not replicate themselves, but they can be just as destructive.
>
> *Virus.* A malicious program or piece of software code that attaches itself to a computer program, usually with unwitting assistance from the computer user. Viruses can replicate themselves, which potentially can clog the system

until it stops working. Some viruses destroy data, transmit themselves across networks, and bypass security systems.

Worm. A type of virus that can replicate itself over a computer network and usually performs malicious actions, such as using up the computer's resources and potentially shutting the system down. Hybrid worms may contain viruses, backdoors, and Trojan horses. (See **www.edweek.org/ew/ewstory .cfm?slug=02virus.h23**.)

Computer viruses are no laughing matter. To combat viruses, antivirus programs detect and eradicate known viruses, and to be effective, these programs must be updated weekly. (See the Antivirus Research Center for more information at **www. symantec.com/avcenter**.)

Spam (unwanted email such as unsolicited email advertisements) has been increasing at an alarming rate, forcing Congress to begin pursuing legislation to reduce spam. Charp (2003) reported that 49 percent of users spend from 40 minutes a day to almost 4 hours a week deleting spam. Many computer users are getting additional email addresses to share with advertisers and thus have protected their personal and business email. [Obviously shared email addresses can end up with unscrupulous advertisers.]

Maintaining Security

The need for security of computer equipment and computer data is significant for a computer system of any size, from a large mainframe system with extensive peripheral equipment to a single computer on a student's desk. Security measures prevent the fraudulent use or destruction of computer equipment. These measures include something a person has (a key or badge), something a person knows (a password), or something about a person (a fingerprint, a voiceprint, a facial feature).

Most large companies have security systems that one must pass through to gain access to the computer room. These systems may use special cards to insert or buttons to press on the outer door of the computer room. Other security measures include allowing only the personnel necessary to perform certain functions to be in a certain place, for instance, in the computer room. Therefore, once programs are written and in place, computer programmers should not be allowed to go into the computer room and should never be allowed to run their programs. Whereas it is reasonable in large organizations to allow only authorized personnel to enter the computer room, in most schools such a security measure would be unrealistic. However, access to the administrative computer containing confidential records should be limited. Security measures in the computer lab and in individual classes should be necessarily broader. Another measure requires the investigation of staff and security clearances for those who work with confidential information. A third measure establishes a system for efficiently investigating suspected breaches of security. No system is ever foolproof, but every effort should be made to ensure the security of both computer and data.

Biometric devices are now being used to ensure privacy, protect assets, confirm identity, and guard against unauthorized access. Biometric devices scan body parts such as fingerprints or retinas. A smart card is a plastic credit card type device with an embedded integrated circuit for storing information. Biometric technologies and smart cards are replacing the antiquated method of using passwords or PIN numbers. Electronic signatures, or e-signatures, represent a new form of technology used to verify a party's identity so as to certify contracts that are agreed to over the Internet.

Individual Privacy

Thus far, we have discussed crimes and abuses committed by individuals for their own personal gain. Some of these crimes affect us only indirectly, through increased prices and lowered standards of quality. However, another computer crime, related to identity theft, may have an impact on each and every one of us: invasion of privacy resulting from improper use of databases or data warehouses. A data warehouse is a collection of data from a variety of sources, which is analyzed for patterns and trends to support decisions. Although data warehouses provide a highly effective problem-solving environment for research (e.g., the Environmental Protection Agency's Envirofacts Warehouse at **www.epa.gov/enviro**), the potential for abuse exists.

Our digital identities are being stored in databases of companies we've never heard of. Private information is not only being captured online via the Internet, it is being collected in our offline world as well. Buying patterns are data mined from point-of-sale terminals via your supermarket club card. Advancements in biometric scanning technologies warrant a closer examination of our networked world of private information.

Until 1974, there was little concern about privacy with regard to databases. Few databases shared their information because access was slow and inefficient. However, as technology advanced and databases evolved into data warehouses, so concern for individual privacy increased. In 1974, President Gerald Ford signed the Privacy Act into law. Its purpose was to protect confidentiality of files generated by the federal government. Its principles are paraphrased as follows:

- There must be no personal data record-keeping systems whose very existence is secret.
- There must be a way for individuals to find out what information about them is in a record and how it is used.
- There must be a way for individuals to prevent information about them obtained for one purpose from being used or made available for other purposes without their consent.
- There must be a way for individuals to correct or amend records of identifiable information about them.
- Organizations creating, maintaining, using, or disseminating records of identifiable personal data must assure the reliability of the data for their intended use and must take reasonable precautions to prevent misuse of the data.

Let's examine the privacy issue with regard to several situations. First, consider credit checks. Today, we are a nation of borrowers. In fact, we have become so dependent on credit that business probably could not exist without it. Cars are bought on time payments, merchandise is charged to credit cards, and homes are mortgaged. All these items are bought on deferred payment plans requiring the establishment of credit.

Problems always arise whenever there is access to credit information. Questions range from who is authorized to access the information to how much information that person is entitled to know. In addition, the information available may or may not be accurate. For example, data might have been entered incorrectly, resulting in denial of credit purchases. Often, information is entered into a system but is never removed. A record of an arrest in a law enforcement database may be entered without indication of whether the person was acquitted of the charge. This same information may result in a university refusing an applicant admission. Another problem results from the unrestricted use of data. The large amounts of data available today often become accessible to more people than originally intended. The growth of government obviously increases the amount of data collected. In addition, data collected by one agency is often shared and used by other agencies for other purposes.

Tax forms are submitted to the Internal Revenue Service each year. The Census Bureau gathers information while law enforcement databases compile criminal records. Motor vehicle departments annually update data on registered car owners and licensed drivers, and voter registration lists abound. With this wide range of available information, these databases could be merged into data warehouses. These mergers could produce a detailed picture of an individual, threatening the individual's right to privacy. Many doctors and other professionals are reluctant to store client information in computer systems because of such a threat.

The shift to networked information environments challenges privacy in additional ways. Some popular email systems allow senders of bulk commercial email to track email recipients' web browsing behavior. Web browser cookies help companies match website visitors with their email addresses. When you receive an email message containing a graphic from a website, an email security loophole allows you to be assigned a unique serial number in a cookie, which is a text file stored in your hard drive and readable by other computers. This serial number or cookie is stealthily transmitted as you browse the web.

Technological advances are increasingly undermining privacy. Safeguarding our privacy is therefore a major issue requiring a thorough understanding of who is warehousing data, for what purpose, and how personal information is collected without our consent. The computer is invaluable in the management and distribution of information. However, it is up to those with access to this information to use it legally, wisely, and ethically. A strong need exists for improved oversight and stricter enforcement of current laws. To ensure that legal protections are not ignored, a public research center, the Electronic Privacy Information Center (EPIC), established a website at **www.epic.org** to disseminate information on emerging civil liberties issues including privacy and First Amendment concerns.

Privacy issues are increasingly a concern for educators as well. The handling of student information is protected under the Family Educational Rights and Privacy

Act (FERPA) of 1974. This federal law provides parents and students with the right to see their school records and to request corrections to records believed to be inaccurate or misleading. Schools must have written consent from parents or an eligible student (18 years or older) before releasing any information on a student. However, exceptions exist for certain entities, for instance, school employees or a contract agency conducting a study.

Referred to earlier in Chapter 3, the Children's Online Privacy Protection Act (COPPA) of 1998 protects the privacy of children using the Internet. Before collecting, using, or disclosing personal information from children under 13, websites or online services must obtain parental consent. Compliance with COPPA requires websites or online services to provide a prominent link to a notice disclosing how personal information is collected, used, and/or disclosed. Passive collection through techniques such as cookies must be disclosed. To find this information look for a link entitled Privacy Policy (see the bottom of Yahooligans! homepage at **www.yahooligans.com** for an example).

So far our discussion of computer crimes and threats to privacy illustrates some of the drastic changes computers are causing in our society. Another key set of issues, ethics and equity, impacts new responsibilities facing educators. The next two sections explore these concerns in education.

Ethical and Legal Concerns in Education

Educators share with parents and society the task of teaching ethical use of computers and the Internet. To help teachers develop a set of ethics applicable to computer and Internet use, schools create and implement an Acceptable Use Policy (AUP). The AUP is a critical part of the school's technology plan and states the rules governing computer and Internet use and the consequences for violations. Parents and their children are held responsible to adhere to this policy. There are many commercial software products that parents can use to screen their children's Internet access including messaging and chat rooms. In fact, most products can limit access to certain times of day and also have the ability to keep logs of the websites their children have visited.

Many schools install filtering software to monitor and block access to questionable materials. Congress passed the Children's Internet Protection Act (CIPA) on December 21, 2000. This Internet Safety Policy was created to protect children against online information considered harmful to children. This legislation is located at **www.ala.org/ala/washoff/WOissues/civilliberties/wascipa/cipatext.pdf.** The use of filtering software is itself controversial, however. Filtering software constitutes a prior restraint of the First Amendment's protections of free speech. For example, forcing adult library patrons to use filtering software in public libraries is unconstitutional. See **www.aclu.org/Privacy/Privacy.cfm?ID=13270&c=252** for more details. Notwithstanding the filtering issues, students need to acquire technology skills, and we need to help students learn to act ethically and responsibly.

Teachers are role models. Therefore, there is no substitute for ethical teacher behavior and proper supervision of students. Teachers must set an example of ethical behavior whenever using or discussing computers. A lecture on the evils of software piracy becomes meaningless if the teacher practices piracy. Understanding current copyright issues and the term *educational fair use* are paramount to teachers' ethical behavior.

The federal agency charged with administering the copyright law is the Copyright Office of the Library of Congress. (Visit its site at **http://lcweb.loc.gov/copyright/ title17** to review the law or **www.loc.gov/copyright/circs/circ1.html** to review the basics.) A copyright gives the creator the exclusive right to reproduce, distribute, perform, display, or license his or her work. When the original work is "fixed" in a "tangible medium of expression," copyright is automatic and notice is not necessary. For example, the email you write is copyrighted. Copyright protection lasts the lifetime of the creator plus 70 years; however, limited exceptions exist for types of "fair use."

Fair use is defined in Section 107 of the 1976 Copyright Act (see **www.loc.gov/ copyright/title17/92chap1.html#107**). Use for criticism, comment, news reporting, teaching (including multiple copies for classroom use), scholarship, or research is not an infringement of copyright. To determine whether a use is "fair" under the above law, the following factors must be considered but are not limited to:

- "The purpose and character of the use, including whether such use is of a commercial nature or is for nonprofit educational purposes;
- The nature of the copyrighted work;
- The amount and substantiality of the portion used in relation to the copyrighted work as a whole; and
- The effect of the use upon the potential market for or value of the copyrighted work."

In 1998 the Digital Millennium Copyright Act (DMCA) was signed into law. The DMCA's purpose is to update our copyright law for the digital age. An overview of the DMCA can be found at **www.asu.edu/counsel/brief/dig.html**.

Teach Act of 2002

On November 2, 2002, the Teach Act of 2002 was signed into law (**www.copyright. gov/legislation/pl107-273.pdf#13210**). The Teach Act of 2002 requires the use of technological measures that reasonably prevent further copying and distribution of copyrighted works. A class is limited to access to copyrighted works for only those officially enrolled. In addition, the access is only for the time period necessary to complete the class session. Finally, the digital transmissions are expected not to interfere with technological measures used by the copyright owners to prevent such retention or unauthorized further dissemination. The Association of Research Libraries website at **www.arl.org/info/frn/copy/copytoc.html** is a good source to acquire current and accurate information on copyright issues.

Plagiarism

Another growing concern among educators is plagiarism while using the Internet. Now Internet-provided information, including enhanced photos and animations can be easily copied and pasted into papers. Because so many sources of information are available on the Internet, plagiarizing the information in papers and reports is a temptation. See Chapter 15 and **www.plagiarism.org/index.html** for more information on this issue. Another growing concern among educators is the accuracy of Internet-provided information. There are no standards or clearinghouses to screen the plethora of information available.

These are a few of the technology-related issues. Teachers can spend class time discussing ethical issues with students. There are many role-playing models that cast students as software pirates, software publishers, and so on. One very important topic for discussion is plagiarism. Finding information on the Internet makes verbatim text very convenient to cut and paste into student papers. Even entire essays can be downloaded and passed off as original works. Entrepreneurs can acquire a repository of essays and research papers for resale. In less than a second after entering the search word *essays* into Yahooligans!, you can find a website listing more than thirty student essays. Giving students opportunities to role play and discuss these issues helps them develop and clarify their own ethical codes.

Equity in Education

Equity issues are a major concern of educators utilizing technology. Gender and equal availability of technology for everyone are the main issues. Research has documented that boys are more interested and involved with technology than are girls. Software generally tends to emphasize male-dominated activities. Games often include violence and competition as motivation. These software characteristics tend to attract males. Therefore, careful student software selection is essential for addressing gender in the classroom.

Student access to technology is dependent on the financial capabilities of a school or school district. Although student-to-computer ratios are steadily improving, many low socioeconomic schools have limited access to computers and the World Wide Web, especially classroom access. The Universal Service Fund for Schools and Libraries, referred to as the "E-Rate," was created in 1996 to provide discounts on the cost of telecommunication services and equipment to public and private schools and libraries. The E-Rate program has connected over a million classrooms to the Internet. Although Congress and state governments have taken steps to increase access through the E-Rate as well as other technology grant programs, the gap is still significant. A new type of poverty—information poverty—has emerged from this gap or digital divide.

Educators are concerned that this digital divide will create a form of technological elitism. In a technologically oriented economy, people with more computer experience will obtain higher salaries. On the other hand, those with little or no computer experience will be disadvantaged. The U.S. Department of Commerce (1999) documents the digital divide and reports a 25 to 30 percent increase in the gap since 1994. Educators have a responsibility to ensure that all students have sufficient access to computers and the Internet, regardless of gender, ethnicity, socioeconomic background, and disability.

Although the U.S. Department of Commerce (2000) documents slight increases in minority access to technology, people with disabilities are only half as likely (based on the national average) to have Internet access. Only 25 percent of the population without disabilities have never used a computer, while close to 60 percent of the population with disabilities have never used a computer. Only 20 percent of the people who are blind or vision impaired have Internet access. When selecting computer hardware and software applications for classroom use, educators need to evaluate the hardware and software to determine their accessibility by students with disabilities. Techniques for ensuring accessibility to a website are documented by the Web Access Initiative of the World Wide Web Consortium (**www.w3.org/wai**).

Vision-impaired students may use screen access software, which translates information on the screen into synthesized speech or Braille. If a site does not offer a text-only version, comprehension problems may occur when the screen access software reads the available text. For instance, when a graphic is a navigational element such as a button or arrow and the image label reads 009.gif or the button's text is labeled "click," the screen access software reads 009.gif or click. Vision-impaired students may not understand the decontextualized text and become disoriented. Even with assistive computer technology installed for students with disabilities, Internet research is not possible with inaccessible web-page design. The Center for Applied Special Technology (CAST) is a nonprofit organization dedicated to expanding educational opportunities for individuals with disabilities through the development and innovative uses of technology (see its website at **www.cast.org/index.cfm**). CAST developed a web-based program that identifies a website's accessibility problems and suggests solutions. The Equal Access to Software and Information (EASI) website at **www.rit.edu/~easi** provides invaluable resources for teachers using technology as a tool toward inclusion and curriculum integration for students with disabilities.

Teachers must take advantage of technology so all students can be involved in more than the drill-and-practice activities often common in lower socioeconomic schools. Teachers need to be aware of web designs that do not take cultural connotations and disabilities into consideration. Access to technology is more importantly about the effective use and careful integration of technology into the curriculum than simply providing access or the acquisition of hardware and software.

How can we ensure adequate and equal access to technology? Two strategies are critical: funding and teacher professional development (Kuperstein & Gentile, 1998). Parent groups, fund-raising, industry partnerships, and careful budgeting in schools can help improve access to technology. Interest groups such as the National Coalition for Equity in Education (**www.math.ucsb.edu/NCEE**) disseminate information. Similarly, the Digital Divide Network (**www.digitaldividenetwork.org**) is an online resource connecting communities with resources needed to address the current inequalities. In addition, the Digital Equity Network (**http://digitalequity.edreform.net**) is an online service providing high-quality resources that help address the digital divide in the classroom and community. Ongoing professional development and technical assistance support teachers' efforts to transform their practice.

Teachers must strive to arrange equitable access and facilitate students' use of technology that addresses their individual needs, including their cultural identity, and promotes interaction with the global community.

Summary

We have only begun to experience the radical changes that computers will make on society, as we know it. Computer scientists and sociologists differ in their estimates of our technological future: Some foresee a stark *1984* type world; others, Toffler among them, predict a bright future in which humans, aided by advanced technology, function with greater freedom than ever before. Who is right remains to be seen, but this much is certain: Computers are bound to change our lives and our society in dramatic and irrevocable ways.

Computer fraud and abuse take many forms: theft of money, goods, and identity; unlawful use of information stored in computers' memories; and unauthorized use of computer time. Hackers enter computer systems without authorization. Software piracy, which is the theft of computer programs, can cause software prices to increase. The computer virus is another major concern of computer security. The entry of a virus can destroy or damage records and shut down computers. Generally, viruses are difficult to detect, but vaccines are available to overcome them.

Computer crimes are on the increase partly because of the increasing number of computers in society. There are various methods of maintaining security in the computer room, primarily by limiting access to the room to authorized personnel. The password is the traditional method of controlling entry into a computer system and limiting access to records. Biometric technology is increasingly being used to maintain security. In addition, many organizations screen potential employees in the hiring process.

In addition to concerns for the security of organizations, there is concern for the rights of individuals. The Federal Privacy Act of 1974 was enacted to protect the confidentiality of files generated by federal government computers. Several state governments have passed laws to further protect the average citizen from illegal use of computer information. Besides computer crime, the issue of change in the labor force is another major concern.

Teachers face new challenges in technology-based education. First, they must strive to provide equal access to computers for all students, regardless of gender, ethnicity, socioeconomic background, and disability. Second, they must promote computer ethics in their classrooms. They can do this by setting an example of ethical computer use and by using tools such as role playing and simulations to examine ethical questions. Educators and parents are concerned about student privacy and access to inappropriate sites. In addition, plagiarism concerns about student assignments utilizing the World Wide Web are becoming a major concern. Technology provides opportunities but also provides concerns to teachers and parents. All must work together to take advantage of this powerful tool!

School Stories

Have you ever "borrowed" a computer program from a friend or coworker? Are copyrighted computer programs currently installed on your home or office computer? If so, do you know whether those programs were borrowed or installed with the permission of the copyright owner? Federal copyright law gives the copyright owner the exclusive right to determine who can install or borrow copyrighted computer software. If you or an authorized University representative purchased software from a reputable vendor, then that purchase probably included the purchase of a license for the purchaser of the software. Before you use, share, or distribute the software, you should understand the terms of the license. If the software was purchased "off the shelf" or prepackaged, then the packaging will include the license terms. This method of disclosing the license terms is sometimes referred to as "shrink wrap" licensing, because the language often provides that by opening the (shrink wrap) packaging, the purchaser agrees to be bound by the terms of the license. If the software was developed or customized for a particular purpose, an underlying written agreement may contain the terms of the license. If University employees developed the software in the course of or as part of their employment, then the copyright in the software will belong to the Arizona Board of Regents. This means that no one can distribute the software or license or allow others to use it without the express, written authorization of someone authorized to contract on behalf of the board. Agreement to license software created by ASU employees should be reviewed by the Technology Collaboration and Licensing Office or the Office of General Counsel. If the University hired a consultant or independent contractor to develop the software, the agreement with the consultant or contractor either should assign ownership of the copyright in the resulting software to the University or should contain the license terms governing the use and distribution of the software. All agreements with third parties (including students) for the purchase, lease, creation, or adaptation of software or other copyrighted materials for use by the University should be reviewed by Purchasing and Business Services or the Office of General Council. License terms may restrict the individuals or sites that are authorized to use the software. The term of the use, the purpose of the use, and the ability to distribute and copy the software may also be limited by license terms. The license may describe penalties for violation of its terms. Unauthorized copying or distribution of software may also result in civil and criminal liability under federal and state laws. The University and the individuals involved in the unauthorized copying may be liable even if the software was copied for an educational or a nonprofit use.

Software publishers have taken aggressive steps to protect against infringement of their copyrighted software. These steps may include an audit of University computers to search for software being used without authorization. The presence of unlicensed software may result in considerable liability for the University and for individuals involved in unauthorized copying. In other words, unless you are an authorized user, that "free" copy of a copyrighted software program may not be free at all.

Source: Arizona State University Office of General Counsel, 1997.

Challenge Yourself!

1. Discuss the gender-related differences in attitudes toward computers.
2. What are the dangers of technological elitism?
3. Describe recent cases of fraudulent uses of computers.
4. Describe the differences between COPPA and CIPA.
5. Research violations of individual rights to privacy through unauthorized access to records.
6. What are your concerns about computer viruses and what are you doing to prevent loss or misuse of your data due to a virus?
7. Research the effects of low-income technology access.
8. Review a popular educational software package and check for male-dominated roles in the software.
9. Review the methods of blocking inappropriate websites for eliminating student access in schools.
10. What dangers do you foresee in new technology? Will new technology render life more impersonal or threaten our privacy?
11. Compare the privacy policy of Yahoo.com at **www.yahoo.com** to the privacy notice of Amazon.com at **www.amazon.com**. (Look at the bottom of the main page for the link to privacy information.) Take note of the "cookies" and personal information sections.

References

Apple, M. W. (2000). The hidden costs of reforms. *Educational Policy, 14*(3), 429–436.

Atwater, M. (1998). Science literacy through the lens of critical feminist interpretive frameworks. *Journal of Research in Science Teaching, 35*(4), 375–377.

Au, K. H., & Raphael, T. E. (2000). Equity and literacy in the next millennium. *Reading Research Quarterly, 35*(1), 170–188.

Becker, G. H. (2000). Copyright in a digital age. *Electronic School, 187*(6), 26–31.

Benner, J., Givens, B., & Mierzwinski, E. (2000). *Nowhere to turn; Victims speak out on identity theft.* Sacramento, CA: CALPRIG's Consumer Program.

Brown, M. R. (2000). Access, instruction, and barriers technology issues facing students at risk. *Remedial and Special Education, 21*(3), 182–193.

Carlson, S. (2003). Survey of college-bound students finds no digital divide among them. *The Chronicle of Higher Education, 49*(34), A37.

Charp, S. (2003). Security and privacy of information. *T.H.E. Journal, 31*(2), 8.

Cruz, J. M. (2000). A closer look: Teaching SMART and beyond point and click. *Equity and Excellence in Education, 33*(1), 91–94.

Dietz, L. D. (1982). Computer security: Not just for mainframes. *Mini-Micro Systems, 15*(6), 251–256.

Eline, L. (1992). Safeguarding online systems. *Technical Training, 9*(2), 24–31.

Emmans, C. (2000). Internet Ethics. *TECHNOS, 9*(1), 34–36.

Engler, P. (1992). Equity issues and computers. In Gary Bitter (Ed.), *Macmillan encyclopedia of computers* (pp. 359–367). New York: Macmillan.

Fleming, P. M. (2000). Three decades of educational progress (and continuing barriers) for women and girls. *Equity and Excellence in Education, 33*(1), 74–80.

Freed, G., Rothberg, M., & Wlodkowski, T. (2003). *Making educational software titles and web sites accessible: Design guidelines including math and science solutions.* Boston: The Media Access Group at WGBH.

Fryer. W. (2003). A beginner's guide to school security. *Technology and Learning, 24*(2), 9–14.

Gardiner, C. S. (2000). The search for bias-free educational software. *ENC Focus, 7*(4), 45–46.

Gonsalves, A. (2003). Web watchers, *Technology and Learning, 23*(6), 7–10.

Gordon, A. (1988). Viruses pose tricky threat to computers. *The Arizona Republic, 114*(133) p. AA1.

Hannah, L. S., & Matus, C. B. (1984). A question of ethics. *The Computing Teacher, 12*(1), 11–14.

Keyboard bandits who steal your money. (1982, December 27–1983, January 3). *U.S. News and World Report, 92,* 68–69.

Koski, W. S., & Levin, H. M. (2000). Twenty-five years after Rodriguez: What have we learned? *Teachers College Record, 102*(3), 480–514.

Kuperstein, J., & Gentile, C. (1998). *The connected learning community technology roadmap.* Redmond, WA: Microsoft Corporation.

Lee, J. (1992). Hacking. In Gary Bitter (Ed.), *Macmillan encyclopedia of computers* (pp. 425–434). New York: Macmillan.

Legal bulletin. (1997). Tempe: Arizona State University Office of the General Council.

Lockheed, M. E., & Frant, S. B. (1983). Sex equity: Increasing girls' use of computers. *The Computing Teacher, 11*(8), 16–18.

Luft, J. A., Bragg, J., & Peters, C. (1999). Learning to teach in a diverse setting: A case study of a multicultural science education enthusiast. *Science Education, 83*(1), 100.

Markoff, J. (1988). Computer "virus" linked to "bored students." *The Arizona Republic, 99*(171), 1–2.

McAdoo, M. (1994). Equity: Has technology bridged the gap? *Electronic Learning, 13*(7), 24–34.

McCaughey, M. (2003). Windows without curtains: Computer privacy and academic freedom. *ACADEME, 89*(5), 39–46.

Nieto, S. (2000). Placing equity front and center. *Journal of Teacher Education, 51*(3), 180–188.

Parker, D. B. (1981). *Computer security management.* Reston, VA: Reston.

Perez, C. (2000). Equity in the standards-based elementary mathematics classroom. *ENC Focus, 7*(4), 28–31.

Perryess, C. S. (2000). Reality check. *Educational Leadership, 57*(8), 78–80.

Puma, M. J., Chaplin, D. D., & Pape, A. D. (2000). *E-Rate and the digital divide: A preliminary analysis from the Integrated Studies of Educational Technology.* Washington, DC: The Urban Institute.

Reilly, R. (2002). Internet crime: What's hot, statistics, reporting incidences. *Multimedia Schools, 9*(5), 68–71.

Revenaugh, M. (2000). Beyond the digital divide: Pathways to equity. *Technology and Learning, 20*(10), 38–50.

Robyler, M., Dozier-Henry, O., & Burnette, A. (1996). Technology and multicultural education: The "uneasy alliance." *Educational Technology, 35*(3), 5–12.

Roth-Vinson, C. (2000). Cybersisters jumpstart girls' interest in math, science, and technology. *ENC Focus, 7*(4), 23–27.

Stabiner, K. (2003, January 12). Where the girls aren't. *New York Times, 153*(52,361), 32.

Toffler, A. (1981). *The third wave.* New York: Bantam Books.

Trotter, A. (2003). Cyber viruses infect schools across nation. *Education Week, 23*(2), 1, 14.

U.S. Department of Commerce. (1999). *Falling through the net: Defining the digital divide.* Washington, DC: National Telecommunications and Information Administration.

U.S. Department of Commerce. (2000). *Falling through the net: Toward a digital inclusion.* Washington, DC: National Telecommunications and Information Administration.

U.S. General Accounting Office. (1998). *Identity fraud: Information on prevalence, cost, and Internet impact is limited.* (GAO/GGD-98-100BR). Washington, DC: Author.

Weissglass, J. (1997). Deepening our dialogue about equity. *Educational Leadership, 54*(7), 78–81.

Websites

10 Big Myths about copyrights explained **www.templetons.com/brad/copymyths.html**

American with Disabilities Act (ADA) **www.usdoj.gov/crt/ada/adahom1.htm**

Antivirus Research Center **www.symantec.com/avcenter**

Copyright and Multimedia Law for Webbuilders and Multimedia Authors **http://bailiwick.lib.uiowa.edu/webbuilder/copyright.html**

Equal Access to Software and Information **www.rit.edu/~easi**

E-Rate and the Digital Divide: A preliminary analysis from the Integrated Studies of Educational Technology **www.ed.gov/Technology/erate_findings.html**

Fair Use Documents for multimedia and distance learning **www.libraries.psu.edu/mtss/fairuse/guidelines.html**

Fair Use of Copyrighted Works **www.cetus.org/fairindex.html**

The International Publication on Computer Virus Prevention, Recognition, and Removal **www.virusbtn.com/index.xml**

ISTE guidelines and related information **www.iste.org**

Milken Family Foundation **www.mff.org/edtech**

National Telecommunication and Information Administration **www.ntia.doc.gov/ntiahome/digitaldivide**

Security Web Portal **www.alw.nih.gov/Security/security-www.html**

The Software and Information Association   **www.siia.net**

Software and Web Site Accessibility   **http://main.wgbh.org/wgbh/access/ access.html**

SPA copying guidelines and related information   **www.spa.org**

Teach Act of 2002   **www.copyright.gov/legislation/pl107-273.pdf#13210, www.umuc.edu/distance/odell/cip/links_teach.html**

Tool (Bobby) to analyze a URL's web accessibility   **www.cast.org/bobby**

Tools to detect plagiarism   **www.plagiarism.org, www.plagiarized.com/index.shtml**

University of Maryland University College—Center for Intellectual Property and Copyright in the Digital Environment   **www.umuc.edu/distance/odell/cip**

U.S. Copyright Office   **www.loc.gov/copyright**

Web Accessibility Initiative (WAI)   **www.w3.org/WAI**

Web Content Accessibility Guidelines 1.0   **www.w3.org/TR/1999/WAI-WEBCONTENT-19990505/#themes**

Women in Technology   **www.ability.org.uk/womentec.html**

Additional Reading

Business Week
Chronicle of Higher Education
Communications of the ACM
Computerworld
Education Week
eMediaweekly
Information Week
InfoWorld
Interactive
International Journal on E-Learning
Learning and Leading with Technology
Network World
Newsweek
PC Week
Technology and Learning
Time
U.S. News and World Report
USA Today
Wall Street Journal

INDEX

CREDITS

23, Courtesy of Apple Computer, Inc.; 27, Courtesy of Panasonic; 29, Courtesy of Sharp Electronics; 36, 276 (bottom left), Courtesy of Samsung Electronics America, Inc.; 58, 275, 278, 280, 296 Screen shots reprinted by permission from Microsoft Corporation.; 49, 50, 51, 54, 182, 184, Netscape Communicator browser window © 1999 Netscape Communications Corporation. Used with permission. Netscape Communications has not authorized, sponsored, endorsed, or approved this publication and is not responsible for its content.; 54, Digital, AltaVista, and AltaVista logo are trademarks or service marks of Digital Equipment Corporation. Used with permission.; 73, Courtesy of Philips; 74, Courtesy of Mitsubishi; 75, Courtesy of Minstrel; 76, Courtesy of NTT Soft; 80 (left), Courtesy of Bausch and Lomb; 80 (right), Courtesy of Wizzard Software; 101, Courtesy of Hunter Digital; 139, Published and distributed by Pearson Digital Learning, Scottsdale, Arizona.; 140, 143, Courtesy of Tom Snyder Productions; 145 (top), This graphic is the property of and is used with the permission of Renaissance Learning, Inc. Perfect Copy is a registered trademark of Renaissance Learning, Inc.; 145 (bottom), Diagram created using Inspiration® by Inspiration Software®, Inc.; 155, © 2001 Education World, Inc.; 160, Courtesy of The Franklin Institute; 161, Volcano World—University of North Dakota; 162 (top), Capitol Advantage, Fairfax, VA; 162 (bottom), Digital History; 163, Xpeditions © nationalgeographic.com; 164, ArtsEdge: The National Arts & Education Information Network; 165, www.goals.com; 166, Ask ERIC Homepage; 265, Courtesy of Curtis Computer Products; 276 (bottom right), Courtesy of Casio, Inc.; 293, Courtesy of FunBrain.com, part of Learning Network; 310, © 1992–2000 ISD Software Design (www.isdsoftwaredesign.com).